C0-AVY-497

THE CORRESPONDENCE

of

HEINRICH MELCHIOR MÜHLENBERG

VOLUME 2

1748 - 1752

HEINRICH MELCHIOR MÜHLENBERG

THE CORRESPONDENCE

of

HEINRICH MELCHIOR MÜHLENBERG

VOLUME 2

1748 - 1752

Edited and Translated by

John W. Kleiner

and

Helmut T. Lehmann

PICTON PRESS
CAMDEN, MAINE

This volume is a translation of Letters 70-127 (1748-52) from

Die Korrespondenz Heinrich Melchior Mühlenbergs:
Aus der Anfangszeit des
Deutschen Luthertums in Nordamerika
Band I: 1740-1752

von
Kurt Aland

In addition, three letters not included in the German edition are published
in this English language edition, making a total of sixty-one letters in all.

All rights reserved
Copyright © 1986 by Walter de Gruyter & Co., Berlin
New material copyright © 1997 by Picton Press, Rockport
Library of Congress Catalog Card Number 93-86108
International Standard Book Number 0-89725-227-6

No part of this publication may be reproduced or transmitted in any form
or by any means, electronic or mechanical, including photocopying,
recording, or any information storage or retrieval system, without
permission in writing from the copyright holders, except for the inclusion
of brief quotations in a review.

First printing October 1997

Available from:

Picton Press
P.O. Box 250
Rockport, ME 04856-0250

Visa/Mastercard (207) 236-6565

Manufactured in the United States of America
Printed on 60# acid-free paper

iv

H. M. Mühlenberg

CONTENTS

CONTENTS

CONTENTS

CONTENTS

ABBREVIATIONS

Atlas

Atlas of Early American History: The Revolutionary Era 1760-1790. Princeton: Princeton University Press, 1976.

Bewährte Nachrichten

Bewährte Nachrichten von Herrnhutischen Sachen. Edited by Johann Philip Fresenius. 2 vols. Frankfurt am Mayn: Buchner, 1747-1751.

Büdingsche Sammlung

Nikolaus Ludwig von Zinzendorf, *Büdingsche Sammlung.* 3 vols. Büdingen: Johann Christian Stöhr, 1742-1744. - Ergänzungsband 9 zu den Hauptschriften. Edited by Erich Beyreuther and Gerhard Meyer. Hildesheim: Georg Olms Verlagsbuchhandlung, 1966.

CSB

Common Service Book of the Lutheran Church. Philadelphia: The Board of Publication of the Lutheran Church in America, 1917.

Detailed Reports

Detailed Reports on the Salzburger Emigrants Who Settled in America... Edited by Samuel Urlsperger. Volume Nine, 1742. Translated by Don Savelle; edited by George Fenwick Jones. Athens and London: The University of Georgia Press, 1988.

Documentary History

Documentary History of the Evangelical Lutheran Ministerium of Pennsylvania and Adjacent States. Proceedings of the Annual Conventions from 1748-1821. Philadelphia: Board of Publication of the General Council of the Evangelical Lutheran Church in North America, 1898.

HN1

Nachrichten von den vereinigten Deutschen Evangelisch=Lutherischen Gemeinen in Nord=America, absonderlich in Pensylvanien. Mit einer Vorrede von D. Johann Ludewig Schulze. Halle: Buchhandlung des Waisenhauses, 1787 (Kurze Nachricht von Einigen Evangelischen Gemeinen in America. Halle, 1744-1787).

HN2/1 and HN2/2

Nachrichten von den vereinigten Deutschen Evangelisch-Lutherischen Gemeinen in Nord-America, absonderlich in Pensylvanien. Mit einer Vorrede von D. Johann Ludewig Schulze. Neu hrsg. von W. J. Mann, B. M. Schmucker und W. Germann. Vol. 1: Allentown, Pennsylvania, Verlag von Brobst, Diehl & Co; Halle: Buchhandlung des Waisenhauses, 1886. Vol. 2: Philadelphia, Pennsylvania: P. G. C. Eisenhardt; Halle: Buchhandlung des Waisenhauses, 1895.

Halle Reports

Halle Reports. Vol. 1. New Edition with extensive historical, critical and literary annotations and numerous documents, copied from the manuscripts in the archives of the Francke Institutions at Halle. By W. J. Mann and B. M. Schmucker, assisted by W. Germann. Translated from the German by C. W. Schaeffer. Philadelphia, 1882.

Journals

The Journals of Henry Melchior Muhlenberg. Edited and translated by Theodore G. Tappert and John W. Doberstein. 3 vols. Philadelphia: Muhlenberg Press, 1942; 1945; 1958. Reprint by the Lutheran Historical Society of Eastern Pennsylvania, Philadelphia, and Whipporwill Publications, Evansville, Indiana, 1982. Vol. 2:773-808, *Travel Diary of Henry Muhlenberg May 1-26, 1772* and *July 20-August 17, 1773.* Translated by Helmut T. Lehmann and John W. Kleiner. Philadelphia: Lutheran Historical Society of Eastern Pennsylvania, Inc., 1982.

Korrespondenz

Die Korrespondenz Heinrich Melchior Mühlenbergs: Aus der Anfangszeit des deutschen Luthertums in Nordamerika. 5 vols. Berlin: Walter de Gruyter & Co., 1986-

Liedersammlung

Erbauliche Lieder=Sammlung zum Gottesdienstlichen Gebrauch in den Vereinigten Evangelisch=Lutherischen Gemeinen in Pennsylvanien und den benachbarten Staaten. Gesammelt, eingerichtet, und zum Druck befördert durch das hiesige Deutsche Evangelisch=Lutherische Ministerium. Philadelphia: Leibert und Billmeyer, 1786.

LBW

Lutheran Book of Worship. Minneapolis: Augsburg Publishing House; Philadelphia: Board of Publication, Lutheran Church of America, 1978.

Lutheran Church in NY and NJ

Lutheran Church in New York and New Jersey 1722-1760; Lutheran Records in the Ministerial Archives of the Staatsarchiv, Hamburg, Germany. Translated by Simon Hart and Harry J. Kreider. Published by the United Lutheran Synod of New York and New England, 1962.

Lutheranism in Colonial NY	Harry J. Kreider, *Lutheranism in Colonial New York.* New York: Priv. printed, 1942.
Lutheran Church in PA	Theodore Emanuel Schmauck, *A History of the Lutheran Church in Pennsylvania (1638-1820).* Philadelphia: General Council Publication House, 1903.
Lutherans in N.A.	*The Lutherans in North America.* Edited by E. Clifford Nelson in collaboration with Theodore G. Tappert, H. George Anderson, August R. Suelflow, Eugene L. Fevold and Fred W. Meuser. Philadelphia: Fortress Press, 1975.
LW	*American Edition of Luther's Works.* 55 vols. Philadelphia: Fortress Press; St. Louis: Concordia Publishing House, 1955-1986.
Minutes and Letters	*Minutes and Letters of the Coetus of the German Reformed Congregations in Pennsylvania 1744-1792 Together with Three Preliminary Reports of the Rev. John Philip Boehm, 1733-1744.* Translated and edited by William J. Hinke. Philadelphia: Reformed Church Publication Board, 1903.
Missionary of Moderation	Leonard Richard Riforgiato, *Missionary of Moderation: Henry Melchior Muhlenberg and the Lutheran Church in English America.* Lewisburg, Pennsylvania: Bucknell University Press; London: Associated Presses, 1980.
Pastors and People	Charles H. Glatfelter, *Pastors and People: German Lutheran and Reformed Churches*

in the Pennsylvania Field, 1717-1793.
Vol. 1: Pastors and Congregations; Vol.
2: The History. Breinigsville,
Pennsylvania: The Pennsylvania German
Society, 1980; 1981.

SBH

*Service Book and Hymnal of the Lutheran
Church in America.* Philadelphia: United
Lutheran Publication House, 1958.

Selbstbiographie

*Heinrich Melchior Mühlenberg, Patriarch
der Lutherischen Kirche Nordamerika's.
Selbstbiographie, 1711-1743.* Mit
Zusätzen und Erläuterungen von Lic.
Theol. Dr. W. Germann. Allentown, Pa.:
Brobst, Diehl & Co.; Halle:
Waisenhausbuchhandlung, 1881.

WA

D. Martin Luthers Werke. Kritische
Gesamtausgabe. Weimar: Hermann
Böhlau, 1883-

INTRODUCTION

This second volume of the English translation of Heinrich Melchior Mühlenberg's *Korrespondenz* contains sixty-one letters written between 1748 and 1752, thirty-six written by him and twenty-five to him. The correspondence is quite evenly divided between international correspondence, linking the Old World of England and Germany with the New World of the American colonies on the eastern seaboard, and local correspondence within and between these same colonies. Of the international correspondence, the most important is that between Mühlenberg (and his colleagues) and "the Very Reverend Fathers" in London and Halle; the twenty-three letters in this category--eight written by Mühlenberg, fourteen by Gotthilf August Francke and one by Friedrich Michael Ziegenhagen--are among the longer letters in the volume and account for almost half of the volume in terms of length. The local correspondence is less focused than the international correspondence; however, from mid-1750 on, "the New York affair"--Mühlenberg's contact with the Dutch Church in New York, his sojourn in that city in the summers of 1751 and 1752, and the possibility that he might take a call to that congregation--accounts for thirteen letters in this volume (to say nothing of the space that is devoted to this topic in the correspondence between Mühlenberg and the Fathers during these years).

The one topic that ties together all of the correspondence in this volume is the *ecclesia plantanda*, the church that is being planted in North America's wilderness, and the ministry that Mühlenberg and his colleagues are exercising "among the dispersed and erring sheep of the evangelical flock" (p. 211) in Pennsylvania, New Jersey and New York. The years 1748-52 were years of high immigration to the colonies, and there was a corresponding growth in the numbers of both clergy and congregations. At the beginning of 1748 Mühlenberg was still supported by only one clergy colleague and two catechists; by 1752 Mühlenberg could list eight pastors and two catechists who were serving a total of twenty-three large and small congregations. In fact, Mühlenberg's ministry impacted on an even larger populace and territory; in late 1751 in Letters 106 and 107 when Mühlenberg reflected on all of the congregations and clergy with which he was in some sort of (not always friendly) contact, he wrote about some sixteen pastors and catechists and thirty-three congregations (plus their outparishes or filials). Although there was considerable turmoil associated with the rapid growth of both the colonies and the churches, the correspondence also makes evident the strong organizational thrust that is

xv

emerging in these years. One of the first letters in this volume (Letter 71A) stresses the importance of the "College of Pastors of the united Evangelical Lutheran congregations in Pennsylvania" and indicates that it has been functioning in significant ways for some time already. However, it is generally 1748 that is seen as the year of important beginnings, marking as it does the formation of the Pennsylvania Ministerium, the first synodical meeting, the first synodical ordination and the creation of uniform liturgies for use in the churches.

If the dominant topic here is the church and its ministry, the dominant personality is that of Henry Melchior Mühlenberg. He is the person we get to know best in this correspondence, in part because he has the most letters (thirty-six) and they tend to be the longest (accounting for nearly seventy percent of the total volume). But we also get to know him well because he wears his heart on his sleeve; his dreams and disappointments, his physical and emotional highs and lows are all laid out here. Thus we rather quickly learn that although the church was being planted and watered with some considerable success in these years, this ministry was placing enormous physical and emotional strains on Mühlenberg. Combined with occasional illnesses and the responsibilities associated with being a husband, father and manager along with his wife of an extensive household, this work brought Mühlenberg to the brink of collapse. The year 1751 was a particularly difficult one for Mühlenberg. In this year, when he reached the age of forty, he appears to have experienced a kind of burnout or even mid-life crisis. He was "sick unto death" (p. 129) early in the year in Pennsylvania and in June he was suffering from "hectic fever" (p. 129) while he was living in New York. In his sick and sorry state he sent off a letter to the Fathers in London and Halle (Letter 93), a letter which he soon termed his "melancholy letter" (p. 133). Late in the fall of that same year Mühlenberg sent off a similar letter to his friend Johann Martin Boltzius in Ebenezer, Georgia. In both of these letters he speaks of his inability to carry on with the ministry; his only goal now seems to be to find a place, whether in Pennsylvania or Georgia, where he can withdraw into quiet retirement and "prepare for a blessed end" (p. 186).

By 1752 Mühlenberg seems to have come through the worst of his crisis. Mühlenberg in 1752 is no longer seeking withdrawal and retirement; in fact, when he proposes the creation of a retirement home for "poor, weak and worn-out brothers in the ministry" (p. 219) he no longer lists himself among the candidates for such an institution as he had done earlier. And a retirement home is only a small part of Mühlenberg's ambitious proposals in 1752; he is now dreaming of duplicating in North America the "blessed institutions" in Halle, complete with a hospital, seminary, retirement home, school, orphanage, "modest book and pharmaceutical store" and a "small printing press" (p. 216).

Mühlenberg's more robust and positive outlook in 1752 appears to be directly related to the fact that in this year he finally addresses a problem that has been affecting him for some time and no doubt played a large part in his "crisis." The problem was his relationship with the Fathers, or at least his perception of that relationship. Mühlenberg felt that he probably compromised his standing with the Fathers because he had "whined and complained" in his journals of 1750 (p. 235). He was embarrassed by his "melancholy letter" (Letter 93) and also fearful that Boltzius might forward his "long letter of complaint" (Letter 107) to the Fathers (p. 258). When two "new brothers" arrived in Philadelphia from Halle on 1 December 1751, Mühlenberg questioned them anxiously about the Fathers' disposition towards him (pp. 204-5). Thus it was a significant moment in early 1752 when Mühlenberg felt secure and self-confident enough to confront head-on this issue of his relationship with the Fathers. In a long letter of 18 February 1752 (Letter 112) Mühlenberg addressed misunderstandings that went back to 1742 (he was supposedly unhappy about having been sent initially to Georgia); in the main, however, he dealt with what he understood were the Fathers' main criticisms of him, namely, his involvement with congregations and clergy that were under the authority of other ministeriums (as had happened in 1745 when Mühlenberg became involved in "the Wolf affair" on the Raritan in New Jersey and as was happening again with Mühlenberg's association with the Dutch Church in New York). Mühlenberg's defence and explanation of his decisions and actions was simply to state that the distinctive North American context made his particular choices necessary. "The right reverend gentlemen in Hamburg," who were the sponsors of both the congregations on the Raritan and the Dutch Church in New York, "may judge as they wish," Mühlenberg wrote, but the reality is that they "are far removed from America" (p. 207). Addressing more directly the Fathers in London and Halle, Mühlenberg went on to write that his "involvement with alien labourers" and his adherence to "the instruction they [i.e., the Fathers] gave" (pp. 207-8) had to be evaluated in light of the "circumstances with their encumbrances." These circumstances, he argued, did not leave him with "any other choice" (p. 207). His comment that he had acted in accord with reason and the grace given to him and that subsequently he had "not yet discovered any reproof of conscience before God" (p. 206) would seem to apply to all the areas where he felt he was being criticized.

It is important to recognize that Mühlenberg was not challenging the authority of the Fathers. He was being quite forthright when he wrote that he considered "the voice of the Fathers to be the voice of God" (p. 209). What he did appear to want from the Fathers was their assurance that they did not see his actions and decisions as acts of disobedience but rather as necessary choices made within the limitations of a context that was quite foreign to them and for which their instructions had given him little preparation.

Francke's letter to Mühlenberg of 13 September 1752 (Letter 124) provides a very suitable capstone to the correspondence between the Fathers and Mühlenberg in this volume. In some respects the letter must have been quite disappointing to Mühlenberg. Although Francke did send over some Halle medicines and books in 1752 (p. 265), his response to Mühlenberg's proposals for establishing North American equivalents of the Halle institutions was essentially negative: at the present time the financial situation of the Pennsylvania congregations precluded such an undertaking, and even in the future Francke indicated that he would need to be persuaded. Francke noted that his father, August Hermann Francke, always carefully "tested the ways of God and was careful not to start anything in which he did not clearly see his footsteps leading the way" (p. 279). Also in relation to "the circumstances in New York," Francke clearly advised against accepting the call (p. 281). On the critical matter of how Francke assessed Mühlenberg's actions and his contributions to the Pennsylvania ministry, however, Francke's comments must have been deeply satisfying to Mühlenberg personally, for the letter is strongly affirmative of Mühlenberg and his work. Francke admits that he had had some initial misgivings about Mühlenberg and his methods but that he now realized that Mühlenberg had acted "wisely in several confused circumstances" (p. 277). The integrity of Mühlenberg's motives is affirmed in this letter, and he is recognized as the one whose presence holds the Pennsylvania congregations together and to whom they "look primarily" (p. 281). On balance, then, Mühlenberg must have felt considerable satisfaction with this letter. Given Mühlenberg's commitment to the unique realities of church life in North America and to the indigenous church structures that were emerging, as well as his equally strong commitment to "the complete authority" of the Very Reverend Fathers "to arrange matters as they wish" (p. 221), there was clearly potential for future difficulties. In late 1752, however, the relationship with the Fathers seemed once again to be quite solid.

These central themes of the correspondence are only a sample of the riches contained in these letters. Along with Mühlenberg's *Journals*, they offer an unparalleled description of life in the American colonies at the mid-point of the eighteenth century. In a review of the first two volumes of the *Korrespondenz*, A. G. Roeber did not exaggerate when he wrote: "Aside from the better-known writings of eighteenth century New England divines, no other body of letters chronicles in such depth the culture, society, and politics, as well as the religious texture of North America" (*William and Mary Quarterly* [Jan. 1988], p. 191).

Readers of this volume of the *Correspondence* are referred back to the Introduction in Volume 1 for general principles that were laid out there about the translating and editing of the *Correspondence*. These principles continue to be the operative principles in the present volume. For assistance in the preparation of this volume we are once again indebted to a number of persons and institutions. We want to thank Professor Dr. Martin Brecht for personal assistance and for permission to use the facilities of the Institute for the Study of the History of Pietism, Münster, Germany. Dr. Karl-Otto Strohmidel, Münster, Germany, was once again most generous in sharing his valuable expertise on the *Korrespondenz*; we have benefitted greatly from his help and friendship and we extend our grateful thanks to him. The Dutch and Latin letters in this volume created some problems for us, and we had to draw on the expertise of a number of colleagues and friends: Dr. Gordon Lathrop of the Lutheran Theological Seminary at Philadelphia assisted with the translation of the Dutch letters; Tim Hegedus, Ph.D. candidate at the University of Toronto, translated most of the Latin letters while he was a student at the Lutheran Theological Seminary at Saskatoon, and Dr. Gottfried Krodel, Valparaiso, Indiana, helped with a couple of particularly problematic letters. We acknowledge gratefully the help we have received from these persons, at the same time accepting full responsibility for the final product.

John W. Kleiner
Lutheran Theological Seminary
Saskatoon, Saskatchewan

Helmut T. Lehmann
Lutheran Theological Seminary
Philadelphia, Pennsylvania

LETTERS OF 1748

Letter 70

To Wilhelmine Sophie von Münchhausen[1]
Providence, 24 February 1748

This fragment of a letter again (see Letter 60, Correspondence *1:311-15) pays tribute to Mühlenberg's noble patron, Baroness Wilhelmine Sophie von Münchhausen.*

Text in German: Korrespondenz *1:309. For further textual information, see* Korrespondenz *1:309.*

Providence, 24 February 1748, old calendar
Honorable Lady,
Gracious Consort of the High Sheriff:
It depresses me that I have already written twice quite extensively to Your Honorable Grace and afterwards had to learn that the first letter, sent via Holland, got lost,[2] and the second one of 1747, sent on an English ship, fell into French hands![3] Nevertheless I console myself that nothing can happen without God's will and permission. Should this present insignificant letter be preserved through God's special providence and be delivered submissively to Your Honorable Grace--if Your Grace has still been sustained in this vale of tears and has not yet been translated into the eternal rest and the blessed homeland--I will humbly praise God for it! What should I now report and in what way could I seek to give some small thanks for the countless most gracious kindnesses, holy zeal and tireless care which Your Honorable Grace bestowed on my insignificant person many years ago and which you are pleased to demonstrate to my beloved coworkers and to the scattered, erring and forsaken sheep in Pennsylvania down to the present hour? If I were to report something of my circumstances I would perhaps try the patience of Your Honorable Grace more than I would give you thanks.

Heinrich Melchior Mühlenberg

---

1. On Baroness Wilhelmine Sophie von Münchhausen, see *Correspondence* 1:18 n. 18. For her significance to Mühlenberg, see especially Letter 60, written to her by Mühlenberg on 20 February 1747, *Correspondence* 1:311-15.
2. Written in 1745; see Letter 43, *Correspondence* 1:227.
3. Letter 60; see *Correspondence* 1:311-15.

Letter 71

Gotthilf August Francke to Peter Brunnholz and Mühlenberg
Halle, 23 July 1748

In general Francke's letter is prompted by his eagerness to hear how Mühlenberg and Brunnholz are faring; specifically he is replying to Brunnholz's letter of 22 September 1747. He expresses concern about Brunnholz's health and about Schaum's apparent desire to return to Germany. Financial matters in relation to the Pennsylvania congregations and relationships with various persons are discussed; Francke gives particular attention to Johann Albert Weygand, a would-be pastor who was known to Francke but who had set off for America with a group of German immigrants without the proper authorization and credentials. The letter is written in Francke's characteristic rather convoluted style and with the usual pietistic flourishes.

Text in German: Korrespondenz *1:309-12. For further textual information, see* Korrespondenz *1:312.*

To Pastor Mühlenberg
and Pastor Brunnholtz
in Pennsylvania

23 July 1748

Reverend,
Dearly beloved Brothers in the Lord:
I cannot refrain from sending off herewith a few lines to you. I am very eager to hear about the welfare of both of you, about how the work of the Lord is proceeding in your midst and once again to receive some report from you. May the Lord soon allow us to rejoice and grant us the particular pleasure of hearing much good news of the happy and blessed arrival of dear Pastor Handschuch.[1] I greatly regret that the many letters and reports got lost with Captain Seimour, particularly because there was among them a significant report on your circumstances.[2] If you could have a copy made of it and sent, it would be very good. I am much grieved to hear that Pastor Brunholtz[3] has been ill again, and my heartfelt wish for him is that the Lord would grant him in the future more constant and somewhat more lasting well-being. I have duly received and answered on 18 September of last year the letters of 30 May 1747[4] along with the report of the worthy

Mr. Weiser on the travels of Count von Zinzendorf among the Indians.[5] The aforementioned report was very welcome to many people and was included by Doctor Baumgarden in the fifth collection of his *Objections* in his last writing against the Moravians.[6] I am pleased that you have received my previous letter of 24 March 1747.[7] It is also gratifying that the patrons and benefactors in Stuttgart have shown themselves to be loving and generous towards the new church in Germantown.[8]

These are God's own unique ways that he has not only allowed it to be so difficult to find a pair of helpers for my worthy brothers, but has also led dear Pastor Handschuch through so many difficulties and round about ways. But we will not allow these things to discourage us again; rather we will reassure ourselves that such trials are in no way to be viewed as a sign that God is not with us; we will much rather put our trust in him, that through such trials he is preparing for us all the more blessing. I am anxious to learn if you have in the meantime been able to ordain the catechists and with them to supply the needs of some congregations. All the same it is not pleasing to me that good Mr. Schaum[9] still speaks of going back. I hope, however, when he has considered the matter more carefully, namely, that it is not good to set aside a loving God's discipline and follow one's own ideas, that he will also allow such whims to pass away. In the accompanying letter[10] I have sought only in more general ways to direct him to a simple yielding to the will of God and his ways. You will continue to hold up before him the reasons that can move him to this: that it is more for his own sake, so that in the future sometime he will not have to regret that he had put his hand to the plow and nevertheless had looked back.[11] Thus for the sake of the work, God could rather, so to speak, make for himself servants and instruments from the stones[12] than that he should leave the work undone if people do not want to do his work. I am very pleased that Pastor Hartwich[13] is siding with you and in his own measure demonstrating a Christian bearing. May God grant him an increasingly clear eye so that he seeks only the salvation of the souls entrusted to him and that he brings himself down to their level in a fine, simple way. To enter into much debate with the Reformed I also consider is not wise; one must not even start it.

I am glad that the Reformed pastor, Mr. Slatter,[14] is showing himself to be very peaceable and is establishing good relationships with you in externals; likewise I am pleased that God has helped to the extent that the church buildings in Philadelphia can be entirely finished and that the aggravations associated with the distribution of the church pews are overcome.[15] May God continue to help! This is as much as I wanted to state at this time on the occasion of Pastor Brunholtz's welcome letter of 22 September 1747.[16]

Additionally the following is also to be noted:

(1) Blessed Deacon Berner[17] of the St. Boniface Cathedral in Halberstadt left one hundred reichstaler in his will towards the construction of the church in Philadelphia. In my letter of 29 May of the current year, I am assigning it immediately for remittance to Court Preacher Ziegenhagen, along with seventeen pounds five shillings sterling, in my letter of 29 May of the current year.

(2) Because according to the accompanying account of 1747 there is nothing more on hand for the congregations than what came in anew during this year, to which belong the five reichstaler which have come in from Pastor Laurentius[18] in the accompanying letter,[19] I will remit it, along with what will still come in, at the time of the fall fair.

(3) If the offering for the Pennsylvania congregations has really been announced in the Darmstadt region for the Ninth Sunday after Trinity, may God awaken their hearts to charitableness and allow a rich blessing to come forth from it for the congregations.[20]

(4) I wanted to pass on the news to you that a candidate of theology, by the name of Weygand,[21] who studied here for a time, also taught in the Orphans' Home and most recently had a position in Frankfurt, is joining as their pastor a new shipment of German people who are moving to Pennsylvania--as he himself reports in the accompanying copy of the letter to Court Preacher Ziegenhagen.[22] From the letter it is already apparent that he is a person who exceeds his grasp; perhaps all too soon he will regret that he has abandoned a regular call and preferred the offer of such people who themselves have no authority to issue a call. So far as one can still remember his disposition here, he pretended at all times to have much that was good in mind, but self-love and pride showed through everywhere. Pastor Sommer[23] of Schortewitz and Court Preacher Allendorff,[24] to whom he appeals among others, are not able to remember much more about him either; I have not yet called in a report from Abbot Steinmetz,[25] but I suspect that he also will not remember much about him. My dear brothers will themselves see from this that they will have to act prudently and test his disposition for themselves; they will also have to treat him as God will give them opportunity to do so. In the meantime if he should see that the Pennsylvania air is different than he had imagined, he may very well think of longing[26] to return as soon as possible, as often happens when people undertake something without sufficient testing of God's will; or perhaps God will achieve his ultimate purpose more nearly under the dear cross. This is truly to be desired. Finally, I leave you in the care of the Lord and remain with sincere love ever

Your,

G. A. Francke

1. On Johann Friedrich Handschuh, see *Correspondence* 1:291 n. 18.

2. Brunnholz had mentioned in his letter of 30 May 1747 that he had sent several letters off to Europe in February 1747. "On 19 February of the current year I wrote to Your Reverences [and sent it] with Captain Semour, and also enclosed with it the eight letters to various patrons and friends in Europe. I have received no confirmation of their safe arrival. However, the letters written on 3 November 1746 will have arrived safely with Captain Messnard." See *Korrespondenz* 1:312 n. 2.

3. Peter Brunnholz (-1757) studied at the university in Halle and in 1744 accepted a call to serve in Pennsylvania. He arrived in Philadelphia on 26 January 1745, accompanied by two catechists, Johann Nicolaus Kurz and Johann Helfrich Schaum. He served Philadelphia and Germantown from 1745-51. His health was frail, and from 1751 until his death in 1757 he had to limit his ministry to Philadelphia. He worked closely with Mühlenberg, was the second ordained pastor sent out from Halle to Pennsylvania (Mühlenberg being the first) and was one of the founders of the Pennsylvania Ministerium. See *Pastors and People* 1:23.

4. Namely, Brunnholz's letter; see n. 2, above.

5. See Brunnholz's letter of 30 May 1747: "I sent along a copy of Mr. Weiser's answer to my preliminary questions about the Count's Indian travels and have kept the original of it. If it were necessary and useful it could be printed or sent to Mr. Fresenius." For further archival information on this letter by Peter Brunnholz and Conrad Weiser's answer to it, dated 16 February 1746, see *Korrespondenz* 1:312 n. 4. Letter 68, dated 17 September 1747, is Francke's reply. - On Johann Conrad Weiser, see *Correspondence* 1:142 n. 7. - On Nikolaus Ludwig Count von Zinzendorf, see *Correspondence* 1:2 n. 2.

6. Siegmund Jakob Baumgarten (1706-57) studied theology in Halle; he became G.A. Francke's assistant in 1728 and professor of theology in 1743. His *Theological Objections*, to which Francke is referring here, appeared in seven numbers from 1743-50. Weiser's letter, however, is printed not in the fifth but in the sixth collection, in the forty-fourth section (pp. 673-703).

7. Letter 62.

8. In his letter of 3 November 1746 Brunnholz had reported: "A man who is a member of the church, Mathias Genzel, is now leaving for Stuttgart. This man has told my deacons in Germantown that he will certainly be given a bell in Stuttgart and perhaps also freewill offerings if they would send along a letter with him. To satisfy them in this matter and also to leave no stone unturned, I undertook to prepare a letter last Sunday in Germantown to the ministerium in Stuttgart. In it I stipulated two points: (1) The letter must first be presented to the Court Preacher to ascertain if it would be useful to pass it on to the ministerium. Consequently the man will go over in this ship and make inquiries in Kensington. (2) In the event that something in the form of money should be given, it would be better to send it to Halle by some pastor or friend than to give it to the man; for even though he is no doubt honest, it is still unsafe. But if a bell would be given, he could bring it with him. I wrote the letter with these conditions; Your Reverences can take the matter under consideration and advise what is best." On 22 September 1747 Brunnholz was able to write to Europe that he had received a "gratifying letter from Counsellor Fischer of the consistory in Stuttgart, dated 13 March . . . . the due reception of which I simply wanted to announce here in a preliminary way and at the same time indicate what great joy this gave me, so that my superiors might be pleased [to learn] that the most worthy patrons in Stuttgart have not yet become weary in caring for our congregation and have taken care of my Germantown church in a fatherly way." For further archival information on these two letters, see *Korrespondenz* 1:312 n. 7.

9. Johann Helfrich Schaum (1721-78) arrived in Philadelphia with newly ordained Peter Brunnholz and fellow catechist Johann Nicolaus Kurz on 15 January 1745. He functioned mainly as a schoolmaster in Philadelphia until 1747 when he was assigned as an assistant pastor to the congregations on the Raritan in New Jersey. See *Correspondence* 1:154 n. 6 and *Pastors and People* 1:115f.

10. Francke's letter to Schaum of 28 July 1748. See *Korrespondenz* 1:312 n. 8.

11. See Luke 9:62.

12. See Matt. 3:9 and Luke 3:8; also Luke 19:40.
13. On Johann Christoph Hartwich, see *Correspondence* 1:323 n. 19. Although Hartwich was sent out by the Hamburg Consistory, his Halle connections brought him increasingly into the sphere of influence of the Pennsylvania Ministerium.
14. On Michael Schlatter, see *Correspondence* 1:342 n. 41.
15. The German term for church pews that is used here, *Kirchenstände*, could also be translated as church boxes or stalls. These pews/boxes/stalls were assigned and rented out, and this process often caused controversy.
16. This letter is extant in a fair copy. See *Korrespondenz* 1:312 n. 10.
17. Johann Friedrich Berner, canon and subsenior of the St. Boniface Cathedral in Halberstadt.
18. This may be a reference to Karl Gottlob Laurentius. He was born in Wölkau in Saxony, ordained on 6 July 1738, and accepted a call to Gross Krausnick in the Doberburg-Sonnewalde region. From 1741 to 1772 he was pastor and superintendent in Sonnewalde.
19. The letter is not extant, but it is mentioned in *HN2/1*:326.
20. On the offering for the Pennsylvania congregations to be taken in the Darmstadt territories, see esp. Letter 37 in *Correspondence* 1:167-70.
21. Johann Albert Weygand (1722-70). On Weygand, see the curriculum vitae which Mühlenberg incorporated into his letter of 16 November 1748 to the Fathers (Letter 72:14-15); see also *Pastors and People* 1:162f.
22. Not extant. In a postscript to this letter Francke writes to Ziegenhagen: "The accompanying letter from a person who is unknown to us, named Weygand, was delivered to us with the regular mail. In regard to his request to the Court Preacher nothing can be done here, particularly since his action is open to question in that he declined a regular call and moved to Pennsylvania with a group of people who themselves do not have the proper authority to issue a call. However, since his arrival in Pennsylvania could be either useful or detrimental to the dear pastors, we request the Court Preacher to make some more careful inquiries about the character of this man, if it is not troublesome and if it is not already known, so that this can be reported to the brethren in Pennsylvania." See *Korrespondenz* 1:313 n. 16.

Francke appended to his letter an undated memorandum from Pastor Sommer. In it he states: "About Mr. Johann Albert Weygand I have noted this much, that: 26 August 1722 he was born in Kempfenbrunn in the Hanau region. 1 July 1745 he came to Broseik and held a position with Lady von Zantbieren. 19 April 1746 he left there again. During his stay in Broseik he once sent a letter through me (if I am not mistaken) to his brother, named Casemir Weygand, who is a police officer in Partenstein near Gelnhausen. He visited me frequently and, as far as I can remember, he conducted himself well; he also went to Communion with me in Schortewitz on the Tenth and Nineteenth Sundays after Trinity, 1745." See *Korrespondenz* 1:313 n. 16.
23. Johann Heinrich Sommer (1675-1758), a native of Silesia, studied theology in Leipzig and served as pastor of a number of congregations. In 1728 he was accused of pietistic practices and for a short time left the ministry. However, in 1731 he accepted the call to Schortewitz and remained there until his death. He was well known as the author of hymns and devotional writings.
24. Johann Ludwig Conrad Allendorf (1693-1773) was born near Marburg and studied theology in Giessen and Halle, beginning in 1711. He was a tutor, first for Count Erdmann Heinrich von Henckel-Pölzig and then for Count Erdmann von Promnitz in Sorau. He became court preacher in Köthen in 1724, pastor and consistorial counsellor in Wernigerode in 1755 and pastor at the Ulrichskirche in Halle in 1759. See also *Correspondence* 1:6 n. 13.
25. Johann Adam Steinmetz (1689-1762) was born in Gross-Kriegnitz and studied theology in Leipzig, Wittenberg, Helmstedt, Jena and Halle. After serving in various places and positions he ran into difficulties and fled to the Duchy of Magdeburg. In 1732 he became general superintendent and consistorial counsellor there and abbot of the Bergen Cloister.
26. Reading *zurücksehnen* for *zurücksehen*.

Letter 71A

Johann Nicolaus Schwingel, Adam Lösch et al. to Mühlenberg
Peter Brunnholz and Johann Friedrich Handschuh
Philadelphia, 13 August 1748

In this letter the officers of the Lutheran congregation in Tulpehocken address the "College of Pastors (collegium pastorum) of the United Evangelical Lutheran Congregations in Pennsylvania" with the request that they provide them with their own regular pastor. They reflect on the very satisfactory relationship that they have had with this body since they first approached them on 8 July 1745 with a request for spiritual care. They list seven reasons why they continue to look to this body for leadership and they promise their support in general to this body and in particular to the pastor that is provided for them. This letter is an important statement of Lutheran ecclesiology and church polity in colonial times; it is also an important witness to the fact that the College of Pastors is coming to be recognized, as it is by the writers of this letter, as a "legitimate and regular presbytery and ministerium" whose leaders function as "chief pastors and spiritual caregivers" for the Lutheran congregations in Pennsylvania.

This letter has been translated in the Halle Reports, *pp. 214-17, and that translation serves as the basis for our translation, with some editorial changes. There is also an excerpt of this letter in* Documentary History, *pp. 21-23.*

Text in German: Korrespondenz *1:313-16. For further textual information, see* Korrespondenz *1:317.*

To the reverend and learned sirs, all the pastors of the united Evangelical Lutheran congregations in Pennsylvania at Philadelphia, Germantown, Providence and New Hanover: Mr. Mühlenberg, Mr. Brunnholtz and Mr. Handschuch, our honored pastors and reverend spiritual fathers in Christ.

To all the reverend and learned,
Most honored Sirs:
It is sufficiently well known to Your Reverences that we, the undersigned, who are all officers and members of the Evangelical Lutheran congregation at Tulpehocken and vicinity, in the county of Lancaster in the province of Pennsylvania, presented to the College of Pastors of the united Evangelical Lutheran congregations in Pennsylvania, in particular to Pastor Muhlenberg and Pastor Brunnholtz,[1] a petition in the English language, that

was dated 8 July 1745 and signed by various members of the said Evangelical Lutheran congregation at Tulpehocken.[2] In it we bewailed the deplorable state of our spiritual lives and especially the lack of upright teachers and pastors and we begged them respectfully to have compassion on our spiritual need, to accept us as part of their pastoral charge, to allow us also to enjoy their spiritual care and, in short, to be our pastors and the shepherds of our souls. Similarly, in a second, detailed petition, written in the German language, we renewed our most humble request.[3] Your Reverences are sufficiently familiar with this. We also acknowledge with due thanks and humble praise to God the faithful care for our souls by the reverend College of Pastors of the united congregations which we have enjoyed since that time. However, since our congregation is growing through the efforts of Your Reverences and God's blessing and the unhappy ruptures have been somewhat healed, we are now in a position through God's grace and have the desire to support our own pastor, and our situation of pressing need requires it. Therefore we, the aforementioned undersigned officers of the Evangelical Lutheran congregation at Tulpehocken, in our own names and in the name of our congregation, most respectfully and obediently petition the reverend and honorable College of Pastors and especially the reverend gentlemen who currently make up this college, namely, Pastor Mühlenberg, Pastor Brunnholtz and Pastor Handschuh,[4] to send to us as a regular pastor for our congregation at Tulpehocken, either someone out of their own midst or some other person who has been examined, ordained and adequately authorized for all priestly functions within whatever restrictions and regulations are established by the reverend College of Pastors.[5] In all this the presupposition is always that we, together with the united congregations, constitute one entire Evangelical Lutheran community which acknowledges and respects all the pastors who make up the College of Pastors, and with whom our own particular pastor remains in the closest association. As we have sufficient grounds to hope that the reverend College of Pastors will grant this our reasonable and respectful request, we want to indicate and set forth adequately both why we have applied to your reverend College of Pastors and requested it to provide a pastor for us, as well as to indicate what it can expect from us. With this in mind we will first of all set forth the reasons which have prompted us in our spiritual affairs, both in the past as well as in the present, to resort to this college; then we will set forth the main points in respect to which we, both for ourselves and in the name of our constituents, will bind ourselves to this college and to the regular pastor who is appointed to us by it.

The reasons that moved us to resort to your reverend College of Pastors in our spiritual need and to call you to care for our souls are, among others, principally the following:

(1) Your legitimate, regular and, therefore, divine call.

(2) The good testimonials you received from such spiritual fathers and public teachers of our Evangelical Lutheran Church in Europe who, by their zeal for the retention of the evangelical doctrine according to the Unaltered Augsburg Confession and by the uprightness of their lives in harmony with the same and with the whole word of God, out of which this confession is taken, have been shining like lights throughout the whole Protestant Church; and especially those which you have from the University of Halle in Saxony, which is like a city set on a hill,[6] which enlightens much with its light and which has already awakened many to the glorification of God. May the Lord continue to keep it as a blessing, defend it against all heresy and make it a place where godliness is united with pure doctrine; may it be a workshop of the great God in which many vessels of honor will be used to the praise of the Lord, the building up of the evangelical truth by the church of Jesus Christ and the eternal salvation of many thousands of souls.

(3) We are moved to do this by your faithfulness to the confession and the teaching of the Unaltered Augsburg Confession which has been fiercely attacked here, sometimes by false brethren, sometimes by fanatical sects, sometimes by Epicureans and various others. You have not only survived such attacks personally but you have also maintained, gathered and increased the numbers of Evangelical Lutheran members. Let this be said to the praise of God who has stood by you.

(4) We are also led to this by the blessed way in which you have conducted your ministry, whereby many were brought from darkness to light and from the power of Satan to God[7] and were sustained by you.

(5) Your gifts for ministry and your good sense, as well as your experience and your willingness to accommodate yourselves to the peculiar circumstances of this country.

(6) Your assembly[8] which allows us to hope not only that something good has been established but also that it will be continued for us and for our descendants.

(7) The faithfulness and conscientiousness which you have demonstrated not only toward the united congregations but also toward other congregations that had recourse to you.

These things, among others, have moved us in our situation of pressing need to put our trust in Your Reverences next to God and to turn to you in our spiritual concerns.

Out of these concerns, the desire has grown among us to be incorporated into and included in the united congregations in Pennsylvania and to be recognized and received as brothers and fellow members of a local congregation of the Evangelical Lutheran Church and, as a result, to participate in the spiritual care of the reverend College of Pastors of the united congregations.

Thus, we do hereby, in a most public and solemn manner, appeal to, recognize and acknowledge the reverend pastors of the united congregations[9] in Pennsylvania as our pastors and shepherds. We also invest them with full authority to care for our spiritual welfare in whatever manner, by whomever and for as long as they are willing to do so. Further, we promise to recognize the reverend College of Pastors of the Evangelical Lutheran community in Pennsylvania as a legitimate and regular presbytery and ministerium and, in particular, as our own chief pastors and spiritual caregivers. We also promise to respect and esteem them as such and to do, arrange, determine or change nothing in church matters without their prior advice and consent. Consequently we will not enter into any agreement with any preacher, and even with the pastor they send to us we will not undertake anything in important church matters without their prior advice and consent. On the contrary, whatever the united reverend College of Pastors may determine in our case and in general church matters, having duly informed and instructed us, we will accept and seek to comply with and bring about with all our might. Further, we promise to recognize, welcome, respect, honor and listen to as our regularly and divinely called pastor the pastor who will be sent to us by the reverend College of Pastors, as long as it may please the reverend College of Pastors to leave him with us. We would also not resist if they should decide for good reasons to call him away and send someone else in his place; rather we would receive and maintain his successor and the one taking his place with the same love and reverence. Again, we give the assurance that if (God forbid) any misunderstanding or division should arise either among the members of the whole congregation, or between some of them and the pastor, or between individual congregation members, we will report this at once to the reverend College of Pastors, to await their decision and to abide by the same.

Finally, we promise to maintain the pastor or pastors sent to us according to their need. To this end we are committing ourselves to a special subscription and holding the congregation to it to the best of our ability, so that our pastor will receive what he needs annually.

We subscribe our signatures to this document, both for ourselves and in the name of our congregation.

Executed at Philadelphia, 13 August 1748.

Johann Nicolaus Schwingel
Adam Lösch
Balthasar Anspach
Johannes Immel
Church Council at Tulpehocken

Abraham Lauck
Martin Batdorff
Deacons at Tulpehocken
Andreas Bager
Deacon at Northkill

1. In June of 1745 Mühlenberg and Brunnholz had determined "occasionally to hold a gathering and fraternal conference in which all necessary things could be considered and agreed upon in cordial love and unity" (*HN1*:43f.; *HN2/1*:100). - On Peter Brunnholz, see Letter 71 n. 3.

2. On the earlier situation in Tulpehocken, see *Correspondence* 1:234 n. 6 and 241-43.

3. The congregation at Tulpehocken was without a pastor since Tobias Wagner's departure from there in 1746. Tobias Wagner (see *Correspondence* 1:128 n. 9) was serving Tulpehocken on a term basis, and in 1746 his term was not renewed; thereafter his relations with the Pennsylvania Ministerium and with Mühlenberg deteriorated markedly. Wagner was replaced by the catechist Johann Nicolaus Kurz (see *Correspondence* 1:154 n. 5 and 341 n. 16). The Tulpehocken congregation's petition in the German language is not extant.

4. On Johann Friedrich Handschuh, see *Correspondence* 1:291 n. 18.

5. Mühlenberg writes in his journal in 1748: "AUGUST 13. Pastor Brunnholtz, Pastor Handschue, Pastor Hartwich and I being present, we drew up the *instrumenta vocationis*, examined Mr. Kurtz, and, in the evening, had the deacons and elders of Tulpehocken who were present sign it, [HN: and also had Mr. Kurtz execute a *revers*]. The deacons and elders were hesitant and fearful concerning several points because Magister Wagner had spoken with them on the way and insinuated all sorts of prejudices. [HD: But after we had enlightened them in a kindly way, we told them that they did not have long to consider because we could ordain Mr. Kurtz anyhow and send him to Raritan. They then changed their minds and signed]" (*Journals* 1:201). See also the nine examination questions, dated 12 August 1748, formulated by Brunnholz, Handschuh and Hartwich (*Halle Reports*, pp. 209f.; *Documentary History*, pp. 18f.), Kurz's answers to these questions (*Halle Reports*, pp. 211-14) and his oath of office (*revers*) of 13 August 1748, which was also signed by two deacons of the Tulpehocken congregation (*Halle Reports*, pp. 208f.; *Documentary History*, pp. 20f). Johann Nicolaus Kurz was ordained at the synod convention in Philadelphia on 14 August 1748; on this, see Mühlenberg's journal entry of 14 August 1748 (*Journals* 1:202) and Kurz's journal for 12-15 August 1748 (*Documentary History*, pp. 6f.). See also G. A. Francke's recommendations for the ordination and calling of a pastor in Letter 62 of 24 March 1747 (Correspondence 1:319-20).

6. See Matt. 5:14.

7. See Acts 26:18.

8. The reference is to the convention of the Synod which was about to meet in Philadelphia: 14-15 August 1748. For further particulars, see *Documentary History*, pp. 8-12; *HN2/1*:208-11.

9. The German word used here, *Kirchen=Gemeinden*, represents an attempt to reflect the unity between the church as a whole and the local congregation.

Letter 72

To Gotthilf August Francke and Friedrich Michael Ziegenhagen
Providence, 16 November 1748

After preliminary apologies to the Reverend Fathers for failing to keep them fully up to date on his life and activities and the promise to get caught up as soon as possible when the situation permits, Mühlenberg gets on with the burden of his letter which is a discussion of what to do with Johann Albert Weygand, a pastor who has arrived from Germany on 7 September 1748 without a call. The letter shows Mühlenberg on the horns of a dilemma. On the one hand, Weygand has not come through the proper channels and may be a fraud. On the other hand, Mühlenberg is quite impressed by his examination of Weygand's "studies, faith and life" and sees the possibility of placing another pastor in the field. Mühlenberg presents to the Fathers the particularly difficult situation of the congregations in the wake of the Wolf Affair (see Letter 42, Correspondence 1:203-26). The letter appears to be both a request for direction from the Fathers and a statement asking the Fathers to confirm what Mühlenberg has already done, namely, to send Weygand to the Raritan congregations for a one year term.

Text in German: Korrespondenz *1:317-24.   For further textual information, see* Korrespondenz *1:324.*

Very Reverend and devout Fathers in God:

The turbulent times of war at sea,[1] the extensive wandering about in this untrodden country, the many different tasks and the alternation of sickness and health have for some time now prevented us from being able to fulfill very faithfully our filial and requisite duty of writing. Herewith a long letter follows which contains some notices of deceased, sick and healthy congregation members and also a few particulars[2] for November 1746 down to approximately April 1747.[3] I would gladly have added the rest of the events which I have noted down to the present time if I had not been stricken with a serious illness, with which I still struggle, just at the time that the ships were leaving. If the most holy God should allow me to survive for another year and once again spade and till me, I would most obediently report at the first opportunity: (1) on my trip through Pennsylvania to Maryland in the year 1747; (2) on my worthy colleague Brunnholtz's serious illness, namely, the measles, which he had in my house;[4] (3) on my hot and cold fevers; (4) on Mr. Kurtz's pastoral work and his honorable marriage;[5] (5) on my pastoral work in 1748 and the necessary taking on of a congregation that has a church fifteen miles from me, is made up of English and Swedish people and previously was served in English and occasionally also in the Swedish language by the Moravians;[6] (6) on the welcome arrival of the faithful and proved servant of Christ, namely, Pastor Handschuh, and of our journey with him to Tulpehocken and Lancaster;[7] (7) on the circumstances and reasons that moved us to place Pastor Handschuh in Lancaster for half a year on an interim basis; (8) on my journey to Raritan in Jersey and the circumstances there; (9) on the necessity of Mr. Kurtz's ordination;[8] (10) on the liturgies we made for our churches;[9] (11) on the transfer of Mr. Schaum to York beyond the Susquehanna;[10] (12) on the second serious and life-threatening feverish illness of my dear colleague Brunnholtz. But what I have to report to the Reverend Fathers most urgently and first of all is this:

On 7 September of the current year a ship loaded with German people arrived outside of Philadelphia on which it was said that there was a young pastor.[11] Colleague Brunnholtz was still sick at the time. A few hotheads in the Philadelphia and Germantown congregations were soon ready to propose in their haste and without examination of the man that he could become an assistant to Pastor Brunnholtz; but on what he would live they did not know. The church councils were calm and cautious. The pastor could not come off the ship until several newlanders (that is what they call those who do not want to work here and for that reason sail off on the ships late in the year; they encourage the German people in the Rhine area to undertake the Pennsylvania trip, borrow their money, buy goods with it and late in the following year they return again with the German people; in short, they are for the most part wandering Jews who support themselves through lies and deceit)[12] who had been with him on the ship were willing to post bond to the merchant for the eight pistoles[13] owing on his passage. As soon as he was released he announced himself to Pastor Brunnholtz, but he had no testimonials with him except that all the German people from his ship testified that he had conducted himself in a pious and Christian manner, had preached to them and prayed diligently. Pastor Brunnholtz examined him about his calling and about the Moravians; he presented to him the many dangerous ways to go astray in this land.[14] He found his manner of speech to be healthy and edifying, and he was able to relate many particulars[15] about our Very Reverend Fathers in Halle. While he stayed in the city for a few days farmers from here and there arrived who wanted to call him as pastor. Pastor Andrae[16] also sent his messengers, inviting him and promising to care for him. But he was silent and asked first of all to speak with me and also soon came to me in the country. As I had previously been informed by my colleague, I immediately asked very pointedly if he did not have a wandering eye and had not run ahead of his God? To this he gave the following explanation: "I, Johann Albert Wygand, was born 26 August 1722 in a village in the Hanau region where my father had been schoolmaster. In 1736 my parents placed me with a pastor for an education, and it was here that I laid the foundation for the humanities.[17]   In 1742 I went to the Illustre Gymnasium in Hanau. I was scarcely there four months when I betook myself to Halle University on my own impetus even though my patrons, like Superintendent Koerber[18] and other pastors, were opposed and said it would be dangerous in Halle on account of pietistic carrying on. In Halle I lived for half a year in the city until I was given permission to teach in the Weingarten School.[19] Afterwards I came to the major institutions for instruction and lived for a time in the senior's quarters and for a time in student rooms. I attained second level in geography and third level in French.[20]   I heard lectures by the Very Reverend Dr. Franck,[21] namely, a course in catechetics on Philipp Spener's catechism[22] and a course in exegesis on the Epistle to the Ephesians, as well as lectures by Dr. Knapp[23] and Dr. Baumgarten.[24]   In these blessed institutions I was first awakened to repentance and faith; in this the worthy assistant Niemeyer,[25] among others, was for me a blessed instrument. In the penitential struggle I was always of the opinion that I would not only have to turn away from all things but also turn to my Jesus, that I would have to follow him to the East or West Indies if I wanted to find rest. In 1744 I was recommended by Inspector Steinersdorff[26] to Mr. von Schloten in Stassfurt.[27]   On this occasion I became acquainted with the Very Reverend Abbot Steinmetz[28] and other faithful servants of Christ. In 1745 I went to Lady von Santhir[29] at Köthen as teacher, and this gave me the opportunity to become acquainted with old Father Somer.[30]   I journeyed to my home in 1746 where I experienced not a few trials because my still unconverted relatives wanted to put me into an office in an inappropriate manner.[31]   This made it necessary for me to leave my native land and to travel to Frankfurt on the Main where I instructed several children of the nobility and merchants. There I came to know Pastor Fressenius[32] as a zealous Elijah, but I experienced no fewer trials. In 1748 a number of my fellow countrymen sailed by on the Main, and a newlander brought to me in Frankfurt the call to be an itinerant preacher in America; at the same time he assured me that there were still whole regions full of German people, such as Virginia, Maryland and the like, that were sitting in darkness and the shadow of death[33] and had neither schoolmasters nor pastors. The newlander could pretend to be even more abject than the man from Macedonia who said to Paul: Come down and help us![34]   But he knew very well that he would receive a good present from the kidnappers in Holland if he brought along a pastor. For if a pastor goes on board ship everyone goes along voluntarily. The newlander offered me free passage and maintenance as well; the merchant in Holland on whose ship I went confirmed the newlander's promise. The hardship, misery and stench that I endured among the people go beyond words; nevertheless the misery drove me all the more to repentance, faith and prayer. As I arrived outside of Philadelphia my newlander absconded, and if the other newlanders had not been willing to post bond for me with the merchant, he would have had the power to sell me as another slave," etc.

As Mr. Weygand spoke with appropriate veneration of our Very Reverend Fathers in Halle and of the blessed institutions, my heart yearned like that of Joseph[35] and I would gladly have given expression to this if one did not have so many examples of hypocrites. I asked him what he would now do in Pennsylvania, if he wanted to be with us or against us.[36] If he wanted to be with us, then we would first need permission from our Very Reverend Fathers. But if he wanted to be against us, then he should just come along; we were not frightened because we had already fought with persons here in this country who had come running on their own. He answered that God should protect him from that! He wanted to have nothing to do with the ministerium in which Mr. Valentin Krafft,[37] Conrad Andrae, Wagner,[38] Stöver[39] and others like them were members, even if they asked him to join. Also, he did not want to stand in our way and would rather go on and start a school somewhere or other. What should we do, Very Reverend Fathers? To cast him aside was not advisable because several of our well-meaning members had already spoken with him and had learned that he was from Halle and was bone of our bones and flesh of our flesh.[40] To ask the Very Reverend Fathers was also not possible within a week. In accordance with love, I hoped for the best, looked at him the way Abraham looked at the ram which was caught in a thicket by his horns in Genesis 22,[41] took him to my house on trial, but not without the consent of my colleague, and made a few inquiries about his studies, faith and life. He is quite well versed in the Latin language, as well as in French. He is no stranger to Greek and Hebrew and can read and understand the Bible reasonably well if he has a lexicon at hand and can look up the difficult words; he also knows something about the accents. He has studied the dogmatic themes very industriously and has also grasped some things in church history. Altogether, in all the areas that belong to theological study, he has a basic grasp of things. If now, in addition, prayer, temptation and meditation[42] are added, he could surely be made into a useful instrument of the church of Christ. He believes that he experienced repentance and faith rationally[43] but not gratuitously[44] from Halle until he was on the ocean.

Evenings and mornings in the household devotions that I hold with my domestics, I let him pray extemporaneously and I find that he uses sound and scriptural expressions. In New Hanover I have involved him in the instruction of the confirmands. He is proving to be a tireless worker, but he preaches too much in his catechetical instruction and cannot yet make the questions to the children simple enough. I have also tested him in preaching. He has a nice tenor voice, respectable gestures; he does not use the new German metaphysical style but rather remains simply with the expressions of Holy Scripture and is edifying to the people. In conversation he is edifying, speaks respectably and uses all sorts of refined phrases which he has picked up in his association with experienced fathers. So at one time I hear a powerful phrase from His Reverence Dr. Francke, then one from another of the workers in those blessed institutions, then one from the Bergen Cloister,[45] then one from Father Sommer, then one from the worthy brothers in blessed Wernigerode,[46] then one from Pastor Fressenius. This tastes so good to me that I forget all my sorrow and think that even if the man is a hypocrite and hereafter should become a punishment to me, the preceding sugar nevertheless tasted very good to me. In terms of his complexion he seems to be a sanguine type, a temperament that admittedly is in danger of growing cold and has a tendency to be changeable, now taking one side and then the other. May God help for the sake of Christ and his church! I, indeed, would like to keep the man with me until the Very Reverend Fathers graciously reveal to us their understanding and advice as soon as possible, but I see two difficulties: (1) My household consists of seven persons but my income is the same as it was in the beginning and is only for one or two persons; it follows that I must look to get by because I cannot place more of a burden on the poor people. (2) Mr. Weygand still owes for his freight and is short of clothing. We considered in our College of Pastors if we could not place him in Lancaster as schoolmaster. He was willing to do this, but we found after more mature consideration that it would not be advisable for the whole. Finally I came up with the idea that in the interim we could send him for one year to the Raritan.

Herewith I will report on the circumstances in the Raritan congregations. (1) That the Very Reverend Fathers were able after much heartfelt prayer and effort only to find, call and send one pastor must have its reasons with the almighty God, and these must be sought out after the fact. (2) That the worthy Pastor Handschuh had to stay in Pennsylvania, close to us and our united congregations, arose out of circumstances which for certain reasons must be seen as God's providence. The situation of the Raritan congregations is currently as follows: First, Magister Wolf[47] is still sitting there; he will not come around at all but would rather rot there as an affront to the congregations than go to another place. (2) Another preacher, by the name of Langenfeld,[48] is also sitting there with his wife and children; a number of years ago he served half of the congregations, but he grew weary of preaching and now pursues the farmer's trade; nevertheless, like Wolf, he remains a spectator. (3) In part the Hamburg Ministerium believes the Hallensians were trying to insinuate themselves there, and Pastor Berckenmeyer[49] is watching how things unfold and would gladly provoke Magister Wolff into starting a lawsuit again with the congregations as soon as they take on a Hallensian. (4) The congregations are in the most extreme state of degeneration as a result of the twelve year long dispute. (5) Out of fear they do not want to underwrite properly any call or to pay much freight and they retain the freedom and power to hire and dismiss a pastor. (6) They still do not have a church, school and parsonage; they would gladly receive assistance from our Very Reverend Fathers. (7) In these last years, according to their own choice, they have wanted to have Mr. Kurtz as pastor, particularly at the instigation of the most prominent congregation member who has a daughter that he wants to marry off.[50] Even if a tried and true Hallensian could have overcome all of these difficulties through the grace of God, the all-knowing God knows best of all when the time is right. (8) In this year, before the arrival of Mr. Handschuh, the godless, so-called Prince Carl Rudolph of Württemberg[51] intruded there as preacher through the recommendation of Pastor Andrae, and he maligned most shamefully our College of Pastors from the pulpit and in his dealings. Because there are still some well-meaning souls among them, there were then two parties: the one fought for the honor of our name and eagerly brought forward all the kindness and spiritual edification that they had partaken of from us; the others fought against and slandered us. (9) Mr. Kurtz and Schaum had worked there--not without blessing--but they were too weak and inexperienced in such a critical situation; they had also not always expressed themselves cautiously enough[52], which the opposition party misused. In a short time the prince conducted himself in such a satanic manner that even the most flagrant sinners joined in chasing him away. In this manner his coarse blaspheming became for our supporters their best defence. When this comedy came to an end, both parties came to us again, asked for forgiveness and further assistance for God's sake, and were given a sound talking-to. Consequently, it was necessary for me, with the consent of my colleagues, to make a trip there last July.[53] By investigating I found that a few hotheads had aroused the people and told them that no pastor from our College of Pastors would ever come to them from Europe and that they should take the prince who was no pietist but rather a zealous dominie. I had all four congregations together and wanted to bow out and have nothing more to do with them.   But the poor youth, the heartbreaking expressions of our awakened souls, and the tears of the widows and orphans affected me so much that I had to promise not totally to withdraw our hand.   They all exhorted us pitifully and asked if we could at least allow our youngest brother, Mr. Schaum, to come if we could not spare anyone else so that they would not be totally abandoned.   I agreed to this for a period of time if my colleagues would not be opposed; I established a little external order and chose for a common church council three knowledgeable men from each congregation who could advise and decide what was best for the congregation.   The twelve church councillors deliberated about a church building.   They wanted to build a spacious stone church in a central location, to which the most distant persons farthest away from all sides would have to travel about ten miles.   Three congregations reached agreement on this.   In the fourth there were some stubborn heads who did not agree but wanted to build their own church in their area.   These persons were given the freedom to act in accordance with their conceit.   The three congregations and several men from the fourth have proposed a building for £300, plus a few pounds, without their work, and among themselves have already paid in advance £240 and started construction.   As we now had a mind to send Mr. Schaum there out of necessity for a period of time, we were to be sure much aware of his weak character for such a critical place, and the poor congregation beyond the Susquehanna was not eager to let him go.   Therefore, if the Very Reverend Fathers have a grasp of all the circumstances here and make a decision according to the high degree of wisdom granted them by God, we ask that they will graciously communicate their fatherly advice to us.   We do not want to do the kingdom of Christ the slightest harm through hastiness, but we also do not want to lose through negligence a nail that could be useful in its construction.

To this end I have written to the Raritan church council under my own name and have not added the names of my colleagues, so that there might still be another way out if things do not work out well.   In my letter I have laid out clearly Mr. Weygand's circumstances and have left it up to their discretion and decision.   I am willing to send along with him a set of instructions for one year as the enclosures, Letters A and B, generally indicate.[54]   On the Raritan one needs to have a knowledge, among other things, of the English and Latin languages because there are many New England Presbyterian pastors in that area who have a great respect for Halle and cherish the blessed orphanage, to the extent that they have read about it in Latin reports, and gladly converse with Hallensians.   An English pastor said to me once that it was unfortunate that we did not publicize more of the wonderful works[55] of these institutions in the English language. Another one wanted to speak Latin or English with Mr. Schaum but, as he complained, received no answer. I said that at first we could not immmediately understand their Latin and they our pronunciation. If the gracious God should in the future grant and sustain for us precious peace and allow our life, which for the three of us, namely, Mr. Brunnholz, Handschuh and me, is very much on the wane, to continue, then we will request each year several boxes of books--for example, Arndt's *True Christianity* in large print,[56]--as well as Bibles and Testaments and dispensaries with medicines that can be sold; and if in the course of time, several hundredweight of characters should also arrive, the Very Reverend Fathers can be sure that we would not use such a small printing press in a prejudicial way, but only so that one might share with the poor Germans, and where possible also with the English, who are sitting in darkness and prejudice a few sparks of light which have gone out and are still going out from blessed Halle in this century.[57] For the rest, I commend to the Very Reverend Fathers, all Christian patrons, benefactors and intercessors myself, my worthy colleagues, congregations, our spiritual and physical need, my wife and two children[58] to your well-disposed remembrance, prayer and further goodwill. I assure you that all the cross and suffering that are laid on you for the increase of your future glory produce compassion through Christian sympathy and incite us more to prayer. May God reward you all with eternal mercy and grace for the measureless effort, care and birth-anxiety you have shown for our cause. May we receive the joyous news of your long life and faithful endurance under the cross for the welfare of the church of Christ. This is the desire for the Very Reverend and devout Fathers in God of

New Providence	Your most unworthy son and coworker,
16 November 1748	Heinrich Melchior Mühlenberg

P.S. Senior Wagener[59] of Hamburg wrote to Pastor Knoll[60] in New York last year and asked that we would submit a report on Wolf's law-suit on the Raritan. If such a report was sent off by me last year and received in London,[61] I would request that it might be communicated to the Hamburg Ministerium if the Very Reverend Fathers consider this to be good.

P.S. Because the postage costs are calculated according to weight and there might be much too much paper, I have retained the enclosures A and B that I mentioned.

1.   The reference is to the War of the Austrian Succession (1740-48) which affected North America particularly in the phase known as King George's War (1744-48). See *Correspondence* 1:306 n. 7.

2.   The text reads *particularia*.

3.   Since this journal/letter of Mühlenberg consists almost entirely of descriptions of congregation members, only the beginning of the letter is reprinted (see *Journals* 1:118-42):

"Very Reverend, much loved Fathers in Christ:

From the lengthy letter of March 1747 [=Letter 62] I have learned, in the midst of the fatherly admonitions, instructions, consolations and warnings from the Very Reverend Fathers, that my letter of 30 October 1746 [=Letter 58] arrived safely. In the following year, 20 February 1747, I sent off a long, most obedient letter to Their Graces and Excellencies the older and younger Countesses von Wernigerode and to Her Excellency the Gracious Lady and Consort of the High Sheriff von Münchhauss [=Letter 60]; but I learned from the newspaper that the ship fell into French hands. The following month, May 1747, I sent off a report on the Wolff proceedings on the Raritan to the Reverend Hamburg Ministerium [=Letter 42] and a letter to the Very Reverend Fathers on the ship of our former governor [Morris] [=Letter 65]; I received a very favorable and unmerited reply [=Letter 68] already in the month of September 1747. Because the external building projects in the country congregations assigned to me are temporarily at a standstill, I will report in childlike simplicity a little about the conduct of my ministry and, first of all, recall some of the circumstances from the time [reading "von der Zeit" rather than "vor der Zeit"] when I was still alone in office . . . ." On this subject, see the parallel letter in *Correspondence* 1, Letter 65, pp. 331f., 340f., along with footnotes 1, 10, 43, and 47-51.

4.   On Peter Brunnholz, see Letter 71 n. 3.

5.   Kurz married Anna Elisabeth Seidel, the daughter of a carpenter, in December 1747. See *Journals* 1:177. On Johann Nicolaus Kurz, see *Correspondence* 1:154 n. 5 and 341 n. 16.

6.   Molatton, located between the Schuylkill and Manatawny Rivers, in what is now Douglassville, Pennsylvania, was in an area known as the Swedes' tract and was inhabited by Germans (both Lutheran and Reformed), Swedes, English and Irish. See *Pastors and People* 1:248 and *Journals* 1:185-87.

7.   On Johann Friedrich Handschuh, see *Correspondence* 1:291 n. 18.

8.   On Kurz's ordination, see Letter 71A n. 5.

9.   See the *Journal* entry for 28 April 1748: "We consulted together in Providence with regard to a suitable liturgy [*Agende*] which we could introduce for use in our congregations. True, we had been using a small formulary heretofore, but had nothing definite and harmonious in all its parts, since we had thought it best to wait for the arrival of more laborers and also until we had acquired a better knowledge of conditions in this country. . . . We therefore took the liturgy of the Savoy Church in London as the basis, cut out parts and added to it according to what seemed to us to be profitable and edifying in these circumstances. This we adopted tentatively until we had a better understanding of the matter in order that the same ceremonies, forms, and words might be used in all our congregations" (*Journals* 1:193). The Liturgy of 1748 is published in *HN2/1*:211-16 and *Documentary History*, pp. 13-18.

10.   On Johann Helfrich Schaum, see Letter 71 n. 9.

11.   Johann Albert Weygand, whose arrival Francke had already announced in his letter of 23 July 1748 (=Letter 71). On Weygand, see Letter 71 n. 21.

12.   We have opted to translate the German term here (*Neu Länder*) literally as "newlanders," following the example of A. G. Roeber, *Palatines, Liberty, and Property: German Lutherans in Colonial British America* (Baltimore: The Johns Hopkins University Press, 1993). Roeber adds to Mühlenberg's above description of these persons who were both promoters and shipping agents when he describes them as "key figures in the creative attempt to get cash-poor migrants to the colonies. Securing in North America a future purchaser for the price of the passage, the newlanders helped invent redemptioner contracts. . . . If migrants could not 'redeem' this contract in two weeks after arrival among the small but successful German-speaking population already living in Pennsylvania, the contracts were put out for general bid. Humane and workable in its early stages, the system

degenerated as the number of migrants swelled" (p. 98).

13. A *pistole* was a gold coin circulating in various German states in this period which was worth slightly less than a pound sterling. See Helmut Kahnt and Bernd Knorr, *Alte Masse, Münzen und Gewichte: Ein Lexicon* (Mannheim/Vienna/Zurich: Meyers Lexiconverlag, 1987), s.v. "Pistole."

14. The no longer extant letter of a former Moravian to Mühlenberg, written in February 1748, gives information about the efforts of Moravians to find new adherents from among the ranks of the Pennsylvania Lutherans. Muhlenberg reports in his journal: "A young man by the name of N. Deyling wrote a letter to me in which he set forth the reasons which prompted him to remain separated from and not have any fellowship with the Zinzendorfian congregation. . . . We received this letter and saw from it that he had been only a beast of burden among them, but that he never really knew or wanted to know the inside of their plan. At the same time he requested us not to publish what he had written because he was afraid that they might, out of *revenge*, publish certain secret sins which he had committed while at school and which he had confessed when he was received into their fellowship, and thus raise a public scandal" (*Journals* 1:182-83).

15. The text reads *particularia*.

16. On Johann Conrad Andreae, see *Correspondence* 1:143 n. 10.

17. The text reads *Humanioribus*.

18. Johann Jakob Koerber (1696-1759) was born in Hanau, studied theology in Giessen and Jena, and served as pastor in Hanau from 1728 to 1759. From 1740 on he served as both first pastor and inspector there.

19. The Weingarten School in the Halle suburb of Oberglaucha was affiliated with August Hermann Francke's Halle institutions and was a school for poor children. See *Selbstbiographie*, p. 200.

20. The references to the second and third level or class (*Secundam Classem* and *Tertiam*) indicate the year of study, with the first level being the highest and final year.

21. On Gotthilf August Francke, see *Correspondence* 1:8 n. 1.

22. On Spener's interpretation of the catechism, see *Correspondence* 1:282 n. 14; see also *Korrespondenz* 1:325 n. 13. On Philipp Jacob Spener, see *Correspondence* 1:315 n.20.

23. Johann Georg Knapp (1705-71) studied law in Altdorf and theology in Jena and Halle. In 1733 he joined the Theological Faculty at Halle and thereafter was both professor on the Theological Faculty and administrator in the Halle institutions. In 1769 he became Gotthilf August Francke's successor as director of the Francke institutions.

24. On Siegmund Jakob Baumgarten, see Letter 71 n. 6.

25. On Johann Conrad Philipp Niemeyer, a close confidant and associate of G. A. Francke, see *Correspondence* 1:33 n. 9.

26. Johann Christian Steinersdorf (1711-80) studied theology in Jena and Halle and began teaching at the Latina in Halle in 1734. In 1749 he became co-rector in Prenzlau and was pastor there from 1755 to 1780.

27. Stassfurt is in the vicinity of Magdeburg. The identity of Mr. von Schloten is unknown.

28. On Johann Adam Steinmetz, see Letter 71 n. 25.

29. Her identity is unknown, although Francke refers to her in a letter to Ziegenhagen as "Lady von Zantbieren" of Broseik. See Letter 71 n. 22.

30. On Johann Heinrich Sommer, see Letter 71 nn. 22 and 23.

31. The text reads *per casum obliquum*.

32. Johann Philipp Fresenius (1705-61) was a noted controversialist who functioned as both professor (at the University of Giessen) and pastor (at Giessen, Darmstadt and Frankfurt). Mühlenberg especially appreciated him for his polemics against Count von Zinzendorf and the Moravians; see Letter 106. See also *Correspondence* 1:121 n. 4 and 310 n. 10.

33. See Luke 1:79.

34. See Acts 16:9.

35. See Gen. 43:30.

36. See Matt. 12:30.

37. On Johann Valentin Kraft, see *Correspondence* 1:52 n. 7.

38. On Tobias Wagner, see Letter 71A n. 3.

39. Johann Caspar Stöver, Jr. (1707-79) arrived in Philadelphia with his father, Johann Caspar Stöver, Sr., in 1728. He had studied some theology informally in Germany and presented himself as a Lutheran pastor to the Lutherans in Pennsylvania. He was irregularly ordained in 1733 and worked together with Johann Valentin Kraft when the latter arrived on the scene in 1742. See *Correspondence* 1:52 nn. 18 and 19, 62 n. 7 and 310 n. 1.

40. See Gen. 2:23.

41. See Gen. 22:13.

42. See Martin Luther's "three rules" for "a correct way of studying theology," namely, *Oratio, Meditatio, Tentatio*: "Preface to the Wittenberg Edition of Luther's German Writings [1539]," *LW* 34:285ff.

43. The text reads *ratione partium*.

44. The text reads *gratuum*.

45. Bergen Cloister was closely associated with Halle pietism through the influence of persons like Joachim Justus Breithaupt (see *Correspondence* 1:62 n. 16) and Johann Adam Steinmetz (see Letter 71 n. 25), both of whom were abbots of the cloister.

46. Julius Leopold von Caprivi (see *Correspondence* 1:17 n. 7), Pastor Bötticher (see *Correspondence* 1:33 n. 8), Werner Nicolaus Ziegler (see *Correspondence* 1:106 n. 11), Inspector Mell (see *Correspondence* 1:322 n. 8), as well as Count Heinrich Ernst von Stolberg-Wernigerode, were all associated with Wernigerode.

47. Johann August Wolf was sent out by the Hamburg Consistory in 1734 to serve the congregations on the Raritan in New Jersey. He was soon in trouble with them, and these troubles escalated into "the Wolf affair" which occupied Mühlenberg a great deal in 1745. On this matter, see Letters 40A, 40B, 40C, 41A, 41B and 42; *Correspondence* 1:187-93, 201-26.

48. On Johann Albert Langerfeld, see *Correspondence* 1:225 n. 44.

49. Wilhelm Christoph Berckenmeyer (see *Correspondence 1:189 n. 1*) was another key player in "the Wolf affair." See Letters 40A, 40B, 40C, 41A. 41B and 42; *Correspondence* 1:187-93, 201-26.

50. On the desire to call Kurz as pastor, see *Correspondence* 1:300. The elder in question was Balthasar Bickel; his daughter, Anna Eva, married Johann Helfrich Schaum on 4 December 1750. On this matter, see Letters 63 and 64, *Correspondence* 1:324-30.

51. On Carl Rudolph, allegedly prince of Württemberg, see *Correspondence* 1:342 n. 40.

52. The text reads *formulas caute loquendi*.

53. On Mühlenberg's trip to the Raritan, see his journal entries from the beginning of July to 7 August 1748; see *Journals* 1:198-201.

54. Mühlenberg's second postscript, below, indicates that the enclosures were not sent, and they are not extant.

55. The text reads *Mirabilia*.

56. See *Correspondence* 1:315 n. 20.

57. On Mühlenberg's earlier requests for a printing press and Francke's response to them, see *Correspondence* 1:181, 198, 229 and 353.

58. Mühlenberg comments on his second child in his autobiographical notes as follows: "In the year 1748, 29 January, according to the old calendar, a daughter was born and she was baptized on 10 February. The godparents were (a) the grandmother, Mrs. Anna Eva Weiser, and (b) Mrs. Elisabeth Schleydorn. They gave her the name Eva Elisabeth." See *Korrespondenz* 1:326 n. 35.

59. On Friedrich Wagner, Senior of the Hamburg Consistory, see *Correspondence* 1:189 n. 9.

60. Michael Christian Knoll (see *Correspondence* 1:189 n. 5) was one of the arbitrators in "the Wolf affair."

61. See *Correspondence* 1:340.

LETTERS OF 1749

Letter 73

Gotthilf August Francke to Mühlenberg
Halle, 26 March 1749

This letter is Francke's provisional reply to Mühlenberg's letter of 16 November 1748 (Letter 72). It is a very positive evaluation of the way Mühlenberg is handling the ministries of Johann Nicolaus Kurz, Johann Helfrich Schaum and Johann Albert Weygand, although Francke does raise concerns about Schaum's administration of Holy Communion without having been formally ordained. In conclusion Francke assures Mühlenberg that the long awaited equipment for a printing press will soon be shipped.

Text in German: Korrespondenz 1:329-31. For further textual information, see Korrespondenz 1:331.

To Pastor Mühlenberg
in New Providence
in Pennsylvania

26 March 1749

Reverend,

Dearly beloved Brother in the Lord:

For some time now--finally--we have been gratified by the many pleasant and very uplifting reports of the work of God among the Pennsylvania congregations, and in particular also by Your Reverence's esteemed letter of 16 November 1748[1] and your reports from November 1746 to April 1747[2] of certain things in which you perceive divine blessing. I find in them nothing but reasons for the praise of God and I heartily extol God's name for them. Only one thing concerns me, namely, that both Mr. Brunnholz[3] and you have been ill several times and that you have still not fully recovered from your last illness. May the Lord of life strengthen you once again and keep you for a long time yet for the good of his work.

In reply to your aforementioned, very welcome letter, which I received on 1 February of this year, I am responding for the time being only to the most necessary things until I am in a position to write more extensively.

1.) The reports which you have sent I have found to be very good, in so

23

far as I have read them (for I am still awaiting their conclusion from England). From them I will have a new continuation made of the Reports from the congregations there. May God lay his blessing on them.

2.) The ordination of Mr. Kurtz[4] and his installation at Tulpehocken, as well as Mr. Schaum's[5] transfer to the congregations beyond the Susquehanna, are as acceptable to me as the answers of the former to the questions that were put to him[6] and the journal of the latter[7] were very gratifying. I was very happy that I could see in these things how they have managed pretty well during the time of their stay in America. In Mr. Kurz's response, it is true, there are still some things that are inadequate, although in part the questions were not specific enough or exceeded his capabilities, so that he was not able to answer them adequately in such a short time. But all in all (which he should not be told, however, at this point), his responses are still much better than you would probably expect to get from scarcely one in ten preachers in consistories here. One hopes that in the future he will continue to seek a firm base for himself; if he allows himself to be led by the Spirit of God so that he keeps to himself in true purity and self-denial, I do not doubt that God will add his blessing to this. The journal of Mr. Schaum is no less well prepared; it pleases me how he starts everything so well with prayer and also the way the faithful God has been with him in various critical circumstances, so that one can indeed say that one sees in these things that the Lord allows the unsophisticated to succeed.

3.) The one thing that is open to question for me in this is that he administered Holy Communion without having been ordained.[8] There are those who could take some offense at this and use it as an opportunity for slander. One could, of course, respond to such persons that he had not done this as a private person but only after he had been assigned to it by you as the evangelical minister[9] of the united Pennsylvania congregations and that he was lacking nothing except the external formality of the ordination ceremony of the Lutheran church that is used in most places. In this case one can quite legitimately appeal to the practice in the Württemberg Consistory whereby the examined candidates[10] for the ministry receive general permission to administer the sacraments;[11] thereafter, without the further ordination, they are permitted to perform all ministerial acts[12] without exception; in this way, as they are directed by the superiors, they assist those pastors who are sick or who want to go on a journey, etc., until they get their own congregations, in which they are only installed. To remove all occasion for slander, however, I think you should really ordain him as soon as possible without further hesitation. I recall that I required as a prerequisite for ordination that you previously had in hand an actual call from a specific congregation[13] and I suspect for this reason you have delayed the ordination. But even if the congregations across the Susquehanna do not yet want to issue such a call, you can call him yourself as your assistant, deacon, adjunct minister, or whatever name you consider most suitable (as is the practice in some territories, that a certain number of ordained general adjunct ministers are created who have no specific congregations but have to allow themselves to be used wherever there is need); or you can also issue the call to a congregation that is requesting him for a trial under your own name and thereafter use him as you find it necessary and useful.

4.) In regard to Mr. Weygand,[14] I can recall nothing negative about his conduct; therefore, as it seems that he means well and does not want to associate himself with other disreputable people, it was a rather good thing that you sought to keep him. Perhaps God will confirm and strengthen him so that he becomes even more useful than we had formerly thought. Those who remember him here, consider him to be a person who can be guided by what he is told, which also appears to be what one could hope for from him on the basis of your account. Therefore, if he has until now shown himself in this way to have a disposition that lets itself be corrected and has avoided irregularities; if he has performed well during the trial period in the Raritan and allows himself to be awakened to greater seriousness in Christianity and to enter more and more into self-denial, then I would have no reservations if you ordained him, for the reason given under the previous point and in the same way. But be sure to get his specific assurance that he will not in future go over to any opposition party.

5.) The characters for a printing press have long since been poured[15] and would have been sent earlier if this had been feasible and advisable during the previous war.[16] Now that this hindrance has been removed, I will send them off from here at once and I have already made inquiries in Holland to see if they can be shipped conveniently on Dutch ships, just like the medicine ordered by Mr. Brunnholz. I am awaiting a reply very soon. I will also provide Bibles and other books.

I herewith commend Your Reverence and your worthy household to the gracious care of the Lord. May he continue to grant you further victory and blessing in his work, and I remain always

Your,

G. A. Francke

P.S. Give hearty greetings to your worthy father-in-law.[17]

1. See Letter 72.
2. See Letter 72 n. 2. Mühlenberg's 1746 Reports were published in the fourth continuation: *HN1*:149-79; *HN2/1*:237-55. Francke observes in the 1751 Foreword (*HN1*:115; *HN2/1*:217): ". . . in part many intervening hindrances delayed the fulfillment of this promise."
3. On Peter Brunnholz, see Letter 71 n. 3.
4. On Johann Nicolaus Kurz, see *Correspondence* 1:154 n. 5 and 341 n. 16.
5. On Johann Helfrich Schaum, see Letter 71 n. 9.
6. Kurz's examination was presumably sent to Halle along with Brunnholz's letter of 19 November 1748.
7. On Schaum's placement in York, see Mühlenberg's journal entry of 2 May 1748: "The poor congregation in Yorktown beyond the Susquehanna had long been petitioning us to come to their aid in their forsaken condition. . . . Pastor Brunnholz . . . decided with us to send Mr. Schaum to Yorktown as a catechist on trial. We would not have ventured this so readily if Pastor Handschuh had not been assigned to the post in Lancaster" (*Journals* 1:194). Schaum's journal, published in excerpts in *HN2/1*:203-6, covers the period from 17 May to 3 June, 1748.
8. The text reads *ordines*.
9. The text reads *Ministerio euangelico*.
10. The text reads *Candidati Ministerii*.
11. The text reads *sacra*.
12. The text reads *Actus ministeriales*.
13. See *Correspondence* 1:319 and 352.
14. On Johann Albert Weygand, see Letter 71 n. 21.
15. See *Correspondence* 1:353.
16. The War of the Austrian Succession (1740-48). See *Correspondence* 1:306 n. 7.
17. On Johann Conrad Weiser, see *Correspondence* 1:142 n. 7.

Letter 74

Gotthilf August Francke to Johann Friedrich Handschuh and Mühlenberg
Halle, 4 April 1749

*Francke here comes to the defense particularly of Pastor Brunnholz
against whom Johann Nicolaus Croesmann, a deacon from Providence, has
complained to the Darmstadt Consistory about the proposed distribution of
the Darmstadt Collection. Francke assures the pastors that Croesmann's
complaints have not been listened to, but offers encouragement and advice
on settling this controversy. He hints that disunity and lack of gratefulness
in the congregations could affect future offerings.*

On the Darmstadt Collection, see Letter 53, Correspondence 1:261-63.
*Text in German: Korrespondenz 1:332-33. For further textual
information on this letter, see Korrespondenz 1:333.*

To Pastors
Mühlenberg in New Providence
and Handschuh in Lancaster

4 April 1749

Reverend,
Dearly beloved Brothers in the Lord:
Herewith I am sending you a letter from the Providence deacon Johann
Niclaus Kressmann[1] with reference to Germantown. From the whole
manner of writing I have recognized that his complaints against worthy
Pastor Brunnholz[2] flow from strong emotions, and as the pastors have in all
things until now cared for the congregations most lovingly with so much
effort, difficulty and self-denial, it concerns me that such faithfulness is not
better recognized. The whole content of the letter is not much better than
what Korah, Dathan and Abiram said back there to Moses who had until
then had so much patience with the people: "Will you put out our eyes as
well?"[3] The same man also wrote to Darmstadt himself.[4] How they
received his letter there can be seen in the accompanying letter of Chief
Court Preacher Berchelmann,[5] which I am including here along with the
letter that Johann Niclaus Kressmann sent over there. In regard to the
collection itself, it is not fitting that the congregations do not come to an
amicable common understanding in this matter. Kressmann should have
kept in mind that the congregation in Providence has already enjoyed so
many benefits from the other collections, which could again be taken back
if they do not want to accept this one with gratefulness; also he should

remember that the Darmstadt Collection was not the result of his letter[6] and would probably never have come to be at all if I had not done most of it. But if the congregations cannot peaceably come to a peaceable understanding about the gifts of kindness, then it will be their own fault if the love of other benefactors gets stopped up because of it. Consequently, I ask that you both, with the assistance of several deacons, if you think it is good, would speak with the aforementioned Kressmann himself and present to him in love the impropriety of his complaints, heartily admonish him to live in peace with Pastor Brunnholtz as his pastor, and to acknowledge with thankfulness the blessing that God has sent the congregations his word and faithful teachers and to use them for the awakening of his soul. In regard to the collection itself, I will report more about it as soon as I have received the money.[7] Finally, please greet all the deacons and members of the church council in my name and admonish them especially not to allow even a single seed of disunity to spring up among them, so that God may continue to give his blessing for the advancement of good institutions in church and school. With this I commend you to God's protection and remain

Your,

G. A. Francke

---

1. This letter is dated 12 November 1748. In it Croesmann complains that primarily Brunnholz but also Mühlenberg have not adequately informed the parish council about contributions in money and in kind that have been received and that in the distribution of these the expectations of the parish councillors have not received adequate consideration. So, for example, Brunnholz wanted to use the Darmstadt Collection for the benefit of all the Pennsylvania congregations whereas Croesmann was defending the sole interests of the Providence congregation. See *Korrespondenz* 1:333 n. 1. On Croesmann, a deacon and prominent lay leader in the Providence congregation, see *Correspondence* 1:53 n. 15.

2. On Peter Brunnholz, see Letter 71 n. 3.

3. See Num. 16:14.

4. This letter is dated 12 November 1748. Croesmann expresses the hope in this letter that the Darmstadt Consistory will assign the collection entirely to Providence.

5. On this letter, dated 25 March 1749, see *Korrespondenz* 1:333 n. 40. The passage in question reads as follows: "Additionally, after a leather worker from Pennsylvania who was born in this region also approached me several weeks ago and gave me the enclosed letter from there, E. H. at once wanted to send it over along with it [namely, the collection], so that people could determine from its contents what was being alleged and requested in relation to this collection. But this letter did not find any acceptance here and was flatly rejected. You will certainly know how to reply to it" (pp. 91f.). - On Friedrich Wilhelm Berchelmann, see *Correspondence* 1:113 n. 4.

6. The letter of request of 21 February 1746 (*Correspondence* 1:261-63).

7. Francke's report is found in the account he established for the Pennsylvania congregations for 1748 and 1749 (*HN2/1*:326): "According to Court Preacher Dietzen's letter the Darmstadt Collection which had been promised for a long time and has finally come in amounted to . . . 384 reichsthaler and 19 groschen." In his letter of 10 June 1749 to Brunnholz, Francke confirms the receipt of the Darmstadt Collection in this amount. See *Korrespondenz* 1:333 n. 6.

Letter 75

Gilbert Tennent,[1] Peter Brunnholz and Mühlenberg to Johann Conrad
Steiner[2]
Philadelphia, 14 November 1749

*In this letter Gilbert Tennent, a leading Presbyterian pastor and friend
of Mühlenberg, Peter Brunnholz, Mühlenberg's pastoral colleague, and
Mühlenberg himself enter into a controversy that was affecting the
Presbyterian churches in Philadelphia and Germantown. The resident
pastor, Michael Schlatter, had alienated some of the elders of his
congregation in Philadelphia, so they dismissed him and offered the call to
Johann Conrad Steiner who had just stepped off the boat in Philadelphia
and who already had a valid call to a Reformed congregation in Lancaster.
The letter is preceded by a copy of Steiner's three arguments that moved him
to accept the call. Steiner had written to Brunnholz about this matter on 13
November 1749 and requested a prompt response. In their reply the three
authors evaluate and reject Steiner's arguments. Their sentiments are
summed up in the rhetorical question they pose in the letter: "Would that
not be to abandon his legitimate call in Lancaster and to interfere in
someone else's ministry?"*
     Text in German: Korrespondenz *1:333-37. For further textual
information, see* Korrespondenz *1:337.*

Copy

Argument 1: The acceptance of the call from Philadelphia and Germantown
     coincides most nearly with the purpose he had in leaving his
     fatherland and travelling to this country, because Philadelphia
     and Germantown are two major congregations.
Argument 2: Consideration of the most pitiful circumstances in which the
     Philadelphia and Germantown congregations find themselves and
     would find themselves even more if they would remain without a
     proper pastor.
Argument 3: The call itself is: 1. spontaneous; 2. full of love; 3. very
     moving.
     These were Mr. Steinert's arguments which supposedly moved him
     to accept the call and which were put forward in the declaration
     with which he tried to justify himself before the public.

Reverend, highly honored Pastor,

Well disposed Friend and Colleague:

Your Reverence sent a letter to me (Brunnholz) on 13 November of the current year[3] and asked that I would read through it, deliberate and share my thoughts about it with you in a brotherly manner before tomorrow. Because I was occupied all day with official duties and was visited in the evening unexpectedly by His Reverence Pastor Tennent and my colleague Mühlenberg, the allotted time was almost up and the matter was too important for me to unravel it all and respond adequately. Consequently I considered it together with them and wanted to respond to only some of it now.

Before we proceed to the response, we want to declare most solemnly in the most holy sight of God and of all reasonable readers, that we are impartial in your whole controversy. We wholeheartedly desire that not only in the Lutheran but also in the Reformed congregations true repentance before God and living faith in Jesus Christ, and the godliness that follow from them, might be furthered and maintained through pure, proper doctrine.

Further, we have to admit that we do not take lightly matters relating to the call between pastors and congregations as do some people who imagine and proceed rather glibly; rather, we have to judge proper as well as improper practice according to the holy word of God and illustrate it with many examples from all sacred ordinances.

If we do not misunderstand your declaration, Your Reverence is presently undergoing an important test before God and the people, and the decision which you reach cannot remain hidden; it will rather be reflected on and judged by the reverend Classis,[4] indeed, by all of Christendom, and the good or evil of it will be driven home to your conscience. Therefore, we hope Your Reverence will permit us only to comment on some of your declaration and to present our humble reservations about it in weakness as well as in sincerity, although we see in advance that our thoughts can have little influence in the matter because Your Reverence seems to have gone too far already. In the meantime our conscience bears witness that we have long and often sighed and prayed in secret to our gracious God in Christ that he would carry the whole matter out so that love and truth will not be compromised.

We also dispatch in advance your three major arguments on the basis of our own experience:

1. There is a real relationship and a binding agreement between Mr. Schlatter and the congregations in Philadelphia and Germantown.

   a) Because the congregations applied to the reverend Synod in Holland for a number of years for pastors.

b) The reverend Classis called, authorized, freely sent Mr. Schlatter there and provided him with satisfactory instructions.

c) Because Mr. Schlatter was presented to the congregations by Mr. Böhm[5] and was accepted by the congregations without objection.

d) Because Mr. Schlatter served the congregations in this relationship with the word and sacraments until now.

e) Because the controversy between the regular pastors and the congregations was provisionally investigated at the most recent Coetus. Mr. Schlatter was declared innocent by all the pastors who were present and they signed their names to that effect.[6]

f) Because the matter has not yet been put before the reverend Classis in Holland for more considered judgment.

Consequently, under these circumstances, we cannot at all see that the congregations in Philadelphia and Germantown are vacant; there is rather a binding agreement there until the matter has been presented to a higher court for judgment and a decision has come down from there. The elders cannot remove him on their own without presenting before a higher court compelling arguments that merit dismissal. Likewise Mr. Schlatter cannot abandon the congregations without the permission of his superiors.

2. In respect to Your Reverence's arrival in this country, the circumstances show:

a) that the reverend Classis did not call Mr. Steinert away from his congregation in Switzerland; rather you left the congregations there on your own; your reasons for this will have to be weighed on the scales in the sanctuary.

b) that the reverend Classis itself in the letter of recommendation to Mr. Schlatter and, therefore, both parties expressly determined that Mr. Steinert should be placed in the vacancy at Lancaster or in some other vacant congregations.

c) that Your Reverence actually accepted the call which was proffered by the reverend Coetus and which they based partly on the synod's order and partly on the congregation's need. On the basis of these premises[7] we respond briefly to your first argument:

In accordance with love we gladly believe that Your Reverence had an honest goal, to leave behind your small door in the fatherland and to seek a wider door in Pennsylvania through the reverend Classis. But we cannot find even the slightest evidence that the door in Philadelphia and Germantown is presently open for you. If we assume the congregations did not want to be their own biased judges, but rather wanted to have the matter decided, as is most equitable, by the reverend Classis, and if the reverend

Classis would find Mr. Schlatter unfit and guilty, they would certainly choose and send a better man in Mr. Schlatter's place, for the fathers in Holland have already shown so many undeserved kindnesses to these congregations. But if the congregations wanted to reject Schlatter without further investigation and to appeal to the, nota bene, misuse of their freedom in Pennsylvania, the reverend Classis would at once dismiss them; then, what vocation and joy could Mr. Steinert have to serve such people who help to debase the Classis? Would that not be *to abandon his legitimate call in Lancaster and to interfere in someone else's ministry?* Is the door in Lancaster perhaps not wide enough? Did there have to be two pastors in Philadelphia and Germantown who tear the poor congregations apart? Do the poor souls in Lancaster who have lain deserted for so long have to be abandoned and simply have no one? Is it honorable that Mr. Steinert accepts the call to Lancaster, to which the Classis has assigned him and which the Coetus has advised him to accept, but then accepts another call before he can even once visit this poor, abandoned congregation that anxiously awaits him every day and looks forward to the arrival of the pastor assigned to them, and before the matter has been decided and the Classis has given him the power to do so?

The second argument, relating to the lamentable circumstances if Philadelphia and Germantown are left without a proper pastor or a proper physician and true shepherd, is based more on the lower than on the higher powers of the soul. It is indeed true that most of those young and old people there can be compared to those pitiful patients who are close to death. But who is the true physician and faithful shepherd? Few, very few ask for the chief shepherd, guardian, and physician of souls;[8] and they quickly get tired of the undershepherds and physicians and are just like physically-ill patients who eagerly send for a new doctor if they hear that a new one has arrived. The same thing will also happen with the spiritual physicians. If they are not afraid to chase away in the heat of the moment and without proper investigation those who have been sent by the reverend Classis which has been their greatest benefactor, what will they do with those whom they have engaged on their own authority, without a proper call?

Due to the shortness of time we cannot respond more fully to this argument at this time.

The third argument is derived from the spontaneity of the call, from the disinterested love, and the heart-rending emotional appeals for acceptance, etc. If the source is pure, the stream will be pure as well. When our king and Lord made his entry into Jerusalem, heart-rending and moving words of love were also heard; but shortly thereafter it was: *Away with him!*[9] If love proceeds from faith, it will endure. Besides, one can no more depend on the affections in their best appearance when coming from passionate hearts than one can on the constancy of the local weather.

Neither time nor circumstances allow us to respond in more detail. As we have done from the beginning so we continue to do. We commit the whole matter to the chief shepherd in prayer and supplication and earnestly desire that the poor Protestant church will also be helped in this country so that God's word might run its course and prevail.[10]

We entrust these lines to our worthy colleague for reflection, deliberation and resolution. We have had no purpose in this effort of ours other than to declare openly our impartial thoughts on this matter. We have attempted to look at the whole matter by itself, without thereby seeking to praise or blame anyone. Whether the blessing of God will rest on it and what kind of effect it will have, we leave to you, and that time will tell.

Philadelphia, 14 November 1749   Gilbert Tennent
                                                   H. M. Muhlenberg
                                                   Peter Brunnholtz

-----

1. Gilbert Tennent (1703-64) was a Presbyterian pastor in Philadelphia. Trained by his father and joined in the ministry by his three brothers, he was a central figure in the revival movement among the Presbyterians which was part of the Great Awakening. An important but controversial personality within his own denomination, he was also a good friend of Mühlenberg, and Mühlenberg's *Journals* contain frequent references to him. See Sydney E. Ahlstrom, *A Religious History of the American People* (New Haven: Yale University Press, 1972), pp. 270-74 and 284-85.

2. Johann Conrad Steiner (1707-62) was sent out by the Holland fathers in The Hague to serve the Reformed congregation in Lancaster. Upon his arrival in Philadelphia at the end of September 1749, the deacons of the Philadelphia congregation pulled him into the conflict they were having with their pastor, Michael Schlatter (see *Correspondence* 1:342 n. 41). On 5 October 1749 the deacons dismissed Schlatter, giving him three months' notice, and offered the Philadelphia and Germantown Reformed congregations to Steiner. After some hesitation Steiner accepted the call to Philadelphia and informed the Holland fathers to this effect in a letter of 28 November 1749. Steiner was vigorously attacked by many Reformed clergy in Pennsylvania because of the irregular way in which he entered into his office. In the present letter Tennent, Mühlenberg and Brunnholz, as representatives of both the Presbyterian and Lutheran churches, are stating their position in response to Steiner's inquiry. On this affair, see *Pastors and People* 2:217f.

3. Not extant. On Peter Brunnholz, see above, Letter 71 n. 3.

4. On the Classis in Amsterdam, see *Correspondence* 1:342 n. 42.

5. Johann Philipp Böhm (1683-1749) arrived in Pennsylvania with a group of Palatine immigrants in 1720. He served as a lay preacher from the very beginning and began to administer the sacraments in Falckner's Swamp, Skippack and Whitemarsh in 1725. According to Glatfelter these actions of Böhm constitute "the beginning of the German Reformed church in Pennsylvania" (*Pastors and People* 1:21f.). He was ordained in 1729 and was an important pastor and leader among the German Reformed congregations in Pennsylvania. See *Pastors and People* 2:35-51.

6. The elders' points of complaint and their explanation that they would only accept a pastor other than Schlatter from the Coetus were submitted to the Reformed Coetus on 20-24 October 1749. In its resolution the Coetus placed itself totally on Schlatter's side and rejected the charges and complaints of the elders. See Marthi Pritzker-Ehrlich, "Michael Schlatter von St. Gallen: Eine biographische Untersuchung zur schweizerischen Amerika-Auswanderung des 18. Jahrhunderts" (Diss. Zurich 1981), pp. 114f.

7. The text reads *Hisce praemissis*.

8. See 1 Pet. 2:25.

9. See Luke 23:18; John 19:15.

10. See 2 Thess. 3:1.

Letter 76

To Friedrich Michael Ziegenhagen, Gotthilf August Francke and Johann August Majer[1]
Providence, 20 December 1749

This year-end letter to the Fathers gains in importance because of the very small number of letters we have from Mühlenberg in 1749. Shocked by Ziegenhagen's severe illness, Mühlenberg is moved to reflect on the perilous state of the Lutheran church but also on God's ongoing favor that is extended to it (as seen in Ziegenhagen's movement toward recovery). These considerations bring Mühlenberg to a discussion of the developments in his own "small and insignificant" part of the world. He reports with sadness that his experience shows him that many persons seek alternatives to the way of "true repentance and conversion according to God's word," and many parties or sects cater to these preferences. Among such groups Mühlenberg lists and discusses (rather unflatteringly) Quakers, "the silent in the land," Seventh Day Baptists, Moravians, Sunday Baptists and Mennonites. Mühlenberg then shifts his attention to another group that causes him problems: unconverted Lutherans, that is, Lutherans who engage in a few external rituals but live worldly lives--carousing, dancing, etc. Mühlenberg lays the blame for some of this at the feet of a group of debauched "so-called Lutheran pastors" who are operating in the New World; but he also points out that many Lutherans had learned these same attitudes from clergy back in Germany. In explaining the difficulties of establishing a church in this new country, Mühlenberg contrasts the established position of the churches in the Old World with the church in the New World that lacks this "external scaffolding, that is, churches and school buildings," etc. Nevertheless, Mühlenberg sees and celebrates great advances in the Protestant church worldwide and in his own corner. He reports on the specific developments in the various congregations and on the life and work of the clergy and catechists associated with him. Most notably he comments on the severe illnesses of both Brunnholz and Handschuh and on his own difficult situation (ailments and overwork). Various financial matters, the state of the Reformed church in the area, some further reports on a couple of clergy, and assorted greetings and commendations complete the letter.

Text in German: Korrespondenz *1:337-47. For further textual information, see* Korrespondenz *1:347.*

A letter to the Very Reverend Court Preacher
Ziegenhagen, Doctor and Professor Franck and
Pastor Mayer from Heinrich Melchior
Mühlenberg of Pennsylvania

20 December 1749

Very Reverend Fathers:

The mercy of God in Christ permits me to hope that my humble letter will find our Very Reverend Fathers still alive, courageous and of good hope at their important posts in the church militant and in Jesus Christ's kingdom of the cross. How painful the sad news of His Reverence Court Preacher Ziegenhagen's prostration and how heartening the news of his gradual recovery was for all of us, only he alone can attest who searches the heart and knows how we have acted and conducted ourselves in our room in secret.[2] Whoever considers with enlightened and dispassionate eyes the present situation of the evangelical church as it is tossed about on the raging world-sea and considers in this context how few are sitting at the helm who have enough experience, ability and strength of mind to steer between the waves and the rocks; in addition, whoever considers that the Lord threatens to reduce the number of those few as a well deserved punishment of us, but in the midst of his righteous anger remembers his mercy and allows grace and forbearance to prevail--this person will experience with us similar emotions of sorrow and joy, the former having moved one to intercessory prayer and the latter to glory and praise. As earnestly as we now ask and pray that the Very Reverend Fathers may be led by Jehovah, our gracious Father in Christ, to remain for many years yet in the church militant and to work for the whole, so eager will those same highly respected Fathers be to learn from our small and insignificant part of the world whether here and there under the refuse and debris of the world a small stone can be found, worked on and made suitable to fill a gap in the whole edifice of the kingdom of Jesus Christ. The Very Reverend Fathers, worthy patrons and benefactors are entitled to this knowledge because their great efforts and gifts of love were not intended to establish a fraudulent, disgraceful, so-called Savior's fund[3] by means of which, for the sake of worldly prestige, one buys and establishes villages for serfs, but rather so that abandoned and scattered souls might be sought out and converted from darkness to light and from the power of Satan to God.[4]

But here I must immediately voice a complaint and acknowledge a truth which daily experience in my ministry makes clear to me: *namely, true repentance and conversion according to God's word proceed slowly and one by one*. I cannot in any way lay the blame for this on the most holy God, his powerful law and gospel and holy sacraments, much less on the ceaseless intercession of our Lord Jesus Christ and his dear children; rather I find it incontestably in the evil hearts of people who after the fall love darkness rather than light[5] and truth, in the many thousand hindrances which Satan and the world throw in the way, and not least also in my lack of experience in so important an office. But experience also teaches this truth that *it is easier to convert persons to a sect and a polity in which one sets certain goals*[6] where our natural inclinations can obtain nourishment by their own powers and find false rest and which can avoid the very repugnant way of repentance, faith and godliness according to the norm of the divine word. The many religious parties in this country are witnesses to this truth. How easy it is to convert unconverted people to the Quaker polity, for many respectable magistrates who govern the country belong to the Quakers! They possess honor, respect, power and wealth, do not trouble themselves with the written word of God and the sacraments and pay no pastors' salaries. They wear the most simple style of clothes and may all teach and prophesy if they have any good ideas. They love one another as the tax collectors also do, help the poor according to their polity, and make a natural, respectable life the basis of eternal blessedness; they have so many plausible written defences[7] for themselves, yet they remain good, converted members even if they appear only twice a year in the large assembly. If such conversion is still too difficult for the flesh, a still easier way is found. For we have many here who cut themselves off from all externals and worship God in spirit and truth[8] and call themselves the *silent in the land*.[9] Such persons are under no polity at all and cannot be disciplined by anyone; they receive no sympathy or support from other members because they are isolated; they interpret the Bible to their own satisfaction, obscure the most clear truths with their gibberish and fantastic language and find therein great mysteries which must apparently remain unresolved for the common man. They write books complaining and lamenting that not all people find the light and the Savior within themselves, with which they are impregnated by nature, that not all hearts are intoxicated as they themselves are. As silent as they and their likes are when they should attend to the common and particular distress and need, they are nevertheless found to be loud, effective and busy enough in the markets, where there is something to be bartered and traded. If there are melancholy types who would gladly be totally out of the world, there is for them a very convenient polity prepared by various cunning men and their concubines who are called the Seventh Day Baptists.[10] They purchase a nice, productive field from the properties of widows and orphans, communal homes, etc., as well as mills, brew houses, and bake houses, and build them up for the unmarried men and women through the blood and sweat of the self-denying members. What astonishing institutions and converts are there! There Christ is regarded as no more than an example, but one should have a high regard for those men who have become like Christ in their holiness and thereby have attained to the status of those who are capable of giving birth again, so that they are able to beget virgins. Nothing is heard there about a righteousness grasped through faith; as long as one affects a righteousness of life through fasting, mortification, hard work in common, and a ridiculous costume, contributes one's possessions to the community chest, immerses oneself in their fellowship and allows oneself to be ruled all of one's life, body and soul, by the chief task-masters, then one is such a convert and feels sorry for all the rest who do not want to be that well off. But such a polity is still too restrictive and is suitable for only one or two types of temperaments; for this reason Count Zinzendorf invented an even more comfortable polity where every kind of temperament finds nourishment. For they accept "cross-atmosphere,"[11] donkeys, pigs, monkeys and birds.[12] Here many a wanton whoremonger and adulterer has given up his house and property to hear from such new teachers that he is absolved without repentance and faith from his gross vices and has been assured that his natural self will fit in well with the other birds and four-footed creatures--if he brings his possessions and makes friends for himself by means of unrighteous mammon.[13] This last conversion would be much more universal if it did not affect so drastically one's goods and left more nourishment for the natural self. If one would rather control one's possessions oneself and still become something extraordinary that has more of the appearance of godliness than the ordinary church ways, then one can be converted to the polity of the so-called Sunday Baptists. One is quickly qualified if one knows by memory a few verses from the Revelation of John about Babylon and the beast and the harlot,[14] while at the same time cutting a good figure with them and letting oneself be immersed publicly by them. Their lessons are very simple and easy for our human nature learns them easily if one can simply mock infant baptism, criticize unfairly all those who disagree with them, in particular pastors and church people, and, among other things, believe that the devil and the damned in hell will again be restored.

Conversion to the Mennonite polity is also very simple, easy and advantageous and almost one of the smoothest. *I must* also, however, complain about those who are our co-religionists and acknowledge that for the most part they labor under the delusion that they are already converted if they have performed the outward ritual[15] and have sung "Now, the hour of worship o'er!"[16] But on other occasions, out of human weakness, they curse so that heaven itself is undoubtedly appalled, they drink themselves into a Christian state of slight drunkenness, do a dance with all due respect, and the like. Such poor people are encouraged in their delusion and given false security about the certainty of their salvation and lulled to sleep for the sake of a handful of barley by some nine or ten so-called Lutheran pastors, some of whom have put themselves forward here as preachers and some who have landed here after having been defrocked in Germany because of gross vices; they even argue vigorously that other pastors who insist so earnestly on repentance have departed from the Lutheran teaching. One should not think that the people have only fallen into this erroneous opinion here in this country; they have, rather, brought it with them from various places in Germany. I can illustrate this with a few examples. Last year I chastised several Lutherans from the congregation in New Hanover because of drunkenness and dancing at a wedding. They were natives of the Hanau region and they appealed to the testimonials they had brought with them from their pastors, in which it was stated that they had conducted themselves devoutly and honestly and had been regularly and attentively present at the Lord's table, etc., etc. When I asked them if drunkenness and dancing contribute to piety, they said that this was no sin as their pastors in Germany had always joined in the dancing at weddings, etc., etc., and entertained themselves honorably (which undoubtedly must have been practised by them as a class[17] and not just as individuals[18]). This year two newly arrived Württembergers announced themselves along with others for Holy Communion and showed me the testimonials from their pastors. When I inquired into their conduct I learned that only a few days earlier they carried on their tavern-fiddling trade all night in disreputable taverns. They did not think this should be reckoned as sin because, as they said, they carried it on unhindered in their fatherland. They appealed to their testimonial in which it was recorded under the pastoral seal[19] that they conducted themselves honestly and devoutly and always presented themselves attentively at the table of the Lord. They said further that there were no doubt pastors in their country who could not tolerate the festivities, but such were not orthodox but rather "penitists."[20] In short, in this country Satan, who deceives the whole world, has his fully stocked fair and almost every possible type of sectarian mode, so that because of the subtleties it is almost impossible to distinguish them any longer according to the principle of indistinguishables;[21] nevertheless they all agree in this that they give the appearance of godliness but deny its real power.[22] This is the extent to which the unlimited, so-called freedom of conscience can lead the mortal and sinful human race.

The Very Reverend Fathers, worthy patrons and benefactors may well ask what we have built to this point. Building involves the removal of obstacles, the preparation of the materials, excavating the ground, and setting up the scaffolding as much as it does the actual putting together of the parts in a beautiful form. Oh! How many obstacles are created by Satan, the coarse and subtle world, the unlimited freedom and especially all the hearts that have lost their original uprightness[23] and without it have become like a confused and tangled ball of weaver's yarn. Into how many branches and leaves has the inborn darkness spread as a result of the hardened understanding![24] How seriously alienated is the will from the life that comes from God! What a confused chaos is found in the emotions! How open are the sense organs[25] to every temporal object and how closed to everything that is godly and eternal! What great readiness have the members for impurity attained, committing one iniquity after another! We had to spend several years before folks were even willing to see us as honest people, because the ministerium is so much degraded and made questionable by such so-called pastors who lead an offensive life and practice gross and subtle knaveries under the black gown! How difficult it is to dig a deep, lasting foundation in the hearts that our Master compares with the path, with rocky and thorny ground.[26] One digs in valiantly with the holy law of God and reproves all kinds of sin, but there is much (stubbornness   and) opposition. How much time we waste on the external scaffolding, that is, churches and school buildings! Our worthy ministerial colleagues in Europe have a great advantage over us because the external scaffolding is already up. They receive their necessary support without worry, and they have an outside fence around their congregations and are protected by the Christian authorities, even though it is more in one place and less in another, so that they can confidently and uninterruptedly cultivate the hearts of those entrusted to them with the law and build with the gospel as a power for salvation! It was certainly very sinful that the papists in the dark ages cheated the poor, unknowing souls out of their goods and chattels, promised them salvation or release from purgatory in return, and erected with the money massive churches, cloisters, school buildings. In the meantime it benefits us in our Protestant countries, because the providence of God brought something good out of what was evil and in this way made the spiritual building easier for us. In many Protestant places it would be just as hard and difficult as it is for us if they would have to begin building the churches and schools in the present without guaranteed funds, on the basis of voluntary gifts. The wealthy of this world have nothing left over for churches and schools, for the maintenance of pastors and teachers; rather they wish much more that such things might be banned from Europe. The poor would gladly give occasionally and cannot. Do we really recognize the difference between the various churches: the one has an external scaffolding and the other has none; the one has a fence and the other has none; the one has authorities as wet-nurses and the other does not have that privilege. Nevertheless, we find ourselves very much under the shadow and protection of the Almighty and have fence and wall enough if we believe the promise of our Master: "Lo, I am with you always,"[27] etc., etc. We can also learn to understand better how far the power of the word of God and his gracious, special providence reach without the secular arm.[28] We also do not want to murmur like the children of Israel and demand a king like the other nations;[29] rather we still want to thank our Jehovah most humbly that he is the help of our countenance and our God![30] The point is also not that we imagine that we alone have made and continue to make the present external scaffolding; rather it remains an everlasting monument that God who is entirely good has awakened so many upright persons in the Protestant church in this century from a variety of estates, dignities and honors and has endowed them with such extraordinary faith that has almost outdone itself working through love[31] and that has had and still has as its special purpose the spreading of the kingdom of Jesus Christ among the heathen, Jews, and even among the lukewarm, so-called Christians. It is to this most gracious God and his worthy children in Europe that the scattered, erring and abandoned Lutherans in Philadelphia, Germantown, Providence, New Hanover, Upper Milford, Saccum, Fork, Birkensee, Tulpehocken, Heidelberg, Lancaster and York need to be most grateful; for, to be quite blunt about it, during the most dangerous wartime and with much effort and great expense, they sent over five pastors; and, when the combined contributions of the first united congregations were far from sufficient to purchase the necessary buildings for church services and schools and the congregations were not in a position to support me in the first year, the Very Reverend Fathers, benefactors and patrons not only allowed my scanty but adequate salary that first year to come to me through Pastor Brunnholtz[32] from the love offerings that were intended for the congregations but also gradually they sent over so much that from these gifts, when combined with the contributions here, a church has been renovated in New Hanover, a new schoolhouse built, and several acres of land purchased; in Providence a solid, stone church and schoolhouse have been completed from the ground up; in Germantown the second half of a church has been constructed; and in Philadelphia a property has been purchased and a church built on it. This last church, however, is the one that is in the deepest debt; this is because construction in the city is the most expensive, the congregation members are mostly poor and still just starting out, and the building had to be the largest of all of them. To make an exact comparison, in the city a pound cannot reach further in construction than a dollar[33] in Germany: as many pennies[34] as one pays a workman per day in Germany, that is how many shillings one has to pay the English artisans per day here. The accounts and receipts which Pastor Brunnholtz has already sent in and will still send in will certify all the aforementioned.[35] Whether some souls have been won and saved through the many efforts, love offerings, and arrangements, or whether, God forbid, we had to use up our energies simply as a witness among them, nevertheless, according to the sure promises of God, the great effort and love offering of our Very Reverend Fathers and all worthy benefactors, yes, even the smallest drink of cold water, will not remain unrewarded and unrecompensed.[36] Accordingly, our great effort and concern, although in great weakness, is so directed that, in accord with the blessed purpose of our Very Reverend Fathers, patrons, and benefactors, we might so believe, teach, live, pray, struggle and fight that wherever possible the congregations entrusted to us and in particular every member in them will be won and saved through our service and that of our successors. With this purpose in mind our worthy colleague in the ministry, Pastor Brunnholtz, is now in his fifth year of working with all faithfulness and patience in Philadelphia and Germantown. He preaches publicly not with words of human wisdom, but in demonstration of the Spirit and power.[37] He holds special prayer meetings in his house. He is edifying in his relations with his own people and with those of various opinions. He concentrates all his speaking on the improvement of understanding and willing. He visits the sick day and night when it is necessary, even if he is sometimes weak and worn out himself. He meditates, prays, fights and struggles in his room for all the congregations, and especially for those entrusted to him, for the Fathers and all the members of Jesus Christ in Europe. He works a great deal at teaching the children. He has the greatest burden with the correspondence, because all our letters for ordering something are handed over to him and also because he has a special gift for correspondence. He faithfully looks after the external burden and debts of the congregations and sees to it that the interest is collected. He is satisfied with the support his congregation members give him out of their goodwill. He is considerate of the poor, chastises no one, manages from hand to mouth, and if he has something left over he lets the poor enjoy it with him. He shows himself in all things as a servant of God and a faithful steward of the mysteries of God.[38] His work is also not without blessing. For the preaching of the Gospel becomes for some a fragrance from life to life.[39] God does not allow the blessing in its entirety to be very evident to him so that he remains in poverty and humility of spirit. He has already cleared away many obstacles, has dug a deep foundation with some, and laid a base by the grace of God. The fire of adversity will test[40] and reveal it. But I do have to inform you now with great sorrow in my heart that he has already burned up most of himself in the process of having shined as a light for others. He suffered almost all summer, so that I was worried that it might be the beginning of a hectic fever. But it manifested itself rather in the highest degree of hypochondria[41] (with such convulsions that he lost consciousness). I took him to my place in the country for a couple of weeks which brought him around again somewhat. But finally in the fall he had an outbreak of miliary fever and it was so deadly and critical that he was twice in his death throes.[42] Admittedly, he had two English doctors, but the Essentia dulcis,[43] next to God, helped to put him on his feet again after a long and difficult confinement. But now the hypochondria is again coming to the fore. If there is not prompt help and assistance so that he can be torn away for a time from the heavy burden of his ministry, then by all appearances he is finished. None of us is in a position to assist him, for we can scarcely help ourselves in our overextended circumstances. Admittedly I have not yet been able to confer at length with Pastor Brunnholtz about this. For this reason I have only wanted provisionally to pour my individual thoughts and opinion into the lap of our Very Reverend Fathers.

Philadelphia cannot and dare not be abandoned. I and Pastor Brunnholtz both have in our call the first united congregations. I and he together are both scarcely as strong as one; therefore, we both need an assistant who awaits our demise. If now, on the strength of your fatherly love to us and our poor congregations, the Very Reverend Fathers could seek out in advance a competent candidate, we would try in the meantime to make arrangements for our congregations to issue a formal call to N. N. whom the Very Reverend Fathers selected. This call should be signed by the most prominent congregation members. Pastor Brunnholtz would indeed remain pastor in our four congregations, only that he would spend most of his time out in the country with me and would work as much as his strength would permit. In this way I and he and all four congregations would be better served. To move about he could also occasionally pay a visit to the other colleagues and give them advice and consolation. Even though my income is rather meager and I am still in debt 116 pounds because of building my house, nevertheless God will not abandon or neglect us. For we have a generous Father over all. I know he is satisfied with the way God ordains things. He shall have as much right in my house and yard as I do myself. In her weakness, my wife will do for him what she can, for she reveres and loves him like her own earthly father here on earth. In terms of the travel costs, the heavenly Father will also certainly find the means. If Pastor Handshue[44] should live and have to remain in Lancaster, as it appears, the

Lancaster people still have to hand over one or two parts of his travel costs. Perhaps my worthy colleague Brunnholtz will also inform the Very Reverend Fathers of his opinion. At one time I was under the impression that Mr. Hartwich[45] would not be opposed to becoming Pastor Brunnholtz's assistant, if the congregations requested him and the Very Reverend Fathers would be pleased to permit it, for he would like to be with and among us. As fearful as Pastor Handshue was initially to go to Lancaster, he is nevertheless finding good acceptance and already his work is a blessing. Late this summer he had to endure a serious illness, so that we almost feared he would die. But God graciously averted it and gave him back to us again. Mr. Schaum, who was ordained this year for the congregation in York,[46] was also seriously afflicted with a fever and had various other trials. Nevertheless, no temptation has overtaken us yet that is not common to humanity; but God is faithful! etc., etc.[47] Mr. Kurtz himself will have reported on his circumstances.[48] In the past summer I had to travel to the Raritan once again.[49] Mr. Weygand is meeting with approval and until now has conducted himself well.[50] The three united congregations gave him a formal call in my presence and are requesting our Very Reverend Fathers in a childlike and humble manner through me that these same Very Reverend Fathers would permit and graciously grant us the power to ordain Weygand at our next Synod meeting.[51] How often this year we have rejoiced and been blessed with letters from our Very Reverend Fathers and worthy patrons and especially with the medicines and the long lost medicine chest of Her Excellency, Lady von Münchhauss,[52] my dear colleague Brunnholtz will humbly set forth in detail, because the correspondence is his responsibility. Among other things, it was very consoling for us to realize that God's special providence had ordained the worthy Mr. Albinus as an assistant.[53] Oh, what a vigorous and valiant mate for East and West at the helm! Help us, O Lord! O Lord, in everything give success![54] "His wisdom never plans in vain Nor falters nor mistakes."[55]

We have drawn the Darmstadt collection and have assigned one-half to Providence and the other half to Philadelphia. Now Providence and New Hanover can rest and can thank our most gracious God and our Very Reverend Fathers and patrons in dust and ashes many thousand times if they truly want to acknowledge it! (We have not allowed our congregations to become aware of the 50 pounds for my first year that it was necessary to draw on for my survival, so that they might not misuse this information foolishly.) If out of paternal graciousness the Very Reverend Fathers would verify the receipts we submitted as opportunity permits, we would greatly appreciate it and this might protect me and my children against charges by contrary-minded people. (May the Very Reverend Fathers not take to heart what Johann Nicol Croesman has written about us,[56] for he has become a drunkard since he has rejected all the good stirrings and workings of the Spirit. May the Lord yet convert and save him.) I have also sent in my paltry journal which runs to the end of the year 1748. I have too little time and too much disturbance; I usually have to write at night, using my glasses because since about two years ago I have had weak eyes which, due to the great heat in summer and the cold and raw winds in winter, have become almost totally ruined and bleary. Otherwise, I would write more and decently. If God will allow me to live this winter yet, I will with his help record a little bit more about 1749, but before anything else I will first of all compose a most humble letter of reply to His Excellency, the older Count of Wernigerode,[57] to His Excellency Count Erdman Henckel,[58] and to Her Excellency Baroness von Münchhauss if the Lord has not already joined their precious souls to the spirits of just persons made perfect.[59]

The situation of the Reformed is badly confused. The licentious deacons in Philadelphia have dismissed without significant reasons their pastor who was sent out by the Synod in Holland. They are using the Pennsylvania coarseness and freedom and say, "No one has the right to dictate to us." Another pastor,[60] who also has just been sent here by the Classis for Lancaster, is allowing himself to be taken on by the disorderly deacons in Philadelphia and Germantown without the knowledge and against the will of his superiors; he is unwittingly helping to evict his colleague who does not want to allow himself to be evicted because he has his following.[61] The third one, who has been taken on as pastor in Tulpehocken, acts as if he had been given some potion and also has terrible convulsions.[62] The fourth one has mostly given up his preaching and is vigorously practising medicine.[63] The fifth one has involved himself in buying cattle and land.[64] The sixth is a poor, cold man.[65] The seventh is the former Zinzendorfer Jakob Lischy who still does his best and gets by.[66] Oh, here pastors are put through their paces! May the Lord confirm us ever more for his purpose in faith, love and unity. And now, Lord, with what shall we console ourselves? Our hope is in you! Deliver us from all our transgressions and do not let us be made the scorn of the fool.[67]

Last summer Pastor Klug[68] of Virginia visited us; he was moved, as he said, to make such a great and long journey of from three to four hundred miles over land out of love for us. The elders from his congregation went to Germany with old Stöver[69] a number of years ago and are said to have brought together between two and three thousand pounds cash, from which they have built a church and have bought a glebe and a number of black slaves to work it. Most recently this fall twenty-four ships full of German people also arrived here;[70] among them there was also a pastor[71] who let himself be called by some of those travelling to Pennsylvania and ordained by three pastors. His little congregation, consisting of thirteen or fourteen men, was dispersed here in this country, and now he is practising medicine here in Philadelphia to earn a living. After this one, a student of theology who was a native of Transylvania also came along here[72] and he is now seeking refuge as a sojourner with Pastor Brunnholtz. Curious people go into this strange land recklessly, without a call, fall into various temptations afterwards and become a burden for us. For they are not easily employed because here there are only three types of vocations: merchant, artisan, or farmer. Almost no one can make a living simply by teaching school, and the preaching places are mostly occupied by all sorts. It would be very consoling to us if the Very Reverend Fathers would once again allow the written reports of the blessed institutions in Halle and other changes in the church of Christ to come to us, so that we would have more promptings to particular petitions and also to glory and praise. For we gladly bear and rejoice with the other members of the body of Jesus Christ. In conclusion, I commend myself, my family, particularly my dear colleagues, congregations, and all other concerns to the continuing goodwill, love and affection and especially the earnest petitions of our Very Reverend Fathers, patrons and all acquaintances in the Lord. I remain with the most sincere esteem and most proper respect,

Providence, 20 December
1749.

Very Reverend Fathers,
Your most obedient and
most lowly son,
H. M. Mühlenberg

---

1. On Johann August Majer, a Halle pastor and friend of the "blessed institutions" in Halle who was often fondly remembered and greeted by Mühlenberg in his letters to the Fathers, see *Correspondence* 1:23 n. 14.
2. See Matt. 6:6.
3. This pejorative reference to a "Savior's fund" (*Heilands-Cassa*) remains unclear.
4. See Acts 26:18.
5. John 3:19.
6. The words in italics were highlighted by Mühlenberg in the original text.
7. The text reads *Apologien*.
8. See John 4:24.
9. The term "the silent in the land" (*Stille im Lande*) is used by Gottfried Arnold in his *Unparteiische Kirchen- und Ketzer-Historie* (1699-1700) to describe separatists and spiritualists of the seventeenth century who had waged an unsuccessful campaign against "Babel" and, having failed, retreated from the overt attempt to reshape the structures of church and world and withdrew into their own private realms. Such individuals and groups continued to exist in the eighteenth century in Germany as well. See the article by E. Beyreuther in *Die Religion in Geschichte und*

Gegenwart, 3rd ed. (Tübingen: J. C. B. Mohr [Paul Siebeck], 1962), s.v. "Stille im Lande."

10. Under the designation of Seventh Day Baptists, Mühlenberg is describing the community of the Church of the Brethren (also known as Dunkers, Tunkers, or Täufers) established by Conrad Beissel (1691-1768) which became the Ephrata Community. "In this 'Order of the Solitary' a seventh-day Sabbath was observed, the sexes separated, and a communal semimonastic economy was inaugurated" (Sydney E. Ahlstrom, *A Religious History of the American People* [New Haven: Yale University Press, 1972], p. 241).

11. This translation is based on the conjecture that the punctuation between *Creuz* and *Luft* is a hyphen rather than a comma. In his homilies on the "Litany of the Wounds of our Lord Jesus Christ," preached in 1747, Zinzendorf spoke of "the atmosphere of the cross and of the dead body which constantly wafts around" the Christian (*die beständige um einen herum wehende Creuz=Luft und Leichnams=Luft*). See Nikolaus Ludwig von Zinzendorf, *Hauptschriften*, vol. 3: *Vier und Dreissig Homiliae über die Wunden=Litaney der Brüder* [1747] (Hildesheim: Georg Olms Verlagsbuchhandlung, 1963), p. 35.

12. Mühlenberg's reference is probably to the rather extravagant imagery and vocabulary that the Moravian Church adopted during the period known as the "time of sifting" (1743-50). John R. Weinlick, *Count Zinzendorf* (New York-Nashville: Abingdon Press, 1956), pp. 199-200, writes that "they spoke of themselves as 'little doves flying about in the atmosphere of the cross,' 'little fish swimming in the bed of blood,' or as 'little bees who suck on the wounds of Christ, who feel at home in the side hole and crawl in deep.' Again, they would call themselves 'bloodthirsty beasts,' 'blood leeches,' 'wound worms,' and 'side-hole hearts.'"

13. Luke 16:9.

14. See Rev. 17 et passim.

15. The text reads *Opus operatum*, literally "the act done." For a definition of this term and the related *ex opere operato*, see *Oxford Dictionary of the Christian Church*, 2nd ed. rev. (London: Oxford University Press, 1974), s.v. "ex opere operato."

16. Hymn by Hartmann Schrenk, "Nun Gott Lob, es ist vollbracht" (1680), v. 1. See *Liedersammlung*, Hymn 11; for an English translation, see *The Lutheran Hymnal* (St. Louis: Concordia Publishing House, 1941), Hymn 45.

17. The text reads *in concreto*.

18. The text reads *in individuo*.

19. The text reads *sub fide pastorali*.

20. The text reads *penetisten*. The speakers clearly meant "pietists" but did not get the word quite right.

21. The text reads *principio indiscernibilium*. According to this principle, there are no two things in all of nature that are absolutely identical. See Johann Heinrich Zedler, *Grosses Vollständiges Universal-Lexikon* (Graz, Austria: Akademische Druck und Verlagsanstalt, 1961 [1743]), s.v. "Unterscheidenden, (Satz des nicht zu) Lat. *principium indiscernibilium*."

22. See 2 Tim. 3:5.

23. The text reads יֵשׁ

24. The text reads διάνοιαν, "mind" or "understanding." (The accent should be on the penultimate rather than ultimate syllable.)

25. The text reads *organa sensoria*.

26. See Mark 4:1-20; Matt. 13:1-23; Luke 8:4-15.

27. Matt. 28:20.

28. The text reads *Brachium saeculare*.

29. See 1 Sam. 8:5.

30. See Ps. 42:5, 11; 43:5 (AV).

31. See Gal. 5:6.

32. On Peter Brunnholz, see Letter 71 n. 3.

33. The text reads *Thaler*. According to the figures in Table 2 of the Appendix in A. G. Roeber, *Palatines, Liberty, and Property: German Lutherans in Colonial British America* (Baltimore: The Johns Hopkins University Press, 1993), p. 334, the Pennsylvania pound was worth approximately five times as much as a Hamburg taler. Therefore, Mühlenberg is suggesting that construction costs in Philadelphia are five times what they are in Germany.

34. The text reads *Groschen*.

35. The church in Philadelphia was dedicated on 14 August 1748. On the accounts of the congregations in Philadelphia, Providence and New Hanover, see *Correspondence* 1:264-67, incl. nn. 3, 9, 12; 303-5, incl. n. 22. The accounts were sent over with Brunnholz's letter of 13 April 1749. For further details, see *Korrespondenz* 1:348 n. 7.

36. See Matt. 10:42.

37. See 1 Cor. 2:4.

38. See 1 Cor. 4:1.

39. See 2 Cor. 2:16

40. See Ecclus. 2:5.

41. The text reads *Malum hypocondriacum*.

42. Mühlenberg's medical term here is *der weisse Friesel* which was apparently a form of "miliary fever." It was characterized by rash or pustules as well as fever. Brunnholz's own comments on his illness are contained in a letter of 25 October 1749 to Francke and Ziegenhagen; see *Korrespondenz* 1:348 n. 8. For a medical description of this illness, see Frank Pierce Foster, *An Illustrated Encyclopedia Medical Dictionary* (New York: D. Appleton, 1892), s.v. "Miliaria."

43. On this medicine which was manufactured in Halle, see *Correspondence* 1:94 n. 48.

44. On Johann Friedrich Handschuh, see *Correspondence* 1:291 n. 18.

45. On Johann Christoph Hartwich, see *Correspondence* 1:323 n. 19.

46. Schaum was ordained on 4 June 1749 at the second meeting of the Ministerium in Lancaster. See *Journals* 1:222f.; for further documentation, see *Korrespondenz* 1:348 n. 9. On Johann Helfrich Schaum, see Letter 71 n. 9.

47. See 1 Cor. 10:13.

48. Kurz wrote to Francke on 15 February 1749. For documentation, see *Korrespondenz* 1:348 n. 9. On Johann Nicolaus Kurz, see *Correspondence* 1:154 n. 5 and 341 n. 16.

49. On Mühlenberg's late July and early August trip, see Letter 72:16ff.

50. On Weygand's assignment to the Raritan, see Letter 72:18f and Letter 73:25. On Johann Albert Weygand, see Letter 71 n. 21.

51. Weygand was supposed to be ordained at the Synod meeting in Providence on 17 June 1750; see *Journals* 1:244-46. However, his ordination was postponed until 2 December 1750; see *Korrespondenz* 1:400 n. 13.

52. On Baroness Wilhelmine Sophie von Münchhausen, see *Correspondence* 1:18 n. 18.

53. On Samuel Theodor Albinus, see *Correspondence* 1:154 n. 8 and 354 n. 5.

54. See Ps. 118:25.

55. Hymn by Paul Gerhardt (1607-76), "Ich singe dir mit Herz und Mund" (1653). See *Liedersammlung*, Hymn 499, v. 17. The English translation is by John Kelly (1833-90) in *Lutheran Worship* (St. Louis: Concordia Publishing House, 1982), Hymn 424, v. 6.

56. Croesmann had complained that Brunnholz and Mühlenberg did not adequately inform their congregations about expenses that had been incurred; see Letter 74.

57. Count Christian Ernst von Stolberg-Wernigerode (1691-1771).

58. On Count Erdmann Heinrich von Henckel-Pölzig (1681-1752), see *Correspondence* 1:11 n. 7.

59. See Heb. 12:23.

60. Johann Conrad Steiner; see Letter 75, incl. n. 2.

61. Michael Schlatter; see Letter 71 n. 14 and Letter 75.

62. Johann Dominicus Bartholomae (1723-68) was born in Heidelberg and studied theology there and in Franecker (Holland). He was sent out to America from Holland at the end of 1747 and was installed as pastor in Tulpehocken by Johann Philipp Böhm in 1748. See *Pastors and People* 1:18.

63. Johann Bartholomäus Rieger (1707-69) was born in Oberingelheim in the Palatinate, studied theology in Heidelberg, came to Philadelphia on 21 September 1731, and was initially active as a Reformed pastor in Philadelphia and Germantown. After studying medicine in Holland in 1744, he earned his living as a doctor and preached only occasionally. Rieger was a member of the Reformed Synod in Pennsylvania. See *Pastors and People* 1:108f.

64. Is this Johann Philipp Leydich (1715-84) who was in Philadelphia since 1748? On him, see *Pastors and People* 1:82f.

65. Presumably Georg Michael Weiss (1700-61). He arrived in Philadelphia in 1727 and supplied various congregations in Pennsylvania and New York, including Goshenhoppen (1746-61), right up to the time of his death. See *Pastors and People* 1:160f.

66. Jakob Lischy (1719-80) was born in Mühlhausen and was originally a linen-weaver. After visiting Herrnhut and Marienborn, he emigrated to America in 1741 where he accompanied Zinzendorf on his journeys. He was active for a short time as a Reformed pastor in Cocalico and then in New York from 1744. In 1747 he turned away from the Moravians. In 1760 he was expelled from the Reformed Church and worked from that point on as an independent Reformed pastor. See *Pastors and People* 1:83f.

67. See Ps. 39:7-8.

68. On Georg Samuel Klug, see *Correspondence* 1:342 n. 37. Mühlenberg comments in his journals on Klug's visit as follows: "For several years he has been the regular pastor of a German Evangelical congregation in the province of Virginia. He lamented that he was so entirely alone in that vast, extensive country and had no opportunity to be cheered and edified by his clerical brethren. He also said that an occasional Zinzendorfer Brother had passed through his parish but had not been able to gain a foothold. Moreover, they cannot easily get into the country because of special laws of the land which are very severe against such vagabonds who cannot produce a regular call and valid credentials. He promised to visit us again, if his life were spared, because he gained encouragement from it, though he lives all of three hundred miles away from us" (*Journals* 1:223).

69. Johann Caspar Stöver, Sr. (1685-1739) arrived in Philadelphia in 1728 with his son, Johann Caspar, Jr. He was ordained in 1733 and served a congregation in Madison county, Virginia. In 1734 he left for Europe to raise funds for his congregation. Stöver raised considerable funds but remained in Germany for a number of years studying theology. He died in 1739 while on the return trip to America. See *Pastors and People* 1:138f.

70. Just before mid-century immigration was reaching new heights. The ships mentioned here by Mühlenberg contained over seven thousand German immigrants, and they had been preceded that summer by twelve thousand Germans. See William J. Mann, *Life and Times of Henry Melchior Mühlenberg* (Philadelphia: G. W. Frederick, 1888), pp. 216f.

71. Johann Friedrich Riess (d. 1791). In his letter of 25 October 1749 to Ziegenhagen and Francke, Brunnholz writes: "During my illness a young pastor by the name of Ries arrived here; some Germans who were coming here had called him and had him ordained. He has studied medicine in Jena and theology in Halle under Doctor Baumgarden. . . . He has gone to New York. Mr. Mühlenberg has offered to look after him in the meantime. . . . When they arrived the people who called him were sold to pay for their passage and scattered, and so he was without a congregation." See *Korrespondenz* 1:349 n. 26. Riess went on to serve various congregations in the province of New York. See *HN2/1*:629f.; *Pastors and People* 1:109f.

72. Lucas Rauss (1723-88). Rauss was born in Transylvania and studied theology at Jena. However, as a non-German he felt he had little prospect of getting a position in Germany and so he came to America in 1749. After some further study and apprenticeship, he was ordained with the approval of the Ministerium on 5 November 1752. A conflict between Rauss and Mühlenberg and Rauss's inability to discharge the responsibilities of a pastor in his Indianfield congregation confirmed Mühlenberg's initial misgivings concerning him. See *HN2/1*:657-63; *Pastors and People* 1:107f.

Letter 77

To Johann Basilius Gabler[1]
Providence, 22 December 1749

More than seven years after he has left his homeland, Mühlenberg redeems his promise to communicate with Gabler by letter. In carrying out his promise Mühlenberg ranges over a large number of subjects, his knowledge of which is an indication of his observation of geographical, political, judicial and religious matters in the land of his adoption. The conclusion of the letter is taken up with acknowledgments and certification of a number of concerns.
Text in German: Korrespondenz *1:349-57. For further textual information see* Korrespondenz *1:357.*

Honorable Sir,
Dearly beloved Friend in Christ and Colleague
in the kingdom of Jesus Christ:
Though no bond of a natural blood relationship exists between us, nevertheless, a transcending relationship in regeneration through the most holy blood and merit of Jesus Christ has created such a close and intimate union between us that from the first day of our acquaintance we immediately became one heart and one soul.[2] In this regeneration we share by grace one Lord, one baptism, one faith and one Father of us all.[3] As has been said, this bond has its basis in the birth from above and is not to be severed by anything as long as both of us on our part remain firm through our living faith in our head, Jesus Christ, and his strong love. Neither death nor life, neither angels nor principalities, nor powers, neither things present nor things to come, neither height nor depth, nor any other creature shall separate us from his love.[4] The most wise and gracious providence of God has situated us very far apart in body and calling but not so far apart that we cannot be together in spirit and manifest our faith in love.

For my own part I must indeed openly acknowledge that the love of my worthy friend for me has now run into its eighth year. I know he has remembered me and my congregations before the Lord in his room,[5] has done much that is good for me during my journey and here in this country; indeed, not only for me and my family but for our congregations as well. If I were to mention every good turn individually, space in this letter would be too limited, and his poverty and humility in spirit would chastise me with the saying of our beloved Master when he says that the left hand should not know what the right hand is doing.[6] I also know very well that he does not and cannot expect a reward either from me or from our poor congregations but believes the promise spoken by the mouth of truth: Your Father who sees in secret will reward you openly.[7] Nonetheless, it is still right and proper to acknowledge every undeserved endeavor and kindness in the presence of the all-knowing God, humbly imploring God to reward it and also publicly giving thanks for it. The first of these I have carried out, albeit in weakness and unworthiness, in secret as well as publicly in the congregations. I have the confidence that the Lord Jesus will reckon this endeavor and kindness to his account and list it under that column on the Last Day in the presence of all elect and holy angels and will say, I was hungry and you gave me food, I was naked and you clothed me![8] The second part of this acknowledgment I am currently carrying out and I certify herewith in his presence, my worthy comrade-in-arms, and before all the remaining well-disposed patrons and benefactors that all mites gathered in the form of money and remaining donations consisting of edifying books and several pieces of clothing and linen have been handed over faithfully and applied in all honesty to the purpose for which loving hearts intended them.

After I have brought these matters up in a preliminary way I must now also indicate the reasons for not having written directly even once to my worthy conrade-in-arms and the remaining acquaintances in the Lord since I had after all promised to do so and was frequently reminded of it. The failure to write must by no means be attributed to forgetfulness or laziness or neglect but rather to a lack of time, being overwhelmed with work, several illnesses and uncertainty in the dangerous events of war on land and sea. In accordance with love, the most charitable construction should be placed on this failure. Since I am now writing to my worthy friend and the remaining acquaintances in the Lord for the first time I want to report on that aspect of the outward and inner circumstances which my memory readily calls to mind and which I think you will most easily understand. Since we saw each other the last time and parted from one another with tears, God's providence has until now arranged for us to be separated from each other by approximately twelve to thirteen hundred miles.[9] Seamen reckon the distance from London to Philadelphia to be seventy-four degrees longitude. Since one degree equals fifteen miles, the total distance adds up to eleven hundred miles. From London to Hannover is another good stretch. That represents a large space between us, yet we can be with one another in spirit and thoughts. By taking this longitude at noon time there is approximately a difference of six hours so that when you observe noon time in Hannover we reckon it to be six o'clock in the morning. At that time you are perhaps occupied with food for the body and we present our supplications in our room before God saying morning prayers in which we include our friends. Consequently, you have our intercession as an added benefit at a time when it is not really suitable for you to be at prayer. When you come to six o'clock in the evening you may be engaged in prayer before God[10] and you also think of us as we are having our noon meal and it is not a particularly convenient time for prayer; and so it alternates night and day. As far as our location according to latitude is concerned we are situated between ten and twelve degrees, that is, 150 to 180 German miles nearer to the sun than you are in Hannover. But Jesus Christ, the sun of righteousness, is equally near to every one who calls on him. Your summer and winter are constant, and you enjoy fairly stable weather. We also have summer and winter but very unstable weather in both. It is only toward the end of April according to the old calendar which is eleven days later than the new style calendar that the woods turn green here. Already in the month of May we have days as hot as you do in the dog days. Here in the months of June and July the heat is occasionally so great that some men and beasts often suffocate and suddenly die; in spite of this in both months the hardest work, haying and harvesting fruit, must be done. The months of August and September still have penetrating hot days and cold nights which frequently cause ague and high fevers and other kinds of sicknesses. Beyond that one barely has two or three days of settled weather; rather, cold and hot winds alternate and attack the body in a struggle between life and death, health and sickness. Our October begins with high winds and makes the trees bare. Yet often very hot and cold days, even hours, alternate with one another. From November to March we have a raw and sustained winter, but with many changes. Snow, one, two and three feet high, can fall in one day and night; in the following twenty-four hours a warm rain, accompanied by wind, falls, consumes the snow and causes fierce, high waters; on the third day everything freezes over again and becomes like a mirror; and so there is constant change and yet it is always still winter. If a person wanted to provide proper clothing for himself in summer and winter and observe a strict diet from the point of view of health, he would always have to cart along a wheelbarrow full of linen and woolen clothing. In this way one could change clothing twice a day, indeed, every half hour until one would gradually become proficient in enduring change and onsets in weather. As much as one would like to stick with this observation, it nevertheless has quite a substantial influence and effect on animal, vegetable and mineral life, yes, even somewhat on the kingdom of grace. One only needs to be an apprentice in chemistry to see the effect of uniform, sustained warmth and cold and tempering and by way of contrast to see what incomplete processes, rapid changes and jumps in heat and cold bring about. In the animal kingdom all animals are smaller, weaker, more imperfect and not as tough as they are where you are. And nature produces all kinds of pests of which no one knows anything where you are. In the vegetable kingdom the members also do not reach the degree of perfection, purity, toughness, maturity and age as they do where you are. In the mineral kingdom well-to-do Englishmen have conducted many experiments. However, one finds nothing better than ironstone. Silver and gold cannot reach maturity and copper is not worth the cost and labor. For in a certain location one comes across a vein which appears to be good and full of promise but all of a sudden it breaks off, and when one continues to dig on several rods one finds only a single clump which is more like a millstone than a proper birth.

No less significant is the effect of unstable weather also on brutish people who possess only a natural soul and are devoid of Spirit from above according to the Epistle of Jude in verse 19. In their customary dealings the greatest fickleness becomes apparent which among other things may be attributed to the many sects and almost innumerable opinions and diversity encountered here. Experience also teaches that this fickleness can also bring about many temptations for these persons living in the kingdom of grace. At one time the heavens are weighed down with heavy, black clouds and oppressive haze and want to saturate the remaining seeds of corruption with anxiety about nourishment, doubt and loss of confidence; at another time the heavens are clear and bright and want to arouse libertinism, rashness and frivolity if one does not have a new and right Spirit[11] from above and does not seriously struggle so that the heart will become firm and certain through repentance and faith. Consequently, there is almost no more convenient polity in this country for changeable weather and brutish people than the Zinzendorfian one because it is changeable in so many ways and adapts itself so well when one turns into a crosscurrent, ass, pig, monkey and little birdie.[12] If, however, one wants to save one's soul that means, "Hasten! Hasten..."[13]

As far as the external constitution of this country is concerned it is under the protection of the most gracious king of England; already in the previous century it was given to the noble family of Penn as its own.[14] The proprietors are in Old England and they have a vice governor and other officers educated in the law who look after their particular rights and interests. The king has an agent here who must see to it that nothing is done that is in contradiction or contrary to English basic laws. The vice governor is confirmed in his office by the king and must at the same time keep in mind the interests of the crown and appoint all justices of the peace in accordance with English laws. The inhabitants of the country have the right and the freedom at the annual election to arrange for a council from their midst[15] which is called the assembly and is similar to the tribunal of the people[16] of the old Romans. Consequently, there are two branches of the legislature which are to administer the rights and interests of the Crown, the proprietors and the inhabitants. As one branch of the legislature, the assembly has for some years now consisted of Quakers because the largest body of people here in this country like the way they conduct government and elect them for this purpose. The other branch is mixed and consists of so-called church people and some Quakers. Although probably all of them have until now governed the country wisely and happily, the prophet Isaiah would, in accordance with the inner condition, not only lecture the poor but also the whole body and say, "From the sole of the foot even to the head, there is no soundness in them," etc.[17] Regardless of whether they are called Quakers or church people, faith and love are in decline; atheism, deism, naturalism and that sort of thing are gaining the upper hand in the whole body so that we might easily become like Sodom and Gomorrah, if the Lord had not permitted a remnant to remain for us, etc., etc.[18] According to the basic laws of this country everyone is permitted to live here provided he acknowledges a higher being or God and in other respects conducts himself peaceably according to the laws. For that reason this country is to be viewed altogether as a hospital where hundreds of kinds of rooms and places for safekeeping are to be found in which patients receive tender care. One finds people here from almost all the nations under the sun, namely, Portuguese, Spaniards, Frenchmen, Englishmen, Dutchmen, Swedes, Danes, Poles, Hungarians, Moravians, Austrians, Salzburgers, indeed, people from every corner of Germany, and even blacks from Africa. In accordance with civil law one finds many honest people, but almost all of them are broken earthen vessels which have been rejected in other parts of the world as useless and incorrigible. For annually they send us several ships full of people who committed criminal offences in Old England, Ireland and Scotland and fought in the distressing rebellion against the legitimate anointed ruler. No less do we also get many of our nationality who have run away from the flag and prisons. In terms of true and false religion we have Lutherans, Reformed, Catholics, Quakers, Mennonites, Schwenckfelders and every imaginable kind of Anabaptists; in addition there are Separatists, Inspired Ones, those who observe new moons, Jews, pagans and among them all many who are practically atheists, deists, naturalists and whatever other names there may be.[19] Each party has its own assembly and seeks to solidify its opinions and increase its party. If one pays a little attention in the city on a Sunday everything swarms about in confusion like bees and yet each one finds its hive. But on the two market days that occur each week one sees the people of various opinions in trade and commerce with each other. Although on Sunday so many different languages are spoken by people who cannot understand each other, they can understand each other very well in trade and commerce. Oh what a gracious God who has also arranged for such a place in the world which is like a sanctuary to which the greatest of all sinners can flee and have the greatest freedom and opportunity for upright repentance and conversion, if only they would still make the most of the time of grace! When taking into consideration governmental policy one does not find guilds and regulations as you have them; rather, everyone has the freedom to carry on trade on land and also at sea, if he is a royal subject. Consequently, we have great and rich merchants among the English who carry on their trade at sea and very cunning shopkeepers among the Germans who could still teach the subtlest Jews something about making deals. Tradesmen excel, depending on the gifts they possess. Farmers do the heaviest work and do not see any money for almost a whole year until they bring cattle and produce they have left to the city of Philadelphia in the fall. In addition, some must travel more than one hundred miles, depending on how close to or how far from Philadelphia they live. Now if a farmer must pay off a certain amount on his land and satisfy craftsmen for a whole year of labor, he has to work himself to death day and night; he probably has to work harder than those outside who have much labor to perform for their overlords. What he does like is that he is his own boss and hired hand who is allowed to serve himself. One also has to pay some taxes annually, the pastor as well as the farmer and everybody else, only one has the advantage of not having to maintain soldiers. Everything is open in this country. The city has neither gates nor walls and, nevertheless, the Lord watches over it. One might well ask in a country as free as this, where different kinds of people live together, whether there is not a lot of murder, theft and the like. Before the last Spanish-French War[20] started and there were still somewhat fewer people, a year often passed without execution of a criminal. In Germany there is hardly a city or place where one does not find all kinds of instruments of torture outside the gates and human bones inside.

Here in this country one finds only one court of law in the city of Philadelphia and one in Lancaster, and they are seldom needed. As long as the war lasted the country was purged of useless people who were used as privateers on water and on land in the military. But now that the war is over and these people are returning again one hears of many highwaymen in the country, some of whom, however, have already been hanged. Besides, there are all sorts of ways of escaping courts of law; supervision is not too strict. Many murders occur involving both children and invalids, and also directly and indirectly in the course of brawls; but they are covered up or the perpetrators vanish. Should the matter, however, come before the high court and the perpetrator has money, the lawyers know how to manipulate things so skilfully that it does not become a capital offense. Thefts occur exceedingly often but they are carried out in such a fashion that one considers them much more as a joke, cleverness and craftiness. Adultery, fornication, bestial sodomy and abominations of that kind may indeed be flourishing but that sort of thing will not come to light until the Lord himself will at some time bring to light everything that has been concealed in darkness here.

You may further ask whether pastors do well in this country. Preachers who come running without having been sent must put up with all sorts of things and live to please the unconverted so they may make a living because they refuse to dig and are ashamed to beg.[21] In the process they still have much trouble on all sides. Pastors who have the confidence of a divine call, though it is indirect, do not seek to do well according to the flesh but teach, believe, live and work by the grace of God as they have been commanded; beyond that they endure what God finds and permits as salutary for their welfare and that of the congregation. When one considers servants of God in the Old and New Testaments who were called directly and indirectly none of them appear to have enjoyed good days according to the flesh. The raw rabble gave Noah little peace. Outwardly he also had a great deal of trouble with ship building.[22] Lot was a troubled soul! In brief, we sing in an old song of cross and redemption something Moses and his brother Aaron experienced. Noah and those who were with him did not see the sun of grace. David, Joseph and Elijah, Peter, Paul and Tobit also bore their share.[23] Accordingly, as long as we retain peace with God through faith in our Lord Jesus and free access to grace we do not lack peace.[24] Though we are troubled on account of sins, mistakes and infirmities clinging to us in our office and position, harassed by Satan and the world and also probably consumed by zeal for the house of the Lord,[25] nevertheless, there remains for us a firm fortress in which we are saved and protected and although we also do not feel completely at home there, a rest still remains for us, etc., etc.[26] Besides, if they want to measure up to their office reasonably well, upright pastors have a rather difficult time in outward matters. For if one considers the congregations in Philadelphia and Germantown one should not imagine that the congregation members all live close together; rather, some live dispersed two, three, four, five, six English miles from Philadelphia, and the Germantown congregation members live even farther apart. That condition always causes a lot of work for the pastor and deprives him of time, especially since people here are subjected to many different kinds of illnesses. At one time the pastor has an emergency baptism several miles distant, at another time he hears confession[27] of a sick person, at another time he has a funeral and in this manner he goes from one congregation and one congregation member to another. In the country the congregation members are dispersed even more. For example, from the most distant member of the Providence congregation to the most distant one of the New Hanover congregation I cover a stretch of thirty English miles in length and approximately seventeen to eighteen miles in width. During certain periods of the year, for example, November, December, January and February when many illnesses are rampant, I am in great fear because, along with the normal, on-going riding from one congregation to the next, I am on my horse almost day and night riding from one patient to the next and all the remaining duties of office still have to be discharged carefully. Moreover, the pastor has to make do with the most basic necessities and get along with whatever each congregation member gives of his own free will, for compulsion has no place here and also is contrary to the purpose of the office.

Since for the most part the congregation members are poor, and one spares widows and domestic servants in any case, and the few rich people do not always contribute gladly one must do nothing further than to seek diligently the kingdom of God and whatever is necessary will come as well.[28] For the congregations are still young; they have a great deal of trouble to complete with their mites and gifts from Europe the most necessary buildings in which to have church and school. If they want to give something to their pastors annually they almost have to do it secretly because they are mocked and laughed at on account of it by the unbelieving Epicureans as well as by the many kinds of sectarian people or, on this account, the German paper[29] makes a display of them. Most of the sects and parties in this country, such as Quakers, Separatists and the remaining kinds of Anabaptists, consider educated pastors outside their circle as messengers of the Devil. They do not believe they can be saved in their office. Of even the most gifted and pious person they are accustomed to say, "It is too bad this person became a pastor." In this respect they agree with all crude blasphemers in that they think and say that educated pastors are like leeches who suck the sweat and blood of people until they burst. They know how to make their cause very plausible, and there is probably not one in a thousand who does not know how to tell several dozen stories of unconverted pastors. From there then they draw conclusions that apply to the whole and everyone would gladly win his spurs by overthrowing pastors.

All of that does no harm if one knows in whom one believes and by whom one is sent, for one must endure honor and dishonor, ill repute and good repute, as impostors yet true, etc. 2 Corinthians 6:1-10 is our instruction and comfort. The largest part of our congregations consists of voluntary members, all of whom could withdraw if they did not take delight in God's word and the holy sacraments and worship. But until now their number has increased even though also some have now and then broken away when one has chastised them for their disorderly and wicked behavior. Nevertheless, gradually they straggle back when they find nothing better and also would not like to be lost. The faithful and true God has not left himself without witness but has been with us. Now and again he has also already allowed us to gain a victory. The seed of the living word of God is scattered diligently and, in so far as we are granted grace, we watch over it so that the Devil may not sow weeds in between.[30] We cannot yet engage in an all-out battle with Satan and his kingdom; but rather we can only create a diversion here and there and dart for an advantage like spiritual hussars until a stronger man assails him and overcomes him, takes away his armor and divides his spoil.[31]

In a postscript to Mr. Gabler only I recorded 1) a compliment to Her Excellence, the spouse of Sheriff von Münchhauss;[32] 2) to the spouse of Hofrat von Hattorf;[33] 3) to Mrs. Cullenius;[34] 4) certified to Mr. Christoph Bötticher[35] that Pastor Brunnholtz[36] has received that black *Camelot* as a gown; 5) certified to Mr. Jäger[37] in Hannover that I had received the beautiful Bible he donated and would promote his genealogical album which he sent; 6) certified to Mr. Gabler that the box with several edifying books and some linen cloth arrived in 1749 and was dealt with in accordance with his instruction; 7) sent greetings to Pastor Winckler[38] and remaining acquaintances in the Lord in Peine and Ilsede; 8) provided a defense on account of the Zinzendorfers who are supposed to have said I had married one of their sisters; 9) certified that I had indeed received and intended to respond to the last letter from *my brother Christoph*, dated 13 February 1747[39] and from Pastor Krome, dated 7 February 1747;[40] enclosed a letter from Friedrich Rehkopf to Johann Heinrich Rehkopf[41] in Möringen and requested Mr. Gabler to attend to it.

Heinrich Melchior Mühlenberg

---

1. Johann Basilius Gabler, a journeyman harnessmaker in Hannover, belonged to the circle of pietists centered around Lady von Münchhausen and Lady von Hattorf. During his stay in Hannover in the spring of 1742 Mühlenberg had access to this circle (see Mühlenberg's entry for 12 March 1742, *Journals* 1:14 and 28 March 1742, *Journals* 1:15) See also Rudolf Ruprecht, *Der Pietismus des 18. Jahrhunderts in den Hannoverschen Stammländern* (Göttingen: Vandenhoeck & Ruprecht, 1919), pp. 156f.
2. See Acts 4:32.
3. See Eph. 4:5.
4. See Rom. 8:38.

5. See Matt. 6:6.

6. See Matt. 6:3.

7. See Matt. 6:6.

8. See Matt. 25:35-36.

9. A German mile is equivalent to 7500 meters or 4.2 English miles.

10. See Daniel 9:18. The allusion in the text is to Luther's rendering of this verse, "...*wir liegen vor dir mit unserm Gebet.*"

11. See Ps. 51:10.

12. Mühlenberg may have the extravagant imagery of the Zinzendorfers in mind as it developed during "the time of sifting" (1743-50), when they spoke of themselves as, among other things, "little doves flying about in the atmosphere of the cross." See John R. Weinlick, *Count Zinzendorf* (New York and Nashville; Abingdon Press, 1956), pp. 198-201.

13. It has not been possible to identify the source or author of the hymn of which the following appears to be one stanza, *Eile! Eile wo du dich erretten und nicht mit verderben wilt! Mach dich los von allen Ketten! Fleuch als ein gieagtes wild! Lass dir nichts am Hertzen kleben! Fleuch vor dem verborgnen Bann! Such in Gott geheim zu leben, dass dich nichts beflecken kann!*

14. William Penn (1644-1718) petitioned King Charles II (1660-80) in June 1680 to grant him a colony in North America. It is not possible to establish with certainty the basis for this request. The repayment of the debt Charles II owed Penn's father, Admiral William Penn (1621-70), was certainly not the only decisive factor. One may perhaps assume that William Penn's close connection with the royal palace, above all to James II, Charles II's brother, may have been a motive in making the grant. The charter for the grant went into effect 4 March 1681. See also *Correspondence* 1:224 n.3.

15. The text should read *ihrem Mittel* instead of *ihrer Mitte.*

16. The text reads *Tribunis plebis.*

17. Isa. 1:6.

18. See Rom. 9:29; Isa. 1:9.

19. For the religious diversity of the population in Pennsylvania and New Jersey in 1775, see *Atlas*, pp. 38; 117-18. For an estimate of the black population, see *Atlas*, pp. 25; 100.

20. On King George's War (1744-48), see *Correspondence* 1:306 n.70.

21. See Luke 16:3.

22. See Gen. 6:13; Heb. 11:7.

23. Stanza 14 of a hymn by Johann Rist (1607-67), *Jammer hat mich ganz umgeben.* See *Liedersammlung*, Hymn 391.

24. See Rom. 5:1-2.

25. See John 2:17; Ps. 69:9.

26. Heb. 4:9.

27. The text should read *berichten* instead of *beichten.*

28. See Matt. 6:33.

29. Christoph Sauer enjoyed publishing items critical of Lutheran pastors in his Germantown newspaper. See *Correspondence* 1:86,193, 336-39. On Christoph Sauer, see *Correspondence* 1:93 n.37.

30. See Matt. 13:25.

31. See Luke 11:22.

32. On Wilhelmine Sophie von Münchhausen, see *Correspondence* 1:18 n.18.

33. On Lady von Hattorf, see *Journals* 1:14; *Correspondence* 1:18 n.18 and 23 n.60.

34. A widow, Cullenien, is identified as belonging to the circle of the awakened with Lady von Münchhausen and Lady von Hattorf. See Ruprecht, *Der Pietismus in den Hannoverschen Stammländern*, p. 146.

35. Ernst Christoph Bötticher was a merchant in Hannover who was one of the most prominent representatives of Pietism and founder of the teachers' college in that city. Peter Brunnholz made his acquaintance during his stay in Hannover prior to his departure for North America in 1744.

While Brunnholz was in Hannover Bötticher gave him seventeen yards of fabric called *Camelot*. See also *Correspondence* 1:17 n.9; 33 n.8.

36. On Peter Brunnholz, see Letter 71 n.3.

37. Identity unknown.

38. Born in Hildesheim, Hermann Erich Winckler (1701-59) served as pastor in Peine from 1729 on. He was the chief representative of Pietism in a chapter attached to the cathedral in Hildesheim and a somewhat controversial figure. See also *Correspondence* 1:33 n.8.

39. Heinrich Christoph Mühlenberg was born 13 July 1702. He married A.D. Weidemann 14 November 1730. By profession he was a shoemaker and tanner. He died 3 May 1786. His letter to H.M. Mühlenberg is not extant.

40. Theophilus Arnold Krome (1694-1758) served at Hullersen (Einbeck) from 1721-43. He served as senior pastor at St. Mary's Church in Einbeck until he died. His letter to Mühlenberg is not extant.

41. The identity of these two persons could not be established.

LETTERS OF 1750

Letter 78

To Johann Martin Boltzius[1]
Providence, January-March 1750

Having failed to write Boltzius as he feels he should have, Mühlenberg cites a number of reasons for this failure. Among the reasons he gives is the growth in demands an expanding number of congregations and outparishes places not only on him but also on his coworkers. Coupled with the identification of the congregations and their location is a description of the difficulties and hazards Mühlenberg, his colleagues and congregation members face in an environment markedly different from that obtaining in Europe. All in all, this letter provides an overview of the work Mühlenberg has done as pastor since his arrival in 1742.

Text in German: Korrespondenz *1:361-66. For further textual information see* Korrespondenz *1:366.*

To Pastor Boltzius at Ebenezer:
Title omitted without prejudice.[2] Dearly and heartily beloved Brother and Comrade-in-arms in the Lord Jesus:
What indeed may my dearly beloved brother think that in the course of so many years I have not written once especially to you? After all, there must be reasons for acting in this way and not in another. You could accuse me of a lack of true brotherly love and gratitude I owe you had not the Lord God poured out such great undeserved love in your heart toward me which looks through all failings and in accordance with its divine nature bears, believes, hopes and endures all things—1 Corinthians 13:7. I do not want to justify myself either but rather sincerely apologize and only bring forward as many reasons as are perhaps necessary to deflect any possible appearance of suspicion and to strengthen the love, founded in God, we have for each other until we die.
1) Next to God I took refuge in my dear brothers in Ebenezer during the first years when I stood alone in Pennsylvania, a total stranger to the way things were in Pennsylvania and its realm of sects, stumbling into the chaos of temptations. I had no experience in matters of ministerial office, no reliable friend and counselor, no letters and specific instructions from our

Reverend Fathers; by way of contrast to these I had to put up with altogether inhuman hardships in places very distant from one another, countless attacks from several godless Lutheran preachers who came running on their own, from the Zinzendorfers, other sects and from my own so-called degenerate and dispersed Lutherans. Along with that I was drawn into the troublesome project of building the external scaffolding. So, next to God, I took refuge in my dear brothers in Ebenezer and flooded them with so many letters of complaint that I still must be ashamed of them for a whole year when I consider the cross and need the worthy brothers themselves endured at the time and how my letters must have made it even more difficult to bear the heavy burden of office! This is the first real reason which moved me to discontinue writing so frequently. However, nothing further emerges from this consideration than the well-known maxim of experience: namely, in our behavior we humans are so frail that we sin in omission or commission, doing too much or too little.

2) God has blessed me with a very valuable colleague in Mr. Brunnholtz who in accordance with God's singular providence has taken up the position in Philadelphia.[3] Having a special gift for writing and using every opportunity for correspondence, he made the promise—which he kept—that he would continue the blessed correspondence in the name of all of us. Consequently, I took comfort in this arrangement and in the years that have passed, had a part in everything the dear brothers communicated to us for our instruction, consolation and admonition.

3) Following the arrival of my worthy colleague, Pastor Brunnholtz, I was indeed relieved and saved from work which had become altogether too much and diffuse. However, I still retained so much work in the country and out-of-the-way congregations assigned to me that I almost had to ride to the point of becoming a cripple. The two churches in my two country congregations are ten miles distant from one another. In length the two members at the extreme end of both congregations live thirty miles from each other. In width the two members at the extreme live eighteen miles from each other. Now, besides the regular services of worship and periods of instruction there are the sick, emergency baptisms, burials which demand the presence of the pastor. There are weak old people, pregnant women and children who cannot come to church on Sunday. Because there are two to three rivers which prevent going to church three outparishes were formed which I must serve on week days. Even if I am to carry out only the general duties of my ministerial office I can hardly be at home for certain a single day but I must be on my horse and away from home most of the time. In addition, in common with my colleague Brunnholtz I have had to serve other congregations which petitioned us for help and assistance against the

Zinzendorfers. Thus, for example, Upper Milford and Saccum are located in a mountainous region thirty miles from my house; Tulpehocken is fifty miles; Lancaster forty-five miles; York, across the Susquehanna, is sixty-six miles; to serve Raritan in Jersey is seventy miles. Such extensive, physical work tires the body, causes the mind to wander and leaves little time for study, meditation and for correspondence which are so beneficial. Now I want to report in brief concerning the state of our congregations and my particular circumstances.

1) My dear colleague, Brunnholtz, is now laboring in his sixth year in the congregations in Philadelphia and Germantown with much faithfulness and great patience. He takes the whole matter seriously but almost every year he has to endure one or several illnesses which weaken him very much. Consequently, it is to be feared that he will be taken home from us too soon and to our great loss. 2) Our worthy colleague, Handshue,[4] is stationed in the city of Lancaster for the second year where he labors in blessing. But he, too, is very weak in body and has had severe attacks of acute fever several times. They are two dear servants of God who possess theological learning, have thorough experience in the ways of God and consume themselves as burning lights in the midst of an untoward generation. 3) Twenty-two miles west of Lancaster on the border of Pennsylvania near Maryland in the newly established city of York across the Susquehanna our catechist, Mr. Schaum, is stationed; our catechist, Mr. Kurtz, is in Tulpehocken. We have had to ordain both of these men because circumstances required it, and the Reverend Fathers approved of it.[5] On their part these two dear brothers are faithful; in studies and conversion they are just beginners. They would probably labor with greater blessing and usefulness if they had experienced servants at their side and were not stationed alone in such burdensome offices among all kinds of people and sects. Along with us may the merciful Lord protect, uphold and support them to an age when they turn grey. 4) The untended congregations at Raritan in Jersey were for some years a burden to us and we could not very well rid ourselves of them. For this reason we wrote our Reverend Fathers and petitioned them for a pastor, but after much prayer and effort they were unable to locate a suitable person. In the fall of 1748 a student of theology from the Hanau area came into this country on his own, persuaded to do so by a newlander. He sided with us and certified that he had studied in Halle and had been an instructor in the blessed institutions for a time. Consequently, we recommended him as a catechist to the Raritan congregations and did not conceal his circumstances. We informed the congregations that, as reported previously, he had come without having been called by us and that he had also not been sent. The same person, by the

name of Johann Weygand,[6] is currently stationed in these congregations under certain conditions and under our supervision as long as he conducts himself without giving offense. The four little congregations in Upper Milford, Saccum, Fork and Birkensee, which are located in part near Bethlehem in Zinzendorfian preserves, are currently being served by an interim catechist who is a student of law and theology. One cannot yet properly come to their aid and one cannot by rights abandon them either. Having come into this country in the spring of 1749 at his own expense, he is a student from Lüneburg.[7] 5) Currently I am still serving my two country congregations in New Hanover and Providence and their three outparishes. In 1748 I was prevailed upon to take on a new congregation[8] consisting of Swedes and Englishmen which, for a time, was upset by the well-known Mr. Folck[9] and most recently by the Zinzendorfers.

Moreover, our Lord and Master who tries hearts and reins knows best the inner condition of our congregations as a whole and individual members in particular. For us, however, it is impossible to render a reliable judgment concerning this condition because we are finite and weak creatures who are not even in the position to render an accurate judgment concerning the external surface of matters lying near us. When I consider the visible church and its congregations since the beginning of the world until now in the light of the most holy word of God and the church histories that have been written with enlightened judgment[10] I cannot find another and better definition than the one the very enlightened, blessed Doctor Anthon[11] has provided, namely, the church has been and still is a society of wretched persons.[12] Our Lutherans were scattered in this country and for the most part had no desire, capability or opportunity to be edified by the word of God and the holy sacraments. The tiny and small spark of goodness that was still present in some was in greatest danger of being devoured in part by a crass worldly spirit and in part extinguished by innumerable subtle sectarian spirits who appear outwardly good. In Europe the merciful God and Father in Christ has awakened so many hearts in a variety of positions and highest honors who according to their best ability adopted the poor, abandoned members who were near death and cared for the welfare of their souls. Now people have the opportunity to make use of the word of God and the holy sacraments; no longer can they blame the most holy God and their neighbor if they are lost. On the basis of outward observation of the members of our congregations one has to certify:

1) They have willingly and gladly contributed their mite to the physical construction of churches. They also voluntarily pool their gifts so that until now pastors have obtained what is most necessary for their physical support.

2) They are not intimidated by heat, cold, bad roads and difficulties but

come from near and far—from one to twelve miles—to hear God's word.

3) They partake of Holy Communion faithfully and arrange for the baptism of their children. 4) They maintain and pay their schoolteachers with mites from their livelihood. 5) In connection with all sorts of occasions they must often allow themselves to be ridiculed and mocked by the sects and made sport of in the newspaper as well that they are such fools and go to church and observe the sacraments and foist what they have earned by the sweat of their brow on lazy parsons and loafers. In brief, in this country our congregations are almost in the same outward circumstances as the first Christian congregations under the Roman emperors, the exception being that the lenient English civil laws protect body, property and possessions and the congregations endure no physical persecution. All sorts of possible opinions are tolerated as long as one acknowledges a supreme Being. Other than that we are completely exposed without restraint. Thus we must be the target and plaything by which every party and faction wants to win its spurs. So one can fairly say that we live here as an oppressed church.[13] One must take into consideration that the Quakers and the remaining parties who disagree with the evangelical church have their manners, prestige and wealth and assist their members whereas our people maintain the church's worship of God from their livelihood and must endure ridicule and mockery on account of it. They gain no honor or material benefit from it; they are not attracted by imposing, elaborate church buildings, bells, organs and church music. Nevertheless, they assist one another and are not discouraged by any difficulties. One must therefore conclude that they are concerned about the true salvation of their souls. As blessed Luther himself said, "One would have to preach for a long time and exhort in vain if a law had not been written into the heart of man which prods a person with accusing thoughts."[14] However, a work performed without reference to faith,[15] old customs and habits brought along by parents can also accomplish something and the like. Nevertheless, in accordance with love one must hope for the best and thank God for the opportunity still to present the means of grace and with them to plant and water.[16] We have no defense against disorderly members other than to deny them Holy Communion. We can not and may not exclude anyone from the public hearing of God's word. When we come upon disorderly members who offend with their living we apply the steps of admonition in accordance with Matthew 18[17] and after the third stage we have them appear before the church council. If they still have some feeling left in them, they appear. But if there is malice they are accustomed to saying, "You have no right to order me to do anything, this is a free country and if you want to exclude me from the Lord's Supper then I don't have to contribute to your salary." There are also other Lutheran

congregations which have godless self-appointed preachers. They say, "Join us; your preachers after all are only pietists and false teachers," etc. Whereupon we are rid of them and receive as a reward scoldings and curses. Although we are under various pressures, we must plant and water in hope and pray God that what he gives will prosper.[18] When souls in the congregations are awakened through the Spirit of God by means of his word we face the danger on the other hand from the specious and flashy sects which love to pounce with fervor on the young and delicate plants and, like pests, kill the roots. Because our congregations are so far apart from each other special care[19] on our part is lacking. However, we may entrust to our faithful Savior general, special and most special care[20] because he has purchased souls with his precious blood. True conversion proceeds slowly and individually. I have already observed at various times that the Lord hastens quickly out of the world with those who experienced in themselves something true. As far as our physical support is concerned, a record book or list is kept in each congregation in which the names of congregation members are entered and a note is made of how much each one wants to contribute annually of their own accord for the pastor. With the exception of Mr. Kurtz and myself my worthy colleagues are still single, get by with the bare essentials, seek first the kingdom of God and see how the Lord who has our hearts in his hand fulfills his promise. It is true that the money comes in in very small and uneven amounts because the congregations undergo change. However, one may not employ another method because the Lord has not so far allowed us to suffer want. According to a strict reckoning, none of us manages to make up to forty pounds sterling.[21] We take it from each person in the way they bring it. For if the deacons were to receive it and would perhaps see a total sum of thirty pounds, poor people would perhaps wonder how rich the pastor was becoming. In comparison with it they do not calculate how much one needs in one year and would have to fear that the newspapers and almanacs would be full of these matters, for in every other way the man[22] is a sworn enemy of preachers and does all he can to make them useless and a stench hereabouts.

To report something about my particular circumstances, you probably know, dear brother, that I entered the state of matrimony in 1745 with Anna Maria Weiser, daughter of Mr. Conrad Weiser.[23] My father-in-law arrived with his parents in New York in 1709 from Württemberg; in his younger years he lived for a time among the Indians and learned their languages. Approximately twenty years ago he came to Pennsylvania with his family. During the time of the most benevolent Queen Anne and through the efforts of Court Preacher Böhm[24] many edifying books were sent with German people into the country among which was the postil of Professor Franck.[25]

Through it my father-in-law was awakened so that he always said good things about it but never found a congregation and a polity in accord with it. He also did not want to side with self-appointed, loose living Lutheran preachers. He also did not want to side any more with the likes of Mr. van Döhren[26] and Mr. Leutbecker[27] who had been sent off as schoolmasters on the recommendation of Court Preacher Böhm because they did not continue in their faith and in humility. Rather they forced their way into the office of pastor with the eyes of a wicked servant[28] for which they had neither calling nor gifts and talent. Consequently, in the beginning he united here in Pennsylvania with a small band of awakened people of all kinds who wanted to establish a congregation which was pure and separated from the world. But he also found no peace in this group because they departed from the word of God and several cunning heads among them put themselves forward as head and founded their congregation on theosophical circulars, etc., etc., and so became a dangerous sect.[29] Barely had he separated himself from them when Count Zinzendorf[30] arrived with his following and worked his way into his life, pretending he was in close association with the Halle theologians. Initially these people found his hearty approval until he observed their weak side and waggish ways. They tempted him not a little with all sorts of wiles, showed him the kingdoms of the world and promised everything if he would fall down and worship them.[31]

Heinrich Melchior Mühlenberg

1. On Johann Martin Boltzius, see *Correspondence* 1:30 n.9.
2. The text reads *S[alvo] T[itulo]*.
3. On Peter Brunnholz, see Letter 71 n.3.
4. On Johann Friedrich Handschuh, see *Correspondence* 1:291 nn.18 and 19.
5. On Johann Nicolaus Kurz, ordained on 14 August 1748, see *Correspondence* 1:154 n.5 and 341 n.16; on Johann Helfrich Schaum, ordained 4 June 1749, see Letter 71 n.9.
6. On Johann Albert Weygand, see Letter 71 n.21.
7. The student Mühlenberg refers to is Ludolph Heinrich Schrenck who arrived in Philadelphia in March 1749. Following matriculation in the University of Erlangen in 1746, he studied "the rudiments of the Wolfian philosophy and law" there (*Journals* 1:220). Following ordination in 1752 he initially appeared to be an effective pastor but eventually his ministry turned out to be less than satisfactory to congregations he served. He returned to Europe in 1764. For more information concerning Schrenck, see *Pastors and People* 1:122-23.
8. In March 1748 Mühlenberg was invited to conduct services at Molatton. In his diary Mühlenberg describes some of the trials and difficulties this congregation consisting of Swedes, Irish, English and Germans experienced (*Journals* 1:185-87). Located on the Schuylkill River near Manatawny Creek, the Swedish Lutheran congregation eventually became Episcopal. Today Molatton is known as Douglassville. See *Pastors and People* 1:248.
9. Gabriel Falk, a native of West Gothland, Sweden, arrived in Philadelphia in 1733. He served the congregation in Molatton, beginning in 1735 and it appears off and on until 1745. *HN2/1:* 442-43. See also *Journals* 1:186 and *Pastors and People* 1:248.

10. The text reads *Judicio*.

11. Paul Anton (1661-1730), professor and counsellor of the consistory in Halle, 1695-1730. Prior to that time he held a number of important positions in the Church of Saxony.

12. The text reads *Societas personarum miserabilium*.

13. The text reads *Ecclesia pressa*.

14. *WA* 16:447, 27f.

15. The text reads *Opus Operatum*.

16. See 1 Cor. 3:7-8.

17. Matt. 18:15-17.

18. See 1 Cor. 13:7-8.

19. The text reads *Cura speciali*.

20. The text reads *curam generalem, specialem und specialissimam*.

21. This is the amount the congregations in New Hanover, Providence and Philadelphia were asked to pay Mühlenberg when he began his ministry among them. *Correspondence* 1:25;29.

22. Mühlenberg has Christoph Sauer in mind. See *Correspondence* 1:93 n.37 and p. 173; Letter 77, n.28.

23. On Anna Maria Mühlenberg neé Weiser and Johann Conrad Weiser, see *Correspondence* 1:142 n.7.

24. Anton Wilhelm Böhme (1673-1722), immediate predecessor of Friedrich Michael Ziegenhagen, and Court Preacher at the Chapel of St. James in London, England. See *Correspondence* 1:11 n.10.

25. See *Correspondence* 1:249 n.13.

26. Johann Bernhard van Dieren, dates of birth and death unknown, came to New York about 1720 on recommendation of Böhme. Unsuccessful in his request for ordination in New York and by Swedish Lutherans, he claimed he had been ordained by Anthony Jacob Henkel (1668-1728), without however being able to prove it. Hence in Mühlenberg's view van Dieren was one of those who "had come running on his own." See *Pastors and People* 1:30.

27. As in the case of van Dieren, Caspar Leutbecker (d. 1738) arrived in Pennsylvania without having been ordained. Mühlenberg says that "he even alleged that Mr. Böhm [the Court Preacher referred to above in n. 24] had ordained him!" (*Journals* 1:170). Both Conrad Weiser and Johann Kurz had reservations concerning the authenticity of Leutbecker's claim to valid ordination which he made while serving the congregation at Tulpehocken (*HN2/1*:191;201). For more details concerning Caspar Leutbecker see *Pastors and People* 1:80-81.

28. See Matt. 18:32.

29. See *Correspondence* 1:143 n.9; 240 and 249 n.14.

30. On Nikolaus Lüdwig von Zinzendorf, see *Correspondence* 1:2 n.2.

31. See Matt. 4:9.

Letter 79

To Johann Caspar Stöver
Providence, 26 May 1750

Almost since Mühlenberg's arrival in Philadelphia in 1742 his relationship to Johann Caspar Stöver was a troubled one. In part their relationship was less than cordial because Stöver was one of those preachers about whose ordination there were some questions. Letter 59 (Correspondence 1:308-10) throws a good bit of light on the reasons for the adversarial relationship between Mühlenberg and Stöver. See also Correspondence 1:50, 53 n.18 and 308-10.

In terms of church polity it is interesting to note that Mühlenberg espouses a collegial approach to church leadership and makes no claim to having episcopal authority.

Text in German: Korrespondenz 1:367. For further textual information see Korrespondenz 1:368.

Esteemed Sir and Friend:

As much as I out of Christian love would like to have seen Your Reverence in my house along with other friends and to have had the opportunity to take away the displeasure you have toward me and to edify myself with you, I nevertheless had to withhold the invitation until a better and more opportune time for adequate reasons, namely: 1) Because in Lancaster Your Reverence did not want to promise definitely that you would come but you were in doubt whether His Reverence, Magister Wagner, would be pleased.[1] 2) Because I was unable to receive the agreement of all the deacons and elders of the United Congregations to issue the invitation. From these reasons Your Reverence will clearly perceive and see that I have no episcopal power, much less lay claim to it but at all times and still to the present consider myself the least of the servants of the evangelical church, Your Reverence's friend and well-wisher,

Providence   Mühlenberg
26 May 1750

1. In his diary Mühlenberg records the substance of his negotiations with Stöver to determine whether or not Stöver should be invited to the Synod assembly on 17 and 18 June 1750 and his discussions with his colleagues concerning the matter. Mühlenberg and his colleagues agreed to invite Stöver on the day after the assembly had adjourned. "After this invitation had been extended, Mr. Stöver became very indignant that he should be invited to come *post festum* and wrote a long acrimonious letter though it was not offensive" (*Journals* 1:243-44). Stöver's letter is not extant. On Tobias Wagner, see Letter 71A n.3.

Letter 80

To Israel Acrelius[1]
Providence, 22 June 1750

*During his ministry on the eastern seaboard of North America
Mühlenberg attempted to forge and maintain good relationships on a
professional and personal level with clergymen of the Swedish Church. This
letter to Israel Acrelius provides ample evidence of Mühlenberg's efforts to
cultivate the confessional ties existing between German and Swedish
Lutheran Churches since the sixteenth century Reformation. At the same time
this letter also provides an insight into Mühlenberg's efforts to enlist the
clerical leadership of the Swedish congregations in southeastern
Pennsylvania, New Jersey and Delaware in warding off the threat Moravians
like Nyberg posed for the unity of Lutheran congregations.*
Text in Latin: Korrespondenz 1:368-71. *For further textual information
see* Korrespondenz 1:371.

To the very reverend, most learned man of the Swedish Church which
is in Pennsylvania and New Delaware, provost, to be honoured with
reverence, Mühlenberg extends many greetings.

Scarcely would I dare, very Reverend Sir, to disturb your affairs but I
must do so, if I am to escape the suspicion of being an ungrateful person
who does not offer any congratulation in writing on your most welcome
arrival in our province. If you would not refuse me, I would come to give
these greetings so that I may satisfy both myself and others. I do not doubt,
most Reverend Sir, that God[2] has sent you by his grace and has designated
you to be a special instrument, a watchman, and the voice of one crying in
the wilderness,[3] so that his name may be confessed among peoples
committed to the Augsburg Confession, scattered and roaming about
Pennsylvania and New Delaware, towns of refuge as it were. I do not deny,
longed for provost of the church, that I might regard you so that some
divine benefit may be imparted to me.

It was a special benefit for me and I give God the greatest possible
thanks for considering me worthy of refreshing myself at the homes of the
gentlemen, Sandin and Tranberg[4] and those deemed most worthy while they
were among the living, and indeed I was refreshed through their faith and
experience in divine matters. I was made glad in God when Pastor
Brunnholtz[5] informed me through a letter that Provost Acrelius, one that
ought to be respected because of his own merits, had promised when asked
to visit our yearly assembly.[6] However, I was puzzled by the ambiguity of

the situation, and joy seemed to contend with sorrow when a certain innkeeper from my own neighborhood asked me whether there were disagreements between the Swedish and German theologians. I detected the reason for this previous and repeated question of the innkeeper in that Nyberg,[7] a man notorious for having publicly joined the Zinzendorfian party when he had proclaimed in the inn that we had invited the venerable ministerium of the Swedish Church to our assembly, and that we had disturbed them by our requests and that we had with one mind decided completely to avoid all who had been invited to our assembly. I can scarcely believe that Nyberg[8] was sent by a majority of the Very Reverend Ministerium to act as a crier in a bar. I recall that shopworn proverb of the lawyers that it is necessary that the other side be heard and that the knowledge of its position ought to take precedence over opinion. According to God's good will we are conscious of a hidden faith because in the universities which are in Leipzig, Halle, Jena, Göttingen, Giessen, Erlangen and other cities we have received pure doctrine according to the foundation laid by prophets and apostles, and the norm of the Symbolical Books. With testimonials concerning the legitimate call and ordination or initiation into the priesthood, we have been sent to take over our own sphere of work; and we have discharged the duties of our office right up to this very day although with great weakness, yet with the help of God, as those who hunger and thirst after righteousness[9] in such a way that we may rejoice if lying people fabricate and hurl all sorts of abuse at us. In our office we believe that we have undertaken the glorious fight of faith in the power of God, with weapons of righteousness for the right hand and for the left, in honor and dishonor, in bane and blessing, as deceitful, yet nevertheless speaking the truth, etc. 2 Cor. 6.[10]   One may not deny that God has protected us in these times and circumstances in which our struggle is not only against flesh and blood[11] but also especially against the spirits of wickedness which are transformed into angels of light just as if roaring lions[12] were unable to devour the church of God. Among other things it must be said that from the time of the apostles no disagreement has been more cunning and pernicious than the recent Zinzendorfian faction, theologians who have pledged themselves to the Augsburg Confession. Though experienced in divine matters, having published mere pamphlets as though they were books, they have demonstrated enough and more than enough that which I—novice in theology though I am—have observed as the last twelve years have slipped by and many trials have been endured. Why is this surprising? If the whole body of the faction mentioned above shall gradually have become dark, then the eyes of the leaders are worthless. That the matter rests precisely here, moreover, can be proven from the attacks of the leaders of the faction. For if those fellows adhered to the Swedish

Church where the true worship of God is, they would have flourished long ago according to the norm of the Symbolical books. I say, they attack the Swedish Church and seek to give a reason for this, drawn from the foundation of doctrine, they are compelled by necessity to respond with a furrowed brow that they themselves are committed with voice and soul to the Augsburg Confession. If those same deceitful practitioners invade Russia and are called on for questioning they concoct the story with the same voice and spirit that they were the firstborn sons of the Greek Church. If those same fellows, transformed into angels of light, should creep through Switzerland, town-by-town, and if they should be asked about the hope with which they have been endowed,[13] they avow with obdurate spirit and snapping teeth that they themselves show from a pious heart faith in the decrees of the Synod of Bern.[14] If they fawn upon the English peoples for an increase in good things, they thereby acknowledge that they are pleased with the teachings of the Anglican Church. To put it briefly, they are chameleons! Wherever they wander about on land, in a field and out in the open, they show themselves to be dry wells and clouds driven about by a storm, a storm which is puffed up and empty.[15] They deceive with desires of a passionate, lustful body those who had almost escaped, those who wander in error, promising them liberty; they themselves are servants of destruction, and they make jests about their followers, rejoicing in their errors. They are not theologians for nothing who, by reputation most worthy, clearly and completely[16] have shown that the Zinzendorfian faction is most dangerous. Indeed, the Tübingen theologians, who out of ignorance had issued a response in favor of this faction, publicly retracted it and declared that they had been deceived by them and that their doctrine and polity differed very much from the Augsburg Confession—but scarcely differed from the Variata.[17] Who is in a position of not hearing with anger what one of them proclaimed publicly and rashly to their bishops—as they are called—in the presence of a large gathering of witnesses, saying that all preachers who teach that God the Father, the first person of the divine majesty, ought to be worshiped are thieves and good-for-nothings! Reason: because the Father is only the father-in-law of the Savior of the world, etc. Erotic poems in which they sing about sin in its type and kind about the Savior, marriage, and other articles of doctrine are so full of obscenity and blasphemy that one is not able to mention them among honorable persons without shame and shuddering! So that I may pass over the remaining matters and not abuse your patience, most Reverend Sir, I ask you to examine the Twelfth Part of their hymns[18] where you will discover that those obscene birds—with your permission—have compared women's genitalia, vagina of the uterus, with the side of the Savior of the world which on the cross had been pierced by a spear. If they are compelled to

bring forth in public anything sound concerning justification from the
writings of blessed Luther and of other men gifted with orthodoxy, they
cautiously steal formulas of speaking and accept them only in so far as they
suppose is sufficient for their deceit! In the meantime not only are these
lofty doctors silent concerning penitence which precedes justification and
concerning renewal which follows, but also, given every opportunity, they
make audacious jokes about the written word of God and especially about
the law, penitence, prayer, temptation, meditation and whatever else
remains. What more? The world wants to be deceived because it lies in evil
and loves darkness more than light![19] But they who are anointed by the Holy
Spirit and have been instructed in matters of the heavenly kingdom can
bring forth from their storehouse both more recent and older things.[20] They
are not ignorant that they have been sent forth to this end, namely, that
through the means of salvation they may open the eyes of the people that
they may not continue in darkness but turn from the power of Satan to light
toward God. Therefore it is considered necessary that we watch and pray
accordingly.[21] As far as especially the Reverend Nyberg is concerned, in
what manner he may have grasped the sacred office and has departed from
the carrying out of it, I have nothing which I could say at this time because
the sacred senate of the Swedish Empire which ought to be highly venerated
- unless I am mistaken - has found out about matters compiled by Peter
Koch,[22] the undoubted author and the public overseer of duties while he was
alive, and he has graciously responded in a splendid letter. Nevertheless,
supposing that the one who confessed, most deserving of ordination, has
handed over to you, most Reverend Sir, the trouble of judging and
examining a lawsuit, and without showing any personal favor, it was
agreeable to you that I would use persuasion to make a ruling at your
command. Given that opportunity, I would arrange the whole matter and,
as far as in me lies, I would relate in your presence or in writing where
matters stand and report the particulars. I would produce the documents and
evidence as much as they are available, hoping perhaps that this would
prove satisfactory to all who love the truth. You yourself may investigate
Pastor Nyberg in matters which have taken place to show the Evangelical
Church in general and his congregation in particular whether he acted out
of ignorance or has given a bad example of malice and has set forth a
dangerous pretense as an example. From these people, O God, protect us
forever! Send faithful workers into your harvest![23] May you be present in
your church forever so it may worship the holy name of God. May your
heavenly kingdom come and your will be done, etc. Forgive us our debts;
preserve us from temptation![24] Grant us repentance so we may fight the
glorious fight[25] and complete the journey and keep the faith. Moreover, God
incline yourself to Acrelius, provost of the church, so that he may live well

and happily and always fare well.

Written at Providence   Heinrich Melchior Mühlenberg
in the county of Philadelphia;
on the tenth day before the kalends of July 1750

P.S.

Our blessed Luther has rightly and properly admonished us that we are battling against two leaders of evil angels, namely, black and white.[26] In one part of the church the members are tempted by manifest works of the flesh, Gal. 5:22ff., in the other they are tempted by numerous opinions departing from true doctrine, 2 Tim. 3:5ff.; Epistle of Jude vv.10-19. Entering through the narrow gate that leads to the hard road we walk most safely, Matt. 7:13-23

---

1. Israel Acrelius, chaplain to the Swedish Admiralty before coming to North America, arrived in Philadelphia on 6 November 1749. While there he served as pastor of the congregation in Wilmington, Delaware, and as provost of the Swedish congregations in southeastern Pennsylvania, New Jersey and Delaware. Among the instructions the Swedish Consistory gave Acrelius prior to his departure for North America was one pertaining to Laurentius Thorstonson Nyberg. He was specifically instructed to look into Nyberg's activities (HN2/1:285). Thus it was appropriate for Mühlenberg to turn to Acrelius to register his complaints concerning Nyberg. For Mühlenberg's assessment of Nyberg, see also *Journals* 1:244-46).

Following his return to Sweden in 1756 Acrelius published a history of New Sweden in 1759 (*Korrespondenz* 1:371 n.1 has 1758). In 1874 the Historical Society of Pennsylvania published a translation on this history by William S. Reynolds under the title *Description of Former and Present Conditions of the Swedish Churches in what was Called New Sweden, Afterwards New Netherland on the River De La Ware, West Jersey, and New Castle County in North America.* - With the perspicacity of a diplomat Acrelius dealt with the concerns Mühlenberg raised in this letter in his history (pp. 248-49) under the title, "Causes of Misunderstanding between Mühlenberg and Nyberg."

2. The text reads *Jova*. Here and elsewhere we have translated *Jova* as God.

3. See John 1:23.

4. The Swedish archbishop H. Benzelius had sent John Sandin to North America where he served as pastor of Swedish congregations in Raccoon and Pennsneck, New Jersey. At the same time he became the first provost of Swedish congregations in Pennsylvania and New Jersey. Sandin died in 1748. - On Peter Tranberg, see *Correspondence* 1:62 n.17.

5. On Peter Brunnholz, see Letter 71 n.3.

6. The Minutes of the Synod's Assembly, 18 June 1750, prepared by Peter Brunnholz, make no reference to Acrelius (*HN2/1:471-73*).

7. In his diary for June 1750 Mühlenberg has entered a fairly extended report on what the innkeeper said and on Nyberg's presumed role in sowing "tares among the wheat" with his version of the actions of the Synod assembly (*Journals* 1:244).

8. On Laurentius Thorstonson Nyberg, see *Correspondence* 1:181 n.10.

9. See Matt. 5:6.

10. See 2 Cor. 6:12. - Mühlenberg's Latin version of this reference departs significantly from that of the Vulgate.

11. See Eph. 6:12.

12. See 1 Pet. 5:8.

13. See 1 Pet. 3:15.

14.   Ulrich Zwingli (1484-1531) influenced the Swiss city of Bern in 1528 to accept the Reformation.

15.   See 2 Pet. 2:17 and Jude 12.

16.   The text reads *plane pleneque*.

17.   In 1733 the faculty of theology of the University of Tübingen had decided that Herrnhut had mistakenly been declared a center of heresy, arguing that the Reorganized Unity of the Brethren had rightly considered itself a member of the Moravian and Lutheran Churches. A year after that the faculty of theology offered to confer the degree of doctor of theology on Zinzendorf, which, however, he declined. When the faculty of theology's opinion was reviewed in 1747 its members rejected Zinzendorf's claim to being an orthodox Lutheran.

18.   This is a reference to the Twelfth Appendix of the hymnal the Unity of the Brethren Church published in 1743, with further additions in 1746-48. This appendix came into being during the "time of sifting." For a complete bibliographical reference see *Korrespondenz* 1:372 n.9.

19.   See John 3:19.

20.   See Matt. 13:52.

21.   See Matt. 26:41.

22.   Peter Koch died in 1749, a year before this letter was written. On Peter Koch, see *Correspondence* 1:53 n.20.

23.   See Matt. 9:38.

24.   See Matt. 6:10,12,13.

25.   See 1 Tim. 1:18; 6:12; 2 Tim. 4:7.

26.   See *Correspondence* 1:93 n.44.

Letter 81

Gotthilf August Francke to Mühlenberg
Pölzig, 29 July 1750

After having told Mühlenberg of his intention to remarry, Francke goes into considerable detail to suggest ways in which Mühlenberg may use persons in ministering to congregations who are not ordained or who have come on their own. Francke makes these suggestions in the light of the expanding field of labor Mühlenberg and his colleagues face and the lack of suitable candidates who could be sent to relieve them from overwork. In view of the lack of funds to support additional pastors needed in congregations and outparishes Francke sets forth a hypothetical proposal. He suggests that Mühlenberg explore with the congregations the idea of having them all share in the financial support of a pastor for a congregation or group of congregations. The implication of this proposal for ecclesiology suggests going beyond the autonomy of local congregations and viewing them as a unity in the body of Christ, the church.

Text in German: Korrespondenz *1:372-75. For further textual information see* Korrespondenz *1:375.*

To
Pastor Mühlenberg
at New Providence

29 July 1750

Reverend,
Dearly beloved
Brother in the Lord:
Since the first of this month I am at this blessed place[1] where I not only drink seltzer water from the spring for my health but in the process I enjoy the refreshing and blessed association here with their gracious lordships and other children of God which also then under divine blessing has contributed very much to the fact that the treatment at the spring has turned out well up to this time. In addition, God has also shown me another benefit in this place since he wants to replace the loss in the departure of my blessed wife[2] and mother-in-law[3] in the person of Miss von Gersdorf,[4] a Christian who in the past twelve years has faithfully continued in the ways of the Lord and whom Your Reverence may still remember. For after I sufficiently came to

know her upright disposition after a number of years and following a mature testing of God's will I became engaged to her in the name of God on 3 April of this year. After the completion of my treatment at the springs, if the Lord wills, I intend to consummate my marriage with her on the twenty-ninth of this month. Along with me she sends sincere greetings to Your Reverence and also requests your intercession.

From here I have just now responded[5] to the letter[6] of the worthy Pastor Handschuh which I received along with the continuation of his diary[7] shortly before my departure. (While I have it read to me here at the springs, I sincerely praise God that he has granted our dear brother not only wisdom but also his blessing. Thus, under the pressures of so much work he has not been allowed to consume his strength in vain; rather he has accomplished more already in the rather short time he has been in Lancaster than one might have anticipated previously.) In addition, I have also had the pleasure of receiving your welcome letter[8] along with the continuation of your reports for the year 1746.[9] In them I have especially observed with sincere sympathy that with his extended and overwhelming amount of work the worthy Pastor Brunnholtz[10] is still so fragile; it almost appears that unless one will come to his aid to a greater extent his energies which have almost already been consumed may be fully dissipated in a short time. In the same way Your Reverence is constantly experiencing an increasing diminution in your strength which after all is also not surprising since every one among you is overwhelmed with so much work that one still has reason to thank God that you have not completely succumbed to it. For that reason it is not only highly appropriate to consider seriously how lasting alleviation can be brought about for all of you through several assistants: it appears rather that your most urgent need also demands it. In my letter to Pastor Handschuh I have already mentioned how this concern has weighed my heart down for some time and I have most eagerly desired that God might furnish means and ways for that purpose. From the preliminary announcement[11] of the worthy Court Preacher Albinus[12] I have concluded that you have in mind an assistant to Pastor Brunnholz, and for this position you would propose a candidate who, among other things, is familiar with the situation there. It was assumed that the salary of such an assistant would be provided or means for it would be found without loss of any of your subsistence. But now I see from your letter that the congregation cannot really provide a salary for two pastors but that out of love for the congregations you want somewhat to reduce your own. Your disinterested pure intention evident in this proposal pleases me very much. However, I also know that none of you has anything left over. At the same time it is, nevertheless, absolutely essential that you should receive help as soon as possible. As far as Mr. Raus[13] is concerned, it still appears to me to be highly questionable for him immediately to receive as important a position as that in Philadelphia since he went to Pennsylvania without a call and, indeed, probably mainly for the sake of finding employment for himself. From what he reported in his curriculum vitae there is still no adequate basis on which to assume a thorough conversion on his part. In the event that you did not discover adequate signs of it in him, I for my part would be of the opinion that you could initially use as schoolteachers persons who come on their own if you held out some hope for them that they could still be useful for the work of the Lord. However, I also see from your letter that there is not always an opportunity to make a living teaching school.

Next to this you also mention Pastor Hartwich,[14] saying that you had thought of calling him to Philadelphia, because he has a desire to be in closer fellowship with you. But that, too, must be considered carefully. Because I do not sufficiently know him I, for my part at least, can say nothing regarding the matter. No doubt by now you have come to know him better. I wanted to offer to search out and send several coworkers. But because I do indeed recognize that especially Philadelphia requires a mature man much still depends on whether and how soon the Lord will point to such a person. Consequently, I cannot make a more definite promise other than that God himself will select and point to a chosen instrument. Since in any event the time for this has passed for this year it is probably no longer possible to find and send someone. Consequently, while letters are in the process of going back and forth I hope to receive an answer from you whether I should actually send one or two persons. However, I would not want my dear brothers to come into physical distress if they still want to share their remuneration with others. You must know best what is advisable according to circumstances there, and so I leave it to you whether following previous common consideration you could not make a presentation perhaps in connection with a gathering of all elders of the congregations: how all congregations themselves see and are aware that you, the pastors, until now have neither sought your own advantage nor have you also permitted frequent weakness to prevent you from laboring with all faithfulness in general and with their souls in particular. In so doing your strength has indeed already declined and you could not know how long, especially in view of such a continuing overwhelming workload, you would be in a position to stand it. The congregations would all suffer if one or the other among you should depart prematurely on account of death: for not only could you not know which congregations would be affected but also, as a consequence of their union, the remaining pastors would have to take it upon themselves to take the place of the departed one. Such an occurrence could not happen without damaging the essential work of the ministry in all of its aspects and without causing even more ruin to your health. Consequently, it would be good if you would in common seek to discover means to support several coworkers through whose supporting aid not only your strength would still be preserved for a longer period of time for the general benefit of the congregations under the blessing of God but also the strength of those whose place could also be taken immediately if God should take one or the other into his rest. By these means also provision would be made that no congregation would in the meantime be in some kind of want of the proclamation of the word of God if its pastor were ill or absent, etc., etc. I do not know to what extent you would consider it advisable in accordance with the circumstances of that country, to propose something like this before the persons themselves for this purpose are available and at the same time could be elected for this purpose. I also do not know how in the light of the circumstances salary arrangements are best put in place: whether the congregations as a whole should in general meet these expenses or whether these should be left in whole or in part to that congregation in which a coworker of that kind is employed. Be that as it may, it is reasonable for congregations to care for the adequate support of their pastors and necessary coworkers. However, I leave to your discretion the manner in which you want to bring about arrangements of this kind.

Besides this I have also thought a number of times that it would be desirable for those among you who are still unmarried that God might show and introduce them to faithful persons whom they might marry and through whose care their fragile bodies might receive refreshment for the further preservation of their energies under God's blessing, especially since they live in a foreign country far removed from all relatives and acquaintances. After all, it can be a source of great comfort to be united with such a person in association with whom one can enjoy refreshment and encouragement. Nothing can be forced in such a relationship: it depends rather on the gracious leading of God. But I sincerely desire that if God looks upon it as beneficial and useful for you he may introduce them to such faithful helpers, as he has granted to Your Reverence, as I have rejoiced very sincerely in what I have heard concerning her upright disposition. No less do I desire also that Mr. Schaum[15] and Mr. Weygand[16] similarly may marry, having made a sufficiently careful choice of such persons concerning whom they may be assured that they would not experience an interference but rather encouragement in their office and practice of Christianity. In this endeavor you will offer them fatherly advice. Especially the slander which Mr. Schaum had to endure[17] has given rise to this desire; for although the enemy will probably be busy at all times fabricating all kinds of slanders, through a proper marriage the opportunity for slander of this kind will for the most part fall away. It is so easy for young people to be overhasty in such matters and afterwards to be woven again into the world and all kinds of impurities through a woman who is not firm in true denial of the world; it is therefore most necessary for you to stand by them in such an instance with warnings and good advice.

These then are the generalities I resolved to mention for the present. Upon my return to Halle I shall not neglect to respond to your letter fully. Through communicating your and Mr. Handschuh's letters I have evoked the special pleasure of the gracious lordships here.[18] They sincerely rejoice in the blessed progress of God's work and praise his name for it. But they also have great sympathy with your burden and infirmity and sincerely pray for you. Herewith they transmit a gracious and heartfelt greeting. Wherewith I sincerely commend you to the grace and faithfulness of the Lord and always remain

Your,

G.A. Francke

---

1. Pölzig was the residence of Count Erdmann Heinrich von Henckel-Pölzig, and his second wife, Charlotta Maria Albertina von Henckel-Pölzig, both generous supporters of Halle's missionary enterprises. In his letter of 23 July 1746 to Brunnholz and Mühlenberg Francke spoke of making preparations to travel to Pölzig to avail himself of the springs. See *Correspondence* 1:290.
2. Johanna Henriette Francke née Rachals died of a stroke 2 July 1743. See *Correspondence* 1:112-13.
3. Henriette Rosine Götze née Bose died 30 June 1749. See *Correspondence* 1:13 n.5.
4. Eva Wilhelmine von Gersdorf (1710-93) was the daughter of Joachim Sigismund von Gersdorf at Reinsdorf near Wittenberg. Before her marriage to G.A. Francke on 29 July 1750 she lived in the home of Count Erdmann Heinrich von Henckel-Pölzig for ten years.
5. Handschuh's letter is dated 16 November 1749.
6. In notes intended for Albinus, dated 8 March 1750, Brunnholz observes that he had sent Handschuh's diary for 7 September 1748 to 14 November 1749 with other letters to Europe. — On Johann Friedrich Handschuh, see *Correspondence* 1:291 n.18.
7. In the form of an outline the reply is dated 8 June 1750.
8. The letter is dated 20 December 1749. See Letter 76.
9. See Letter 72 n.2.
10. On Peter Brunnholz, see Letter 71 n.3.
11. This announcement is not extant.
12. On Samuel Theodor Albinus, see *Correspondence* 1:154 n.8 and 354 n.5.
13. On Lucas Rauss, see Letter 76 n.72.
14. On Johann Christoph Hartwich, see *Correspondence* 1:323 n.19.
15. On Johann Helfrich Schaum, see Letter 71 n.9.
16. On Johann Albert Weygand, see Letter 71 n.21.
17. Schaum's difficulties in York had to do with his illness resulting from fever and disciplinary matters in the congregation in York. See Letter 76:44 and *HN2/1*:203-7.
18. Francke has Count Erdmann Heinrich von Henckel-Pölzig in mind. - See *Correspondence* 1:11 n.7.

Letter 82

Israel Acrelius[1] to Mühlenberg
Wilmington, 15 August 1750

In this letter Acrelius, who had recently arrived to serve as provost of the Swedish congregations in southeastern Pennsylvania, New Jersey and Delaware, clearly looks upon Mühlenberg's complaints concerning Laurentius Thorstonson Nyberg as justified. At the same time Acrelius maintains in an adroit fashion his independence in forming an opinion concerning the manner of dealing with the conflict between Mühlenberg, his colleagues, especially Brunnholz, and Nyberg.
Text in Latin: Korrespondenz 1:376-78; Landsarkivet, S-7510 Uppsala, Sweden; Swenson Swedish Immigration Center, Augustana College, Rock Island, Illinois. For further textual information, see Korrespondenz 1:378.

Reply
To the most excellent Reverend, senior and most capable director of the German Lutheran Ministerium which flourishes in America, my beloved brother in Christ's ministry who is always to be honored with inward respect and outward allegiance:
Although you have written letters to me twice, I have received only one.[2] I have not spoken lightly, most Reverend Sir, of the pleasure I have received from it. For not so long ago I began to admire the name of Mühlenberg. Long before I was commanded to leave my fatherland your praises rang out, your deeds in the vineyard of God, your labors alone in America, your hard work, your sorrows. It did not escape me that the throne of Satan is where you dwell. I shudder at your severe battles with false brethren and with false apostles! I delight in your reported victories and I congratulate you on them. Indeed, what is heard in Sweden, is extolled in America and proven in Pennsylvania. Is it then a surprise that I desire to experience your friendship and was and still am eager to participate in the assembly over which you preside annually?[3] I esteem you, most Reverend Sir, as one more advanced because of your age and experience. With my whole heart I embrace your coworkers, partners in the ministry of our Augsburg Confession. Necessity presses us to do battle with our forces joined together. The unity of believers recommends that we act in harmony, thinking and speaking in one and the same way. This is the reason, most Reverend Sir and Pastor, I have aligned myself with your most recent synod; nor has any inconstancy and fickleness of soul caused me to withdraw from this purpose. What kept me at home was above all my care

for my health alone in such burning heat of the sun to which I was unaccustomed; in this I was persuaded by those who had my best interests at heart. I am silent concerning other reasons, both ecclesiastical and domestic, that came up unexpectedly on the same days. I am saying nothing about the unusually small size of the Swedish ministerium which I would have preferred to see increased rather than reduced in rank. I am silent concerning certain responses from our archbishop which were expected sooner. I have provided these and other reasons, of greater and lesser importance, for the information of the most Reverend Sir, Pastor Brunnholtz,[4] urgently requesting that out of his own human feeling and with sincerity of mind he would forgive the promise I did not keep and that my absence from the most honorable German Lutheran Ministerium be interpreted in a better light. But perhaps our friend and brother, Dominie Brunnholtz, was absent, and this certainly would have been unfortunate; or the messenger did not know that he should tell my words to the most esteemed Mr. Schleydorn.[5] On the other hand, there was *that* troublesome Zinzendorfian spirit by the name of Nyberg,[6] to our pain a Swede by nationality! In brief, I do not know by what means and method all these things have been investigated in Philadelphia. From there that vagabond traveller has seized an excellent opportunity for vomiting blasphemies and sowing seeds of discord everywhere. For who doubts that the always vigilant enemy is sowing tares among the wheat?[7] He has aroused emotions of the mind on both sides. He has provoked your spirits. It has rendered us suspect of unfaithfulness and has stained piety. To be brief: he has gained everything he has pursued. This is how the drama unfolded. I have never seen Nyberg with these eyes. He came once to see me when he knew I would be away. I grieve over this miserable apostate. I am even ashamed of this fellow countryman. May Jehovah have mercy on him! The Zinzendorfian crowd is not unknown to me, and with their cunning they have wriggled their way almost into the whole world. I have read, reread, gone over their writings, lists, histories and criticisms of them in our own country. Already it almost hurts me to read further. I greatly wish to be informed of happenings in America and I acknowledge you as teacher whom I will have come to know in a little while.

Not even one iota of which the Zinzendorfian ferment smells is part of the truly Swedish Church nor is it fitting for its ministers. This is my confession so that you may see me as I am.

And, most Reverend Sir, permit me to ask a question. Does your most reverend ministerium have so little influence on this Nybergian nonsense? Let me say, by your leave: Too much has surfaced in the inquiry even if I have doubts about the one invited. Could it have been that he was sent by our own ministerium for the purpose of telling this untrue story, is it not so?

If we follow legal rules in hearing the other part and afterwards pass judgment, why should you trust an unsuitable witness, even if he should relate what is true? It is hateful to you, odious to us. I grieve over conflicts about which I do not know how they came about. I marvel at the credulity which supports the opponent but not friends. Simply my absence and Nyberg's destructive language, what do they have in common? Also, when we study both the moral and the natural realm, we shall see many things living side by side without one having anything to do with the other. Having duly considered them I am drawn to interpret the words of Nyberg as Nyberg's, that of which three words together make a symbol: lie, deny, blaspheme, three "Ls,"[8] the worst evil words by which to be influenced and always to repeat them. Nevertheless, a little while ago the words were most frequently ready at hand to me, especially in Philadelphia, where a little after his return from synod the most reverend brother Brunnholtz excused me with wrinkled brow. Now a second time most Reverend Sir: I see you labor with the same anxiety which the loss of your earlier letters did not lessen. I grieve over your sorrow and I delight in the innocence of both. Certainly if Nyberg had known how much agitation of souls he concocted before his departure, he may have something concerning which he may congratulate himself in his heart. This is my defense of whatever value it may be.

As for the rest, if you judge me to be worthy as one whose close friendship you enjoy, both impartial and honest, you may consult me most promptly for whatever service you wish, second to no one in candor. Nothing is more important to me, nothing than the glory of God and the advantage of his church. We desire a yearly synod, nevertheless in such a way, as the invitation indicates, that it be carried out by both sides that it not be for the vainglory of one or the other side, as was already done some time ago. I think that Philadelphia should serve us as a place of convenience by the grace of heaven in about the months of May and September. Let it be yours, best patron, at the first opportunity to appoint the best time and place in accordance with accustomed practice. As far as in me lies, I shall truly do energetically unwearied work to deserve your favor, to preserve what is deserved, always preserving respect.

Written at Wilmington   Most respectfully in honor
18 September   of your most Reverend Name,
in the year of our Redeemer 1750   Israel Acrelius

1. On Israel Acrelius, see Letter 80 n.1.
2. Only one of these two letters, dated 22 June 1750 (Letter 80), has come down to us.
3. The Third Convention of the Pennsylvania Synod took place on 17 and 18 June 1750. The record of this meeting in the *Documentary History* is a translation of the report prepared by Peter Brunnholz and found in *HN2/1*:471-73. Mühlenberg's record of the meeting is found in *Journals* 1:245-46. In his report Mühlenberg comments on the absence of Acrelius saying, "The Swedish provost did not come as he had promised, and sent no letter of excuse, which confirmed the conjecture that Nyberg and his followers must have attempted to exert some influence." Because "the affair with the Swedish ministers weighed heavily" upon his mind Mühlenberg wasted no time in writing Acrelius four days after the conclusion of the Convention, 22 June 1750. See Letter 80.
4. On Peter Brunnholz, see Letter 71 n.3; see also *Journals* 1:244, "My colleague, Mr. Brunnholtz, reported personally and in writing that he had already had a conversation with the newly arrived provost...."
5. On Heinrich Schleydorn, see *Correspondence* 1:53 n.22.
6. On Laurentius Thorstonson Nyberg, see *Correspondence* 1:181 n.10.
7. See Matt. 13:25.
8. Here Acrelius inserts three words in German, each beginning with the letter "L": Lügen, Leugnen, Lästern, followed by *tria* in Latin and two words in Greek, λάμδε κάκιότα.

Letter 83

To Lucas Rauss
Providence, October 1750-March 1751

Because Mühlenberg has misgivings about Rauss's fitness for the ministry he begins this letter to him with a rather extensive lecture on what is required of a pastor in the American provinces. Mühlenberg has reservations about Rauss's suitability for the ministry because he was one of those persons who had come running on his own. Rauss arrived in Philadelphia without having been sent or requested to come. Furthermore, he was a graduate of the University of Jena and not of Halle. In the view of Rauss Mühlenberg was a "Hallensian" and a pietist. Consequently, the two men never developed a collegial relationship even though the Pennsylvania ministerium ordained Rauss on 5 November 1752.

Text in Latin: Korrespondenz 1:378-80. For further textual information see Korrespondenz 1:380.

Mühlenberg extends most respectful greetings
to Reverend Rauss[1]
his most honored Brother:

I have received two letters[2] from you, each of which is delightful; from these I have understood that, with the help of God, you are experiencing the good fortune of good health and a fairly joyful spirit so far. Therefore, most humble thanks is due to the immortal King of kings and Lord of lords. By his goodness and grace he invites us to health and by his power he wants to and is able to deliver us from the power of darkness and transfer us to the kingdom of his most beloved Son.[3] Most honorable sir, shortness of time and infirmity of health have hindered us from responding to you sooner than now. As far as the gist of your letters is concerned I have noticed that some human temptations have attacked you in your present station. Why is this surprising if, as blessed Luther said, prayer, meditation and temptation make a theologian[4]—and although those temptations may be small, they are bound to bring good. For if on our part we want to manage the office committed to us well, and do not want to be lazy bellies, we want to show ourselves as faithful in all small things, and then we commend ourselves as ministers of God with much patience, in misfortune and adverse circumstances, in precarious situations, beatings and imprisonments, in tumults, in labors and watchings, in hunger and purity, in knowledge, mercy and generosity, in the Holy Spirit, in genuine love and speaking the truth, in the power of God, with weapons of righteousness on the right hand and the left, through glory and dishonor, through cursings and blessings, as deceitful and nevertheless true, as unknown and nevertheless known, as dying and yet we live; as sorrowing and nevertheless always rejoicing, as poor when we make many rich, as possessing nothing and nevertheless having all things, 2 Corinthians 6.[5] Who is truly sufficient for these things?[6] We are so far from the perfection of these qualities we can hardly lay the foundation we intend! For that reason I pray from my heart that Jehovah will make us qualified to be ministers of the new covenant, not of the letter but of the spirit[7] lest at the acceptable time and day of salvation[8] we should not receive the greatness of mercy and longsuffering and other kindnesses. Then one would have received the benefits of God in vain lest as salt that has become tasteless we be thrown out and are trampled under foot by people![9] Therefore, I should like you not to receive it badly if I ask you to consider in your mind in what state your affairs have been: when as a complete foreigner and lost son[10] in great, great poverty you sailed to the American provinces without a regular call and without letters of recommendation.

I ask that you often call to mind with what kindness and uprightness and integrity the Reverend Brunnholtz embraced you: how he took pains to provide those things which are necessary for food and clothing. Or were not our souls and pulpits so far continuously open to you? If the best and greatest God in his mercy toward you had not had a concern for your safety the captain of the ship could have brought harsh servitude on you. For as long as certain affairs of office have been handed over to you in the name of our God so long you have not been left without purse[11] and shoes just as you have not been without anything most necessary for food and clothing. Most honorable sir, you are not unaware that I am the least of my brothers who have been sent into the American harvest; indeed, I call God and you yourself to witness that we all on account of labors, sweat, hindrances and severe struggles in God's vineyard during the years which have slipped by, have been content with moderate and available care of the body. For it is a great gain to be contented[12] with genuine godliness and one's own lot. We have brought nothing into this world, and surely we shall carry nothing away.[13] Therefore, to praise God together with us I entreat you not to refuse the Father of our Lord, Jesus Christ, who has prospered you with the divine abundance of heavenly things in Christ. The time and hour is now that we should awake from sleep,[14] acknowledge the sins of our youth before God, not conceal guilt, be justified by true faith through Jesus Christ, bring forth fruits worthy of a changed life, crucify the flesh together with lusts and desires and living in the Spirit also walk in the Spirit;[15] let us take the divine armour, let us fight the good fight, let us finish the course, let us keep the faith and finally obtain the crown of righteousness.[16] Concerning your sincerity toward us I have nothing for which I can blame you. For I think that in Pennsylvania you have shown yourself to be an honest man, human errors excepted. From that time in which you were joined to me and in which you discharged the duties of your office in the province of New York,[17] your diaries you sent us have been satisfactory to me, and will satisfy me, if done in moderate style so that sternness is joined to kindness, prayer and meditation to temptation. Thus may you endure and make progress!

Henry Melchior Mühlenberg

---

1. On Lucas Rauss, see Letter 76 n.72. For more details concerning Rauss and the troubled relationships between him and the Pennsylvania pastors who were "Hallensians" in his eyes, see *Pastors and People* 1:107-8.
2. Both letters are not extant.
3. See 1 Peter 2:9.
4. See *LW* 34:285-88; *WA* 50:658-61.
5. See 2 Cor. 6:4-10.
6. See 2 Cor. 3:5.
7. See 2 Cor. 3:6.
8. See 2 Cor. 6:2.
9. See Matt. 5:13.
10. This phrase is in Greek: υἱός ἀπολωλός. See Luke 15:24 which reads υἱός ἀπολωλώς
11. See Matt. 10:10.
12. See Phil. 4:11.
13. See 1 Tim. 6:7.
14. See Rom. 13:11.
15. See Gal. 5:25.
16. See 2 Tim. 4:7,8.
17. Since Rauss did not move to New York City until 1758 this is probably a reference to the province of New York. The text reads *Eboracensi.*

Letter 84

The Dutch Church Council in New York to Mühlenberg
New York, 11 August 1750

*The church council members of the Dutch Lutheran congregation in New
York appeal to Mühlenberg in this letter to be their pastor for a period of
time of his own choosing so as to bring an end to the divisions among them.
To encourage Mühlenberg to accept their invitation to be the pastor of their
congregation the council members go so far as to promise Mühlenberg an
assistant who is "virtuous and zealous."*

Text in Dutch: Korrespondenz 1:380-81. *For further textual information
see* Korrespondenz 1:381.

Most reverend Mr. Meuhlenberg,
Most reverend and highly learned Sir:
We are without a shepherd or teacher in our congregation and are afraid
that if we continue thus much longer without a virtuous and faithful
Seelsorger, our church, which is already partly fallen away and divided, will
be entirely destroyed. This event can only be hindered if the ancient and
true shepherd, Jesus Christ, is pleased to send into our congregation or
harvest not only a man but, indeed, a father, who as a mother hen might be
able to gather the lost or divided and ruined ones again under the peaceful
wings of our pure evangelical doctrine. And since, after long consultations
with each other, we have identified no one more competent than you, most
Reverend Sir, it is our heartfelt request that you, most Reverend Sir, would
be pleased to help us in this our great spiritual need by accepting the
preaching office here over our congregation.[1] We are sure that you, most
Reverend Sir, who take to heart the upbuilding of Christ's church in this
place and who would dedicate all your abilities to God's glory and to the
preservation of so many poor souls who otherwise might possibly choose
estrangement from our pure doctrine, not only for their own persons but
also for their descendants, will not be able to refuse to accept our offer.
Although, if you, Reverend Sir, would not want to accept staying here
forever, then at least for one, two or three years, or as long as you, most
Reverend Sir, yourself would think good, until our expelled members can
again be gathered into one body. And we promise you, most Reverend Sir,
to procure as assistant a virtuous and zealous man for relief for you, most
Reverend Sir, to which the Almighty will give his blessing. We would
request that you, most Reverend Sir, would be pleased to apply all diligence

to be here with us, the sooner the better, for our church runs a great risk of falling away if it is not speedily succored.

In expectation of Your Reverence's resolution to this matter, we have the honor to sign ourselves

New York   Most reverend and learned Sir!
8 November   Your Reverence's faithful and humble
1750   servants
                        Charles Beckman   C.R. Herttel
                        Lourens van Boskerk   Jacobus van
                                                         Boskerck
                        Johann David Wollff
                        George Petterson   Henry Scheffer
                        Jacobus Tiedemann   J.M. Magens

---

1. See *Journals* 1:260 for Mühlenberg's summary of this letter. In addition to this letter, the following letters in this volume are related to Mühlenberg's dealings with the Dutch and German Lutheran congregation in New York: 86, 90, 95, 96, 97 n.1, 100. Because Wilhelm Christoph Berckenmeyer had to be considered in these dealings and the ones Mühlenberg had with congregations in Hackensack and Raritan, New Jersey, the content of the following letters in *Correspondence* 1 needs to be taken into account: 40A, 40B, 40C, 41A, 41B, 42. On his return voyage by boat from Rhinebeck, New York, Mühlenberg had stopped over in New York. *Journals* 1:254-58. An extended account of the origin, history and development of the Dutch and German Lutherans in the city of New York and of Lutheranism in the state of New York from 1632-1885 is found in *HN2/1:* 616-54. An account of the problems deeply disturbing Dutch and German Lutherans in New York City and Mühlenberg's involvement in them is provided in *Lutheranism in Colonial NY*, pp. 58-64; 103-5. An overview of the language problem among Dutch and German Lutherans and the relationship of Mühlenberg to Berckenmeyer is found in *Lutheranism in N.A.*, pp. 14-17. Extended references to the tension among Dutch and German Lutherans brought on by language differences in New York City are also present in Simon Hart and Harry J. Kreider, eds., *Protocol of the Lutheran Church in New York City 1702-1750* (New York: Lutheran Synod of New York and New England, 1958), pp. 305-9.

Letter 85

To Thomas Cockson[1]
Providence, 26 November 1750?[2]

This letter may serve as an example of the many times parishioners and acquaintances sought the advice of Mühlenberg as pastor in matters affecting their personal lives. In this particular instance Mühlenberg seeks to establish whether a suitor of a daughter who was a member of his New Providence congregation has the character and integrity the daughter's relatives expect him to have.
Text in German: Korrespondenz 1:382. *For further textual information see* Korrespondenz 1:382.

High and noble Sir,
Kind Patron:
Mr. Koppy,[3] the bearer of these lines, has been down here twice already and has honorably requested to become engaged to the virgin Schrack.[4] Although the relatives asked for my sound advice, in such delicate matters I may give my opinion but not definite advice. I have therefore committed myself to ask my closest friends privately whether said Mr. Kopp has conducted himself among them as a good evangelical Christian and honest fellow citizen and whether you think it will turn out to be a happy marriage? High and noble sir, because you are not only a deacon of the church but also a magistrate of the police[5] you can judge best in this matter and have the most immediate and best opportunity to get to know his character. I am looking for nothing more in this matter other than to promote the glory of God and what is best for my neighbor; however, I am also to assist in every possible way in averting harm to my neighbor. If Your Grace should consider it unnecessary to respond to these few lines, I shall remain silent from now on and consider that I have done my duty. Should you, however, honor me with a response I shall tender my humble advice accordingly. As for the rest I indicate that I am

	High and noble sir,
Providence	Kind patron,
26 November	Your obliging servant
	Mühlenberg

1. The name of the addressee is Thomas Cockson who was a member of St. James Anglican Church in Lancaster, Pennsylvania. As a prothonotary and justice of the peace he was highly respected by the governor of Pennsylvania and, like Conrad Weiser, frequently consulted in affairs related to Indians. He died 20 March 1753 at the age of fifty-three. See *HN2/2:679* n.153; *Correspondence* 1:260 n.3.

2. The dating of this letter is determined by its location in Mühlenberg's diary in which it immediately follows his letter to J.C. Stöver, 26 May 1750 (Letter 79).

3. The name of "Koppy" may be identical with the Palatine, Ulrich Coppy, who arrived in Pennsylvania toward the end of September 1749. See I.D. Rupp, *A Collection of Upwards of Thirty Thousand Names of German, Swiss, Dutch, French and Other Immigrants in Pennsylvania from 1727 to 1776, with a Statement of the Names of Ships, Whence They Sailed, and the Date of Their Arrival at Philadelphia, Chronologically Arranged Together with the Necessary Historical and Other Notes, Also, an Appendix Concerning Lists of More Than One Thousand German and French Names in New York Prior to 1712* (Leipzig, 1931), p. 213.

4. The reference is probably to the daughter of Jacob Schrack and his wife, Eva Rosina. In his diary Mühlenberg points out that the Schracks and their four children came to this country and settled in an area which came to be known as New Providence (*Journals* 3:370; *Pastors and People* 1:379).

5. I.e., justice of the peace.

Letter 86

To the Dutch Church Council in New York
Philadelphia, 3 December 1750

*In replying to Letter 84 of the Dutch Church Council in New York,
Mühlenberg agreed "to make a trial for the space of two years" in serving
the Dutch speaking Lutheran congregation there. His agreement was subject
to a number of conditions. Among the ones he enumerates, the one
concerning his present lack of proficiency in the Dutch language implies his
desire to preach the gospel in a language people understand. In this instance
Mühlenberg feels he will need two to three months to perfect his skills in
speaking the Dutch language. For further information concerning
Mühlenberg's relationship to the Dutch Lutherans in New York, see Letter
84 n.1.*

Text in English: Korrespondenz *1:383-84. For further textual information
see* Korrespondenz *1:384. This letter, written in English, is given here in
its original form.*

Worthy Gentlemen of the Vestry,

The lamentable Description, you have given me, of your present
Church's Affair, in a letter dated the 8 t of November ac:[1] exactly agreeth
with the Idea I conceived in my being at NewYork, and is very strong to
move every patriot and Wellwisher of our holy Religion to call for
Assistence from Heaven and to pray, the Lord of the Harvest would please
to send faithful Labourers into his Harvest,[2] and especially to chuse a father
for gathering the scattred Children of Covenant together under the Wings of
our Saviour Jesus Christ!

But I can't comprehend, what arguments you are induced by, to
concenter your Affections on me, so unworthy subiect videl[icet][3] a Tiro[4] in
the learned world, an unexperienced Soldier in the Church of Christ
militant, a Child in Grace, a half-worn man in age and Constitution, gross
in Manners and Conduct, incumbred with a family, imperfect in the Low
dutch Language, a man that rather would live in an unknown Corner of the
Globe, then to preach at Athens! You will give me leave Gentlemen and
Brethren to render thanks for your undeserved Confidence you put in me,
and let me answer the weighty Matter in question 1) The Lord allmighty and
most gracious be praised, that in this present time wherin faith and love,
hope and holy zeal vanish away, He hath pleased to preserve some sparks
of Light in your Intellect, and some accusing and excusing thoughts and

Motions in your Conscience,[5] to see and have yourselves and your late posterity built and edifyed in the sound and saving doctrine of the Apostels and prophets, which so many Millions of Christians have sealed with their sanctified Blood and our fore-fathers at the blessed time of Reformation confessed with danger of life, and pray your Light and Zeal may grow and continue in the Midst of Storm and Waves. 2) the condition of our Church in your province is woful enough! Head and Heart is sick, and fainting and the whole Body agonizing and torn to pieces by an inward Corruption and several unskillful spiritual Empiricks, and will be very hard and tiresom/: though not impossible unto them that believe:/ to apply Remedies suitable to the disease, because there are left some old and young Struglers, cunning and bold enough to beat the air,[6] to fight and to huzz, for some indifferent rotten pieces of Cerimony and against the power of Godliness, like barking dogs for shadow against the Moon! 3) Admitt Gentlemen, you would in Respect of your Affections wink at my aforesaid disability, and insist to have me a scrifice for your Church, don't you think it should be hard to leave my beloved Congregations dear Relation, faithful Brethren of the Ministry and might be to become burdensom to you with a family You had to maintain according to our Saviour's Demand Luc 10:7. I Cor. 9:14. Galat: 6:5,7. I Thess: 5,12,13? But it seemeth you have wisely foreseen and considered all the difficulties, and desire therefore only that I should accept the Ministerial function and make an Experiment for one, two or three years. In Consideration of this proposition, I answer in the following Manner and condition. 1) the decaying Congregation should needs be supported without delay. 2) I am willing to deny all Commodities for Christ's and his Church's sake. 3) I depend entirely from the Mercy and Assistance of the Lord, who only can enable me for so heavy an office. 4) It is my duty to supply my Congregations with a faithfull successor, lest I commit the folly as to stop a hole in the sheephouss and leave the door open to ravening Wolves.[7] 5) I stand under Inspection of the Right Reverend Master Zigenhagen, His Majesty's German Preacher at Saint Jamses's in London and other Worthy Members of the Society[8] in Europe and need to acquaint them with my Change. 6) I want liberty to assist the Reverend Ministry of our Church on the yearly Synodical Meetings in Pennsylvania and in other good Cases, and to visit now and than a desolate Congregation in your Province, to see, wether any Amendment may be made by my poor mediation. 7) In the beginning I can preach only in the high dutch and English Languages, and ought to have two or three Months for perfecting the Low dutch tongue. 8) I must settle my temporal Affairs and order my little Estate.

Seing, that the above mentioned Conditions require a certain time for preparation and searching after the gracious Will of God, I shall wait for your Answer, in the which you will, according to best Judgement and impartial love either discharge me and look for a better Subiect, or send a lawful Vocation or Call to make a trial for the space of two years. Ad utrumque paratus sum.[9] And in Case you should chuse the last and send a lawfull Vocation unto me,[10] I shall impartialy seek after the will and pleasure of the Lord by the concurring Circumstances and prayers, and having found it, move and come as soon as God and the circumstances will permit. In the mean while I recommend you and you Worthy families, together with the Rest of the Congregation unto Grace, peace and Mercy of God, and myself Gentlemen and Brethren to your Benevolence, remaining your Faithful

Philadelphia
the 3th day of
December 1750.   H.M. Mühlenberg

---

1. This is an abbreviation of the Latin *anno currentis*, meaning "in the current year".
2. See Matt. 9:38; Luke 10:2.
3. This is an abbreviation of the Latin *videlicet*, meaning "namely".
4. The Latin *Tiro* is the equivalent of the English *tyro*, meaning a novice or beginner.
5. See Rom. 2:15.
6. See 1 Cor. 9:26b.
7. In his diary Mühlenberg refers to Wilhelm Christoph Berckenmeyer's attempt to restore unity and order in the New York congregation. Mühlenberg reports that Berckenmeyer prophesied that "after his departure the ravenous wolves would come." See *Journals* 1:260.
8. Mühlenberg is referring to the Society for the Promotion of Christian Knowledge.
9. The Latin text means, "I am prepared for both ways."
10. The call of 1 February 1751 is not extant. For Mühlenberg's reference to receiving the call and the difficulties he recognized in dealing with it, see *Journals* 1:269.

Letter 87

To Johann Conrad Weiser
Providence, 27 December 1750

Because we have only fragments of a letter in the form of three postscripts and because the identity of two persons to whom Mühlenberg refers only with an abbreviation remains unknown, it is difficult to establish the point of the first postscript. Furthermore, there is no connecting thought running through the three postscripts which were part of a letter no longer extant which Mühlenberg wrote to his father-in-law. Notwithstanding these textual and literary difficulties the postscripts give us an insight into Mühlenberg's personal feelings at this juncture in his ministry and into his relationships to the Weiser family.

Text in German: Korrespondenz *1:385-6. For further textual information see* Korrespondenz *1:386.*

P.S. While I was in the city recently I delivered the commission I had been assigned to J. Ev.[1] and said that the mother could not do without her pearl. But he thinks it cannot be otherwise because he now wants to complete the house altogether, also buy an organ and install it. He goes to school, is learning to write with great diligence and will probably write a letter himself. He would rather free a maidservant for mother and assures that M[2] will have the best days while with him because he has no children and otherwise has enough of everything, etc. This much I have accomplished that he does not believe my words and clings to his old hope. If the man had a little more knowledge and the power of godliness then... There is probably nothing lacking in outward respectability and daily bread. He has shown me his baptismal certificate, from which I was to gather that he is supposed to be only thirty-one years old. And he also claims that he has never done his blessed wife any harm but lived peaceably with her.

Herewith I am returning Mr. Volck's[3] book and a biography of Doctor Luther in which the father now and again reads a bit. Perhaps some long comfortable evenings will turn up for reading through it.

P.S. I would request the favor of returning this and my first letter[4] because I have no copies of them; and it is after all necessary for me to transmit the main concerns in them in their connection to each other to the fathers so they may see how we confer concerning such matters and do not make light of them. If sufficient time is left perhaps Samuel[5] could make copies of them without the postscripts which do not belong there.

If an inclination is of any consequence, I have an inclination to remain here for I fear change.[6] But because these are not private but public matters I must leave the judgment to the dear God and my closest friends whom the Lord has given me. Along with them I must search in diligent prayer for the Lord's will and follow in simple obedience to it. God is faithful and in accordance with his mercy and faithfulness will grant that the temptation will come to an end so that we can endure it.[7] I am no longer of any use to this world. I would probably be best off if the Lord were to forgive my many sins incurred in my office and position for the sake of Jesus Christ, take me to himself from this vale of sins and would also guide and preserve my family on the narrow path to heaven.[8]

P.S. As I heard from brother Friederich,[9] the dear father will perhaps travel to Philadelphia in the beginning of January and around that time dear mother will not be able to neglect visiting beloved Benjamin[10] in Reading. From this one can almost conclude that the mother will come down with father again to her little grandchildren, if health, weather and strength permit it and the dear God would grant us the pleasure. In expectation of this I close with cordial greetings to our remaining brothers, sisters and friends. I remain your dutiful

Providence, 27 December 1750   Son Mühlenberg

---

1. It was not possible to identify the person Mühlenberg had in mind here.
2. It was not possible to identify the person Mühlenberg had in mind here.
3. Mühlenberg is probably referring to Gabriel Falk, a pastor sent from Sweden to serve the congregation in Wicaco. On Falk, see Letter 78 n.9.
4. This letter is not extant.
5. Samuel Weiser, Mühlenberg's brother-in-law.
6. Mühlenberg has his imminent move to New York City in mind. See Letter 86.
7. See 1 Cor. 10:13.
8. See Matt. 7:13-14.
9. Friedrich Weiser, Mühlenberg's brother-in-law.
10. Benjamin Weiser, youngest brother of Mühlenberg's wife, Anna Maria, born 12 August 1744. See *The Weiser Family: A Genealogy of the Family of John Conrad Weiser the Elder (d. 1746)* (Manheim, Pennsylvania: The John Conrad Weiser Family Association, 1960), p.8. –On John Conrad Weiser, Jr., see *Correspondence* 1:142 n.7 and Paul A.W. Wallace, *Conrad Weiser 1691-1760: Friend of Colonist and Mohawk* (Philadelphia: University of Pennsylvania Press, 1945).

LETTERS OF 1751

Letter 88

To Israel Acrelius
Providence, 25 January 1751

Troubled about the failure of Acrelius to be present at the 1750 meeting of the German ministerium of the United Congregations, Mühlenberg goes out of his way in this letter to assure Acrelius of his continuing high regard. Though there may be differences in rites and ceremonies between Swedish and German Lutheran congregations, theirs is a unity in the proclamation of the gospel and the administration of the sacraments in accordance with it. Though unable to prove it, Mühlenberg suspects Nyberg may have had something to do with the unexcused, though excusable, absence of Acrelius from the 1750 meeting.

Text in Latin: Korrespondenz 1:389-90; also in Landsarkivet, S-75104 Uppsala, Sweden; and Swedish Immigration Center, Augustana College, Rock Island, Illinois. For further textual information see Korrespondenz 1:390.

Mühlenberg extends respectful greetings and highest regard to the most learned Reverend Provost of the Swedish Church which has been renewed in Pennsylvania and New Jersey:

I was prevented from extending my humble thanks earlier (in a way that my respect would have been equal to yours) to you, most Reverend Sir, for your letters[1] to me because of the great extent of my journey and the weariness when that was finished, scarcity of time to undertake necessary business I had neglected and ill health, and winter time. However, lest I abuse your patience and the shortness of time with the excess of my words I pray with my whole spirit and mind that Jehovah might be and remain your protection and abundant great recompense for your kindness toward me. As far as the content of your very delightful letters is concerned when I passed over your praise which is not appropriate for me, I most freely acknowledge that you, most Reverend Sir, have so clearly illuminated and openly discerned the scene that was played out between us that henceforth I shall hope without hesitation that you with God's help throughout your whole career will remain the pride and joy and protector of the true evangelical church. May you prove to be one who until death increases continuously in the Holy Spirit in the power and great patience of God. As for the rest, pardon me if I constantly ask whether my prejudiced opinions, which do not arise from cunning but from circumstances and conjecture or from the wrinkled brow of the sickly brother, Brunnholtz,[2] or from my dull style of writing, bring pain! For we are human beings and we realize that no error is foreign to us. Most Reverend Sir, we may indeed not ignore that all things are possible which, strictly speaking, do not allow contradiction. Therefore I have thought it possible that Nyberg, out of his own craftiness with which he has first deceived the sacred senate of the Swedish Empire, then a large number of men, both illiterate as well as educated, in the American provinces, has put us to shame among the most reverend Ministerium of the Swedish Church, most eagerly desiring its friendship and wanting to win it over for himself.[3] The church has suffered damage,[4] especially since (as has been told, provided that the story is true), that scoundrel having been given the opportunity of turning confidentially to the most Reverend Sir, Mr. Unander, insisted on getting permission to preach a sermon for a church service of Mr. Unander which had already started.[5] All of these things which were mentioned before in one Nybergian rumour and the unexpected absence of the provost of the church, without any letter of excuse and considering the message and weighing the thought, I wonder how much can be done since Nyberg has sown bad weeds among the grain.[6] I had experienced the wickedness of Nyberg before with its danger, and about the members of the most reverend Swedish Ministerium recently sent to the American provinces I had no certain information. Had they read— yes, even reread ad nauseam—the writings, lists and histories of the new Zinzendorfian party? Is it therefore a surprise if from arguments in the realm of philosophers and not in the usual way I conceived an opinion by chance or casually? Meanwhile I replied to those who asked for the reason for the absence of the most Reverend provost of the church since it is appropriate for my office through these humble letters to search out the reason for your absence; in the meantime I recalled to memory that it is not at all valid to conclude from what may be possible that it is so as to the consequence and that the opinion is only a proposition that has not been sufficiently proved. Given these facts I more certainly expect that the most reverend Ministerium of the Swedish Church is well clothed with divine armor against the wiles of the devil[7] and its house has been built on a rock.[8] Therefore blessing, glory and thanksgiving be to our God throughout all ages. Still, I truly say that our invitation had no other purpose than the presence of the most worthy provost of the church or that of a venerable member of the Ministerium at our annual gathering that we might be refreshed with your counsel through mutual faith, struggling with united strength, acting in harmony, feeling and speaking the same thing. Thus we shall construct the whole building on the foundation of the apostles and prophets and the Symbolical Books in the American wilderness where the true church exists surrounded by innumerable factions and temptations. "For the true unity of the church it is enough to agree concerning the teaching of the Gospel and administration of the sacraments. It is not necessary that human traditions or rites and ceremonies, instituted by men, should be alike;" Augsburg Confession, Article VII.[9] Concerning rites and ceremonies in the service books and liturgies of the church which is truly evangelical which flourishes in Sweden, Germany and London, we have established them with the agreement of our superiors. We are of the opinion that much of our infant church, the German one in particular, has in the meantime come together and moved forward. Therefore in like manner it will prevail whether or not we attend to rites and ceremonies the same way, if only we preserve true unity both in teaching and acting on the one foundation of salvation, Jesus Christ, and do not build on gold, silver and precious stones.[10] Away with all pompous display of vainglory! Among us, the obedience to the Savior's commandment is to make the greatest like the least, the one who presides like the one who serves, and according to divine law ministers of the church equal in terms of dignity. Nevertheless, we think that in terms of man-made law, custom has introduced a certain dignity into this equality, and we shall with all strength given us dedicate ourselves to the caring of souls and obedient service. Farewell and support

the most dedicated servant
of your highly esteemed name

Written at Providence   Mühlenberg
25 January 1751

---

1. See Letter 82.
2. On Peter Brunnholz, see Letter 71 n.3.
3. See Letter 80 n.6.
4. The text of "The church has suffered damage," is barely legible because insertions have been made between the lines.
5. Erik Unander, a Swedish pastor, had arrived in Philadelphia on 11 June 1749. Until 1755 he was pastor in Raccoon and Pennsneck and until 1760 in Wilmington, Delaware. See Israel Acrelius, *A History of New Sweden; or the Settlements on the Delaware*, trans. W.M. Reynolds (1876; reprint ed., Ann Arbor, 1966), p. 399; *HN2/1*:286.
6. See Matt. 13:25.
7. See Eph. 6:11. In the text "wiles" is in Greek: μεθοδέιας.
8. See Matt. 7:24.
9. Theodore G. Tappert et al., ed. and trans., *The Book of Concord* (Philadelphia: Fortress Press, 1959), p.32
10. See 1 Cor. 3:10-12.

Letter 89

Gotthilf August Francke to Peter Brunnholz,
Johann Friedrich Handschuh and Mühlenberg
Halle, 18 March 1751

In this wide ranging and extensive letter we gain an insight into the way Francke brings his mind, imagination and administrative skill to bear on directing, counselling and cautioning the three pioneer Pennsylvania pastors who have to deal with a myriad of problems and challenges. Most pressing among these challenges is the need for additional pastors to serve an ever expanding field of work. There is Francke's usual word of caution against accepting candidates too readily for the ministry who had come running on their own. And there are personal problems, like the poor health of Brunnholz and Handschuh, the diminishing strength of Mühlenberg and difficulties arising from the marriage of one of the younger and less experienced pastors. But especially noteworthy is Francke's consent to a proposal of entering into a closer working relationship with three Swedish pastors who had just arrived to take up their responsibilities.

Text in German: Korrespondenz *1:391-99. For further textual information see* Korrespondenz *1:399.*

To the Pastors
of the United Congregations in Pennsylvania
Messrs. Mühlenberg, Brunnholz and Handschuch

18 March 1751

Reverend,
My dearly beloved Brothers in the Lord:

From the enclosed Letter A[1] it will be evident what I have received from each you, what I have sent to you and concerning the arrival of which I have not yet been assured. I shall reserve separate letters for that which concerns each worthy person individually. However, by this means I have resolved to report on concerns related to God's work in general among you.

1. First of all it grieves my heart that not only worthy Pastor Brunnholz[2] and the worthy Pastor Handschuch[3] still find their bodily strength very impaired and have been subjected until now to severe illnesses but also that the strength of worthy Pastor Mühlenberg has diminished somewhat. This condition has caused some anxiety in my soul on your account, especially since the first two mentioned are not equal to the overwhelming work in their large congregations, and one can well see in advance that they will

succumb to it shortly without receiving relief and more help.

2. Consequently, Court Preacher Ziegenhagen and I, having appealed to God, have reached the decision, in response to the desire mentioned in a number of previous letters for several new helpers, to search for two new coworkers and to cover the cost of travel from the charitable donations that are flowing in here and in England. Not only had one candidate by the name of Schulze[4] already indicated his willingness to accept the call last year, but there was also at the beginning of February a second person, H. Gieseler from Minden,[5] who was willing to follow him. For this purpose he had already received the consent of his mother who was still living at the time. However, when his mother changed her mind completely, the latter candidate permitted himself to be weakened and affected by her and her lamentable letters and he reneged on his word. But then also a number of difficulties surfaced with respect to the first candidate. One harbored all the more reservations about allowing him to travel by himself since Pastor Brunnholz had written in his letter of 21 August 1750: *We are afraid to request some one from Halle on account of the heavy expenses for travel and other difficulties.*[6] For even if the reason on account of the travel expenses had fallen away and I had not had reservations about proceeding, nevertheless the necessity of sending off several laborers would have been evident to me, had I seen that God in his providence had taken the lead with his footprints. Moreover, I did not have the courage to proceed further in the matter without the guidance of God since the obstacles and reservations which had developed suggested that his time did not appear to have come. This is especially the case now, since I did not see the slightest possibility of finding one, much less two persons quickly who could still be sent off in May on departing ships. However, if God wants to direct us to capable persons and you request it, both for the sake of your own weakness and on account of the desire of several congregations I am in all sincerity prepared to send a couple of persons next year. Before I add anything further which should be taken into account with this intention I must explain my opinion concerning several other points contained in your letters. In so doing it may please Court Preacher Ziegenhagen to have Court Preacher Albinus[7] report whether they agree with my opinion or what else they still find that they want to call to mind.

3. I cannot consider it advisable to separate the congregations in Philadelphia and Germantown as the former requested at the Synod assembly.[8] For, (1) as far as I know, acceptance of the latter occurred with the consent of the former; for that reason it does not now have occasion to complain concerning the arrangement. (2) The latter contributes to the support of the pastor without which it would not be possible for him to

manage in this location where it is most expensive to live and where he has
the greatest following. For Pastor Brunnholz[9] even though until now he has
remained unmarried was not able to save anything but has had to manage
carefully; furthermore, if he wanted to marry in accordance with God's will,
since in view of his frailty a helpmeet appears probably necessary for him,
he could not make ends meet. (3) I also think it is beneficial for the welfare
of the congregations that Pastor Brunnholtz retain both congregations
together, partly so that both congregations develop closer relationships,
partly on account of the greater experience and authority of Pastor
Brunnholtz which a junior person would first have to attain. However,
because in the meantime he is not equal to his task alone an assistant pastor
or helper must be appointed in both congregations. It is indeed highly
appropriate for the congregations to pool their resources for the required
support of such a person without burdening the pastor. I also do not doubt
that the members of both congregations will recognize that it is all the more
appropriate that they exert themselves somewhat more in contributing to the
support of their pastors, each one in accordance with what the Lord has
given them in temporal means. For Court Preacher Ziegenhagen and I spare
no pains to provide them not only with faithful and upright pastors who also
in their conscience will be known as upright servants of Christ but also to
gather charitable donations for their very costly building of churches. With
the help of these charitable donations more than half of the debts incurred
in Philadelphia, not to mention others, can be paid off. To this endeavor we
likewise hope that God will also continue to grant his grace and blessing. At
the present time both congregations, but especially the one in Philadelphia
which has just been mentioned, still have a debt which is not insignificant.
Indeed, I recognize very well that the interest they have to pay on it will
make it burdensome for them to raise a large salary for such a second
pastor. Under these difficult circumstances one will be quite satisfied if
enough comes together so that such a person could just manage to scrape
through either until circumstances surrounding the congregations improve
or he can be moved to other congregations and receive a better salary. All
auditors will be convinced that we do not at all require their pastors have a
large surplus or lay up treasures, that this has not been the intention of those
who have until now walked among them--they do not seek the wool of the
sheep but the sheep themselves. However, in the meantime they do want to
live. It is the congregations which would suffer the greatest loss if as a
consequence of their frailty and much work the pastors would suffer from
the lack of necessary care and on that account bring their life and work to
a premature end. One will gladly have patience with those who do not have
much if only each one also contributes a little to their support. I hope,

however, that they whom God has blessed more richly or those whom he still will bless will also contribute from their surplus all the more for the good of the whole congregation. Among those who have until now remitted several contributions for payment of church debts there are some who have nothing left over for themselves; from their poverty they have given a mite almost beyond their capability. Why should not the members of the congregation also apply something that is in their best interest? They also cannot bequeath to their children a greater treasure than when in their time they bring the institutions of church and school into a good and better state, for this is something their children after them will also enjoy. Now because in addition to that which is specifically designated for the payment of church debts, many a contribution has come in and presumably will come in for the advancement of church and schools, for this reason we want to assume the travel expenses of several assistants for this time. As mentioned previously, one of them could be engaged for a time as assistant pastor in Philadelphia and Germantown. I leave the arrangement of this completely to the discretion of the worthy pastors. Since we intend to assume the travel expenses, the congregations will no doubt be willing to provide for the necessary support. In return, the congregations will have the advantage that when a church service is held every Sunday in both places all the more will also come in via the collection-bag. Besides, this arrangement whereby both congregations would have two pastors in common would also have the great benefit that if one of them should become ill either congregation could make use of the ministry of the other one in cases of emergency among the sick and the dying. That same person could alternate in attending to the church service on Sundays.

4. From the diary of Pastor Handschuch[10] I gather that he, too, is overburdened with more work than the strength of one man can bear. Consequently, in view of his frailty an assistant is similarly indispensible for him. In this situation the congregation can no less fail to provide for that one's support. The pastors will therefore present this matter in a variety of ways both to the congregation in Philadelphia and Germantown and the congregation in Lancaster in accordance with the reasons contained under the previous point. These reasons also apply in part to the latter congregation, of which still many more could be adduced. In Court Preacher Ziegenhagen's and my name the congregations could be admonished to contribute willingly and requested to contribute to the maintenance of their pastors, not grudgingly but freely and out of sincere love for those who instruct them, Galatians 6:5, as well as with a joyful heart, 2 Corinthians 9:7, and out of a concern for the salvation of the souls of their children and children's children. I submit for your further consideration whether in

Lancaster perhaps at first and for a time you would want the assistant at the same time to attend to the school, as relief for the congregations and to provide a better livelihood for him. Perhaps then the one who had been used as a schoolmaster could easily be assigned to a school in another place. However that may be, if there is an assistant in Lancaster he can more readily at the same time serve a congregation situated nearby. Consequently, assistance in support of both pastors can be attained in this way.

5. Next: it is still a highly questionable matter for me that you want to call Pastor Hartwich[11] from his congregation to one that is vacant in Pennsylvania. (1) Such an arrangement could lead to some reproach on the part of the Ministerium in Hamburg and Doctor Kreuter[12] in London for it gives the appearance of seeking to attract to oneself men who have been sent by them. (2) Even more to the point, I find it very offensive that this man longs so much to get away from the congregation to which he has been duly called on account of adversities he encountered there. This longing is not a sign of a faithful servant of Christ who ought rather to labor for souls with continuing patience in prayer and struggle until he either wins them over or until God calls him to another place without his own doing.[13] For that reason doubts remain concerning his integrity. (3) Even if in the main matters are fairly correct, the question still remains whether the basic nature of Christianity has developed in him and whether a sincere disposition directed only to the honor of Christ has been effected in him, so that one might expect him to be joined to you all in one mind and spirit in the same way as all of you together stand as one in a bond of union before the Lord. (4) Also, it should be observed that a disposition of this kind is inclined to be domineering from which in the future evil consequences would arise. It would be a different matter if he were driven out of his own congregations through no fault of his own. That is the way I understood the situation when I stated in previous letters that, other things being equal,[14] I would leave it to your discretion.[15]

6. As far as Mr. Rauss[16] is concerned, I cannot deny that I got the idea from the curriculum vitae he drafted that he may not have decided to go to Pennsylvania for the best of reasons; also that his whole disposition is such that you have reason to be on your guard dealing with him. Nevertheless, the sincere love with which you have received him is certainly in accord with the spirit of Jesus Christ. Consequently, I do not disapprove that you have retained him and have sought to use him as much as you can in view of such a shortage of workmen.[17] Only in the future you will also employ the necessary care and test him sufficiently before you involve yourself with him further. It would at least not be advisable to accept him as assistant pastor or helper in Philadelphia in such a manner that thereby a door would

be opened to him to attain there at some time a position of chief pastor. In fact, it would be most advisable in both places either to take a helper on temporarily, as was just mentioned in the case of Philadelphia, or at least to arrange matters in such a way that in future situations this helper would not necessarily succeed the chief pastor. Rather it should be at the discretion of the United Ministerium whom they would elect to this important position and how they would consider it appropriate to place the assistant somewhere better after he has persevered for a time in less favorable circumstances.

7. As far as Mr. Weygand[18] is concerned, his father-in-law, van Dieren,[19] is not known to me; but, as much as I can gather from the addition that he no longer has a congregation, he must otherwise have served well as pastor and, according to Weygand's diary, the people must have considered him a Moravian. However, the diary does not report whether this marriage took place in consultation with you and with your consent, as would be appropriate, and whether he has hit it right in the choice of this person in respect to both the nature of her disposition and the circumstances of her parents. Consequently, I can also not know whether the congregation has reason to be angry with him, especially since similar discontent and grumbling also surfaced on the occasion of the worthy Pastor Handschuch's marriage presumably because previously others had hoped to get him for their daughters.[20] Otherwise, I learn this much from Mr. Weygand's diary[21] that he appears nevertheless quite faithfully to take to heart the congregation in accordance with his understanding. More experience and wisdom, however, are required under these circumstances, and it would be desirable for you to be nearer to him and thus better to help him in his difficulties. You will know best, at least better than we in Europe can know, what may be significant in the whole context of his conduct. Also, at one time a complaint was registered against him, communicated in private correspondence, and he was taken to task for a matter, which however, was not identified.[22] Should his disposition therefore not be quite dependable it would be better if he were near you for a time. But I also do not know whether a change for this purpose would be advisable or also feasible, especially since he has married, and moving would be complicated and expensive. Under these circumstances I must leave everything to your good judgment alone. Even if he only demonstrates a measure of true faithfulness in the care of souls, one can still thank the Lord that he is there and he can keep the Raritan[23] congregation in fairly good order.

8. I hope it has not come to pass that Mr. Hartwich is serving the congregations to which you were willing to some degree to call him. If this has happened[24] the congregations for which Mr. Hartwich has cared until now could be looked after most suitably first of all for a time by an

assistant, as occurred in Tulpehocken, York and Raritan.

9. If therefore you should request sending two new laborers next spring, then, with Mr. Rauss, you would have three assistants. One of these could remain in Philadelphia, the second one could go to Lancaster and the third one could be sent for a time to the congregations now under discussion. Of these one or another could get away sometimes for a few weeks to relieve Pastor Mühlenberg and to visit other congregations on their request. Should the congregations in Philadelphia and Lancaster not agree to an adequate contribution for their support at the very beginning, I hope God will bestow that much in the collection so that if need be what is still required can be extended to them from here. In this way these responsibilities will not become a burden exceeding the ability of Pastors Brunnholtz and Handschuch to bear it. It is not necessary, however, to say anything about this arrangement to the congregations or assistants either in advance or afterwards, so that the congregations do not rely on it. I also find it acceptable that Mr. Rauss's transportation costs will be compensated for out of the collections. Also, if you should have reservations about ordaining Mr. Rauss, the two co-workers sent from here could also be used all the better in the administration of the sacraments. Also, it has already been approved by Court Preacher Ziegenhagen that these men would be ordained in Germany before sending them. With this in view it would not be unsuitable for you to submit a brief document, signed by the three of you, in which you would request two ordained candidates as assistants in your Ministerium which could be enclosed or inserted in the call. For this purpose it should be only directed to me because otherwise Court Preacher Ziegenhagen would have to subscribe the call before the ordination which would greatly complicate matters.

10. It would be entirely satisfactory to prepare Mr. Schrenck,[25] candidate of law, as catechist and use him in that capacity inasmuch as you have found him to be quite satisfactory until now.

11. I am also very pleased that Mr. Schaum and Mr. Kurtz are still getting on well in their congregations and that their progress in experience, faithfulness, docility and wisdom is becoming apparent; also, that the marriage of the latter is turning out well.[26]

12. Especially and above all, however, I praise the Lord that he has bound the hearts of all of you to one another in fraternal and intimate love and that you are engaged in promoting God's cause so splendidly in one and the same spirit, seeking the salvation and well being of souls and assisting, counseling and helping one another in a brotherly way in the process. In this way you can compensate for the lack of not having anyone nearby through whom you could be strengthened and refreshed. Such compensation can

offer you a great deal of relief under your heavy burden. May the Lord sustain this bond of love also as the chief means whereby the good organization which has been established may be maintained and all disturbances can be precluded or quashed which strange heads may stir up in the congregations.

13. Since the three new Swedish pastors[27] also seek your love and friendship and it has even become evident to their superiors that the Lord has blessed your undertaking until now, so that they have been moved to direct them to unite with you, this development should also be viewed as a kindness of God. And if, as Pastor Brunnholtz writes, all three are upright men, it will probably contribute to some advancement of what is good if you receive them into the fellowship of your Ministerium at their request. It should, however, be done in such a way that you and they remain two divisions. The Germans should not interfere nor prevent something that is good among the Swedes nor should the Swedes do so among the Germans; rather all could in common promote the work of the Lord and all good arrangements and order but restrain all disorders.

14. The decision at the last synod[28] to elect annually a superintendent of all congregations can no less serve the cause of good order. Such an arrangement is similarly very good as long as the three of you are alone and others do not enter your assembly who are not completely of one mind with you.

15. I still want to call to mind that it would be good if you were to agree at the Synod that nothing be undertaken without prior consultation with the pastor and without his explicit consent when building and making necessary repairs here and there in the churches. For afterwards the pastors still have to do the most in the collection of the money necessary for payment. For this reason they are also entitled to judge in advance whether the undertaking is not only useful but also necessary and indispensable.

16. By the way, I was greatly saddened that the Reformed in Philadelphia have brought about such a great split, and so many irritating upsets have occurred in the process.[29] Consequently, you have done well not to get mixed up with it. Would that God would also control such offensive and damaging behavior and heal that which is rent among the Reformed for, as a result of numerous relationships, this split will also exert an influence in Lutheran congregations.

17. Concerning your salaries it just occurs to me that at least in the future (even if at present it might still be a problem) it would be a better arrangement if the one who keeps the church accounts were to collect the contribution of each one and deliver it to the pastor (in that way, whatever is not received, could be replaced from church monies). This procedure

would be better than that the pastors themselves do the collecting (if that has been the practice until now, since I am not aware of a different way). This method is not only a great burden but also becomes more burdensome when urging those to give who do not gladly do so; on this account I presume that you must suffer many a loss in membership.

18. Finally, I hereby pass along to you a letter under Letter B[30] from Colonel von Münchhausen at Steyerberg[31] (who several years ago paid out the legacy bequeathed by Canon Berner,[32] from which the Pennsylvania congregations received a portion). In the Memorandum, Letter C,[33] I report in what way I think this gentleman could be served reasonably well. It could be that by obliging such a gentleman in this way he could be persuaded to render some benefactions. For that reason I also do not wish to turn down his request altogether. Perhaps Mr. Vigera,[34] to whom I extend sincere greetings, would be so kind as to provide for a collection, preservation and sending of several kinds of seeds because I know full well that you have too much work to occupy yourselves with the matter.

May the Lord graciously continue to assist you, to strengthen you mightily in all weakness and refresh you with ample fruits of your ministry in the congregations! With the arrival of the first ships I expect an answer to the most necessary points. With sincere commendation to the protection of the Lord, I remain

Halle, 18 March 1751   Your Reverences'
                                       My dearly beloved Brothers
                                       in the Lord,
                                       G.A. Francke

Letter A
Sent off to Pennsylvania:
1750, 20 February. Letter to Pastor Brunnholtz
8 July. Letter to Pastor Handschuh
9 July. Letter to Pastor Kurtz
29 July. Letter to Pastor Mühlenberg
25 September. Letter to Pastor Schaum
Arrived from there:
Letter from Pastor Brunnholtz, dated 3 July 1749. Various matters sent off from Philadelphia on 8 March 1750 along with their identification by Pastor Brunnholtz.
Letter from Pastor Handschuch, dated 21 May 1750.

Letter from Pastor Brunnholtz, dated 21 August, along with a written statement listing all enclosures.

Letter from the same, dated 13 November, along with a beaver pelt.

Letter C
Memorandum

To satisfy the request of Lord von Münchhausen somewhat, an experiment could be made to collect some of the most rare flowers and smaller plants and to send seeds from these. To make sure these do not spoil while under way, the seeds would have to be thoroughly ripened, gathered during dry weather, also in addition dried out a bit in the open air and placed in well secured glass containers. These would then be packed in a small box sealed with pitch. The glasses could be secured with a cork and tied up with a moistened bullock's bladder which, however, must be thoroughly dried before packing. A little note should be pasted on each glass with bookbinder's paste on which the name of the plant is entered. For each plant a complete report should be made along with instructions about what should be observed in its tending and propagation. If you incur some expenses in the process Lord von Münchhausen will compensate you for them. Also in the process some one knowledgeable in gardening could also be called on for advice.

---

1. See p.109.
2. On Peter Brunnholz, see Letter 71 n.3.
3. On Johann Friedrich Handschuh, see *Correspondence* 1:291 nn.18 and 19.
4. Born in Königsberg in the former German state of East Prussia in 1726, Friedrich Schultze studied theology at the university there from 1743-48. Thereafter he studied in Halle where he became a teacher in one of the schools. With Johann Dietrich Heinzelmann he travelled to Pennsylvania at the request of Francke. See *Pastors and People* 1:124-25.
5. Born in Minden in 1726, Johann Arnold Gieseler studied in Halle from 1748 on and subsequently became a teacher there in the orphanage school. For further details see *Korrespondenz* 1:399 n.3.
6. This quotation from the letter of Brunnholz is in italics in the text.
7. On Samuel Theodor Albinus, see *Correspondence* 1:154 n.8.
8. Francke is referring to the request of the congregation in Philadelphia to the Synod assembly, 18 June 1750. The request is contained in the minutes of the assembly and reads, "8. The humble petition of the Church Council of the congregation of Philadelphia, to keep Pastor Brunnholz for themselves alone, and free him from the Germantown congregation, was read by Pastor Mühlenberg, and the information given them that without the knowledge and permission of the Fathers in Europe, we were not authorized to make any changes; we had written to the Superiors in Europe in November already of the previous year; they must have patience until the answer is received. With this they were satisfied." See *Documentary History*, p. 31; see also *HN2/1*:472.
9. See *Pastors and People* 1:23.
10. Francke may be referring to Handschuh's diary of 1749 which indicates that Handschuh was overly conscientious in discharging his responsibilities to his congregation in Lancaster. In this diary he expresses the feeling that he does not know how long he will live since his strength and energy

are diminishing daily. See *HN2/1*:542. - From this and similar references in Handschuh's diary Francke may have inferred that Handschuh needed an assistant.

11. See *Correspondence* 1:323 n. 19 and *Korrespondenz* 1:400 n.4 for details concerning Johann Christoph Hartwich.

12. Philip David Kreuter was a pastor of the German Hamburg or Trinity Church in Trinity Lane, London, England. He demitted the ministry and settled in a county seat near Bath. See Johann Gottlieb Burckhardt, *Kirchengeschichte der Deutschen Gemeinden in London nebst historischen Beilagen und Predigten* (Tübingen: Ludwig Friedrich Fues, 1798), p. 107; see also *Korrespondenz* 1:400 n.8.

13. Hartwich had expressed the desire to receive a call to Pennsylvania. See Letter 76:44.

14. The text reads *ceteris paribus*. At this point Francke deleted the following sentence, "But if this should already have occurred that you have involved yourself too much with him, then may God turn everything for the best and graciously ward off that which is to be feared. Besides I recognize very well indeed that in the circumstances obtaining there you could get into such a predicament that you would do something which one would not do if one could help one's self the way one wanted to." See *Korrespondenz* 1:400 n.10.

15. As of October 1750 Hartwich was installed as assistant to Peter Brunnholz in Philadelphia. At the same time Hartwich was to serve the congregations in Old Goshenhoppen and Indianfield. Lucas Rauss took Hartwich's place in Rhinebeck and Camp, New York. See *HN2/1*:517; *Journals* 1:259.

16. On Lucas Rauss, see Letter 76 n.72.

17. The text reads *in tanta penuria operariorum*.

18. On Johann Albert Weygand, see Letter 71 n.21.

19. On Johann Bernhard van Dieren, see Letter 78 n.26.

20. *HN2/1*:321 introduces Handschuh's report of his marriage and related matters saying it is "interesting." Found in *Journals* 1:238-40, the report tells us how Handschuh had determined never to marry but that God changed his mind, that the girl he married had been his housekeeper for three months, was of rather lowly social origin and that most members of the Lancaster congregation's council were up in arms for not having been consulted previously concerning the matter, etc. Nevertheless, Mühlenberg himself officiated at the wedding of Handschuh and Susanne Barbara Belzner in the Lancaster church on 1 May 1750.

21. See the excerpt from Weygand's diary in 1749 in *HN2/1*:207.

22. It was not possible to establish what was involved.

23. See *Pastors and People* 1:50-51.

24. Concerning this occurrence, see n.15.

25. On Ludolph Heinrich Schrenck, see Letter 78 n.7.

26. On Johann Nicolaus Kurz, see *Correspondence* 1:154 n.5 and 341 n.16. On Johann Helfrich Schaum, see Letter 71 n.9.

27. Israel Acrelius (arrived 1749), Olaf Parlin (arrived 1750) and Erik Unander (arrived 1749). In a letter of 21 August 1750 Brunnholz reported, "They [the three Swedish pastors] have under consideration a plan to create a Ministerium with us and to maintain fellowship because, as the new Provost Acrelius says, he has an order to this effect in his instruction. Provost Acrelius occupies the position of Mr. Tranberg in Wilmington, Mr. Unander is where Provost Sandin had been, and the third one, Mr. Perlin, is here in the city in Mr. Naesman's place." See Letter 80 nn.1 and 3; Letter 88 n.3.

28. At its meeting 18 June 1750 the Synod adopted the following resolution, "Pastor Mühlenberg's proposition concerning the necessity of a Superintendent over all our United Congregations, to be elected yearly. To this office, although one of the Philadelphia Council objected because of his delicate health and numerous duties, Pastor Brunnholz was elected for this year." See *Documentary History*, p. 30.

29. See Letter 75 n.2.

30. Not extant.

31. Baron Otto von Münchhausen (1716-74).

32. See Letter 71:4 and the account of the Pennsylvania congregations for 1748 and 1749 in *HN2/1*:326.
33. See p.110
34. On Johann Christoph Vigera, see *Correspondence* 1:145 n.3.

Letter 90

To the Dutch Church Council in New York
Providence, 2 April 1751

The conversation and correspondence Mühlenberg had with the Dutch Lutheran congregation in New York has culminated in his acceptance of their call on a temporary basis. The uneasiness his acceptance, though temporary, has caused in his congregations has contributed to his decision to leave his family behind as "hostages or pledges," as he says, that he will return to his congregations. Also it seems that competing religious groups who Mühlenberg feels did not wish him or his congregations well have made it difficult for him to make the move to New York.

Text in English: Korrespondenz 1:402-3. *For further textual information see* Korrespondenz 1:403. *This letter, written in English, is given here in its original form.*

Gentlemen and Brethren in Christ.

After having received your favour, both in a lawfull vocation and kind letter, dated 1t of Febr. 1750,[1] I aquainted our Congregations with the Contents of them, called the Ministry of our Church and conferred the notes about the matter in question. I humbly thank you Gentlemen for the Confidence you repose in me and give the following Answer: 1) Myn intended removeal createth a great deal of uneasiness amongst the good and well-minded peopel of our Congregations, and occasioneth many speculations and reflections amongst the sects and parties where our Congregations are surrounded with. The uneasiness of our peopel ariseth not for want of love to our brethren in New York, but they think it hard to se me absent, before death us do part because we have lived together about nine years as it were in a state of spiritual Matrimony, in sickness and health, forsaken all other and born many Hardships for preserving sound doctrine and promoting true piety and Godliness according to the Word of God, and the Augustan Confession in spite of our foes. Sectarians will no less find faults in my removing to New York, making a noise for their Interest. They tell the peopel, I had no other Argument for leaving Pensylvania then to get more money, though I have never complained about salary, and must indeed confess by Experience, the Lord hath added the Rest, when I sought his Kingdom first.[2] The speculations of the latter I dont mind, being well used in Pensylvania to wade by the Assistance of God, on the right and left hand through honour and dishonour, through evil and good report, as deceiver and yet true—as having nothing, and yet possessing all things 2 Cor: VI.[3] 2) All the concurring Circumstances will at present allow no more, then to accept your lawfull vocation together with its contents first for one part of the time, mentioned in your Call. In the which, we may, if the Lord spareth my life, see, how things will, go on; both in New York and Pensylvania.

3) As to my temporal Affairs, I must leave my family behind for many reasons, and especially for Hostages or pledges to my beloved Congregations, and come perhaps with a waitman, that is able to attend and to help me keeping shool in the personage, if young peopel of the Congregation desire to be instructed and the Rev: Vestry will allow it.

4) the day of my departure from Pensylvania can be no sooner, then the 13 of May,[4] and if I could reach New York in two days, would give the first sermon on the sixtenth of May, that is on the Ascension day of Christ. It is impossibel for me to come sooner, being incumbred with many sorts of Labour, and besides all, must take my leave from several Congregations, before I can begin the Journey. In the mean while the Reverend Mr. Hartwich,[5] will if possibel return to his respective Congregations and pass through New York. He may give a sermon, if the Rev. Vestry desire it. May it please the Lord to enable me with strength for soul and Body to serve for the Glory of his holy Name and the well fare of my fellow=Christians, and to uphold and encrease your good zeal for the Edification of our destitute Church in New York, whose humble servant I remain, with humble respect and love to you, Worthy Gentlemen and your families.

Providence the 2 day
of April 1751   H.M. Mühlenberg

---

1. While the letter itself is not extant, Mühlenberg's entry in his diary in February 1751 gives us a clue to its contents: "*In the meantime* I received a call from New York for a two-year trial...*I looked upon* this as having come not altogether without divine influence and I expected...to move away for several years with my family and install Pastor Handshue in my residence and congregations. I mentioned the matter confidentially to the deacons of both my congregations in a preliminary way..." See *Journals* 1:269. Mühlenberg has erroneously dated the letter 1750 instead of 1751.
2. See Matt. 6:33.
3. 2 Cor. 6:7,8,10.
4. On 14 May 1751 Mühlenberg and Hartwich set out for New York, the latter to his former congregations in Rhinebeck and Camp; see *Journals* 1:276. On 17 May in the evening they arrived in New York; see *Journals* 1:278.
5. On Johann Christoph Hartwich, see *Correspondence* 1:323 n.19.

Letter 91

To Tobias Wagner
Providence, 24 April 1751

*Perhaps because differences of opinion existed between Mühlenberg and
Tobias Wagner from time to time, Mühlenberg seems to have gone out of his
way to extend an invitation to Wagner to the forthcoming synod assembly in
an especially cordial manner by providing reasons for appointing a date
earlier than expected for the meeting.*
Text in German: Korrespondenz *1:403-4. For further textual information
see* Korrespondenz *1:404.*

Reverend Pastor,
Very learned Magister,[1]
Most worthy Patron and Colleague:
With these present lines I am taking the liberty to inquire concerning
your well-being and that of your worthy family and dutifully to carry out the
assignment given me by our Assembly to invite Your Reverence to our
forthcoming fraternal conference. Initially we were minded to postpone our
gathering to the fall. However, because my trip to New York will require
one or another minor changes during the coming year; also because all of
those present selected the month of May for the ensuing conference; and
because various elders of congregations who were present also insisted on
this appointment; therefore we had to move as quickly as possible and we
have to convene on the twelfth day of the coming month of May.[2] Dear
colleague, we cherish the certain hope that you, along with several
congregation elders, will accede to our well intentioned plea to honor us, if
possible, with your personal presence and to allow us to profit from the gifts
of grace and office God has granted you for the benefit of our young
congregations in general and especially for our edification.[3] With a thankful
heart we shall acknowledge this before God as an expression of special love
and good will and for the rest of our lives we will consider ourselves, and
in particular I will consider myself

Providence   Your Reverence's,
24 April 1751   Our kind patron's and colleague's obliging servant
                    Heinrich Melchior Mühlenberg

---

1. On Tobias Wagner, see Letter 71A n.3. Wagner was awarded the master's degree from the
University of Tübingen in 1725.

2. Mühlenberg refers to the revised schedule for holding the conference in his diary on 2 April 1751 saying, "I had agreed with my colleague, Mr. Brunnholtz, that we would postpone our synod until I returned from New York, but several elders from the Philadelphia and Providence congregations insisted that it should be held before I went away and at the time which had been appointed at the preceding meeting, that is, in the month of May. Consequently we were required to make preparations for it. The president set the date for May 12 and 13 and sent notice to all the United Congregations and preachers and ordered me to write to Magister Wagner." See *Journals* 1:275.

3. The Fourth Convention of the United Congregations was indeed held on 12 and 13 May 1751. Its proceedings appear in the form of Mühlenberg's report in his diary (*Journals* 1:276), in Johann Friedrich Handschuh's report (*HN2/1*:688-89) and in *Documentary History*, pp. 33-35. However, the *Documentary History* report does not include the name of Wagner as among those who were present at the Convention. Only Mühlenberg's report of the Convention's proceedings on 13 May mentions Wagner as being present.

Letter 92

To Peter Brunnholz
Providence, 26 April 1751

This letter, in the form of a memorandum, lays bare Mühlenberg's reasons for desiring a closer relationship with pastors of the Swedish Church in southeastern Pennsylvania, New Jersey and Delaware. The invitation Mühlenberg issues to the Swedish Lutheran pastors to the forthcoming synodical meeting provides an insight into his churchmanship and into the discretion with which the invitation is extended.

Text in English: Korrespondenz *1:404-5; Landsarchivet, 575104, Uppsala, Sweden; Swenson's Immigration Research Center, Augustana College, Rock Island, Illinois. For further textual information see* Korrespondenz *1:405. This letter, written in English, is given here in its original form.*

Memorandum

Dear Brother Mr. Brunnholtz.[1]

Whereas Necessity requireth to call the Ministry and some Elders of our united german protestant Lutheran Congregations together for the yearly brotherly Meeting towards Philadelphia on the 12 day of May before I go to Newyork, I beg the favour therefore, you will humbly invite and beseech the Reverend Ministry of the Swedish Church, if they would please to honour our Meeting with their presence.[2] I have the following reasons for it: 1) We had the honour in our time, to live, though but a short period, with the late Right Rev: provost Sandin,[3] the Rev: pastor Tranberg,[4] and Mr. Kock[5] in a blessed Harmony and true love. 2) We are sure of the present Right Rev: provost Mr. Acrelius[6] and the Reverend Ministry, that our Meeting will, by their blessed Gifts, talents and Experience in spiritual matter be edifyed and instructed. 3) We stand in the nearest relation with the Rever: Ministry of the Swedish Church according to the Augustan Confession and its Oeconomy. 4) We live in a country where our infant protestant Lutheran Church is surrounded with allmost innumerable parties, sects and enimies and need therefore to keep together as close as possible for the common Wellfare of the whole Church. 5) The Rev: Ministry of the sw: Church will, I hope, not be afraid, as if we would impose the least upon their rights, ordres an Constitutions lawfully setled and used from the beginning of their divine service in America, much less do we expect to reap any temporal Advantage, Interest vain Glory or the like by our invitation, but desire only to wait upon the Reverend Gentleman as our brethren in Christ, as Administrators addicted together with us to the same principles and Augustan Confession, as Counsellors for the spiritual Increase and Interest of the whole Church. 6) And in case the Reverend Ministry should fear, their Visitor presence in our Meeting would give an Umbrage or preiudice to their Superiors in Europa, They might please to frequent our Meeting at first once or twice in Quality of charitable Neighbours, or Evidences or impartial Judges and see, wether the Meeting is agreable unto them, of some service for the whole in general or for its parts in particular or not? this is at present my opinion, to which I add: prove all things; hold fast that which is good.[7]

Provid: th. 26 of April 1751   H.M. Mühlenberg

---

1. Presumably Mühlenberg requested Peter Brunnholz in this memorandum to issue the invitation to the Swedish pastors to attend the synod meeting on the 12 and 13 May 1751 because Brunnholz understood the Swedish language. In his letter to the Swedish Provost, Israel Acrelius, Mühlenberg seems to have relied on Brunnholz to serve as intermediary between him and Acrelius because Brunnholtz understood Swedish (Letter 80:71). In a letter of 21 May 1750, addressed to the Court Preacher Friedrich Michael Ziegenhagen in London and Gotthilf August Francke in Halle, Brunnholz refers to the arrival of the three Swedish pastors: Israel Acrelius, Erik Unander and Olaf Perlin. Brunnholz says they brought with them Swedish tracts directed against the Moravians, some of which they gave him "because I understand the Swedish language" (*HN2/1:*530). As a native of the Danish region of Holstein he understood Swedish because of his understanding of Danish (*HN2/1:*83). However, the letter Brunnholz wrote to Acrelius inviting him and his colleagues to the synodical meeting on 12 and 13 May is in German. Dated 4 May 1751 the letter is in Svenska församlingen i Amerika, Uppsala Domkirka, Landsarkivet, S-75104 Uppsala, Sweden, and on microfilm at the Swedish Immigration Center, Augustana College, Rock Island, Illinois. On Peter Brunnholz, see Letter 71 n.3.
2. Mühlenberg is referring to the Fourth Convention of the United Congregations held in Philadelphia on 12 and 13 May 1751. See Letter 91:116 n.2.
3. On Johann Sandin, see Letter 80 n.4.
4. On Peter Tranberg, see *Correspondence* 1:62 n.17.
5. On Peter Koch, see *Correspondence* 1:53 n.20.
6. On Israel Acrelius, see Letter 80 n.1. See also *Journals* 1:276: "The Swedish Provost [Acrelius] visited us and I had a long conversation with him concerning Pennsylvania church affairs. He excused himself and expressed his regret that he would not be able to attend our convention on the following Sunday and Monday, as he had received notice of it too late and had extremely necessary work to do in his congregations. His colleague, the Swedish preacher in Philadelphia [HN: Mr. Berlin], would be present."
7. See 1 Thess. 5:21.

Letter 93

To Gotthilf August Francke and Friedrich Michael Ziegenhagen
New York, 15 June 1751

In this extensive report on pastors and congregations in Pennsylvania, Mühlenberg intermingles descriptions of his own inadequacies in body and soul to carry out the responsibilities of his high office with pleas to the Reverend Fathers in London and Halle to send capable and qualified pastors to minister to people in an ever expanding field.

Ill and depressed after being in New York for six weeks, Mühlenberg points out in this letter that he has accepted the call to the New York congregation to heal the rift between the disaffected Germans and the Dutch. He complains especially about the Germans who are disinclined to reestablish harmony and stubbornly have gone their way in calling a pastor whose credentials are open to question. Mühlenberg also reports on the work of his fellow pastors and some personal matters relating to them. He asks his superiors not to reveal his comments to them even though he discusses their ministries in his journals. All in all, the poignancy apparent in Mühlenberg's openness in personal and professional matters makes this one of his more engaging letters.

Text in German: Korrespondenz *1:406-15. For further textual information see* Korrespondenz *1:415.*

Very Reverend Fathers and Sirs,
Most kind Patrons and Benefactors:
Though my present circumstances leave little time for me to write to the Very Reverend Fathers in a well ordered way, duty, nevertheless, demands that I grasp the opportunity which has presented itself and submit a bit of something to the best of my ability, having the certain confidence that the Very Reverend Fathers will deign to excuse what is not well ordered in it.
At the present time I am living in New York and my family in New Providence.[1] The purpose of my being here is to make an attempt at uniting the Dutch and German Lutheran congregation which is torn apart.[2] The reasons for accepting the call[3] without having consulted the Very Reverend Fathers first appeared adequate to me and my brothers; they will most humbly be presented in their context in my journal to the Very Reverend Fathers for their opinion at the earliest opportunity.[4] These reasons will also clearly indicate, as I hope, that I was not intentionally hasty or negligent but wanted to look to the guidance of God. Accordingly, on this occasion I shall

speak to my Very Reverend Fathers in childlike simplicity with complete openness and obediently request that you excuse my indiscretion and not communicate to others what I have written here.

1) During the past nine-and-one-half years of my being here I have experienced many challenges and temptations in part on account of my person, in part also because of my calling. According to the measure of my gifts, the position of a catechist or a rural school teacher would still be too lofty and important for me, to say nothing of the kind of position which because of the circumstances is dangerous, complicated and delicate and for which I do not possess the aptitude or gifts. This situation shows clearly the great lack of able and adequate laborers in the harvest for which we should pray.[5] Given the physical shortage in external buildings and scaffolding, the thought has troubled me why the Very Reverend Fathers did not send laborers ten or twelve years earlier? After all, the charge had been given them and, from an external point of view, they could have gained several hundred pounds because land and equipment were still readily for sale and easily acquired. Moreover, people were not yet so pitiably scattered and poisoned by Moravian sectarianism. What could have been bought for one hundred pounds ten years before my arrival now costs a thousand pounds and more. Hence sects and parties have established themselves firmly, are in possession of the best opportunities and funds for schools and propagation of their teachings which are antichristian as well as damaging to the kingdom of Christ and counter to it. However, there is no opportunity for the propagation of pure doctrine for which material support for those who serve school and church is lacking all over. This mist of unbelief has often been a source of temptation for me, but I also know that the Lord has his own time and moments and that his thoughts are infinitely different from mine.[6] The kingdom of the Lord Jesus is not of this world, etc., etc.[7]

As far as the administration of my office of the ministry is concerned, its success demonstrates that the all wise and gracious God has not exposed my great errors and weaknesses to the light but for the sake of his name and honor has covered them. He has used me as a noisy gong and clanging cymbal,[8] to call together some of his poor, scattered, straying and badly lost sons and daughters. Given my feeling of great incompetence and uselessness for this important office of care of souls, I had no regard for life and health and charged headlong against my health. I thought that the sooner the ice is cracked a little, the sooner the door is opened, the sooner I am out of the way, the sooner the Very Reverend Fathers will have an opportunity to put better and more able laborers in place. They can spread the kingdom of Christ in America, build on the foundation of apostles and prophets[9] the sinners who have been called together and plant something which is permanent. *But* even in that respect I find very much imperfection. I am a poor wornout human being. I can no longer get on with my work as in the early years and still I cannot get the slightest relief in physical, crude work and hardships. Also, I do not have the gifts and skills to make the enterprise a distinguished one because it is indeed very difficult to turn a hoe into a pen, etc., etc.

My worthy brother in the ministry, Pastor Brunnholz,[10] entered an open door in Philadelphia and Germantown. He came full of spirit and life and put his shoulder willingly to the burden of outward building and inward care of souls; he advanced both areas beyond expectation and with blessing. He has been marvellously sustained by God, was rescued from death several times and has become the object of love and respect in the whole region, especially in our congregations. But it appears that one trial after another is hard on him and his condition is weak, so that I am afraid something to the disadvantage of all could occur if the Lord in his grace does not have mercy. For he has a young, choleric half-converted maidservant who may have become somewhat familiar with him in his sickly, weak circumstances and I suspect he may perhaps have had ideas to marry her or to be with her in the manner of brother and sister. Mr. Schleydorn[11] complained about it to me with alarm and young Rauss[12] also talked about it with me. I talked with him privately in love and earnestness and advised him to dismiss the maidservant, the sooner the better, etc., etc., for even if the matter was not what it appeared to be one should, nevertheless, also avoid even the appearance of impropriety.[13] Most obediently I beg the Very Reverend Fathers not to let anything at all of my letter become apparent but only to take the matter into consideration in their prayer. I cannot express how many temptations one is subjected to in Pennsylvania! One is all alone in one's outpost, lives far from others and is certainly in the most intense school between the black and white devils, as Luther puts it.[14] May the Lord save us from these and other temptations. No person in the world is more suitable for Philadelphia and Germantown than he if God will continue to strengthen and preserve him.

I and my colleague, Brunnholtz, have had indescribable trouble *with* the congregation in Lancaster, wresting it from the claws of the Moravians.[15] The door was open, but indeed to a wild, rough and foolish people. In accordance with the circumstance God pointed out to us, we appointed Pastor Handshue to that place.[16] He now had the opportunity to apply his learning, but especially his experience of the power of divine blessedness, to his office and position and to demonstrate his gifts, because at the time not a single pastor, the Moravians excepted, was as yet in the city. In brief, we had great hope that things would turn out well. And things went well into the second year: the congregation was brought together, the Moravian matter was pretty well dispelled, and the many sects pricked up their ears and said, "What is going to become of this?" But a great deal of patience and a great deal of wisdom are required to persevere under such trying circumstances, so that one continues in a middle course and does not go too far or not far enough. The dear brother has been in Europe a long time among awakened and pardoned children who always try to help one another to keep their spirits up and to keep their equilibrium, sometimes also lovingly to entertain and uplift one another. But here there was an entirely different situation, namely, it was like sheep being among wolves. Satan employs schemes and we are still poor apprentices and babes nourished with milk.[17] He is also harassed by a strange hypochondriacal illness;[18] for that reason somersaults and capers occur as a result of inexperience and weakness and not of malice. Out of sincere love and faithfulness he wanted to convert all at once the will of a congregation which was corrupted for so many years and whose understanding was still profoundly darkened and weighed down with many prejudices. We were intent on comforting him by word of mouth and in writing. When I now and then introduced my simple farmer's rules which I learned from Pennsylvania affairs, the dear brother was of the opinion that I did not understand and appreciate his many years of experience. But to convince him that I had indeed gained an insight into his conduct, gifts and experience from what he had told me, I put the course of his life into verse in several off hours during the night. In these I showed the grace and patience the Lord had already manifested in him and what he could still do in the future. I did this with the intention to cheer him up and support him in his despondency. In his sincere desire to convert his people he employed all kinds of reasons to move them, e.g., "I am on loan to you for only a short time," etc., etc. When a paroxysm of hypochondriacal illness[19] took hold he would say, "I am only here as a witness against you," etc., etc. "If only I knew of an upright man among elders and deacons," etc., etc. "What could my brothers have had in mind when they assigned me to this country and placed me in Sodom and Gomorrah?" etc., etc. People with little understanding could not comprehend this and were of the opinion that he was losing his mind. Sycophants also turned up diligently and played the hypocrites so that under the appearance of advancing what is good they might sneak in their private hatred of others. Nevertheless, everyone had to admit that his teaching was pure and his life without fault. A number of souls were awakened and some were also attracted from other sects and incorporated into the congregation. All of them showed patience with his weak and inaudible voice. Just as things were in fine fettle and people in their naivete thought their pastor was an angel who had only taken on a body in order to be visible but was no longer in need of anything transitory —because, to avoid slander but contrary to our advice, he also did not want to take any perquisites for the performance of marriage ceremonies for persons outside the congregation, etc. All of a sudden a marriage contract came into play with his housekeeper, a poor, common, yet chaste, honest person whose father was a tailor and deacon in the congregation. We knew nothing of it but were notified of it after the contract had been concluded.[20] The deacons and elders, with the exception of the father-in-law and brother-in-law, would have none of it, being of the opinion that his authority would cave in because the person in question was of common origin and had grown up with and among crude people in the city. Because she was also quite respectable and careful in her dress but previously frequented the fairs as a huckster with trinkets, gingerbread and that sort of thing, the ill-mannered gang of young men gave her all sorts of jaundiced names and epithets. Matters of this kind, they feared, would devolve upon the pastor, as I shall indicate in my diary.[21] The women in the congregation were also very offended at having to acknowledge and honor a girl so inexperienced as the spouse of their father confessor, etc.

Good brother Handshue was indeed confident but not as wise as the children of this world.[22] He extolled his loved one as a precious present and noble gift of God. He also said that she would become the crown of all women; but the women would not believe that and said she probably had danced at weddings like other crude people, and that sort of thing. In short, the contract was concluded and the marriage ceremony was performed. Now a great deal of commotion, grumbling, slander, abuse and backbiting arose in the whole countryside. Nevertheless, no one could truthfully prove that the couple had done anything wrong. The most prominent mopheads, elders and deacons for example, distanced themselves in part and did not concern themselves with the pastor's salary. Also, there was not much by way of perquisites. On Sundays the church was always full of people and remained that way, but they did not ask themselves whether he had something on which to live. Once authority, love and respect among rowdy people give way, matters take a wretched turn. We invited and asked delegates of the congregation to our annual conference but they sent none.[23] Pastor Stöver also profited from this, held meetings and administered the Lord's Supper now and then near the city among the dissatisfied.[24] The young married couple had to get along very miserably for a time because no salary came in. Several elders were surprised that we did not remove him from there since it had always been said that he was only on loan, etc. Finally we were obliged to call Pastor Handshue away from Lancaster and to take him for service among our first United Congregations, especially since I had to be away in New York for a time.[25] Thanks be to God, everyone, also Pastor Handshue's enemies, have to acknowledge that until now he has taught correctly and lived blamelessly in his married estate. Since we are human beings and can indeed see our failings as we look back but not in advance, it is not surprising that a person makes mistakes from time to time in how he proceeds,[26] and does not exactly hit the mark as the complex circumstances in this country might demand it. The faithful God can also create something good out of our weaknesses and mistakes. Once again I would humbly beg the Very Reverend Fathers not to let anything show or to make a remark concerning what I have noted here concerning my brothers, otherwise my colleagues will become suspicious of me and a rift could occur. However, as far as my own failings are concerned I shall gladly allow them to be censured and chastised. It is better for us to pray in secret[27] and have sympathy for we are weak instruments and surrounded with countless temptations. There is a time to complain as well as to rejoice. Among his saints no one is without fault, etc., etc.[28]

Our brother, Kurz, has a large field and many large congregations.[29] From earliest times on there have been hidden away among them not a few awakened and slumbering souls who should continue to be directed and strengthened. The dear brother has already experienced many a painful ride and hardship but he still continues to do gladly what he is able. His strong shouting voice is applauded among the country folk, and his ascetic phrases and expressions awaken; however, in other respects there is a lack of a natural and artificial logic,[30] the knowledge of natural and revealed theology[31] and the gift of edification in special relations. Consequently, the work he does remains static. But that sort of thing could probably be improved if the means of support were not so scarce. As far as material livelihood is concerned he has the best place and housing of all of us.

Mr. Schaum[32] is a poor sick brother. Last December he married the daughter of Balthasar Bickel, the most distinguished elder in Raritan.[33] During the long journey in cold weather he suffered bodily injury so that on one side he had a heavy swelling from the foot up to his hip and was burdened with severe pain. Finally, a wasting away set in so that on that side nothing but skin and bones could be seen on the leg. Some four months he lay in bed and he could not turn over on his own. Messrs. Handshue and Kurz visited him and preached in his congregation. They say he has reached the point that he can walk to church on crutches.[34] In body and soul he is weak and sort of muddles his way through with his voice and loud shouting. At one time also the poor child allowed himself to be taken advantage of while he was still living in Philadelphia. There was a flighty married woman who outwardly professed she belonged to our church but had the reputation of being a prostitute. Now and then he would go to bring her around to a better way of life. One evening he removed the gold or silver ring from the finger of the woman, put it in his pocket and took it home with him. When the husband came home and became aware that the ring was no longer there he asked his wife about it and she said Mr. Schaum had taken it away. The next day the man went to Mr. Schaum and brought the ring back. This came out and a godless, talkative shopkeeper who gads about in the region said everywhere that Mr. Schaum had indulged in fornication and committed theft. When Mr. Schaum was already in York this man also came there and announced it publicly. This annoyed the deacons and they bound the informer over to the next court session in Lancaster. The deed had not occurred but there was the appearance of evil. I knew nothing about it for I was just on an extended journey to see Mr. Hartwich in the New York region.[35] Otherwise I would have come to his assistance at his appearance before the magistrate, for the matter had already gone that far. Now when the public court day had begun, Mr. Schaum and his deacons did not put in an appearance against the accused. Consequently, several pounds for court costs and procedures devolved upon Mr. Schaum. The matter became known in the whole area and in neighboring regions. Good, well-meaning souls on our side put the best construction on it and believe that he endures such slander for the sake of the truth. He himself had nothing evil in mind but said that it was not proper for her to wear a ring but that she must humble herself. In this way innocent careless actions can serve as Satan's darts[36] and weapons.

With a great deal of effort and work we brought the congregations in the Raritan area[37] to the point that there was an open door[38] for cultivation. On account of the lack of faithful laborers we had to relinquish them to a stepbrother. Nevertheless, after several hard blows things still seem to be going tolerably well. The congregation is coming together, has completed the building of its church and is free of debt for the most part. Mr. Weygand[39] also engaged in several capers, but it appears he will recover if the work has staying power and is continued. The young man, Mr. Rauss, is in the congregations of Mr. Hartwich for half a year, and Mr. Hartwich has been with us in Pennsylvania. Both are not yet really suited for our inexperienced young Pennsylvania congregations because the congregations demand a great deal of work and rigorous exertion and the salaries are low. However, necessity has compelled us to take Rauss back again and to place him on trial as assistant in the congregations ruined by Pastor Andreae[40] in Old Goshenhoppen, Indianfield and Birkensee because they have placed themselves under our supervision and care.[41] Mr. Schrenck[42] is still situated as assistant in Saccum, Upper Milford and Fork. He conducts himself quite well, applies effort and diligence in gathering his congregation. It also appears that he is serious about his own conversion.[43] We thought of placing Pastor Handshue in Tulpehocken or Indianfield and Goshenhoppen and to take Mr. Kurtz for our congregations but people do not want to take Mr. Handshue on account of his weak voice and do not like to do without Mr. Kurtz on account of his strong voice. I am sorry that our undertaking should decline on account of a lack of able laborers who are strong and faithful in body and soul since the Very Reverend Fathers, patrons and benefactors have gone to so much trouble and expense! We have to trouble ourselves with people whom our Very Reverend Fathers have not sent. You never know where you are with persons of that kind. They do not always seek the common good, are unsteady, changeable, want to be masters and not servants, etc. To put it succinctly, they are stepbrothers.

The true brothers, however, sometimes come here weak and sickly and greatly fatigued from their journey; they lose energy, acquire families, receive poor salaries and income as long as they are able to attend to their ministry. But when they are no longer able to work they do not know where to turn because the lowliest form of service in the widely dispersed areas here makes greater demands on physical strength than the largest village parishes over there. For poor pastors who have become exhausted and unserviceable not the slightest arrangement and care exist here. From a human point of view I have often considered this situation. Already for several years I have thought and written that 1) I had a modest piece of property and 2) the opportunity to correspond with Germans in seven provinces; 3) discovered that the blessed Halle medicine was very effective in this country and could be obtained quite cheaply; 4) that Bibles, copies of *True Christianity*,[44] hymnals and that sort of thing were quite inexpensive in terms of our currency and could still quite easily be sold. For that reason the thought occurred to me to maintain on my property with the help of Mr. Vigera[45] or other schoolmasters a small pharmacy and bookstore supplied from Halle. For this, however, a small printing press was necessary to put out a newssheet every two to four weeks, one side of which would deal with political matters, the other with matters related to the building of the kingdom of God and with advertisements of books and medications. I had people with the free time for this purpose who could very well carry this out in addition to their school work. I lacked only the initial capital because I did not know that my mother had died and that I might still expect something from my inheritance. With it a good portion could have been supplied. Sauer, the book publisher, can keep three to four people on salary with his publication of newspapers and calendars. On top of that he can administer the most serious blows to the Christian church and its adherents and do more damage than ten preachers can repair. The German printer in Philadelphia[46] has published Arndt's *True Christianity* in an octavo volume for twelve shillings and he had about eight hundred subscribers. We could also have secured from eight hundred to a thousand copies from Halle, paid for them and sold them here for a profit. As soon as Sauer observed that we had procured medicine from Halle a couple of times and that people were singing its praises, he placed a notice in his paper that he himself could produce the genuine Halle medicines. He also faked all sorts of them and sells them at quite a price. It was hardly possible for us to begin with and maintain a stockpile of books and medicines without a printing press. In a situation like that Sauer can paint us as being so diabolical in seven provinces that people would not accept a Bible as a gift. And who is in a position to be in pursuit of his lying newspapers and to rescue innocence? Indeed, on top of it all, like soldiers who have run the gauntlet, one must be grateful for the gracious punishment because he had a monopoly and presently still has it twice over.[47] The one in Philadelphia serves the black devil with ribald jokes and Sauer serves the white devil with froth.[48] God and the truth amount to nothing. Although in this country a printing press makes no profit from publishing books it is useful nevertheless in minor matters and is like a bulletin board in universities where many things can be publicized and posted. I have always been of the opinion that a small printing press in circumstances prevailing in this country could bring about more good than three pastors. Though greed does not bother me I could have wished for myself and my brothers such an establishment in whose service retired pastors could have some sustenance and could have extended the kingdom of Christ somewhat among so many thousands.

However, as God's providence and the circumstances do not yet want to ordain and permit it in this way I shall also remain calm and silent: he will indeed bring it to pass.[49] *My* two original congregations in New Hanover, Providence and its outparish, along with the Swedish-English one, are now vacant. In my absence they were supposed to be served by Pastor Handshue and visited now and then by Pastor Brunnholtz in so far as the strength of both of them would permit it. No matter how I now turn it, this way or that, a highly gifted man who is courageous and strong in body and soul is very much needed quickly if the enterprise is to continue. If I were to remain in New York, then one would have to provide my original Pennsylvania congregations with a competent person; or if I were to return to Pennsylvania, a competent person would have to be appointed in New York. The Lord will be gracious and merciful to us, also provide ways and means so that we can get the travel costs together. It is generally difficult when a pastor is assigned to a particular congregation and the travel costs are imposed on it alone because the congregations are still almost generally poor. It is also easier when many support one man than when one or two alone have to eke out the travel costs. In addition, they fear they will have a burden hanging around their neck if things do not turn out well. The congregations in the province of New York have always turned to the consistory in Amsterdam and Hamburg and paid forty pounds in local money toward travel costs. Most of the time, however, they were unhappy and have now become very skittish. If the Very Reverend Fathers and patrons would be inclined to take the poor, scattered, neglected little band of Lutherans in New York under your fatherly supervision and to care for them, it would make us very happy and comfort us. We well know that Your Highly Esteemed Sirs will have nothing in doing so than much trouble, vexation, anxiety, worry and expense. But we also know that it is your intention and kind inclination to expand and build the kingdom of Jesus Christ in every possible way. Nothing other than an apostolic salary can be expected here while there a glorious reward awaits enjoyment for ever.

In the end the Dutch and some Germans sided with their pastor, Mr. Knoll. However, he reached an agreement with the congregation on account of certain matters and surrendered his call in return for money.[50] A large section of the Germans have separated from the Dutch and their church. They have purchased for themselves a large building, gone into debt to the tune of three to four hundred pounds and fetched the young Pastor Riess[51] from Pennsylvania and accepted him as pastor. From the governor they also received permission to take up a collection.[52] They did not have sufficient cause and basis to sunder themselves from the old Lutheran church and to start their own for the church has space and room adequate for church services as well as beautiful appointments. But some of our Germans are arrogant and stubborn heads who do not want to submit to any kind of order; rather they want the freedom to accept and dismiss--without justification--any vagabond who pretends to be a preacher. The party which sides with Mr. Ries wants to send several men to Germany soon and have collections taken up for the church they started out of envy because here they will not get much. For the people say, "It is not necessary to build a new church," and in derision they add, "The old one is big enough." Now that Mr. Knoll is gone the Dutch have called me to try to bring the congregation which was split together again. Mr. Riess is also still in New York and braces up his party. I, however, work with those Dutch and Germans who still side with the old privileged Lutheran church. I preach each Sunday once in Dutch and once in German, occasionally also in English. It would be a pity if the disorderly party of Mr. Riess were to receive collections in Europe for it is only out of spite that they are starting a separate church, now that they have the opportunity to hear a sermon in German every Sunday. Their collection agents will turn toward Frankfurt, to the region of Württemberg and thereabout and present their frivolous undertaking in a pitiable and mendacious enough manner. If these wayward people would reunite they would have church to spare. However, if they remain divided then both parties must perish. The Moravians are also beginning to build a church here in New York and to recruit all over again after they have already wandered through all sorts of places. Toward the end of September of the previous year I returned again from Mr. Hartwich's congregations and passed through New York for the first time just when Mr. Knoll had abdicated and Mr. Berckenmeyer was also present to remedy matters. The elders and deacons of the church asked me to preach. I promised to do this and I preached in German on Sunday in the forenoon and in the afternoon in English.[53] Some time afterwards the following letter to me arrived unexpectedly in Pennsylvania.[54]

This was the beginning. If God keeps body and soul together I shall present it all in continuity as soon as possible. What I have written in the present letter concerning my brothers is confidential.[55] It could well be that in one or another point I go too far in my opinion, perhaps I should rather have remained silent because the Very Reverend Fathers are only distressed and made tired with such matters. It could also be that a hypochondriacal illness[56] had an influence on my writing, for the change is almost too great. In Pennsylvania I was almost always on horseback. Here in New York I am now almost six weeks as in a prison and immediately as I close this letter I am overtaken by a hectic fever so that I have to quit and lie down in bed. Barely four months ago in Pennsylvania I was also sick unto death because of a serious illness. Forerunners of death come often enough, if only it would finally be completely overcome! If the Very Reverend Fathers would continue to look after the undertakings which have been begun and select and call a qualified person as my successor or assistant either in New York or New Hanover and Providence, we would take care of the travel costs and thank the Lord. If with due deference the Very Reverend Fathers would not oppose this, it would probably be best that the ordination be performed in London by His Reverence, the Court Preacher, because here in New York there are foolish persons and learned ones who still carry on that period of conflict.[57] I have just learned that Pastor Brunnholtz's box of books is in Albany[58] with Mr. Berckenmeyer, and Mr. Berckenmeyer's box is still with Mr. Brunnholtz. P.B. appears on both boxes but with the difference that Philadelphia appears on the latter; nevertheless it reached New York and even Mr. Berckenmeyer. I must close because my illness is getting worse. May the faithful God and Father in Christ generously reward and replace all the fatherly concern, anxiety, labor and endeavour of our Very Reverend Fathers, kind patrons and benefactors with an endless reward! May he help them to bear their burdensome cross and still allow them to serve as the crown of our evangelical church for many years so that through them and their institutions the name of God may be hallowed, his kingdom increased and his will accomplished. Amen.

This is the wish, Very Reverend Fathers, most kind patrons and benefactors, of your poorest servant

New York, 15 June 1751   Mühlenberg

P.S. To the best of my knowledge my worthy colleague Brunnholtz has sent the Very Reverend Fathers all acounts of monies collected and received here. Most obediently I would request a receipt for the account from the Very Reverend Fathers so people here could not say that I or my brothers had committed fraud. And as I withdrew fifty pounds sterling from the first year of my being here with the permission and at the behest of my Reverend Fathers, I would request them to note this separately with a word or two. For the way the Fathers prescribe it over there is the way it is, and it is approved here. Here we have distributed the collections conscientiously and to every congregation in accordance with the greatest need. Now if the Very Reverend Fathers would be pleased to certify that we have not received more and have distributed the sum we received in accordance with their approval, then the matter is clear and agreeable.

---

1. See Letter 90 n.2.
2. See Letter 85.
3. The call is dated 1 February 1751. See Letter 90.
4. In the entries into his diary for December 1750 Mühlenberg recites the reasons for accepting the call to New York. The reasons he gives provide an insight into his assessment of how far he felt his work had progressed up to that time and what the exigencies were, both personal and professional, which moved him to accept the call. See *Journals* 1:261-62. - In *Journals* 1:288 Mühlenberg refers to the transmission of his diary for 1749 and 1750.
5. See John 4:35.
6. See Isa. 55:9.
7. See John 18:36.
8. See 1 Cor. 13:1.
9. See Eph. 2:20.
10. On Peter Brunnholz, see Letter 71 n.3.
11. On Heinrich Schleydorn, see *Correspondence* 1:53 n.22.
12. On Lucas Rauss, see Letter 76 n.72.
13. October 1750 Mühlenberg reports that because of Rauss's innuendos he told his dear colleague "to discharge the maid." See *Journals* 1:259.
14. For Mühlenberg's use of the imagery of black and white devils, see *Correspondence* 1:93 n.44.

15. See *Correspondence* 1:291 n.27.

16. Handschuh went to Lancaster in May 1748. See *HN2/1*:386-87. For more details concerning the difficulties and tentative solutions Mühlenberg and his colleagues had to deal with in Lancaster, see *Journals* 1:191-93. See *Correspondence* 1:291 n.18.

17. See 1 Cor. 3:2; Heb. 5:12.

18. The text reads *Malo Hypocon[driaco]*.

19. The text reads *paroxismus Mal: hyp:*.

20. See Letter 89 n.16.

21. See *Journals* 1:238-40.

22. See Luke 16:8.

23. See *Journals* 1:245; *Documentary History*, p. 27.

24. Johann Caspar Stöver, Jr. (1707-79) had acquired 376 acres of land about twenty-five miles northwest of Lancaster where he lived and from where he continued to minister to congregations in the area. See the extensive narrative of his life and ministry in *Pastors and People* 1:139-43; see also Letter 72 n.39.

25. In March 1751 the decision was made to recall Handschuh from Lancaster and to have him care for the congregation in New Providence in the absence of Mühlenberg (*HN2/1*:405-6; *Journals* 1:271). Handschuh became pastor of the congregation in Lancaster in 1748, but following his marriage to Barbara Belzner on 1 May 1750, tensions between him and congregation members mounted. A reflection of these difficulties becomes apparent from an examination of the proceedings of the synodical meetings of the United Congregations in 1750 and 1751. Members at the synodical meeting must have found Handschuh's assessment satisfactory for they proceeded to elect him "President or Superintendent" for the year (*Documentary History*, p. 34; *Pastors and People* 1:50-51). Prior to the synodical meeting in 1751, on 25 March of that same year, Mühlenberg and Brunnholz drafted a letter to the Lancaster congregation in the presence of Handschuh which contained the following, "We handed him [Handschuh] a letter to take with him which he was to read publicly in the congregation. In it we informed them what our intention was when we appointed our brother to serve in Lancaster on a trial basis for a time, and how they were to conduct themselves in relation to us and to him. We also desired that after a few weeks he should deliver his farewell sermon and come to us because we were in need of him more than they and that we could make better use of him in view of my planned move to New York" (*Korrespondenz* 1:416 n.13). Handschuh had the Lancaster congregation's schoolmaster, Jakob Loeser, read the letter to the congregation 31 March (*HN2/2*:68). On 5 May Handschuh preached his farewell sermon (*HN2/2*:69). On his return to Philadelphia Handschuh did not supply for Mühlenberg in New Providence but became pastor of the congregation in Germantown.

26. The text reads *modo procedendi*.

27. See Matt. 6:6.

28. See Job 4:17; 15:14 and Eccles. 3:4.

29. Johann Nicolaus Kurz "served the numerous congregations in the Tulpehocken charge (1746-1770). This was a large, well-populated frontier parish which had never before sustained pastoral leadership" (*Pastors and People* 1:76). On Kurz, see *Correspondence* 1:154 n.5 and 341 n.16.

30. The text reads *Logica naturalis und artificialis*.

31. The text reads *Theologia naturali und revelata*.

32. On Johann Helfrich Schaum, see Letter 71 n.9.

33. Mühlenberg includes some details related to Schaum's marriage in his diary not found in this letter (*Journals* 1:259).

34. Mühlenberg refers to the visit of Handschuh and Kurz with Schaum in York in his diary (*Journals* 1:270; 271).

35. In August and September 1750 Mühlenberg stayed with Pastor Hartwich in Rhinebeck and the surrounding congregations. (*Journals* 1:247-52).

36. See Eph. 6:16.

37. See *Correspondence* 1:189 nn. 4 and 6; 201 nn. 1 and 4.

38. See Col. 4:3; Acts 14:27.

39. On Johann Albert Weygand, see Letter 71 n.21.

40. On Johann Conrad Andreae, see *Correspondence* 1:143 n.10.

41. On 20 May 1751 Mühlenberg made the following entry in his diary, "Today I prepared a draft of a call and instructions to Mr. Rauss, since it had been decided at the last synod at the request of the congregations to transfer him for a limited time on trial to Indianfield, [*HN*:Old] Goschehoppe and Birkensee [Perkasy] as an assistant or catechist" (*Journals* 1: 279). - On 5 June 1751 Rauss was at the home of Mühlenberg in New York with letters and testimonies from Hartwich stating that he had conducted himself satisfactorily. On the following day, 6 June, Mühlenberg sent Rauss on his way to begin his ministry on trial in the three congregations there (*Journals* 1:285).

42. On Ludolph Heinrich Schrenck, see Letter 78 n.7.

43. An allusion to persons like Weygand, Wagner, Schrenck, Rauss and perhaps others.

44. See *Correspondence* 1:315 n.20.

45. See Letters 112; 114; 115; 116. - On Johann Friedrich Vigera, see *Correspondence* 1:145 n.3.

46. Mühlenberg is referring to Christoph Sauer. See *Correspondence* 1:93 n.37. - *Korrespondenz* 1:417 n. 24 refers to the publication of Arndt's book in 1751 by Benjamin Franklin and Johann Philipp Böhm, with a preface by J.C. Hartwich.

47. The text reads *duopolium*.

48. See *Correspondence* 1:336-39.

49. See Ps. 37:5.

50. For the relationship of Michael Christian Knoll to the New York congregations and Mühlenberg's involvement in it, see *Correspondence* 1:187-93; Letters 40A, 40B and 40C together with the accompanying introductions and notes.

51. On Johann Friedrich Riess, see Letter 76 n.71.

52. They purchased a large building for 250 pounds. An additional fifty pounds were applied to the purchase of furnishings (*HN2/1*:625; *Journals* 1:255).

53. See *Journals* 1:256.

54. See Letter 84:89, 8 November 1750; Letter 86, 3 December 1750, is Mühlenberg's reply to it.

55. The text reads *Sub rosa*.

56. The text reads *Malum hypo[condriacum]*.

57. The text reads *saeculo*.

58. On Wilhelm Christoph Berckenmeyer, see *Correspondence* 1:189 n.1.

Letter 94

To Samuel Theodor Albinus
New York, 18 June 1751

*This letter is actually a postscript to Mühlenberg's previous letter to
Francke and Ziegenhagen (Letter 93). Having just received letters from
Albinus and Francke, Mühlenberg now regrets some things that he has
written in his "melancholy letter." However, there is much in the letter that
is important so he does not want to destroy it; he pleads for charity on the
part of his readers and reminds them that his thoughts are "confused and
strange" because he is quite ill. This postscript is clearly intended for all
the Reverend Fathers, and his request of them is that they send two assistant
pastors to "the ravaged American vineyard," one to serve the Dutch
Lutheran congregation in New York and the other one to serve Mühlenberg's
own congregations in New Hanover and Providence.*

Text in German: Korrespondenz *1:418-19. For further textual
information, see* Korrespondenz *1:420.*

P.S. to Court Preacher Albinus[1]   New York, 18 June 1751

Very Reverend Court Preacher,
Highly esteemed Colleague in Christ:
Just as I am lying seriously ill in New York and am about to hand over
my melancholy letter to the bearer, I have at this moment received from
Pastor Brunnholtz[2] in Pennsylvania:

1) A long but very succinct letter from Court Preacher Albinus, dated 24
August 1750.[3] 2) An extensive, fatherly letter from His Reverence Doctor,
Inspector and Professor Franck, dated 20 March 1751.[4] 3) An especially
fatherly letter to me from His Reverence Dr. Frank from blessed Pölzig,
dated 29 July 1750.[5] These most worthy and precious letters demonstrate
once again that the Very Reverend Fathers have not yet forgotten us in our
poverty and unimportance, but rather they want to commit themselves to us
and to the work of God even more. Consequently Your Reverence will be
so kind and, according to your former love, excuse the confused and strange
manner in which I have expressed myself. I would gladly have torn the
letter[6] in two and written another one because of a few statements, but there
were some things in it that it was necessary for me to report. For in whom
besides God should I take my refuge other than in the Very Reverend
Fathers? No doubt my approaching illness which clouded my senses was

responsible for my writing in such a melancholy manner. During the hot weather I got a chill, then had severe diarrhea along with a gnawing pain in my abdomen; this continued for three days and three nights as with a difficult, debilitating fever. It is still accompanied by fever, and I do not know what will become of it.[7] I did not come to New York out of curiosity or for a thrill or with improper intentions; I came rather for the sake of God's honor and my office and conscience, as my journal[8] and the linkage of the circumstances will show--if I live. For my conscience is my witness that in the past nine years of my difficult calling, I have gladly--albeit very imperfectly--had the honor of my Redeemer and of my Very Reverend Fathers as the center of my attention. Because Christ has given himself for the redemption of *all*, this must be preached in due time in Pennsylvania, Jersey and New York, etc., etc. The Lord will not allow everything to be in vain. I had an iron constitution, but one and another illness has filed away at it for so long that it is getting weak. *Consequently, my most humble petition to the Very Reverend Fathers is for two upright, capable and qualified coworkers who are suited to the ravaged American vineyard, in particular for two assistant pastors, one for the old Dutch and German* evangelical Lutheran congregation of the Unaltered Augsburg Confession in New York and the other for the two congregations entrusted to me in New Hanover and Providence in Pennsylvania. If the one who should go to New York were a Low German, he could perhaps learn the Dutch language here that much more quickly. The small group here in New York has 500 pounds bearing interest and a nice little parsonage. Consequently it is not very difficult for them to support a single man because their capital is earning thirty-five per cent at the current rate, etc., etc. The necessities of life will no doubt be looked after if one seeks first the kingdom of God.[9] The other one will also find the basic necessities of life in New Hanover and Providence. If the candidate for New York could be ordained in London, etc., etc. But these are once again my foggy ideas, because here in New York there are still so many old, prejudiced fighters lurking about. May it be as is pleasing to God and the Very Reverend Fathers. God will no doubt see to it that all is well. Pastor Handshue will probably have to go back and forth between Germantown and Philadelphia.[10] I cannot deny that he is a strange colleague who is least suited for the circumstances in Pennsylvania. He dallies too much with his wife. He is better suited to a place where there are strong children of God who carry him on their backs and will thank him if he says they are not carrying him gently enough, etc., etc. But this is all in confidence,[11] otherwise there will be a split! God will provide help and improvement!

N.B.: The man who is bringing these letters is called Matthias Ernst;[12] he is a member of the Reformed church and a respectable merchant in New York. He is glad to do a good deed to us preachers; he gladly plays the host and would like to meet the honorable court preachers. Whatever is done to him out of love is also done to us. More in the future, if I live.

---

1. On Samuel Theodor Albinus, see *Correspondence* 1:154 n 8 and 354 n. 5.
2. On Peter Brunnholz, see Letter 71 n. 3.
3. Mühlenberg notes the receipt of this letter in his journal under the date of 12 June 1751; *Journals* 1:289. There he records that it was written on 24 August 1751, but this is obviously an error in transcription. The letter is not extant.
4. Letter 89, which is actually dated 18 March 1751.
5. Letter 81.
6. Letter 93.
7. See Muhlenberg's journal for 10-12 June 1751 for further descriptions of his illness; *Journals* 1:287f.
8. See *Journals* 1:261f.
9. See Matt. 6:33.
10. See Letter 93 n. 23. On Johann Friedrich Handschuh, see *Correspondence* 1:291 n. 18.
11. The text reads *sub rosa*.
12. Although Matthias Ernst is mentioned a couple of times in the *Journals* (1:288-89 and 343), nothing more is known about him.

Letter 95

The Dutch Congregation in New York to Johann Friedrich Riess[1]
and His Congregation
New York, 15 July 1751

The following "articles and proposals for reconciliation" (Journals 1:293) were the attempt by the Dutch Lutheran congregation in New York which Mühlenberg was serving to heal the division that had separated them from their German Lutheran brothers and sisters since 1749-50.

Text in German: Korrespondenz 1:420-22. *The only copy of the letter is Mühlenberg's German translation of the Dutch original which is found in his journals of 1751. We have used the English translation of this letter in* Journals 1:293-94 *as the basis for our translation with minor revisions.*

New York, 15 July 1751[2]

Be it known to all before whom these presents come that our forefathers and we, the undersigned, some of us having come from Europe, others born in these North American provinces, residents of the city and provinces of New York and Jersey, did band ourselves together through God's grace, and, with our God-given mites, along with beneficent contributions from our brethren in the faith in Europe, did some years ago build a church in the city of New York and have maintained it down to the present day. This church was built, consecrated and publicly dedicated to the sole use of the evangelical Lutheran congregation in general and each member in particular who confesses and holds the doctrine of the apostles and prophets, the Unaltered Augsburg Confession and the other Symbolical Books, regardless of his nationality and language. Since God is a God of order, and since no church can be governed, built up and maintained without order, our blessed forefathers and we, along with the regularly called pastors, did therefore lay as its foundation a general evangelical Lutheran church order, in accord with which the Lutheran church and congregation at New York was to be governed, maintained and propagated.[3] The aforesaid church order, which consists of thirteen articles, is modeled after the pattern of our Lutheran church in Europe and has been approved and subscribed to by all the regularly called preachers, elders, and deacons of our congregation and it shall and must be retained as a standard in our church and congregation at New York and be added to and perfected by succeeding regularly called pastors, elders and deacons, that is, by the whole church council, as may be necessary from time to time. Because our church at New York was built, consecrated and dedicated to no other use except that of a congregation in accord with the doctrine of the apostles and prophets and the Unaltered Augsburg Confession and the other Symbolical Books; and because in recent years many fellow believers have come to this province from Europe and settled in and around New York, and some have openly accused us of being partial, as if we would not[4] receive any and every regular adherent of the Unaltered Augsburg Confession into the fellowship, privileges, use and enjoyment of our church and divine services; therefore, we, the undersigned, the present regularly called pastor, elders and deacons, that is, the entire church council, and other invited members of the congregation, do make known through this open letter before the face of God and his esteemed Christendom, that we have recognized and still recognize as fellow members any and every adherent of the Augsburg Confession, of the German nationality and other nationalities, who are already here or who may come hereafter, on the following conditions:

I. Each and every member who confesses the Augsburg Confession must be bound by our aforesaid established church order and any supplements which may be added to it, and conduct himself in exact accord with its content.

II. There shall be no respect of persons, apart from discernment and adequate reasons, between Germans and Dutch or other nationalities; rather all as a whole and each member in particular shall have, subject to the church order, equal rights, privileges, use and enjoyment of the church and its divine services as long as they remain true members.

III. On every Sunday and high festival day, when the preacher is present, a sermon in the Dutch language and a sermon in the German language *shall* be preached, the sermons to be alternated and continued as long as necessary and as the two languages remain in use.

IV. The election and appointment of elders and deacons *shall* proceed in accord with the church order without partiality or respect of persons or nationalities, and in every case such members shall be chosen who have the testimony of a blameless life and a sincere love for our divine service and the upbuilding of the congregation.

V. The preacher *shall* have the liberty to preach a brief sermon in the English language in the church on Sunday evenings if his strength permits, in order that the youth may again be attracted, the congregation increased and the treasury better maintained.

VI. *However, in case* the preacher should be too weak to preach an English sermon on Sunday evening, he shall retain the liberty occasionally to preach English during the day in place of the German or Dutch sermon in order that the language may not be neglected, for our young people are learning the English language of themselves, regardless of our wish, and go over to other denominations if they do not have the opportunity of enjoying the confession of faith of their parents in the prevailing language of the land.

VII. *Each* and every member of the entire congregation *shall* write his name in a church book provided for this purpose and set down what he will contribute annually from a sense of love and duty toward the support of the regularly called preacher, in order that as far as possible the savings in the church treasury may be spared, kept and increased until such time as we, or our descendants, as it may please God, shall be able to maintain the church and school with the interest therefrom.

VIII. If our German brethren and fellow believers should sell the lot and house[5] which they have been using heretofore as a meeting place as advantageously as possible, and if the income from the sale should not be sufficient to pay off the debt of £300, the remaining debt shall be liquidated by means of charitable collections from the whole congregation, by freewill gifts from the Christian congregations of adjacent provinces, and also by drawing upon the alms treasury of our entire congregation to the end that neither part of the congregation may suffer loss. Or, if this can be done in a better and more convenient way, the way remains open for both sides to confer on the matter.

IX. All disorder, party-feeling, division and unmannerliness shall be avoided to the utmost; if not, it shall be punished, for where such prevails, there God removes his blessing.

X. The church council *shall* take care to the best of its knowledge and conscience that the Christian congregation shall be and continue to be provided with faithful shepherds and teachers who hold the pure doctrine as the mystery of faith in a pure conscience[6] and adorn it with a holy life.

XI. To this end, the whole church council of the Lutheran congregation in New York shall conscientiously take care that they do not sin against their own souls and the blood of their children and descendants through neglect of pure doctrine and godliness; they shall use the freedom granted by God and the provincial government to report fully and forthwith the lack of a faithful shepherd and teacher to the reverend ministeria mentioned in the church order, or to other pure and godly consistories or ministeria of the evangelical Lutheran church; and shall come to agreement with them in order that, through their paternal care and aid, our congregation may at all times be provided with upright, learned, orthodox and godly shepherds.

XII. The church council shall see to it that, in accord with our church order, no preacher teaches or administers the sacraments in our church and congregation who has not been called and ordained according to the order of the evangelical Lutheran church, for it is on account of such men that grievous divisions arise and our religion and practice is only brought into more disrepute and scorn. The Lord Jesus have mercy upon us and grant us his peace!

---

1. On Johann Friedrich Riess, see Letter 76 n. 71.

2. Mühlenberg's journal entry of 15 July 1751 makes it clear that this letter is an attempt to reunite the German and Dutch congregations in New York: "JULY 15. The church council met at my house. Mr. Magens and several other prominent members of the congregation were also present. At this time we agreed to complete the articles and proposals for reconciliation, to write them in the church's protocol as a matter of record, and to submit a copy and translation of them to the separated party. Since I do not have at hand a copy of the German translation which was submitted, I shall translate it again from the Dutch original" (*Journals* 1:293). On the break-up of the congregations, see Letters 84, 86 and 93 n. 51. The Dutch congregation had hoped that Mühlenberg would succeed in reuniting the two congregations, but this did not happen. The reasons for this are not quite clear. Mühlenberg's *Journals* contain the following entry for 24 July 1751: "(1) Our deacons and elders said that it was not advisable to have anything further to do with Mr. Riess's party because the heads of the party were seeking, not the glory of God, but their own glory and the ruin of the church" (*Journals* 1:300). Issues surrounding the church buildings (see Article VIII in this letter and Article IX in Letter 96) and the suggestion that Riess be the pastor of the reunited congregations may help to explain the negative response.

3. The church order of the Dutch congregation was based on the Amsterdam Church Order of 1689.

4. Following *Journals* 1:293 in conjecturing that "not" should be inserted here.

5. See Letter 93 n. 51.

6. See 1 Tim. 3:9.

Letter 96

Johann Friedrich Riess[1] and the German Congregation in New York
to Mühlenberg and His Congregation
New York, 17 July 1751

*This unsigned letter, included in Mühlenberg's journal of 1751, sets forth
the position of the German party of the New York congregation in reply to
the proposals of the Dutch party in the preceding letter, Letter 95.*

Text in German: Korrespondenz *1:423-25. For further textual
information, see* Korrespondenz *1:425. We have used the English
translation of this letter in* Journals *1:295 as the basis for our translation
with minor revisions.*

Dear Brethren in Christ Jesus:

From the letter sent to our German united evangelical Lutheran
brotherhood we, all the undersigned, united members,[2] have learned that an
evangelical Dutch and Lower Saxon congregation, moved by God and
peace-loving minds, has begun to take into consideration an agreement to
hold divine services in our language, an agreement long but vainly
requested, sought and prayed for by us, but refused for demonstrable
reasons, and we heartily wish that God's blessing may rest upon it. Since
nothing else but a friendly union of the two congregations has for eight
years been the wish and desire of our German congregation, we hasten to
transmit to you our favorable and humble reply and opinion, framed to
correspond with the articles submitted to us, and beg a final friendly answer.

I. According to the promise given, each and every adherent of the
Augsburg Confession, whether of German or other nationality, *shall* have
equal rights and privileges in, and use and enjoyment of, the church and its
property.

II. At the election of church elders, in other important changes and in
principal matters of business, *each* member of the whole congregation *shall*
have one vote in the decision of the matter which shall be legally accepted.

III. Each and every member who confesses the evangelical Lutheran
doctrine *shall* be bound to a properly established Christian church order
which is in accord with God's word and local conditions of the country.

IV. There *shall* be two sermons every Sunday and festival day, one in
German and the other in the Dutch language, alternately, and this
arrangement shall be retained as long as there are enough members of either
side to hold the services. V. *Our* preacher shall have liberty and power to

preach English sermons and instruct the children, not only on Sundays but also during the week if his strength will permit and he can do so without neglect of the other two sermons. VI. Every Sunday there *shall* be instruction of the children and during the week a school visitation. However, when the weather will not permit because of too great heat or cold, he shall have the liberty of holding them in his residence.

VII. Each and every member of the whole congregation *shall* write his name in the church book and indicate what he is willing to contribute out of love and duty toward the proper support *of our regularly called pastor*.

VIII. Each member *shall* at the same time indicate how much he will contribute toward paying for the place of worship purchased for us.

IX. The place of worship or church, purchased by us, and invested with privilege and public authority, *shall* not only be taken over by the whole congregation with all encumbrances and debts, but shall also be retained for sacred use as a schoolhouse, kept in repair and paid for in the aforementioned manner; and furthermore a German sermon shall be preached in it every four weeks.

X. All disorder, party-feeling, division and unmannerliness *shall* be avoided, failing which, it shall be punished.

XI. The church council of our congregation *shall* take care to seek out a faithful shepherd according to the heart and mind of God, one who, in his doctrine and life, exhibits the teaching of Jesus and his apostles as a pattern and example to the whole congregation. To this end, it is also our advice that the teacher and preacher who has already been *regularly called* by our congregation and found by us to be *devoted, diligent and upright* in *doctrine* and *life*, the Reverend Mr. Johann Friedrich Riess, be *requested* the sooner the better, through a new, regular call, to continue in the future among us, to administer, with the help of the Holy Spirit, the grace of preaching the gospel of Jesus Christ with which he is so *richly endowed*, and to accept the call sent to him. However, in case the *aforementioned* Mr. Ries should not be willing to accept such a call (though we *all* sincerely desire that he should) and should he (in conformity with a statement he once made), for the sake of peace and harmony, prefer to serve some other congregation that may call him, our duty and conscience demand that we dismiss him in peace,[3] furnished with honorable testimonials, after he has preached a farewell sermon in the old church, and that in his place we call as our teacher another honored preacher who is already known to us and reputed for his faithful ministry, Mr. Peter Sommer,[4] of Schoharie, or Mr. Brunnholtz.[5] However, if neither of these can be obtained, another lawfully ordained preacher shall be called. In order that all these lengthy controversies may hereby be terminated, we give our assurance to the beloved brotherhood, by these sincere and *honestly meant* proposals, that not one of all the above articles shall be broken, but rather more and more confirmed by actual demonstration. Given and signed at a meeting of the German church council and of other delegated members at New York, 17 July 1751.

---

1.   On Johann Friedrich Riess, see Letter 76 n. 71.
2.   Mühlenberg notes in his journal at the end of his transcript of this letter: "When Mr. Riess handed me this reply, there was not a single signature on it. He made excuses and said that he had written it out in a hurry because he had learned that I was setting out for Hackinsack the next day and desired that I should think over the reply while I was in Hackinsack" (*Journals* 1:296).
3.   Riess stayed in New York until October 1751. From December 1751 he served the congregation in Stone Arabia (Montgomery County). Weygand had advised him to accept the call to Hackensack and Remersbach, but Riess refused to do so. See *Korrespondenz* 1:425 n. 2.
4.   Peter Nikolaus Sommer (1709-95), the son-in-law of Wilhelm Christoph Berckenmeyer, was serving Schoharie since 1743. He also served congregations in Stone Arabia, Palatine Bridge and Cobleskill. See *Pastors and People* 1:217f.
5.   On Peter Brunnholz, see Letter 71 n. 3.

Letter 97

The Deacons of Hackensack to Mühlenberg
Hackensack, 19 August 1751[1]

The Dutch Lutheran congregation at Hackensack, New Jersey, lay about seventeen miles from New York, and when Mühlenberg visited it in June 1751 he learned that it had "been united with New York from almost the beginning of this century" (Journals 1:285). Thus it was not surprising, when the deacons at Hackensack learned the New York congregation was attempting to obtain Mühlenberg's services, that they should follow suit. The Hackensack deacons ask Mühlenberg to include the following letter of call with the New York application to the Reverend Fathers.

Text in English: Korrespondenz 1:426. For further textual information, see Korrespondenz 1:427. This letter, written in English, is given here in its original form. It is also reprinted in Journals 1:309-10.

Whereas We, the subscribers, His Majesty's loyal Subjects and Freeholders of the County and Township of Bergen and Hackinsack in the province of Jersey have from the first settling of the aforesaid County and Township enjoyed the free use and exercise of our protestant Lutheran Religion under the powerful protection of God and the protestant Realm of Great Brittain to this very day and are left destitute of a learned and lawful ordained Minister; And Whereas We, the subscribers, have got Acquaintance with the Reverend Henry Melchior Mühlenberg, being a lawful ordained Minister, called from the protestant Lutheran Congregation at Newyork[2] and formerly sent by Recommendation of His Majesty's Chaplain and German preacher at St. James's in London,[3] the Reverend Dr. Ziegenhagen and Professor Franck, Worthy Members and Trustees of the Society for promoting Christian Knowledge, We do therefore by these presents beseech and call the Rev. Mr. Mühlenberg to take upon him besides his other congregations the pastoral Care and Inspection of our Church and School, of us and our Children and to be the sole Minister of our Congregation during his stay in our American parts upon the following conditions: I, to keep divine service in the fore- and afternoon on every first Sunday in every current Month of the year and once at least a Catechetical Exercise in the Week after the appointed monthly Sunday when Health, Wind and Weather will permit it. II, to administer the Holy Ordinances and what belongeth to the Ministerial Office in his appointed Turns, according to our introduced Ordres and Rules of the Church. And for the true performing of his Ministerial Function, We the subscribers oblige ourselves and promise by these presents 1, to keep the personage clear and ready for his Abode and quiet possession 2, to bring or cause him to be brought to and fro, between here and Newyork at the appointed Meetings, be it by Water or Land, as it may suit best for him 3, to delivre as much fire wood as He and his family want, when they are abiding and dwelling amongst us in Hackinsack 4, to pay to our aforesaid Minister or cause to be paid unto him every year the sum of thirty pounds current lawful Money, and to delivre one Half of the aforesaid sum to the Minister yearly in the Beginning of May and the other Half in the beginning of November.

This our lawful Vocation and Obligation shall take and stand its ful power and virtue from the time and date, when our Minister hath received permission from his Superiours, and when he setteth out from Newyork with Intention to begin the divine service in our Congregation.[4] In Whitnesse whereof, We have set our Hands and Marks, this 19th day of August 1751 in the 24th year of the happy Reign of our Most Gracious Sovereign King George the second, whom God preserve.

Lucas van Hoorn
Joan van Hoorn
Gerhard Halenbeek
Jan van Orden

---

1. Mühlenberg's journal entry for August 19, 1751, reads as follows: "In the evening the elders and deacons met together, handed me a call [= Letter 97], and earnestly begged me to accept it and serve them every four weeks. Since they had learned that the New Yorkers were applying to our Reverend Fathers for my services, they asked me to include a copy of their call and in their name to beg the Reverend Fathers to give heed to their spiritual need and gladden them with a favorable reply" (*Journals* 1:307). On August 4, 1751, Mühlenberg had informed the New York church council that, at the urgent request of his wife, he would have to return to his country congregations in Pennsylvania toward the end of August. In the course of the conversation the Dutch deacons expressed the hope that "since there were already so many good preachers in Pennsylvania, might not the Reverend Fathers consent to placing Mühlenberg in New York for several years, just as they had done for the Pennsylvanians at the beginning? They were confident in their hope that the Reverend Fathers would more easily find a competent man for my place in Pennsylvania, than for New York, because in Pennsylvania the German language is enough, whereas here more languages and more experience of American conditions are necessary. . . . There was nothing else for me to do than give this decision: If my Reverend Fathers order me to accept the call to New York I should have to obey. They thereupon requested Mr. Magens to address a petition to our superiors and send it from New York at the first opportunity" (*Journals* 1:302). The petition, in Dutch, is printed in *Korrespondenz* 1:427 n. 1.
2. See Letter 84.
3. See Letters 8 and 9, *Correspondence* 1:24-30.

Letter 99

Gotthilf August Francke to Peter Brunnholz, Johann Friedrich Handschuh
and Mühlenberg
Halle, 27 (or 29) September 1751

*Francke is communicating to the Pennsylvania pastors the good news that
an unnamed benefactor was committing several thousand gulden to the
congregations in Pennsylvania. There are strings attached to this gift,
however, and Francke's letter gives his reflections on how these conditions
can best be met and also asks for the Pennsylvania pastors' thoughts and
advice on this matter.*
    Text in German: Korrespondenz *1:429-30. For further textual
information, see* Korrespondenz *1:430.*

To
Pastors Mühlenberg, Brunholtz[1] and Handschuch[2]
                                 29 September 1751[3]

Reverend,
Dearly beloved Brothers in the Lord:
From the copy of the accompanying letter of a Christian merchant
outside of Germany, whose name will be made known to you in the future,[4]
you will learn among other things that a friend who is still unknown has
been awakened by God to dedicate several thousand gulden of his wealth for
the congregations in Pennsylvania; nevertheless, for the duration of his life
he requested the interest, at six or five per cent, for his own maintenance.
In this I recognize with heartfelt thanks the fatherly provision of God which
he also demonstrates in this matter to your dear congregations. I also
rejoice inwardly that it pleases God to begin meeting the external needs, in
the sure hope that he will further open his merciful[5] hand and, if only the
congregations make themselves ever more receptive to his spiritual blessing,
he will also permit his physical blessing to well out over them for the
continuation of good institutions in church and school. However, because
the condition about the interest for the rest of his life[6] is tied to the gift; and,
because, on the one hand, the safe investment of a capital sum here involves
many difficulties and, on the other hand, the congregation in Philadelphia
is still so heavily in debt as a result of its church construction and has to pay
six per cent interest on this gift; therefore, I can find no better way to invest
this capital which the unnamed benefactor is willing to dedicate to the

congregations than to loan it in the meantime to the congregation in Philadelphia as a formal debenture towards the payment of a part of its debts. It would have to be done in such a way that they would commit themselves in the debenture to pay the interest of it annually, at six percent, and deliver it into the hands of the pastors and leave the disposition of it to me. Thus, on the one hand, if God will give enough gifts into my hands annually that I could pay the annual interest to the benefactor with them, I would nevertheless retain the freedom to determine how the interest that was collected there, in lieu of the gifts that have come in here, would be used; on the other hand, in case the gifts here would not suffice to pay the interest, the interest from there could be used for this purpose and to that end could be remitted to Europe by a bill of exchange. In terms of the capital itself, I can at present report even less about its future use, as the benefactor appears to want a better arrangement for it so that it would be a secure fund for the future. In that case we still have to wait and see what he himself decides about it when he makes the actual payment. In the meantime, so far as I am able, I will try to make sure that the congregation in Philadelphia at least has some advantage from it for paying off its debts and that the reception of this capital does not simply become a burden[7] for it. Although in this situation the congregation would not in any case experience any disadvantage because of it, because it is a matter of indifference, since the congregation is already in debt, to whom it is in debt. I have made this proposal to the unnamed benefactor and I am awaiting his reply.[8] But the matter cannot be completely settled until I will have examined the statement of the Philadelphia congregation. Would you please present the matter to the aforementioned congregation and its church council and deacons and let me know their answer as soon as possible. Would you also prepare and send over a draft of the debenture, in the English or German language as the circumstances there require. The formal preparation of the aforementioned debenture will thus be left until the amount will actually be paid out and transferred. In expectation of such an answer, I remain ever

Halle, 27 September 1751   Your,

                                                 G. A. Francke

P.S. Please communicate to me your thoughts and advice about the future use of the capital and what you perceive to be the most useful arrangement of the matter, for I believe the benefactor will go along with what we propose. I almost see this as a means by which one can to a certain extent bind the congregations so that in future they will be more obliged to submit to good arrangements.

---

1. On Peter Brunnholz, see Letter 71 n. 3.
2. On Johann Friedrich Handschuh, see *Correspondence* 1:291 n. 18.
3. Francke here dates the letter 29 September; at the end he dates it 27 September.
4. The letter Francke is referring to was written to him by Johann Michael Wagner from Venice and dated 10 February 1751. In this letter Wagner relates that a Lutheran merchant, by the name of Sigismund Streit, would like to bequeath several thousand gulden to the Lutheran congregations in America. Wagner is asking if Francke can arrange the transfer of the money and if he knows of a safe investment opportunity for it. See *Korrespondenz* 1:430 n. 1.
5. See Ps. 146:16.
6. The text reads *ad dies vitae*.
7. The text reads *onere*.
8. A few weeks later Francke reported that the capital was designated for the East India and not the American mission. See Letter 104, dated 30 October 1751. However, the benefactor later changed his mind and let the Pennsylvania congregations have 15,000 gulden. See Letter 124:279 and 285 n.11.. For information on an undated draft of the Philadelphia trustees' and deacons' debenture in German, see *Korrespondenz* 1:430 n. 2.

Letter 100

C. R. Herttel[1] to Mühlenberg
New York, 30 September 1751

*Herttel informs Mühlenberg that Pastor Weygand will very shortly be
leaving the New York congregation. With this news and with many flattering
comments and other devices, Herttel clearly hopes to persuade Mühlenberg
to return to New York.*
Text in English: Korrespondenz *1:431. For further textual information,
see* Korrespondenz *1:431. This letter, written in English, is given here in
its original form.*

To M: Mühlenberg at Providence:

Sir, I was very sorry to hear of your sickness at Philadelphia in your
voyage home! which I hope, you have recovred and found your family in
good health! I am informed that Mr Weygand[2] doth not intend to stay
longer with us till the 8 of october,[3] and then we shall be left alone in case
you should not come, which would make me very sorry to see, since you
had made such a good beginning. A great many Friends of other
denominations as well as of our own, are dayly inquiring, to know, when
you return, so that I am rejoyced to see, what Impressions your preaching
has had, and what Veneration they have for your person *I hope* God will
bless you with Health and strength to bear the fatiguing voyage, that we
may have the pleasure to see you again, at the time appointed which we are
all heartily wishing for. I conclude after giving my kind Respect—Sir your
most humble servant

Neuyork Sept: 30, 1751   C. R. Herttel

P.S. I have forwarded the Petition[4] to the Reverd: Mr. Ziegenhagen.
P.S. The Clerk of your Church is gone a voyage to sea, so that we are
quite poorly off, when Mr. Weygand goes away!

---

1. C. R. Herttel was a member of the church council of the Dutch Lutheran congregation in New
York and one of the signatories of the call letter to Mühlenberg of 8 November 1750 (Letter 84).
2. On Johann Albert Weygand, see Letter 71 n. 21.

3. Mühlenberg left New York on 26 August 1751 to travel back to his Pennsylvania congregations; see *Journals* 1:308. It is evident from his journal that Weygand was supposed to care for the New York congregation in his absence. We read there: "None of my colleagues in Pennsylvania could take my place in New York, but, on the other hand, I could not leave the little congregation alone in these critical circumstances without danger. Consequently I wrote to Mr. Weygand and his congregation and asked that he should stay in New York for six weeks until I returned, for he understands a little English and Dutch" (*Journals* 1:302). After his return to Pennsylvania, however, Mühlenberg had to change his plans: "The work had so piled up that the six weeks elapsed all too quickly and made impossible my return to New York, more particularly as I had learned through letters from Europe that two new preachers for Pennsylvania were about to set out on their voyage. The New Yorkers were deeply dismayed and grieved when they learned that I would not be able to come before winter" (*Journals* 1:308). Mühlenberg did not return to New York until May 1752.

4. Not extant. Presumably the petition related to the proposed new settlement between the Delaware River and Rochester, which Mühlenberg discusses in the first paragraph of his 9 January 1751 letter to Herttel (Letter 109).

Letter 101

Gotthilf August Francke to the Pastors and Assistant Pastors
in Pennsylvania
Halle, 15 October 1751

*Here we see Francke exercising a ministry of pastoral care of the clergy
in Pennsylvania, particularly those who have been in the field for a longer
period of time. He trusts that the presence of new coworkers--who are now
on their way in the persons of Johann Dietrich Matthias Heinzelmann and
Friedrich Schultze--will offer renewed joy and encouragement. He recognizes
the importance of the close fellowship that the clergy enjoy and worries
about whether some who have come into the fellowship in an irregular
manner might not endanger the fraternal relations. He holds up the annual
conference of the ministerium as a key to maintaining and building up the
fellowship in their setting. It is also necessary for the newer, younger
members of the group to look to the older ones for advice, especially on
major issues like marriage. Francke devotes considerable space to a
discussion of the significance and uniqueness of clergy marriages. He
concludes the letter by acknowledging the difficulties the clergy face in a
sinful world, but calls on them to persevere and to trust in the grace of God.*

Text in German: Korrespondenz *1:432-36. For further textual
information, see* Korrespondenz *1:436.*

To
all the pastors, assistant pastors
and adjunct pastors of the united congregations
in Pennsylvania[1]

15 October 1751

Reverend,
Dearly beloved Brothers in the Lord:
From my provisional letter of advice, dated 17 June of the current year,[2]
you will have seen that the Lord has finally pointed to a pair of coworkers
for you in Mr. Heintzelmann[3] and Mr. Schultze.[4] As they will presumably
already have started the additional sea voyage, I also see the divine direction
in the hastening of their voyage, even though I would have wished that their
stay in London had been somewhat longer. These lines that I had hoped to
be able to send over before their departure will now apparently have to wait

for the next ship.[5] Other hindrances prevented me from sending them over sooner. Nevertheless I rejoice that God has hastened the new coworkers on their way, as you, the older pastors, are most in need of their help. The approval they met with on the way and the frame of mind in which they set out from here give me hope that in time their work in Pennsylvania will also not be without blessing. The older ones will look after them in love and instruct them in the circumstances there so that they learn to accommodate themselves to them. Because I do not know what may have changed in the circumstances there in the meantime, I leave entirely to the three pastors the arrangements about their placement.

It is my heartfelt wish that through the arrival of these new helpers the Lord would richly comfort and encourage those who for a longer time already have been longing for relief under the manifold burden of their work. The missionaries in India have always testified that they were always reawakened through the arrival of new coworkers to gather up their courage when it wanted to sink under various afflictions and to attack the work of the Lord with new joy. Therefore, I also do not doubt that you will experience similar encouragement through the arrival of these fresh workers.

Although I wanted on this occasion to mention what would be most useful and necessary to say to you from here at this time to give you new encouragement, nevertheless I cannot hide the fact, first of all, that it has caused me anxiety at times about whether one or another person not sent out from here who has been taken up into your fellowship might not in time create an opportunity for some discord in your ministerium. As your numbers will now be increased through these new helpers, I have made every effort to select such persons of whom I could hope that they would carry on the work of the Lord harmoniously with the older pastors, allow themselves to be led willingly by them and enter into a cordial relationship with them. Because I have some experience in how easy it is when a number of people begin to work together at some project that something arises which can become the occasion for all sorts of misunderstandings; and because it is always to be seen as a special kindness of God when he knits hearts together in such a way that each person always accommodates himself to the other, prefers the insights and reminders of the other to his own thoughts and opinions, and ultimately seeks to maintain the collegial bond of peace with everyone in true brotherly love:[6] therefore, I ask both you and the newly arrived coworkers most heartily and fraternally in the Lord that you would together heartily petition the God of peace for this grace that he himself would bind your hearts in such close and inward love that the enemy might find no opportunity, even in insignificant matters, to cause mistrust and misunderstanding among you. As the sincere and intimate relationship you have had together until now has always helped to give you much consolation and support and has contributed greatly to the blessed continuance of God's work, there is surely nothing more important to maintain and nothing can ease your often difficult circumstances more than just this sincere spirit of mutual trust among yourselves and its constant maintenance and increase. Therefore if one or the other person should occasionally think that his opinion in this or that matter was more solid than his brother's insights, it would nevertheless still be better, as far as it can be done in good conscience, rather to follow the reminders of the other and conversely to deny one's own insights, even one's own comfort, rather than to deprive oneself even partially of the great advantage which you have in the collegial relationship. Another factor affecting you is that you live quite far from one another and therefore do not have the opportunity to explain what you have in mind to each other. For this reason it is all the more important to avoid all offence, because at a distance it cannot be easily resolved, and conversely not to entertain any untimely suspicions. In such circumstances it is also necessary for this reason that one often give preference to the advice of the other to one's own: so that the other person is not made hesitant in other instances in turn to take the part of another with his advice. As it is, more often than not another person who is not so involved in a matter, and therefore can reflect on it with more composure, hits the mark much better which one cannot always grasp initially as one is still so preoccupied; nevertheless afterwards it sometimes becomes obvious to oneself, and through the outcome it is confirmed, and one has to admit that he was not able to grasp it then but now recognizes clearly that the proposal or advice of the other person had been good and sound.

It would be my heartfelt wish that you had more opportunity to come together more frequently to complain to one another about your troubles and ask for advice, to console and support one another, and to cheer each other up. Because this is not always possible on account of the distance, it is that much more useful that you at least have the opportunity to strengthen one another once annually at the conference. Consequently, this conference is in this respect a very useful and necessary arrangement. May the Lord allow it to continue to be a rich blessing for your common refreshment and unity. As all of this actually deals with relationships and harmony, therefore in particular the older as well as the younger pastors and coworkers will also continue to acknowledge the gifts, insights and experience of the three pastors so that they follow them most willingly in all things. As these latter have accepted them in all things with fatherly love and will continue to accept them in the future, so the former also have to demonstrate their compliance with even more willing hearts. If matters proceed in this way, both sides make their lives easier. Because the outward circumstances for a pastor more often than not have a great impact on his ministry, and the selection of a wife affects them more than anything else, I have previously indicated that I will not think the worse of anyone in those circumstances if he marries; rather, for the sake of sparing the energies of the workers, even for the sake of the ministry itself, and so much more for the prevention of all slander, I am always happy to see you enter into marriage; similarly, it is quite pleasing to me that you are mostly provided with helpmates. In this matter, however, a well considered choice and the discernment of the traces and leading of God are essential. Therefore, the newer ones, if circumstances should arise in which they desire to make a change, should not undertake anything in this matter without consultation and deliberation with the pastors, just as I do not doubt that Mr. Kurtz,[7] Mr. Schaum,[8] and Mr. Weygand[9] similarly will have drawn on the pastors' advice in this matter. This reminder takes into account what is best for your own good as well as what is best for all. There is a great deal that has to be considered when a pastor marries. He not only has to look for a true fear of God and a disposition that is peaceable and appropriate for him, as do other Christians, so that in future his wife does not become more of an annoyance and a hindrance than an assistance to him in his inner and outer circumstances; for a pastor, there are in addition many special considerations to be observed if he does not want to lose all the respect and confidence of his hearers through a hasty marriage--as often happens. In Pennsylvania this is of even greater importance than in Germany, for the congregations can be kept in order and obedience by nothing other than the authority and esteem which a pastor gains for himself with them. Consequently, if a pastor does not select the kind of person who is highly praised by all and who is and was already in the past highly respected both on account of her estate as well as on account of her true piety and Christian, virtuous conduct; or if he blunders in some situation, concerning which foolish people, even without cause, are given an opportunity to speak evil; he can in this way suddenly lose his authority and consequently make his ministry ten times more difficult for himself than it has been previously. Therefore, when I particularly ask the new helpers to do nothing in this matter without advice, I am asking of them in this matter nothing other than what their own Christian consideration, even without this, can teach and remind them. Especially as they have not known a person for as long a time as have the older pastors, and some matters could be known to these latter which might raise a reasonable doubt, it would therefore be an indiscretion if one wanted to undertake something in such an important matter without first making careful inquiries of others, and especially of one's superiors. In this one should also beware that one does not take a person too much to heart before one has also adequately assured oneself of all the circumstances, much less proceed further in this matter, because afterwards it is not easy, if hindrances and doubts do arise, to extricate onself again--even as it is much more difficult to give advice when a matter is no longer entirely undecided.[10]

My intention in this, however, is not at all that I want to exclude the individual reflection and examination before the Lord. Similarly I also have the assurance of the older pastors in any case that they are not persuading anyone to marry or that they will not, as it were, compel anyone by argument if he is not certain of God's will or if he also does not feel so inclined. For it is a foregone conclusion that it is better for the sake of dissuading a faithful brother to refrain from something in marriage matters which one might later regret or which one has only reason to fear could damage a spirit of mutual trust; conversely, just as it can never be approved if someone would want to persuade someone against his inclination, which I consider to be most inappropriate and injurious, so it can also not be approved if one would simply do something on the basis of another person's persuasion about which one still has doubts. I have gone on at greater length in discussing this subject than I had intended because I know it is of great consequence; also what my blessed father[11] was accustomed to say continues to make a great impression on me: when everything else has gone extremely well, it can often all be destroyed suddenly by a single marriage, etc., etc.-- as experience itself teaches.

As for the rest, I am well aware that the ministerial office is not only a heavy burden in and of itself but also in some respects is even heavier for you in Pennsylvania, particularly because you cannot always be there for one another for consolation and encouragement because of distance. Consequently, if each one of you in his place has to carry his own trials and tribulations and has no one else to complain to about what weighs him down and is difficult for him, one's heart then becomes very downcast and depressed and consequently is prevented from seeing the other side and discerning the help and the support of God, which everyone of you has previously experienced, and from recognizing the encouragement and the blessing which he has graciously conferred on your work according to all previous reports. Therefore I have to add this reminder, that one must arm oneself against this temptation and strengthen oneself in faith. For in the evil world in which everything is lying in wickedness,[12] one must be glad if a few hungry souls still acknowledge the word as not without all power. On the other hand, one must not allow it to strike one as strange, given the great corruption of the world, when some disobedient and stubborn fellows show their insubordination; one must not allow oneself to be too much distressed by these things but rather retain one's peace of mind before God and continue to work also with them in love and gentleness, without allowing it to show that one has been affected and grieved by their behavior. But of course to do this requires a special power of faith, to which one also needs to awaken oneself daily and continuously, recognizing, however, that such a power is actually only a grace of God which one cannot grasp on one's own. May the Lord himself support you graciously and powerfully, take care of you in a fatherly way in all circumstances and continue to save many souls through your service so that his name may be glorified. With this I remain in cordial love and devotion ever

Your,

G. A. Francke

---

1. Francke is addressing all the pastors and catechists that have been sent out and is using terms to describe the various offices that he had previously suggested to Mühlenberg. See Letter 73:25.
2. Not extant.
3. Johann Dietrich Matthias Heinzelmann (1726-56) studied theology in Halle. From 1749 he was a teacher there at the girls' school, the orphans' school, and the Latina. After his ordination he went in July 1751 to America, together with Friedrich Schultze. He was first of all an assistant to Brunnholz in Philadelphia; in the summer of 1753 he was called to be associate pastor there. In 1754 he married Margarethe Weiser, sister of Anna Maria Mühlenberg née Weiser, and thus became a brother-in-law of Mühlenberg. See *HN2/1*:262f.; *Pastors and People* 1:55f.
4. On Friedrich Schultze, see Letter 89 n. 4.
5. Heinzelmann and Schultze arrived in London on 2 September 1751; they left London again on 28 September 1751. See *Korrespondenz* 1:436 n. 4.
6. See Eph. 4:3.
7. On Johann Nicolaus Kurz, see *Correspondence* 1:154 n. 5 and 341 n. 16.
8. On Johann Helfrich Schaum, see Letter 71 n. 9.
9. On Johann Albert Weygand, see Letter 71 n. 21.
10. The text reads *res . . . integra.*
11. August Hermann Francke (1663-1727), the founder of the famous institutions at Halle that bore his name.
12. See 1 John 5:19. The text is an allusion to this passage in Luther's translation into German.

Letter 102

Gotthilf August Francke to Mühlenberg
Halle, 20 October 1751

*This is another pastoral letter (see Letter 101) by Francke, this time to
Mühlenberg alone. In addition to expressing his concern for Mühlenberg's
welfare, Francke also considers how best to limit the damage done by Pastor
Handschuh's hasty marriage.*
Text in German: Korrespondenz *1:436-39.   For further textual
information, see* Korrespondenz *1:439.*

To Pastor Mühlenberg in Providence

20 October 1751

Reverend,
Dearly beloved Brother in the Lord:
Although I cannot deny that I was very distressed by your esteemed letter
from New York, dated 15 June of the current year,[1] nevertheless I thank
you heartily that you lay bare your heart in it to Court Preacher
Ziegenhagen and me and want to report everything that is burdening and
troubling you. I am very glad to participate in your trials and tribulations,
and to help your sighing and pleading to God for the work in Pennsylvania,
so that God having once stretched out his hand to this people would not
withdraw it again or allow his work to decline.

What most affected me and caused me to worry is your weakness and the
repeated serious illness that you were experiencing at the time you were
sending off your letter. With all my heart I wish that through God's
gracious help it may not only be happily over, but also that the Lord would
sustain and strengthen you in the future for the sake of his work. I also
trust the faithful God not to take you away prematurely, for you are now
still so necessary.

In terms of the other questionable matters, I cannot deny that, although
I knew nothing of the previous circumstances of his wife, I was not pleased
from the very beginning with the report about Mr. Handschuh's marriage,
as he himself makes reference to it in his diary. My reason for this is
because he took her in as his housekeeper without having previously totally
dismissed her again for a period of time from his house.[2] I am all the more
puzzled because he was so hasty in the matter and did not once discuss it

beforehand with his dear colleagues.   And now, as a result of this inadequately considered action and of the dear man's manner of dealing with the people, which was obviously neither evangelical nor cautious enough, such great harm has been done to the kingdom of God that the previous work in the congregation at Lancaster now appears to have been in vain (in that it is now vacant and open to the Moravians, who will be triumphing greatly, and to other faithless workers).[3] May the faithful God forbid that dear Mr. Brunnholz should make the same mistake so that not everything that has already been built up should collapse.[4]

All the same, I feel genuine sympathy for dear Mr. Handschuh and, although he blundered in this matter, I consider he was simply overhasty and therefore like you I for my part gladly pardon him.   Dear Mr. Handschuh, of whom I am otherwise very fond, is admittedly of a rather timid nature; added to this is his frailty.   Consequently, one must have just that much more patience with him, for much can be attributed to his timidity and frailty.   What otherwise pleased me in his most recent diary[5] was that he mentioned several times how he had been corrected by you, both orally and in writing, and testified that he was grateful for it.

To what conclusion does our consideration of these somewhat awkward appearing circumstances lead us?   Should we allow our courage to falter, weighed down as we are in our leadership of God's work both outwardly and inwardly by so many other heavy burdens?   For we see that many things in which we placed our highest hope do not appear to be going forward (according to our understanding) but rather are going backward. Or should we rather, even if we cannot always bring ourselves in faith to overlook all such things with great joyfulness, nevertheless with tears commend the matter to God, believing that even out of the mistakes and trespasses of his servants and the evils that result from them, he will still bring forth something good and direct everything so that finally his kingdom can always be extended further?

Well, my dear brother, you have persevered faithfully until now under all sorts of very heavy burdens, you have spared no effort and work, and you have undertaken many a difficult and extremely dangerous ride at the expense of your strength.   And the faithful God has also given his blessing to your work to the extent that your diaries are full of his particular traces. Especially the Lord has also given you wisdom to come through many a difficult situation in the way you did and to find a means by which the cause of God has always been advanced. May the Lord continue to give you wisdom, on the one hand, to deal with your colleagues who are for the most part upright, so that above all the bond of peace is maintained[6] and that whatever could occasion any disadvantage to the cause of God might be averted through helpful presentations; and, on the other hand, with God's help also to put back on track again one or the other thing that seems to have gone astray.   It is extremely pleasing to me that the two new coworkers, Mr. Heintzelmann[7] and Mr. Schultze,[8] can still be sent off before winter. I hope that their arrival will restore you once again. The first one, Mr. Heintzelmann, has a considerable advantage over Mr. Schultze in terms of knowledge; the foundation of his Christian faith also goes deeper. I also believe he will do quite well with the large amount of work, for he has demonstrated that he has soundness of health and would choose for himself the kind of position where he would have to be constantly occupied, something which he probably will not lack.   Mr. Schultze does not have the steady character of the former. Nevertheless I hope he will let himself be instructed, for he always demonstrates a willing obedience, and, if he will allow himself to be ever more securely placed on the right track, that in the course of his activity he will not prove to be unsuitable.

I have already sent off in the previous mail to England a letter to all the pastors[9] into which I incorporated in general terms[10] such reminders as seemed necessary to me on the basis of the circumstances you reported. It is my wish that these will be received well and might have the desired effect. How and in what way I could continue to be of some further help to you from here, please inform me.   I still intend to write to Mr. Handschuch in particular and perhaps also to Mr. Brunnholz; in this I will exercise the necessary precaution so that they cannot become suspicious of Your Reverence. I will also still compose a letter to all the congregations to impress upon them their duties to their pastors who are set over them and how they should conduct themselves over against the word of God that is proclaimed to them.[11]

I would wish I could be helpful to Your Reverence in particular by providing some easing of your manifold burden and I regret that I could not from the very beginning fulfill your request for a printing press.   I was preoccupied with the idea that the new printer in Philadelphia had started his printing press at your suggestion; otherwise I would have had no hesitation about sending over at that time the characters for the printing press which were ready to go. I would also gladly have sent them afterwards if you had only informed me to that effect. From your last letter I cannot quite tell if you still require them, because in particular I do not know if you still have the opportunity to get the people required to keep it going. I am therefore only requesting a brief response to determine whether I can be of service to you; if so, I will send over the characters without delay at the earliest opportunity.

May the faithful God who has been with you until now continue to keep you alive and in good health for his service. With his own empowering strength may he replace in you the energies you have already lost and graciously help you through all particular circumstances so that his name may be glorified--and also so that we may be gladdened by good news. With cordial greetings also from my dear wife, I remain ever

Your,

G. A. Francke

---

1. Letter 93.
2. Francke is drawing on Handschuh's journal of 20 and 21 November 1749 and 8 March 1750. See *HN2/1*:684f. and Letter 89 n. 17. On Johann Friedrich Handschuh, see *Correspondence* 1:291 n. 18.
3. See Letter 93 n. 23.
4. See Letter 93 n. 12. On Peter Brunnholz, see Letter 71 n. 3.
5. The reference is to Handschuh's journal of 7 September 1748 to 16 May 1750, extracts of which are printed in *HN1*:392-421 and *HN2/2*:531-48.
6. See Eph. 4:3.
7. On Johann Dietrich Matthias Heinzelmann, see Letter 101 n. 3.
8. On Friedrich Schultze, see Letter 89 n. 4.
9. Letter 101.
10. The text reads *in generalioribus*.
11. Here Francke initially continued the letter as follows: ". . . with the intention of determining —whereby I would not give any indication that I knew anything about the removal of Mr. Handschuh—whether the congregation in Lancaster might thereby possibly be induced once again to accept one of the new assistants, so that at least the Moravians do not attract everyone to themselves again. Should I still send over such a letter? I am hereby stating beforehand that I leave the decision up to you because you can best evaluate the present circumstances. Do you think it will be advisable to address it to the still favorably inclined deacons, as they were the ones who presented it to the others, or would you want to have it read to the congregation, or would you rather that it simply not be sent." This passage has been stricken. The letter to the congregations in Pennsylvania is not extant.

Letter 103

Gotthilf August Francke to Peter Brunnholz, Johann Friedrich Handschuh
and Mühlenberg
Halle, 29 October 1751

*Francke here communicates to the Pennsylvania pastors the proposal of
a Mr. J. G. Krause of Glogau that German colonists settle in the Bahamas
rather than Pennsylvania and solicits their response.*
Text in German: Korrespondenz *1:440. For further textual information,
see* Korrespondenz *1:440.*

To the three pastors in Pennsylvania

29 October 1751

Reverend,
Dearly beloved Brothers in the Lord:
Herewith I am sending a letter from a man in Glogau which contains a
proposal about how, in the opinion of this man who is otherwise unknown
to me, the poor and superfluous German colonists in Pennsylvania can be
helped in some way.[1] My reaction to this proposal can be seen in my
response; for this reason I enclose a copy of it.[2] When you have an
opportunity please report to me very briefly your thoughts which I can in
turn report to the author of the letter and thereby convince him that I have
sent his letter as promised. Undoubtedly I will have further correspondence
with him, which I am quite happy to maintain. With this I remain

Your,
G. A. Francke

---

1. The letter of the town councillor J. G. Krause to Francke is dated Glogau, 8 September 1751.
In this letter Krause comments on reports he has seen in the Halle newspapers that the German
colonists in Pennsylvania have a hard time finding places for themselves. He therefore suggests they
should go to the Bahamas because these islands are only sparsely populated. He requests that this
proposal be shared with Mühlenberg and Brunnholz. See *Korrespondenz* 1:440 n. 1.
2. Francke's response is dated Halle, 28 October 1751. Francke thanks Krause for his letter of 8
September 1751 and reports that he has passed on the proposal to England and Pennsylvania.
Nevertheless, he does raise concerns about sending colonists into a country in which their economic
and religious support cannot be guaranteed. To send pastors to the Bahamas would entail
considerable difficulties and expense. See *Korrespondenz* 1:440 n.2.

Letter 104

Gotthilf August Francke to the Pastors in Pennsylvania
Halle, 30 October 1751

This letter, which is actually a postscript to Letter 103, squelches (for the time being) the hope of a substantial gift to the Pennsylvania congregations from an as yet unknown benefactor (see Letter 99).

Text in German: Korrespondenz *1:440-41.* *For further textual information, see* Korrespondenz *1:441.*

To all
the pastors
in Pennsylvania

30 October 1751

P. S. The copy of the accompanying letter is just now being made.[1] I will send it over immediately so that if you should already have received my previous letter of 22 September,[2] in which I led you to hope that a certain benefactor outside of Germany had made a substantial gift of several thousand reichstalers for Pennsylvania, with the reservation of the interest for the duration of his life, you may now see from this letter that this was an error on the part of that merchant who reported this to me at that time. I hope you will not have said anything to the congregations yet about it. But if that has already happened, there is no other advice than to undeceive them again. The congregations could in the meantime see from this that the disorder that still prevails among them is the reason many other benefactors would hold back.

Halle, as in the letter, 30 October 1751

---

1. Not extant.
2. Letter 99, dated 27 (or 29) September 1751. The benefactor, however, later changed his mind a second time and let the Pennsylvania congregations have 15,000 pounds. See Letter 124:279 and 285 n.11.

Letter 105

Friedrich Michael Ziegenhagen to Mühlenberg
Kensington, 7 November 1751

*In this postscript to Francke's letter of 20 October 1751 (Letter 102)--
apparently Ziegenhagen's first direct communication with Mühlenberg in the
more than nine years since Mühlenberg left for America--Ziegenhagen
echoes Francke's concern for Mühlenberg's well-being and makes a two-fold
request: (1) That Mühlenberg stay with his Pennsylvania congregations. (2)
That he help to squelch rumors about Brunnholz's conduct and thus help to
preserve Brunnholz's reputation.*
Text in German: Korrespondenz *1:441-42.* *For further textual
information, see* Korrespondenz *1:442.*

P. S. to Pastor Mühlenberg, etc.

Dear Dr. Francke has sent me unsealed the preceding letter[1] to our dear
brother and was kind enough to communicate the content of it to me. As
I was reading through it I felt in myself a desire, through the addition of
several lines, to assure my most worthy brother that although I myself have
not written in a long time, I am and remain of the same disposition toward
him as Dr. Francke. The compassion, love and cordial wishes which he
expresses in the accompanying letter, I repeat herewith as my own, and I
ask you to believe confidently that it would be a heartfelt joy for me to be
able to come to your help in any way. What my situation is, however, and
how great are my weakness and incapacity are already well known to you
from before, and you will receive a further report of them from the new
assistants, Mr. Heinzelmann[2] and Mr. Schultze,[3] who will already have
arrived there by the time these lines reach you. But what I want to add to
what Dr. Francke has written consists in a double request, namely:
    (1) That you would not change your present station, and least of all
exchange it for another one in New York. God has sent you to the poor,
unruly and torn apart congregations in Philadelphia, New Hanover and
Providence; also, in his mercy he made a beginning of improvement through
your service and work, with good hope for the future. This is therefore
your post which he has assigned to you and at which you can most
confidently trust in his grace, help and blessing. Consequently it is not to
be abandoned in any way, for any reason--unless it be the clear and
undoubted will of God. The harm that would result from this, as well for

yourself as for the previously mentioned congregations, could be very considerable. For this reason I am taking the opportunity to lay on your heart the words from Hebrews 10:35-36, and may God's Spirit himself call out to you: Therefore do not throw away your confidence, which has great reward. For you have need of endurance, so that you may do the will of God and receive the promise abundantly at the right time and be comforted. Amen.

(2) The second thing I am requesting relates to your concern for dear[4] Mr. Brunnholz. I have to admit that the serious mistake that was made in the marriage matter at Lancaster has greatly affected me.[5] But there would be more of this sort of thing if the same thing would be repeated at Philadelphia. I hope, however, that the distressing consequences of the Lancaster mistake will not only serve as a warning and instruction to others but also that Mr. Brunnholz possesses more grace, wisdom and vigilance than to allow himself to be so overtaken and carried away.[6] Just for this reason I am requesting you not to give quick or total credence to the rumors that are circulating but rather to deny them and suppress them with all your power, so that in every way the reputation of Mr. Brunnholz is preserved and remains unharmed. From this it naturally follows that the dear brother will show others through his cordial relationship with Mr. Brunnholz and the way he deals with him that the former brotherly love and harmony certainly continue between the two of you, and therefore the gossip that has arisen must be without foundation.

In the meantime would you be so good as to report very openly in your next letter how this matter is proceeding or has proceeded.

May the gracious God have mercy on all his servants for his Son's sake; may he sanctify and purify you of everything that is harmful not only to your own soul but also to the congregations entrusted to you; may he make you very useful and blessed to him, to the honor of his name and to the true salvation of many thousand people. May he bless you and your dear family with rich grace for Christ's sake, etc.

Kensington   Wholly yours,
7 November 1751   Fr. M. Ziegenhagen

---

1. Letter 102.
2. On Johann Dietrich Matthias Heinzelmann, see Letter 101 n. 3.
3. On Friedrich Schultze, see Letter 89 n. 4.
4. Reading the "L." as an abbreviation for "Lieben." On Peter Brunnholz, see Letter 71 n. 3.
5. On Handschuh's marriage, see Letter 89 n. 17. On Johann Friedrich Handschuh, see *Correspondence* 1:291 n. 18.
6. See *Journals* 1:258f.

Letter 106

To Johann Philipp Fresenius[1]
Providence, 15 November 1751

Johann Philipp Fresenius was among other things a noted opponent of Count Zinzendorf and the Moravians. (Zinzendorf is said to have called him a "devil incarnate"!) It is particularly in this capacity that Mühlenberg writes to him; with strong military images, Mühlenberg commends Fresenius for his zeal in attacking the Moravians.

Mühlenberg also takes the liberty of acquainting Fresenius with the situation of the Lutheran church in Pennsylvania, New Jersey and New York. Along with some general observations about the church that are intended to provide some orientation to the North American scene for Fresenius, Mühlenberg also gives a quick sketch of each parish and of all the pastors (including some of the more recent and more troublesome imposters) that he has had contact with over the years. Thus, the letter gives the reader insight into the breadth of Mühlenberg's involvement and a good overview of the ecclesiastical situation at this time.

Text in German: Korrespondenz *1:443-53. For further textual information, see* Korrespondenz *1:453.*

Most reverend and learned Doctor,
Most honorable Senior,
Most well-disposed Patron:
The most important office that Your Reverence occupies, the many and most necessary tasks that are connected with it, the time which is short and carefully scheduled--these should really have kept me from dispatching an insignificant letter from America, if more reasons had not tipped the scale in favor of my taking the liberty: I have not had the honor in my life to know Your Reverence personally, but this deficiency has been all the more richly compensated for inasmuch as I have received from various public writings and private letters a clear conception of your inner being, the beautiful talent of your sanctified spiritual powers and gifts used faithfully to the glory of God and the benefit of our Lutheran church.   The more solitary and rare such pillars and guardians are in our Lutheran church at the present time, the more zealously and earnestly the little flock should plead that the gracious and merciful God would crown these few with long life, continuous strength and steadfast faithfulness; and that he would make large the number of those who could place themselves in front of the crevice and become a wall, so that we would not only have to be left standing at the song of lament in Psalm 12 but might also go on with joyful hearts to sing

the psalms of praise as well.

What has come into my unworthy hands and heart from Your Reverence's public and private writings consists in the following: (1) Nine years ago while I was with the reverend Royal Court Preacher in London, I read a letter from you about the German congregations in Pennsylvania.[2] (2) I profited from a well-disposed writing seven years ago dealing with Valentin Krafft which Your Reverence sent to the deacons of the congregation in Providence, in which you shared wise, well-intentioned proposals for the building up and spread of our Lutheran church in Pennsylvania.[3] (3) The priceless, thorough writings against the Zinzendorf faction.[4] (4) A letter to the Lutheran pastors in Pennsylvania, occasioned by Mr. Weygand,[5] in which especially your fatherly love and conscientiousness for our poor, scattered Lutherans and your good advice about how to help our congregations shine through. (5) The confession and communion book which is very necessary and edifying for our church.[6] (7) The choice and pithy meditations on the Sunday texts.[7] Your Reverence, with the wisdom granted you by God, has sufficiently experienced, grasped and understood that the true church of Jesus Christ has had no more destructive, dangerous and crafty enemies since the time of the apostles than the Zinzendorf sect. For the last twelve years the lot has fallen to me to be in their neighborhood, to note their movements, plans, writings, and attacks, and to observe the defence and preparations of our Lutheran church. With sadness I have learned that we did not seem to be a match for their stratagems of war and their serpentine deviousness, because they advanced mightily and like a plague creeping in the dark they gained the upper hand. The commanding officers and generals of our church were in part badly trained to stand against such a crafty enemy, because they had learned only the theoretical part of the divine knowledge and had not encountered the praxis; also they had more military exercises on paper than in their hearts. Consequently they often beat the air, and when they thought they were on target they lacked the right judgment, insight into the point of the controversy[8], the most essential truths, and the power of godliness. Thus, they often opened the door and gate to the enemy, put the sword into his hand, or themselves fought against the heart[9] of our Christian religion when they dared to do battle and attack.

I have read various writings by our scholars against the Zinzendorfers which fought more against our blessed Luther, Johann Arndt,[10] Dr. Spener[11] and other resplendent theologians than against the Zinzendorfers and did more damage than good. Great, elaborate, literalist learning, mere worldly wisdom and imposing orators[12] were not frightening to enemies of this kind for they had taken shelter behind a summary of selected teachings from the essential dogmatics and ethics of the great world Savior, which they had carried off from the armory of our Lutheran church and which will confound the doctrine of reason. Even *when* other combatants arose and fought against these foes out of secondary motives or personal hatred or with a roguish eye, this was even less helpful. For they used to answer: Jesus we know, and Paul we know; but who are you?[13] Another group of overseers and leaders of our Lutheran church had sufficient theory and praxis, insight and experience of the Lutheran doctrine and the power of godliness that flows from it; but hope, love and forbearance, as well perhaps as insufficient experience to grasp the depths of the disguised angel of light[14] and the fear of damaging the wheat through an untimely uprooting of the weeds,[15] held them back. In the meantime the enemy gained the upper hand and became so mighty that I and other lower servants like me who were vainly standing sentry were in danger of losing our courage and having our hearts break as we saw countries, cities, towns and houses taken in by trickery and so many people from a variety of estates made into slaves in body and soul. Congregational pastors and teachers such as I and my peers have very little time, vocation and skill to take the offensive against such a powerful enemy; we are more committed to standing at the posts to which we have been assigned and proceeding defensively in accordance with the gifts and faithfulness God has granted. But those who are in high offices and honors should be all the more watchful, stouthearted and courageous so that they might engage the enemy in good time and give us, as undershepherds, news and warning at the right time because that is what their office and duty demand. Oh, how I rejoiced, how I bent my knee before God when I saw Your Reverence's and other highly experienced teachers' writings against the abominable sect! Here and there a few individual skirmishes had taken place, but the thorough, incisive, conclusive, two-edged, unaffected, impartial, clear, on target and stouthearted writing style of Your Reverence and other divines attacked the enemy in his entrenchments in the name of the Lord and gave rise to the first general battle. "A mighty fortress is our God, a trusty shield and weapon," etc., etc.[16] *Oh, that* more of the same will occur in the name of the Lord, and such ringleaders will be disgraced and their hearts converted so that they might give back again their booty, the many thousand poor souls and particularly the innocent children! We would certainly have deserved it if God had removed his lampstand from us[17] and allowed the powerful errors to get the upper hand because we did not give careful consideration to and make appropriate use of the many gracious visitations of the present century, much less of all those since the Reformation; rather, unfortunately, in our unrighteousness we all too frequently obstructed the bright light of truth. But because there may still be many who seek and fear the Lord, he will have mercy for the sake of Jesus Christ, as a father has on his children[18], and he will allow his holy word and sacraments to remain with us. Having said this, the major purpose of my insignificant letter is to give humble thanks to Your Reverence from the bottom of my heart that you were willing to endure so much trouble, dishonor, contempt and abuse of the enemy for the sake of Jesus Christ and that you have borne witness to and defended the truth. "Fear not," says the Lord, "I am your shield and your very great reward."[19]

After this I thought Your Reverence would not construe it amiss if I would give a small report about our congregations and circumstances, because you as a teacher and leader of the Lutheran church rightly participate in what we encounter in our part of the whole. In the city of Philadelphia the number of members in our congregation grows every year, but it consists mainly of the materially poor because the people who have just arrived tend to settle in the city first until they find further opportunity in the country. Those that stay in the city have to support themselves as day laborers and artisans and they have to work very hard if they are supposed to pay for their transportation alongside their daily bread. The church is now completed, furnished with an organ from Heilbronn,[20] and suitable for divine worship. Unfortunately, however, it is still heavily in debt because construction in this country, particularly in the city, is very expensive, and the congregation is poor. Because our congregations remain with the Augsburg Confession and its polity and because in this country, under the rule of Great Britain, there is free practice of religion and the political laws do not touch our church constitutions but consider only the material welfare of the subjects, it is therefore necessary to maintain a council[21] of the oldest, judicious, settled members who, in accordance with 1 Corinthians 6,[22] judge lesser matters, preserve the privileges and property of the church, keep an eye on external discipline, and, within their limits, are governors of the congregation and above all are to see that churches, schools and divine worship will be passed down to our descendants. The regular pastor always presides at this council, and it is called a church council because, in accord with their responsibility, they are to counsel and promote what is best for the church. In addition to the council, every one or two years two deacons are elected by majority vote who are to serve tables in accordance with Acts 6,[23] so that the pastors might devote themselves more completely to prayer and the ministry of the word.

The congregation in Philadelphia is presently still being served by Pastor Brunnholtz.[24] Until now he has made a great effort to work openly and with the old and the young in particular, to show the way to life. The second congregation is in Germantown, a German city or borough seven miles from Philadelphia. Within a few years this congregation has grown a great deal and at present it is increasing still more because Pastor Handshue, who was first placed in Lancaster for a couple of years for a trial period,[25] is now located there. The faithful ministry of Mr. Handshue does not remain without blessing but already displays an occasional blossom and fruit, even though the congregation is still in debt on account of the construction of the church and because it has many materially poor people who are more able to support the pastor by wishing him well than to make a contribution. The congregations in the Providence and New Hanover township, along with their outparishes, are served by me alternately, in great weakness because I have pretty much forfeited my strength and health. The congregation members of the church in Providence live scattered and very far apart among all sorts of sects. With mites from their own sustenance[26] and through the liberal provisions for the future of our very reverend overseers and the benevolent collections from Europe, they have a fine stone church and schoolhouse; they also now have an organ and the opportunity to edify their souls through God's word and the Spirit who is united with it.

The congregation in New Hanover is one of the strongest in terms of the number of members. They had built a church of wood and roofed it when I came into the country.[27] But wood construction does not last in this country, and the church is much too small for the congregation. Therefore we will be forced to build a larger one of stone. We do not yet have anything set aside for this, and we have many materially poor members who would gladly help if they could. It would be desirable if our Fathers, patrons and benefactors might also be kind enough to hasten to the aid of this poor little group and help them with benevolent collections for the construction of a church, even though they already have a fine sum to give to the construction of the schoolhouse and the payment of the first church and the land. North of Providence approximately eight to twelve miles there were three congregations, named Old and New Goshenhoppen and Indianfield. They had two churches as well as a schoolhouse, and in the beginning I served them on weekdays. But in 1743 a pastor named Johann Conrad Andreae came into the country with some other German people and wangled his way into the congregations.[28] He had been in the Zweibrücken region and, as we learned, had been dismissed in good standing on account of gross misdeeds. He then travelled to many universities in Germany where he underhandedly obtained favorable, one-sided responses dealing with his dismissal. Eventually he came to Pennsylvania. During the past seven or eight years he has practised the most dreadful vices, including drunkenness, adultery, whoring, slander, etc., etc., of which I have the formal report[29] in hand. In short, he did not only sin himself, but he made the people sin and made our religion foul in front of all the sects. To cite only a few cases: The wives were not safe: he showed an old deacon an herb which permitted one to whore without fear of causing pregnancy, etc., etc. In another deacon's house he was found by the woman of the house with a disreputable woman; his hand was bloody because he had contact with her while she was menstruating.[30] Several times he filled the pulpit and chancel chair with vomit during the service, etc. He performed marriages for all kinds of people against his better knowledge: for example, a man with his stepdaughter, a man whose wife was still alive to another woman, another man to his wife's sister whom he had impregnated. Finally he also gave two living men to one woman, for which charges were laid with the authorities. In connection with this last case he was twice put into prison and was given a cash fine.[31] Because he had no money the governor pardoned him. The congregations in Old Goshenhoppen and Indianfield discharged him and asked us if we could place a candidate there as a catechist, which was done. At present Andreae is still serving the congregation in New Goshenhoppen and several other groups. He continues on his sinful journey, rebukes us at every opportunity as Moravians and pietists, and boasts of his responses from so many universities. The various sects and enemies of the church laugh about this and draw conclusions from individual cases to the whole.

Thirty to forty miles north of Providence there are four little congregations,[32] not far from Bethlehem where the Moravians have their center. These congregations are united with us and are served by a fine candidate who is a catechist.[33] These little congregations are very poor, lie far apart, but still do not want to be Zinzendorf servants and so they remain firm in our teaching. Thirty miles west of Providence a new city[34] is being established on the river called Schuylkill. Magister Wagner lives there.[35] For several years he was a pastor in Horkheim. From there he moved to New England with a colony and his family. But a quarrel arose within the colony and it scattered, and Mr. Wagner was persuaded to come from New England to Pennsylvania where he has taken on several congregations and has served till now with much outward hardship and grief. He is, indeed, poor but he leads an honest life to the extent of his abilities and he makes a great effort to keep his congregations from falling away and going over to the sects. Fourteen to twenty miles from there, to the northwest, lies Tulpehocken where our Assistant Pastor Kurtz[36] is and where there are presently four churches. The Moravians had built one of these churches on a Lutheran tract of land and torn down an old Lutheran church. But the Moravians lost their usurped right and church because most of the members fell away from them and became Lutheran again. Mr. Kurtz also makes a great effort, and his work in the congregations is not without blessing. Several miles farther up there is a preacher named Mr. Stöver.[37] He came into the country several years ago with his father; he has not studied theology but he has learned some Latin and Greek and has a lively disposition. On account of the shortage of workers[38] at that time he was ordained in Providence by a well-known young renegade preacher named Schultze.[39] He had no one who could have given him further instruction and taken him in hand with good advice. As a result of much riding back and forth in the country he became confused and led astray by some self-appointed preachers and groups, and was overtaken in his trespasses.[40] Now the more sensible years are coming along, and the dear God has brought him through severe illnesses, so that he is more inclined to enter our fellowship and to take better care of his soul, and to spend his energies on others in accord with his ability and God's proffered grace. He is presently still serving several congregations in the time that he can spare from his business enterprises.

About thirty miles southwest of Tulpehocken lies the city of Lancaster where there was a large congregation that had called a pastor from the archbishop of Sweden and had received a crypto-Moravian. The man, by the name of Nyberg,[41] was very troublesome. He gained for himself a following from among the most prominent people and formed them according to the Zinzendorfian model. He made all sorts of stringent rules and regulations, set traps and nets so that at the proper time he could suddenly pull the net shut and hand the congregation and the church over to the Zinzendorfers. But he pulled up the net before the fish were all in it, so that he caught only the fattest third of the congregation. Two thirds, however, stayed behind and fought back for the sake of the church and its rights. The matter came publicly before the secular court. At their earnest entreaties we stood by the two thirds so that they retained their church; for our part we were forced to feel the weight of "the triple L" that they mount on their shield and to experience their lying, denial, and slander.[42] I have in hand the court proceedings[43] of the whole process, but they are too extensive to include here.[44] Thereafter the Zinzendorfian party built its own church, and Mr. Nyberg himself eventually moved with his wife to Bethlehem, even though before the controversy broke out publicly he uttered the most awful curses from the pulpit on several occasions and said that if he were a Moravian brother or even had any fellowship with them, then let him have no part in the blood of Jesus Christ, etc., etc. But the Moravian party did not flourish for a long time, and the members are in part either dead or corrupt. The remaining Lutheran group, however, is very unruly as a result of the wearisome, lengthy controversy and will accept almost no discipline. We visited them occasionally; we also permitted our colleague Mr. Handshue to work there on trial into the third year. The congregation revived again, heaps of young people were instructed and confirmed, many poor congregation members were awakened and set on the way of peace; but the leaders who make up the church council and should be promoting what is best had a falling out and carried on so childishly and perversely that we finally had to call Mr. Handshue away from there[45] and place him in Germantown where he is presently working with more blessing. The group in Lancaster is now vacant and is totally losing all discipline and respectability. Magister Wagner goes there occasionally to preach and to administer the Lord's Supper. I have heard that several people would like to call Mr. Stöver there, but he is said to have declined.

Twenty miles west of Lancaster beyond the large river called the Susquehanna there is a new city, York, in the Pennsylvania region. Quite a large congregation is located here which is served by our Assistant Pastor Schaum.[46] This congregation has also suffered many trials and attacks from the Zinzendorfers. But because they had a few sensible leaders as deacons they were not overpowered but rather until now they were kept in order.

Forty miles from Philadelphia in the eastern part of the province of New Jersey there is a small group of Lutherans[47] which Pastor Brunnholtz visits occasionally. The Zinzendorfers had also crept in there and created confusion. In the western part of New Jersey there are four congregations called "on the Raritan," approximately sixty to seventy miles northwest of Philadelphia. In former times these congregations had applied to the Very Reverend Ministerium in Hamburg and received from there Magister Wolf.[48] The man was a good philologist; his Latin was excellent, and no doubt he had also mastered the theological doctrines,[49] and he had a sharp memory for temporal matters.[50] For some reason, however, he could not deliver a sermon from memory[51], but rather read off the sermons from old rough drafts. He also did not know how to relate to the country people. He married one of them and led an offensive married life, finally living in a divorced state[52]. He got into a grievous lawsuit with the congregations which lasted nearly twelve years, until the congregations were almost dispersed and the young people had almost totally run wild. Those who were left in the congregations turned to us and entreated us, for the sake of God and the last judgment, to help them. The matter was finally negotiated with a great deal of effort in the presence of three pastors so that Magister Wolf came to an agreement with the congregations and relinquished his office for ninety pounds.[53] Our ministerium served the congregations for a time by turns and brought back large numbers of young people and of old dispersed people.

A number of years ago a student of theology, Mr. Weygand by name, who was a native of the Hanau region, arrived in Pennsylvania with German people and did not know which way to turn. The so-called newlanders-- whom one could in part, according to the old fable, more fittingly call the pied pipers of Hameln[54]—had called him and promised to pay his passage. When he arrived in Philadelphia they left him sitting on the ship and did not pay his passage. If he had not found some friends he could have been sold like other servants and offered to anyone. Because he had most recently been a teacher in Frankfurt, we asked him if he had not brought along a few lines from Your Reverences, but he had not. We took him in and let him stay with us for several months. Because he led a Christian life and seemed to be orthodox in his faith, we placed him on a trial basis as a catechist for a year in the congregations on the Raritan. As the congregations gradually indicated, he proved himself to be faithful in his duties--to pass over in silence a few irregularities--and, at the request of the congregation and with the approval of our overseers, he was consecrated by the local ministerium to the office of the ministry when he had completed the trial period. The congregations have built a fine, spacious stone church in their midst, have had an organ built into it; they have also bought a piece of land for a parsonage and have not spared the mites from their livelihood; they are, however, still in debt. Because of this, as you know, Mr. Weygand petitioned Your Reverences and entreated your help for the Raritan congregations. Your Reverences saw the matter in the right light and in your well-disposed answer you displayed a fatherly love for the whole of our American church and what is generally best for it. Because in this country the congregations that hold to the Augsburg Confession and its polity and also its pastors who have the good name and the welfare of the church as their object are--thank God--in quite good fellowship and hold a conference together annually in a certain place, the whole body could, according to Your Reverences' well-disposed, fatherly advice, humbly issue the letter of petition. In my humble opinion it would be very beneficial if a fund could be established in Europe by our Very Reverend Fathers and patrons; with the interest from this fund a helping hand could be held out to one or another upright pastor who is in a poor congregation, because poverty is a hindrance in the spread of the gospel. In those congregations that are out of debt we could perhaps add the few pounds that are left over in the poor relief treasury to the fund when the church accounts are closed every year, etc., etc. These, however, are only preliminary ideas. Our Very Reverend Fathers and benefactors are wiser and will know how to do it best.

In the province of New York there are presently three Lutheran pastors who were assigned and sent from the Reverend Ministerium in Hamburg via London. The senior of that ministerium, Mr. Berckenmeyer, died this year.[55] He had been located up country in Loonenburg. The next one was Mr. Christian Knoll who served the Dutch and German Lutheran church in the city of New York; last year he gave up his office for a little over one hundred pounds and moved farther up in the country.[56] The third one, Mr. Sommer by name, is also up in the country in a congregation called Schoharie.[57] The fourth one, Mr. Hartwich by name, also still lives in the country, in the villages called Rhinebeck and Camp.[58] This last man is known to us; as far as we can judge he is preaching a pure, healthy evangelical Lutheran doctrine and leading a becoming life. He has been persecuted bitterly by his three ministerial colleagues and especially by the deceased senior. In print he was proclaimed a Moravian, but without evidence or a hearing, because in accord with the teaching of Luther he urged not only the article of justification but also daily sanctification and renewal. *That* justification that is without repentance and faith is still allowed among our people in a pinch; but justification on the basis of the apostles and our Symbolical Books and the sanctification that flows from it are called suspect, pietistic and Moravian things. In the province of New York there could be the biggest and best Lutheran congregations; but the pastors have never been much in agreement; they have always gotten in each other's hair, lived offensively, scattered the congregations, and driven them to other denominations; they have laid such a severe illness on our church that it is at death's door, etc., etc. At the end of last year the elders and deacons of our German and Dutch church in New York called on me to make an attempt to see if by God's grace their scattered congregation could again be helped.[59] I went there for several months and found there a fine stone church with a beautiful bell in the middle of the city; in addition I found a church council composed of Dutch and German members and also a small congregation of German and Dutch members. They showed me their church account book from which I learned that the church has almost 500 pounds earning interest and a good parsonage. They have an imported church constitution and liturgy which were produced by the Lutheran church in Amsterdam and which are very fitting and edifying for the American circumstances. Every Sunday I had to preach once in German and once in Dutch and to conduct a class for the children. After a while I also made an attempt to preach in the evening in English in the church; a great many English people came by for this and gave evidence of great pleasure in the Lutheran teaching and its hymns. Some also expressed great surprise that the Lutherans had such teachings because our confession had previously been held in such contempt. To my great sorrow, however, I found that a group of Germans had severed their connections with the church and bought a brewery on credit in a remote part of the city and gathered there with a German pastor. I found in the church records the documents and the reports[60] of this separation and I found no reasons for this separation other than that a couple of stubborn fellows from among the Germans wanted to be the masters of the church and its properties; they also did not like the church constitution but rather wanted to rule without discipline and integrity according to their own arbitrary ideas. These two leaders who have a very bad reputation in the city had alienated from the church a large group of German Lutherans and Reformed on the basis of all kinds of pretences and accusations and a few years earlier they had already taken on a pastor who was driven out of Württemberg on account of gross misconduct.[61] But when the authorities forbade him to preach, they returned to the church again. Afterwards they had gotten themselves involved with a notorious villain who calls himself Carl Rudolph, prince of Württemberg[62] and who has already passed through all the waterless places[63] in America. Finally they brought a young preacher from Pennsylvania whom the newlanders called a couple of years ago in Odewalde along with several families from there whom they had also persuaded; they also had him ordained for the families by three pastors. As long as the young pastor, Johann Friedrich Riess by name,[64] was at sea he had his congregation, consisting of the ten families, with him, as well as the newlanders as the patrons of the parish.[65] But when they arrived at Philadelphia the congregation dispersed along with its patrons and left Pastor Riess alone. But in this difficult situation he was able to help himself because he had some knowledge of medicine and had brought a medicine chest with him. When the fickle German party in New York heard that they called him as their pastor. I warned him and entreated him not to meddle with that party and to give no occasion for separation, because Mr. Knoll was still in the church and preaching in German and Dutch; but it was of no use, and he accepted the call. Now this German party bought the aforementioned brewery; with all kinds of lies[66] they were able to obtain permission from the governor[67] to collect in the country for a German Lutheran meeting house because they still owe 300 pounds on it. But because the collection did not go very well, as most people said there was already a Lutheran church and it was not necessary to build another one, their next scheme was to send a couple of men to Germany with touching letters to gather funds for their unnecessary church. A newlander in New York related to me that he had conferred with His Reverence Dr. and Senior Fresenius about these New York circumstances and had received fair words only. It is a matter of great regret that people undertake such things, and themselves want to build churches according to their own unsettled minds, using other benevolent Christians' contributions and credit, even though the regular church in New York is big enough for all of them and has good regulations and discipline! If the congregation at the church, which presently still consists of respectable Dutch and German members without the separated party, should not be taken by a man who understands English, German and Dutch and who is upstanding in doctrine and life, then the church with all the rest of its properties is lost and the heirs will be laughing up their sleeves. Already last year the Zinzendorfers stopped by and said that they wanted to rent it, etc., etc. I did my best to get the separated party to return but neither pleading nor imploring helps, their irrationality is too much in control. Mr. Riess was already tired of his ministry under his party because there is not the least order, discipline, honor or shame among the ringleaders. As soon as he had broken with them, they called the well-known Johann Conrad Andreae of New Goshenhoppen, but he has not moved there yet.

This is what I wanted to report to Your Reverence at present about our circumstances through a young congregation member from Providence who is the bearer of this letter. I am confident that Your Reverence will forgive my impertinence, will graciously allow me to write in future about more pleasant matters and to call myself for the duration of my life

> Your Reverence's, my well-disposed patron's,
> Most devoted servant,
> H. M. Mühlenberg

---

1. On Johann Philipp Fresenius, see Letter 72 n. 32 and *Correspondence* 1:121 n. 4.
2. Not extant.
3. See *Correspondence* 1:121 n. 5. On Johann Valentin Kraft, see Letter 72 n. 37.
4. See *Bewährte Nachrichten,* pp. 877-976.
5. On Johann Albert Weygand, see Letter 71 n. 21.
6. Johann Philipp Fresenius, *Beicht- und Communionbuch, wobey allenthalben nach vielfältiger Erfahrung die bewährteste Wege gezeiget werden wie die Sünder bekehret, die Bussfertigen für gefährlichen Abwegen in der Bekehrung bewahret, die Schwachen gestärket, und zu einem recht evangelischen Gebrauch des heiligen Abendmahls zubereitet werden können* (Frankfurt and Leipzig, 1746).
7. Johann Philipp Fresenius, *Heilsame Betrachtungen über Sonn- und Festtags-Evangelien; nebst einem Anhang einiger Casualpredigten* (Frankfurt, 1750).
8. The text reads *statu controversiae.*
9. Literally: "the apple of the eye."
10. On Johann Arndt, see *Correspondence* 1:315 n. 20.
11. On Philipp Jacob Spener, see *Correspondence* 1:315 n. 20.
12. Literally: "oratorical characters."
13. See Acts 19:15.
14. See 2 Cor. 11:14.

15. See Matt. 13:29.
16. Martin Luther's famous battle hymn. See *Liedersammlung*, Hymn 429; see also *LBW*, Hymn 228/229.
17. See Rev. 2:5.
18. See Ps. 103:13.
19. See Gen. 15:1.
20. Heilbronn was a free imperial city in what is now Württemberg, Germany.
21. The text reads *collegium*.
22. 1 Cor. 6:1-4.
23. Acts 6:1-7.
24. On Peter Brunnholz, see Letter 71 n. 3.
25. See Letter 93 n. 13. On Johann Friedrich Handschuh, see *Correspondence* 1:291 n. 18.
26. See Luke 21:2-4.
27. See Letter 14, *Correspondence* 1:48.
28. On Johann Conrad Andreae, see *Correspondence* 1:143 n. 10.
29. The text reads *Species facti*. In legal terminology *species facti* refers to the formal presentation or report of a controversial matter that could be used in court.
30. The text for the latter part of this sentence reads: *quia istam tetigerat mensium fluxu laborante.*
31. On this incident, see *Journals* 1:259.
32. Saccum, Upper Milford, Fork and Birkensee, Pennsylvania.
33. Ludolph Heinrich Schrenck. On him, see Letter 78 n. 7.
34. Reading, Pennsylvania.
35. On Tobias Wagner, see Letter 71A n. 3.
36. On Johann Nicolaus Kurz, see *Correspondence* 1:154 n. 5 and 341 n. 16.
37. On Johann Caspar Stöver, Jr., see Letter 72 n. 39.
38. The text reads *Penuria Operariorum*.
39. On Johann Christian Schultze and this ordination, see Letter 14, *Correspondence* 1:50 and 53 n. 19.
40. See Gal. 6:1. Mühlenberg mixes elements of Greek and Latin into his citation of this passage: παραπτοματibus.
41. On Laurentius Thorstonson Nyberg, see Letter 80 n. 1.
42. The "triple L" is a reference to the "lying, denial, and slander" which in German all start with the letter "L": *Lügen, Leugnen, Lästern.* See also Letter 82:84.
43. The text reads *Acta Species facti.*
44. On the controversies in Lancaster, see Letter 39 n.10 and Letters 45-52, *Correspondence* 1:181 and 235-60.
45. In March, 1751. See *Journals* 1:274f.; see also Letter 93 nn. 12 and 13.
46. On Johann Helfrich Schaum, see Letter 71 n. 9.
47. A different writer has added here: "Cohanzey."
48. On Johann August Wolf, see Letter 72 n. 47.
49. The text reads *Systema Theologicum*.
50. The text reads *temporalio*.
51. The text reads *ex memoria*.
52. The text reads *Divortio*.
53. See Letters 42, 45, 63 and 64 in *Correspondence* 1:203-26, 235-50, 324-30.
54. The text reads *muscipulatores Hamelensos*. On the "newlanders," see Letter 72 n. 12.
55. Wilhelm Christoph Berckenmeyer died on 25 August 1751. See Mühlenberg's journal entry for 29 August 1751, *Journals* 1:308. On Berckenmeyer, see Letter 72 n. 49. See also *Correspondence* 1:189 nn. 1 and 2.
56. On Michael Christian Knoll, see *Correspondence* 1:189 n. 5.
57. On Peter Nikolaus Sommer, see Letter 96 n. 3.
58. On Johann Christoph Hartwich, see *Correspondence* 1:323 n. 19.

59. See Letters 84, 86, 93, and Mühlenberg's journal entry for 28 May 1751 (*Journals* 1:308).
60. The text reads *Species facti*.
61. Johann Ludwig Hofgut had been dropped from the clergy roster in Württemberg because of adultery but he tried to pass himself off in New York as a pastor through the use of false documents. See *Correspondence* 1:292 n. 30.
62. On Carl Rudolph, allegedly prince of Württemberg, see *Correspondence* 1:342 n 40.
63. See Matt. 12:43.
64. On Johann Friedrich Riess, see Letter 76 n. 71.
65. The text reads *Parochiae Patronos*.
66. The text reads *falsis*.
67. George Clinton, Governor of New York (1743-53).

Letter 107

To Johann Martin Boltzius
Providence, 23 November 1751

Much of this letter parallels Letter 106: it is a discussion of the congregations and pastors in Pennsylvania, New Jersey and New York that are in some form of association with Mühlenberg. At the end of this presentation Mühlenberg pauses to reflect on his own state, some ten years after he accepted the call and made the journey to Pennsylvania. He sees himself as exhausted and worn-out as a result of extremely hard work under difficult conditions. In this mood he reflects on his desire to go once more to Ebenezer, Georgia, and perhaps to retire there. He even discusses how he could support himself and his family. Mühlenberg then proposes an alternative plan he has been developing in his mind: once again he presents his dream of having a small printing press that would enable him to publish and distribute a newspaper and calendar to German people in New York, New Jersey, Pennsylvania, Maryland, Virginia and North Carolina to counteract the publications of Christoph Sauer of Germantown. Mühlenberg concludes by citing what he sees as the advantages of Ebenezer over Pennsylvania and warning any malcontents at Ebenezer not to think the pastures are greener in Pennsylvania.

Text in German: Korrespondenz *1:454-63.   For further textual information, see* Korrespondenz *1:463.*

To Pastor Bolzius[1]
at Ebenezer[2]

Title omitted without prejudice[3]
Highly and dearly prized Colleague
In our Immanuel,
What may my most worthy colleague have thought about me during this long time? Sometimes too much, sometimes too little! At the beginning I was too burdensome to you with my letters of lament and complaint; after that I stopped all of a sudden and did too little. I am asking for forgiveness and the disposition to listen to my explanation and to put the best interpretation on it according to the tender and constant love you have for me. When my colleague Brunnholtz[4] came into the country and, in accordance with God's guidance, took charge of the congregation in Philadelphia, he promised to replace me and to carry on the blessed

correspondence with Ebenezer in all of our names and to allow us to share in everything that came from there. The dear brother acted to the best of his ability and faithfully shared with us all the letters coming from there. May God be most sincerely and humbly praised for the many admonitions, encouragements, consolations and edifications which dear Ebenezer bestowed upon us without our deserving from year to year! But my highly prized brother will say, Why were there not occasionally a few lines to me personally? Four years ago I wrote to you personally[5] and two years ago I once again wrote a long letter of several pages and poured out my heart in it; but I received no answer and concluded that the letters must be lost. This pains me a great deal because there were numerous particulars in them. At present I would have the finest opportunity to write in greater detail because Mr. Conrad Rahn[6] is again setting out from here; if only there were enough time to compose calmly a coherent letter. But before the opportunity slips away from me I will report somewhat confusedly rather than reporting nothing at all.

In terms of the external state of our congregations, colleague Brunnholtz is still in Philadelphia. The congregation there grows every year in the number of members because so many people from all sorts of places in Germany are arriving. What kind of members are these, my most worthy brother will ask? They are people who were born, baptized, brought up, educated, confirmed and tended, but for the most part they bear bad fruit. For it appears they are sending us the chaff from the old countries and are holding back the wheat. When one believes that the old ones are somewhat tractable and to a certain extent capable of being called congregation members of the visible church, then a new swarm of misfits who curse, carouse, quarrel and the like descend on us again every year. Even to see and hear it from a distance is enough to make one's hair stand on end. Nevertheless, the Lord has his hidden seed among this multitude--Isaiah 9:1. Pastor Handshue[7] is presently in the Germantown congregation; he served for three years previously on a trial basis in the city of Lancaster.[8] He worked there with blessing among some old and young people; but because he afterwards married the daughter of a poor deacon and this annoyed the other elders, the leaders of the crowd[9] were divided, separated themselves, made much trouble and made Pastor Handshue tired and discouraged. They planned to starve him out like a besieged city. We saw that the leaders of the congregation were misusing us and their pastor and that there was nothing to be gained in the long run. So we took him away from there and placed him nearby for the present in Germantown where he is working with blessing and gathering the congregation. Occasionally he and Pastor Brunnholtz also make an exchange. He is a valiant and edifying man in doctrine and life but he is too weak for the extensive, coarse work and raw weather of Pennsylvania. He is not accustomed to putting up with our various national groupings because in Germany he conversed most of the time with people who were awakened and had experienced pardon. Consequently, when one has preached repentance for some time, one would sometimes gladly rather flee from Sodom and Gomorrah before one is dragged or chased out; or one would look to Nineveh on the mountain to see how things will turn out. In an area and situation like Pennsylvania one has to keep watch that indifferentism does not creep in; but one also has to take care that Pelagianism[10] is kept at bay, for it would be extremely dangerous if we were ultimately to become lukewarm and just like the world. But it is also impossible to convert a single soul with our own power. It is best that we wait and hurry: hurry with the putting off of our old person who holds us back and the putting on of the new, etc., etc.; hurry with the faithful use of the means of grace and the carrying out of the duties of our office and position, with which we will encounter the future of our Master! Wait when we have planted and watered;[11] wait under cross and suffering, etc., etc. For the Lord is not slow about his promise as some believe, but is forbearing toward *us*,[12] with the coarse, secure world, but also with his children and their thousandfold known and unknown failures. To what end? He does not wish that anyone should be lost,[13] but that everyone should be helped! If I were to weigh my countless failures over against the works of darkness of some unbeliever, God's sheer grace, forbearance and mercy have to endure the one as much as the other! The deeds of both come from unbelief, and both parties need God's mercy and patience as long as this time of grace prevails.

The congregations in Providence and New Hanover, along with their outparishes, are served by me in my weakness. I plough with the law and sow with the gospel. Three parts of the seeds fall among the thorns, on the rocks and the path, and the fourth part on the soil prepared by God's prevenient grace.[14] But the condition of this seed on the last soil is nonetheless very tenuous and not without weeds. Things in this country are far too spread out. My congregation members are so scattered that the two farthest members are thirty miles apart in length and eighteen miles in breadth. This makes the ministry so difficult that one can barely attend to the general care of souls, to say nothing of the special care.[15] One becomes a cripple before one is old. About thirty to forty miles from my home, there are four little congregations,[16] not far from Bethlehem, the district of the Zinzendorfers. I used to serve these congregations on the side. Presently we have placed a substitute or catechist there, namely, Mr. Ludolph Schrenck;[17] he is making a great effort to gather and feed the poor, scattered sheep. This aforementioned young man had studied some law and the basics of philosophy in Germany; he was moved by a report from Georgia that was translated into German to take refuge there. Because his funds were not quite sufficient for that, he arrived first of all in Philadelphia. Because we recognized in him an honest Low German temperament and because as a stranger he did not know where to turn, we took him in and gave him an opportunity to apply himself to the study of theology, and particularly catechetics. According to our moderate judgment, he made headway in theory and praxis, so that we were able to use him. If he continues to give room to the good Spirit of God in his soul, he can become a valiant man and a faithful coworker. Unfortunately, he has too little care and too many hardships and he is already getting stiff and old before his time, for he has to be on horseback almost all the time, riding between cliffs and rocks and exposed to the ravages of the weather which seem to be attacking and damaging his lungs. Our most worthy brothers in Ebenezer probably would have a greater claim on him, and we would not dispute this if he would seem to be more necessary and useful to you in divine and domestic matters.[18] In the meantime it is good that the gracious God is refining the most course elements out of him and making him ever more fit and useful. Eight to twelve miles from my home there were three congregations[19] which in the beginning I also served on the side. But after that they took on a vagabond who calls himself Johann Conrad Andreae;[20] he is from the Zweibrücken region, was dismissed on account of gross misdeeds, and came into the country one year after me. The poor fellow could in his own way be called a second Jeroboam,[21] because he has defiled —and still does so—himself, his people and the land with his sins. He is a disgrace to us and to our religion, and he causes much harm and hindrance to the course of the gospel! He slanders us and proclaims to the ignorant folk in the land that we are pietists and Moravians, and he has another two or three scoundrels of his stripe who help him. The civil authorities do not attend to such matters, and the editor of the German newspaper[22] is on his side, so we have to keep silent and let everything go until God himself will judge. Two congregations have discharged him and asked us if we would take them into our fellowship and look after them. Accordingly at their request we have placed a theological candidate[23] as a substitute or catechist into the two congregations which are greatly corrupted. He also came into the country on his own a few years ago and was examined by us. His name is Lucas Rauss,[24] and he is a native of Transylvania; until now he proves to be faithful in doctrine and life and is much liked by most people.

Thirty miles from my house a new city has been established.[25] Magister Wagner[26] lives there. Ten or eleven years ago he moved with a colony out of the Württemberg region to New England, and from there he came to Pennsylvania after the colony was scattered. He is serving some four congregations and, after having quarreled with us for a time, he is now living with us in neighborly amnesty for as long as it lasts. Twenty miles farther up, our Pastor Kurtz[27] is living and looking after four congregations.[28] His work is not without blessing, according to the measure and the grace that God proffers. Thirty miles from Mr. Kurtz is the city of Lancaster. We have had much trouble with it and we were forced to withdraw. Magister Wagner goes to the city every three to four weeks and preaches there and provides that coarse crowd with the Lord's Supper. Twenty miles from Lancaster, across the large river called the Susquehanna, but still in Pennsylvania territory, there is also the new city of York; our Assistant Pastor Schaum[29] is located there and has to look after a fairly large congregation. Last year he entered into marriage with the daughter of a deacon from Raritan in New Jersey. He suffered a misfortune on the journey, so that he became almost paralyzed on one side and has developed an atrophy on one leg. According to his measure and gifts he is exercising his ministry which, in spite of many a difficulty, is not without blessing. Forty miles from Philadelphia in the eastern part of New Jersey there is a small congregation[30] which Pastor Brunnholtz occasionally visits. Sixty to seventy miles from Philadelphia in the western part of New Jersey there are four congregations[31] which had Pastor Wolf,[32] who was sent out from Hamburg, as their pastor. After they were involved in a bitter lawsuit with this man for twelve years, were largely scattered, and finally set free by him for a sum of money, they turned to us, were alternately served by us, and provided with a candidate of theology after he had been with us for a quarter of a year and with them for a year on a trial basis. The name of this man is Albertus Weygand.[33] He is a native of the Hanau region, taught for a time in the blessed institutions at Halle and then came to Pennsylvania from Frankfurt through the persuasion of a newlander. After a trial period he was ordained by our ministerium at the request of the congregations. As I hear, he is working with blessing in proportion to his ability.

Last year I had to travel 210 miles from my house to a pastor and congregations in the province of New York which were on friendly terms with us. The name of the pastor is Mr. Christoph Hartwich.[34] He was called to Rhinebeck and Camp by the Reverend Ministerium in Hamburg in the name of the congregations and through old Pastor Berckenmeyer.[35] This man had studied in Halle for a time, had visited us several times in Pennsylvania and requested a return visit--and help because he was being persecuted and also challenged by many congregation members. At the request of the congregations I took him along to Pennsylvania for a half year and promised, with the consent of my brothers, to place Candidate Rauss in his place for that time. On the return trip I was prevailed upon to stop over in the city of New York. Our little Lutheran congregation was torn apart and vacant because the old Low German pastor, Mr. Christian Knoll,[36] had resigned his office by agreement for a sum of money. This same congregation is still made up of Dutch and German members. A group of the Germans separated itself from the church and took on a young pastor who was also called by a newlander in Germany and came to Philadelphia. This group bought a brewery on credit in a remote part of the city; they also received permission from the governor to take up a collection in the country. But because they are not getting much in this country, they want to send collectors to Germany and collect money. Now there are two so-called Lutheran churches, and the one true church would be big enough for all, without the brewery. Both parties requested me to preach. I did not want to get involved with the disorderly party but I did preach on one occasion in the church: in the forenoon in German because the most respectable Germans are still holding to the church; and in the afternoon I preached in English because I did not have command of the Dutch, and the Dutch also understand English. Our old friend Captain Grant[37] and two other awakened Englishmen were at the afternoon service; they took me and Mr. Hartwich home with them and made an edifying and enjoyable evening for us. After I returned home again the elders and deacons of the New York Dutch and German congregation at the church sent a call to me in the month of November. They entreated me to take on their abandoned congregation and church for one, two or three years and to make arrangements so that during this time a competent man from our College of Pastors could take my place and relieve me. After many wearisome consultations and considerations, we came to the point that I moved to New York by myself in the month of May, 1751, and stayed there four months. In the beginning I preached in the church once in German, once in Dutch, and had instruction for the children. The separated party also continued in its brewery with its pastor and did not want to join us again even though we made the most reasonable proposals. In the last two months I preached three times every Sunday: once in Dutch, the second time in German, and in the evening in English where we had the largest congregation of respectable people, so that the church was much too small. Finally I was prevailed upon to come home again.

The New York congregation and the other Dutch Lutheran congregation in New Jersey which is seventeen miles from New York and which I served every fourth Sunday, have written imploringly to our Reverend Fathers, asking for my miserable person.[38] What will come of this I do not know.

Our Pennsylvanians are proving to be obstinate and disheartened.   The obstinate souls say that they will have nothing more to do with churches and pastors for the rest of their lives if I should go away.   It is a poor foundation to build on a human being.   The disheartened ones think that everything would collapse again and the sects would rejoice and get ready to steal, etc., etc.   The New Yorkers think even if a new pastor is assigned to them by our Reverend Fathers such a one would not immediately know the languages and circumstances of America; moreover, their church is in crisis, indeed, is on its last legs, etc., etc.   I am afraid as well for New York as for Pennsylvania, for they are two similar hospitals, and the strength of body and soul is burned out.   In the last ten years on the road and in Pennsylvania my energies have been continually dissipated.   As a result of the heavy work in wind and weather in various situations and through all sorts of things,[39] I have ruined myself; my chest seems to be damaged and my eyes are failing, so that I have to read and write almost everything using my glasses.   I almost feel like a criminal whom one relegates to misery and no longer worries whether he lives or dies.

If our Reverend Fathers should still send us a pair of coworkers from Europe, as they promised, so that one could attend to the ministry in New York and the second one could become my substitute and successor, and if the Lord would keep our body and soul together, then it would be my firm resolve to go once to dear Ebenezer with my wife and to see Zoar[40] once again! In fact, if I could obtain the permission from my most worthy brothers and the grace from God to go there with my family, to raise my poor children, and to regain my composure there and prepare for a blessed end, I would consider myself truly blessed.   I hope our Reverend Fathers would not reject this because I am becoming incapable of persevering in the Pennsylvania calling.   For no one will pretend that I should do more than is possible.[41]   My most worthy colleagues will also not begrudge me such a retreat, if I should seek out a little corner in Ebenezer.   To tell the truth, there is in Pennsylvania not yet a single institution or opportunity for wornout and unserviceable pastors; the sentiment rather is: Do it or die.[42] If I want to keep the congregations on my own, then I either have to work myself to death or leave some of the most necessary ministerial duties undone; if the latter should happen, the congregations will fall apart.   If I want to have a coworker, the congregations are not yet in a position to maintain two pastors and I cannot live on what I have but have to support myself by the work of my hands.   Consequently I see no better way than that a younger, still vigorous man succeed me and I seek out a little corner where I can honestly support myself and bring up my children in the fear of the Lord.

My most worthy brothers would not need to worry that I would become a burden and a bother to them. No, I understand the work on a plantation. My wife can do tailoring, gardening, boil all sorts of soap, distill and prepare basic medicaments.[43] She could also be helpful with the silk-culture and the like. I know something about making potash, tar and the like. In short, I would like to support myself honestly under God's blessing and yet have enough time left over to edify my soul and to look after my family. If I should die soon my wife would not need to become burdensome; she could return to her own people if she wished because, if it pleases God, she still can expect something from her parents. For several years already I have foreseen that in time we would be lacking an institution for emeriti. For when one has become unserviceable here, one cannot simply return to Europe; as it is, the young and poor congregations are not in a position to support more than one pastor, and this cannot suddenly be forced on them because everything proceeds step by step. Accordingly, my simple, humble idea was as follows: I had a dwelling close to a public road. I could have one or two schoolmasters at the church who understood the art of printing. In the summer there is hardly any school, and such a schoolmaster has considerable time apart from teaching. I was quite well-known in the provinces of New York, New Jersey, Pennsylvania, Maryland, Virginia and North Carolina where German people live. A small printing press would have served for the purposes of translating an extract out of the English newspapers and editing a newspaper of half a sheet every four weeks or fourteen days. This could just about support one person, for Sauer gets for his monthly half-sheet two shillings six pence--and that times 600. Such a sheet would have been like a bulletin board at the universities where one could have advertised all necessary matters. Along with this one could have printed a calendar, of which Sauer[44] sells over 1000 copies and it costs him no more effort than to translate the English calendar. Further, I also thought I could have a small shop with the necessary books and medicines from the blessed institutions at Halle, and it would give a good discount. Finally, such a little institution could have been of more use to the kingdom of God than five pastors; for Sauer does not leave off maligning in coarse and subtle ways the pastoral office in his calendars and newspapers and instilling in people a revulsion toward them. The most scandalous pieces about godless pastors that he can hunt up he enthusiastically disseminates and always draws a conclusion from the particular to the universal.[45] We cannot run around after these stories every month six, seven, eight or nine hundred miles and tell the people what is true or false. Indeed, when the most dreadful lies are published about us, the vagabonds, our enemies, rejoice and say openly from their pulpits: There, there you see what kind of people the Hallensians are! In short, we do not have the least thing with which we can defend our innocence; rather we have to surrender and place our hand over our mouth when many thousand poor Germans are being fed lies and slanders and their souls are being put to death every day. To cite only a few examples: our black clergy gowns are called Satan's uniforms; our collars are certificates and testimonials that we whored and caroused at the universities; the churches are called houses of the Baals and whorehouses; the pastor's salary is called blood money which the clerics who are useless and injurious to the republic suck out like leeches, etc., etc. Even dear Ebenezer had to suffer and be maliciously dragged through it, etc., etc. Would it be a sin if one were to distribute such a sheet every two or four weeks and sought to spread the truth and to rescue God's cause? Did not the apostles themselves write their letters so that the truth would be rescued, the lies put to shame and the church of Christ built up? It could be said that there is still another German printing press in the city.[46] Yes, the printer in the city until quite recently served the black devil, and the other one served the white devil.[47] For God and the truth there has not yet been a printing press! I have complained enough about it and written many times about a small printing press, but it did not want to come to pass. It is impossible to be without cross and suffering; but it is more than cross when the devil devours so many thousand sheep and one is supposed to look on and say, "To your health!" We are dependent on means, etc., etc. Indeed, the sect of the Seventh Day Anabaptists has a large printing press for the sole purpose of being able to defend themselves when they are attacked. Perhaps it would be better if we made friends for ourselves of the printers. That could only happen if I gave up my ministry and adopted the religion of the printers, etc., etc. O dear Ebenezer, how many advantages you have over Pennsylvania. There only one church, religion and constitution exist. There shepherds and sheep are close together. There general, specialized, and very specialized pastoral care[48] are practised. There body and soul are cared for with spiritual and material medicines! There justice and righteousness are applied, evil is punished, and goodness is rewarded! There the youth hears only good things and sees examples that are worthy of imitation, etc., etc. There is Peniel[49] and Jacob's ladder, with the angels ascending and descending on it.[50] O dear little group, fear not little flock,[51] but recognize also the time of your visitation[52] and consider in this your day the things that make for peace.[53] Walk while you have the light![54] The souls under our care that know God and call him Father from the heart are calling out to you: Go forth! Go forth! Zion, go forth in the light![55] "Oh, may everything that is contained in earth and heaven be most joyously welcomed by us a thousand times over!"[56] Soon the voice will ring out: Arise, the bridegroom is here! Keep your lamps and flasks ready and never let them be without oil![57] Oh that no one may be left behind and fail to attain eternal rest! See to it that you fight the good fight, finish the race, and remain faithful.[58] It is a matter of a crown of honor,[59] of life,[60] and of glory. Think of us too in your faithful prayer, and let us call to one another in doctrine and life: Holy, holy, holy is God! Amen

Additionally, I still wanted to have issued the warning that no one should leave the fertile and green pastures of the divine word at blessed Ebenezer out of malice or mistaken intentions and come to our confusing Pennsylvania. For those who have come to us with such intentions are unfortunately for the most part dead, ruined and have suffered shipwreck. Zwiefler[61] has died and his wife is ruined. Andreas Grimmiger[62] has to live among the sects; when he wants to hear the word of God he has to go about four or five miles and cross two rivers. His wife has wept bitterly on several occasions and asked that I might beg the dear pastors in her name for forgiveness because she was disobedient to their word and claimed out of ignorance that they were not teaching correctly! Only now has she come to realize how well intentioned they were for her soul! There are others I could speak of as well. I would like to report the following about young Caspar Rahn who is arriving with his brother Conrad:[63] he was instructed and confirmed by me several years ago, but he has little knowledge of the truth because he was neglected in his early youth and grew up among all kinds of sectarian people. Afterwards, when he lost his parents, he was again with the kind of people who are content with a respectable life, etc., etc. I hope he will not leave Ebenezer without blessing and awakening, because he demonstrates the desire to learn something and he was not without feeling when he came to me for instruction. He is just timid and nervous when he is supposed to stand up for himself. It is my greatest sorrow that the young people get so scattered when they have been confirmed and do not remain under our watchful eye; rather they come in contact with all kinds of people and easily forget again what they have learned. We have not been able to do anything about the deceiver Curtius[64] because he was already on the way to Germany before the power of attorney arrived and until now he has not returned. Please pass on my heartfelt greetings to dear Brother Lemke,[65] to the two honorable sisters and to all the dear children! I was greatly depressed that the Lord called your beloved son and daughter out of the world.[66] But how fortunate for them that they attained to the crown at such an early age! "Whatever God ordains is right"[67]--once the pain is overcome! Please greet many thousand times all the dear souls who still know me. Finally, I greet and kiss you all in the Spirit! And I remain your faithful and most devoted

Providence, 23 November 1751   Mühlenberg

P.S. Please excuse the two pieces that I have inserted.[68] I had read through once again, like many another young beginner, the letters from our Fathers, and I composed a few rhymes to lift my colleagues' spirits a little at our annual special conference. My father-in-law came across them and printed them just as they were and added the later part to them.[69] It was meant well but was not quite on the mark.

---

1. On Johann Martin Boltzius, see *Correspondence* 1:30 n. 9.
2. On Ebenezer, see *Correspondence* 1:30 n. 8.
3. The text reads *S[alvo] T[itulo]*.
4. On Peter Brunnholz, see Letter 71 n. 3.
5. Not extant.
6. On Conrad Rahn, see the last paragraph of the present letter.
7. On Johann Friedrich Handschuh, see *Correspondence* 1:291 n. 18.
8. See Letter 93 n. 15.
9. The text reads *tribuni plebis*. Mühlenberg is obviously referring to the church council members.
10. Pelagianism is the theological teaching that salvation is ultimately based on merit rather than grace. This teaching was vigorously combatted by Augustine in the fifth century and by Luther in the sixteenth century.
11. See 1 Cor. 3:6.
12. See 2 Pet. 3:9.
13. See 2 Pet. 3:9.
14. See Matt. 13:1-23; Mark 4:1-20; Luke 8:4-15.
15. Mühlenberg uses Latin technical terms to describe two kinds of pastoral care: *Curam generalem* and *[Curam] specialem*.
16. Saccum, Upper Milford, Fork and Birkensee, Pennsylvania.
17. On Ludolph Heinrich Schrenck, see Letter 78 n. 7.
18. The text reads *in rebus divinis oder domesticis*.
19. Old and New Goshenhoppen and Indianfield, Pennsylvania.
20. On Johann Conrad Andreae, see *Correspondence* 1:143 n. 10.
21. See 1 Kings 12-14.
22. Christoph Sauer. See *Correspondence* 1:93 n. 37.
23. The text reads *Candidatum Theologiae*.
24. On Lucas Rauss, see Letter 76 n. 72.
25. Reading, Pennsylvania.
26. On Tobias Wagner, see Letter 71A n. 3.
27. On Johann Nicolaus Kurz, see *Correspondence* 1:154 n. 5 and 341 n. 16.
28. Tulpehocken, Heidelberg, Northkill and Earltown, Pennsylvania.
29. On Johann Helfrich Schaum, see Letter 71 n. 9.
30. Cohansey, New Jersey.
31. On the congregations on the Raritan, see Letters 42 and 45 in *Correspondence* 1:203ff. and 235ff.
32. On Johann August Wolf, see Letter 72 n. 47.
33. On Johann Albert Weygand, see Letter 71 n. 21.
34. On Johann Christoph Hartwich, see *Correspondence* 1:323 n. 19.
35. On Wilhelm Christoph Berckenmeyer, see Letter 72 n. 49.

36. On Michael Christian Knoll, see *Correspondence* 1:189 n. 5.
37. Unknown.
38. See Letter 97, including n. 1.
39. The text reads *per varios casus per tot discr[epantias ?] rer[um]*.
40. See Gen. 19:22.
41. The text reads *ultra posse*.
42. German proverb: *Vogel friss, oder du must sterben.* Literally: Eat, bird, or you must die.
43. The text reads *simplicia*. On *simplicia* see Johann Heinrich Zedler, *Großes Vollständiges Universal-Lexikon* (Graz, Austria: Akademische Druck und Verlagsanstalt, 1962 [1743]), s.v. "*Simplicia.*"
44. On Christoph Sauer, see *Correspondence* 1:93 n. 37.
45. The text reads *a particulari ad universalem*.
46. Mühlenberg is probably referring here to the printer Anton Armbrüster. Earlier a German printer by the name of Johann Philipp Böhm had been employed by Benjamin Franklin, but Böhm died in 1751. See *Korrespondenz* 1:463 n. 17.
47. On the theological distinction between the black and white devil, see *Correspondence* 1:93 n.4.
48. The text reads *cura generalis, specialis und specialissima*.
49. *Peniel* means "the face of God" in Hebrew. See Gen. 32:22-32, esp. v. 30.
50. See Gen. 28:12.
51. See Luke 12:32.
52. See Luke 19:44.
53. See Luke 19:42.
54. John 12:35.
55. Hymn by Johann Eusebius Schmidt, "Fahre fort, fahre fort" (1704), v. 1. See *Liedersammlung*, Hymn 388.
56. Hymn, "Ach! alles was himmel und erde umschliesset, Sey von mir viel tausendmal schönstens gegrüsset," v. 1. See *Liedersammlung*, Hymn 424.
57. See Matt. 25:1-13.
58. See 2 Tim. 4:7.
59. See 1 Pet. 5:4.
60. See Rev. 2:10.
61. On Johann Andreas Zwiefler, see *Correspondence* 1:52 n. 6.
62. Andreas Grimminger was a member of the Lutheran congregation in Providence; see *Journals* 1:229.
63. Caspar Rahn returned to Philadelphia and is listed as a member of the Lutheran congregation in Philadelphia until 1781. Conrad Rahn apparently stayed in Ebenezer.
64. Curtius appeared in Ebenezer around 1746 and presented himself as the son of a Württemberg pastor. He claimed to have a rich cousin who was engaged in the wood trade in New York. Ebenezer furnished him with a large quantity of boards, and he disappeared without paying.
65. Hermann Heinrich Lemke (1720-68) was born in Fischbeck and was a student in the Latina in Halle. He also studied theology at Halle and was a teacher in the boys' school there. After the death of Israel Christian Gronau in 1745, Lemke was selected to be his successor and arrived in Ebenezer on 7 February 1746. He married the widow of his predecessor and was active in Georgia until his death.
66. Samuel Leberecht and Christina Elisabeth Boltzius both died within a week of each other in 1750 of *roten Friesel*. See *Korrespondenz* 1:463 n. 29. *Der rote Friesel* was a type of "miliary fever." See Letter 76 n. 42.
67. Hymn by Samuel Rodigast (1649-1708), "Was Gott thut, das ist wohlgethan" (1675), v. 1. See *Liedersammlung*, Hymn 410; for an English translation, see *LBW*, Hymn 446.
68. Not extant.
69. The text reads *absque grano salis*; literally, "without a grain of salt." Since "the two pieces" are not extant, Mühlenberg's reference remains unclear.

Letter 108

C. R. Herttel to Mühlenberg
New York, 25 November 1751

Having received no reply to his letter of 30 September (Letter 100) and having learned that Mühlenberg had informed the church council in New York that he would not be returning to them until March 1752, Herttel writes to apprise Mühlenberg once again of the plight of the "poor destitute Church" in New York which is "meeting one disappointment after another." As in Letter 100, the underlying aim is to convince Mühlenberg to return to New York as soon as possible.

Text in English: Korrespondenz *1:464. For further textual information, see* Korrespondenz *1:464. This letter, written in English, is given here in its original form.*

Newyork, November 25th 1751

Sir, My last to you of the 30 Sept:[1] I hope is come save to hand; since which have been favoured with none from you. I have been upon our Land to make a Road, and am just come home, and my Expectation was, to find Mr. Mühlenberg in Newyork, but to my great surprize heard, that there was a letter,[2] who mentiones we may not expect you before March next, which is a great Mortification to all Wellwishers of the Church for, our Countre = party,[3] when they could not perswade Mr. Ries[4] to stay, and found that Mr. Mühlenberg did not come, they have been post half and brought a New Minister in order to draw all what they can, while we are without a Minister, and even without a good Reader, because our Clerk is absent yet! So God knowes what will become of us. I never was more concerned for our poor destitute Church then at present. For the other party hath all the Oportunity, that they can wish for, and we meeting with one disappointment after another, gives them fresh Courage to go on! I verily believe had Mr. Mühlenberg been here at the appointed time it would have been an easy Matter, to have united both parties, for they could by no means perswade Mr. Ries to stay, and Mr. Andrew[5] would not come. So at that present juncture, we would have had an Oportunity, to bring them to the Church again, which I am afraid, will now hardly happen, as they now have got a Minister[6] again Mr. Petersen[7] told me, that he yesterday afternoon out of Curiosity went to hear the New Minister, and said, the Man delivred a very good sermon. How it will farther go with our poor distressed Church, the

Lord allmighty knows! I conclude after giving my kind respects to you and your good family --

C. R. Herttel.

---

1. Letter 100. On C. R. Herttel, the writer of these two letters, see Letter 100 n. 3.

2. Not extant. There is, however, a journal entry which indicates that Mühlenberg informed the church councils at New York and Hackensack that he could not return before winter but only in March 1752. See *Korrespondenz* 1:464 n. 2.

3. On the split in the New York congregation, see Letter 84 n. 1 as well as Letters 93, 106 and 107.

4. On Johann Friedrich Riess, see Letter 76 n. 71.

5. Johann Conrad Andreae. Mühlenberg comments on this development in his journal as follows: "The New Yorkers further reported that Mr. Riess had left his party and resigned his position and that the party had called as their preacher our nasty Pennsylvanian, Pastor Andreae" (*Journals* 1:309). On Johann Conrad Andreae, see *Correspondence* 1:143 n. 10.

6. Philipp Heinrich Rapp who in 1754 became Andreae's successor in Germantown, served the congregation in Tohickon from 1765-71 and ultimately committed suicide in 1779. Mühlenberg comments on Rapp and on the developments in 1751 in his journal as follows: "Mr. Andreae would have been glad to accept the call, but he was involved in such great indebtedness that he could not get away. He, however, had recommended another man from here who calls himself Rab or Rapp and who came to this country about a year ago with other *servants*. He is supposed to have been a *studiosus theolog[iae]*, the son of a preacher, who caused his father bitter sorrow, deserted with his deceased brother's wife, and fled to this country. . . . Finally the New York Germans brought Rapp up and introduced him as their preacher" (*Journals* 1:309). On Rapp, see *Pastors and People* 1:106f.

7. George Petterson was a member of the Lutheran congregation in New York and a supporter of the project to bring Mühlenberg to New York.

LETTERS OF 1752

Letter 109

To C. R. Herttel
Providence, 9 January 1752

In response to Herttel's two letters (Letters 100 and 108), Mühlenberg attempts to put his commitment to the New York situation into the broader context of his prior commitment to his "first and lawfull call" to his congregations in Pennsylvania. He lays out what he has tried to do and he shows Herttel that the situation of the Dutch congregation is not as bleak as he sees it. With their capital and their adherence to their "Confession and saving doctrine" they are in better shape than the German congregation that is being served by vagabond preachers. Mühlenberg promises that he will make every effort to come to New York again in the spring and to bring with him one of the new pastors that has just arrived from Germany.
Text in English: Korrespondenz *1:469-71. For further textual information, see* Korrespondenz *1:472. This letter, written in English, is given here in its original form.*

Provid: d 9. Jan: 1752

Worthy Gentleman Sir[1]
I received your favours dated the 30 of Sept.[2] and 25th of November.[3] In the first I was acquainted with an Account and proposals of a New township situated between Delaware River and Rochester laid out for thirty families to settle upon.[4] I told some honest people of my perswasion of it and think I could find the number you have appointed, if the Land is fit to be improved. On the 22d day of November last I did send 3 Men from Pensylvania upon my own Expence and Charge to view the land laid out for the Townships. The aforesaid came so far as to A place where Immanuel commonly called the Spaniard liveth upon. Said Spaniard would not give a true Account of the Land, being not well pleased with Mr. Livingstown[5] but at last after many Questions, he told our people they should go five Miles farther, there they could see a new road laid out for the said Township. The people found the Entrance of the Road and went up about ten miles till they came to a Creek on the other side of which, the road ended. The people came back on the second day of Decembr and assured

194

me, that it would be very hard to drive and to carrie any weight on vaggons within them ten Miles of the new Road and that it was impossible to improve the Land on both sides of the New Road, because there was nothing else to see and to feel then Rocks and stones. But when they went back one Man met them on the road near Delaware River and told them, that the new road was not so far done and made, where the Land of the Townships beginneth etc. Now I have the Expence and no true account and the people are disappointed. If therefore Worthy Gentleman you should send some people there in the Next spring to finish the road, then you could send some word, what time or days they will be there, because our people is willing to go once more and to see the Land, when some people is there to give 'em Directions. If the Land is fit to be improved, then I hope to bring thirty families of honest Lutherans over especially, when the proprietors stand at their promise and assist, that a Minister is provided for which I will care, if the Lord spareth my life.

The Contents of your second letters are full of Griev and sorrow about your Church in New York. In answer to the point I must confess 1) I am a finit creature and can't be present in two places at once. 2) My first and lawfull call is for Pensylvania. I can't run like other Vagabunds from one place to another, neither can I move to another place, without Consent, and leave of my superiors and ordinary Congregations. 3) I came by accidens to Newyork last year and became acquainted with the critical Church Affairs. 4) I was called quite unexpected to assist my distressed brethren. 5) I was willing to do that little what lay in my power, and intended to make a trial for a certain time, therefore I desired a lawfull call for a certain term to act by Authority as an ordinary Minister. 6) After I had received your Call, it was my duty to confer with my fellow=Labourers and Elders of our Congregation to see how long I could be abroad without hurting my Congregations at home. But all the concurring Circumstances would allow no more, then to assist my brethren in Newyork for one part of the appointed time in your Call. 7) I acquainted the Vestry in my last English letter,[6] that I could only assist one part of the appointed two years. 8) I came accordingly in the Month of May and stood there allmost to the End of August.[7] 9) I tried within that time, wether by any Means the seperated Germans could be brought. But all the means were used in vain. for the Germans would force our Vestry to pay their Brew-houss,[8] and our Vestry couldn't agree with their proposals. I endeavoured therefore to unite the little flock of Hackinsack with the rest of our Congregation at Newyork[9] because I fore saw, that the swamp people[10] would carrie on their own stif necked Contrivance to the utmost desperation. 10) I told our Vestry that the utmost Necessity of Church and domestical Affairs urged and pressed me to go home, and advised them to lay their Complaints before our superiors in London and Germany and to ask, if they thought proper to send me to Newyork, and promised to come back to Newyork. NB: *if possible.* 11) When I came home, loads and weights of labours waited for me. I was obliged to bring my neglected Congregations in order again. I was forced to write night and day to give an Account of the Circumstances in Newyork and Pensylvania, and especially to send letters to some high stationed divines in Germany,[11] desiring them not to assist the swamp people, whenever they should call for Assistance. In the mean while I received a letter from London[12] advising that there were two Worthy ordained Ministers on theyr Journey for Pensylvania, sent by our superiors, for our Congregations in Pensylvania, because we had desired our superiors to send two Ministers for our Assistance. What could I do more?

Should I come back to Newyork and leave all my necessary buisiness undone? My dear brother Hertel thinks I could have united the seperated swamp people, in that time, when Mr. Ries[13] went away. But it was and is impossibel to unite them without damage. If you will have them joined you most take several hundred pounds from the Cash of our Church and pay their houss, and give them ful power and liberty, to be masters of the Church, to overset the Orders of the Church and to introduce every vagabund that appeareth with a black jacket from year to year. If I had been there, they would no less have fetched the scandalous vagabund Andrew[14] or him, which they have at present. The Question is not according to my humble opinion, wether the swamp people have a Minister or not, wheter they have applause or not? But we ought to consider or inquire, if God is with us or not? if truth is on your side or not, If our Church is able to keep a true and faithful Minister and to carrie on the work and service of God, without the running and disorderly Germans? The parlament and good laws support our King and not the Mob.   It is not the Multitude of disorderly people that maketh a good state, but the law and the Rulers. You have by the blessings of God a Capital in Your Church. You need only the Interest to pay to the Minister for his utmost maintenance. If there are but two or three orderly and pious Members, you have a Congregation and may continue Divine service. The Congregation in Hackinsack is united again with your Church, let your Minister go there the third or fourth Sunday. If the Germans won't stay with you, and will run and be tossed to and fro, let them have their Choise and liberty, and let your Minister serve in the Low dutch and English Language. If you preserve your Confession and saving doctrine, let it be in what language soever, you have done Your duty and your Children can not call you to an Account at the dreadful day of Judgment. Commit your Care and Concern to the promises and Directions of God with humble and fervent prayers, go into the sanctuary of God and look upon the End of the wicked and pious peopel. It is not our Wit and Contrivance that bring things aright, but the blessings of God. That man,[15] which the swamp peopel have taken for their Minister, is come upon his own Account to Pensylvania, without call. He brought a Woman a long which died desperately at Philadelphia. The peopel said she was his brothers Wife etc. this poor man hath a bad Character in Pensylvania etc. Let him grow warm at Newyork, they will soon find the difference between him and Mr. Ries. He is a brother of that filthy Rag called parson Andrew. These two Vagabunds have never been received into the fellow ship of our Ministry, because they are scandals and offences of our Religion, and therefore they blame and call me a Hernhuter or Moravian among the Mob, according to the old custom of the world, where the devil and his servants are stiled shepherds and christ and his followers, wolves and Samaritans. I can say and do no more. My call and buisiness in Merica hath ben this nine years past, to gather our poor and scattred Lutherans into Congregations and to introduce lawful called and ordained pious Minister. If I can do the same by the help of God at Newyork, I will not fear and mind any trouble, persecution, Evil and good Reports. But then good people must not depend on my staying or living here or there, but thank God if they are provided with sound and faithful Ministers and give me liberty to go from one place to another and to see how far I made add my mite to the Edification of our Lutheran Church in America, by the Assistance of God! In this Respect I am intended to come to Newyork and Hackinsack once more if it pleaseth the Lord, as soon in the spring as weather and health will permit, and to bring along one of our two capable Ministers, which are save arrived to my great Comfort and satisfaction on the first day of December at Philadelphia.[16] But if you think Dear Brother it be to late to take your Affairs once more in Hand, please to send me a few lines, then shall we remain in Pensylvania, because we have work enough and more then we can perform. With these I recommend You Worthy Gentleman and your Worthy Relation to the particular providence, Grace and Mercy of God and myself together with my Brethren and family to Your benevolence, remaining your humble servant Mühlenberg.

---

1. On C. R. Herttel, see Letter 100 n. 3.
2. Letter 100.
3. Letter 108.
4. Presumably this is a reference to the no longer extant petition that is mentioned in the first postscript to Letter 100. See also Letter 100 n. 4.

5.   This is probably a reference to Peter Livingston (1710-92) who was a New York merchant and whose father was involved in the acquisition of properties for the building of churches in New York. See John P. Dern, ed., *The Albany Protocol: Wilhelm Christoph Berkenmeyer's Chronicle of Lutheran Affairs in New York Colony, 1731-1750*, trans. S. Hart and S. G. Hart-Runeman (Camden, ME: Picton Press, 1992), pp. xlii, 38 and 60.

6.   Letter 90. This letter of 2 April 1751 is Mühlenberg's response to the no longer extant call from New York of 1 February 1751.

7.   On Mühlenberg's sojourn in New York from 17 May to 26 August 1751, see *Journals* 1:278-308.

8.   On the purchase by the New York congregation's German faction of a former brewery for a church building, see Letter 93:128, as well as Letters 94 and 95.

9.   On the relationship between the Hackensack and New York congregations, see the introduction to Letter 97.   Shortly before Mühlenberg became involved in the New York affairs, the congregations at Hackensack and Remersbach had called Johann Friedrich Riess to serve them as well as the New York congregation.   At that time Johann Albert Weygand who was serving the congregations on the Raritan convinced these congregations that they should stipulate that Riess should place himself under the authority of the Pennsylvania Ministerium. Nothing, however, came of these plans because Riess, after a long delay, returned the call in July 1751. See *Journals* 1:285-97.

10.   The so-called Swamp Church in New York was the church of the German party which stood over against the Dutch party that was served by Mühlenberg.

11.   See Mühlenberg's letter of 15 November 1751 to Fresenius (Letter 106). Two further letters to Albinus (30 November 1751) and Pastor Majer in Halle (28 November 1751) are not extant.

12.   Probably a reference to Ziegenhagen's letter of 7 November 1751 (Letter 105).

13.   On Johann Friedrich Riess, see Letter 76 n. 71.

14.   On Johann Conrad Andreae, see *Correspondence* 1:143 n. 10.

15.   Philipp Heinrich Rapp; see Letter 108 n. 6.

16.   On Johann Dietrich Matthias Heinzelmann and Friedrich Schultze, see Letter 101 n. 3 and Letter 89 n. 4 respectively. See also *Journals* 1:319.

Letter 110

To Peter Livingston[1]
Providence, 27 January 1752

The person to whom this letter is written is apparently a promising young gentleman in Mühlenberg's eyes, but also a person who is perhaps too much caught up in "gay, modern and mixted Companies." Mühlenberg's letter seems to be an admonition and exhortation to a deeper commitment to the Christian faith and life. The letter and the concluding poem/hymn offer an interesting summary of how a moderate pietistic Lutheran like Mühlenberg could sum up the themes of conversion and the Christian life.

Text in English: Korrespondenz 1:473-74. For further textual information, see Korrespondenz 1:474. This letter, written in English, is given here in its original form.

Dear Sir,

the Remembrance of our candid and sweet, though short Conversation we had together in Newyork affordeth Motives, to write these few lines to you, humbly desiring, You will lay the best Construction on, and wink at the imperfections and faults of them. I am very much obliged Dear Sir, to rendre humble thanks for your honest, kind and civil underserved behaviour towards me, during the time of our Conversation, and I must confess, that one essential point rendred the Acquaintance of You dear Gentleman and Your noble relation more respectful unto me vdel.[2] When I looked through the veils of some airy Actions, passions and words, which do easily and unaware beset young Gentlemen in gay, modern and mixted Companies and penetrated into the bottom of the Heart, I found and spyed a noble Education. Joined with deep Impressions on the Christian laws, displaying sometimes their Rays like the beams of the sun through the Clouds, perceiving the aforesaid hidden noble principles in You, Dear Sir I hope to God a serious Meditation, faith fully continued in the revealed law and Gospel, and other selected edifying Writings, joined with fervent prayers, and a following period of the wholesom Christian Cross, together with the Assistance and Moving of the Holy Ghost, will awaken the Heart to inward penitence and rouze the hidden principles to shine brighter than ever and scatter the Clouds, that hung dark upon the Evidence of grace. Such a blessed turn, will bring the Heart nearer to God, make the Grace of Christ sweet to the soul and the Commands of Christ easy and delightful. It will enable us, to mortify the habits of our sins, to vanquish temptations, and wean us from all the Enticements of this lower World and its sinful transient pleasures. It will bear us up, above all the disquietudes of life and fit us for the hour of death, and make us ready and desirous to appear before Christ our Lord! Acquaintance, Relations and Conversation established upon the aforesaid foundation, is the surest and everlasting, but that which doth not tend to the Edification of our immortal soul, is vanity and transient shadow!

Must friends and kindred drop and die? Must Helpers be with drawn? While sorrow with a weeping Eye counts up our Comforts gone. be thou our Comfort mighty God our Helper and our friend nor leave us in this dangrous Road, till all our trials end. How is our Nature spoild by sin! Yet nature ne'er hath found the way to make the Conscience clean, or heal the painful wound.

in Vain we seek for peace with God by Methods of our own. There's nothing but the saviour's blood can bring us near the throne. God, the great God, who rules the skies, the gracious and the Just, made his own son our sacrifice. And there lies all our trust.

O never let my thoughts renounce the Gospel of my God! Where viless crimes and cleans'd at once in Christ's atoning blood! Here rest my faith and ne'er remove! Here let repentance rise, while I behold his bleeding love, his dying Agonies.[3]

Please to excuse my freedom Dear Sir, remember my humble Respects to your Lady, to dear Mother, Madame de Ranzow to Captain Kiersted,[4] and to the whole noble Relation, and give me leave to remain, W: Gentleman your affectionate and obedient servant

H. M. Millenberg VDM[5]
Providence in Pensylvania th 27 Jan: 1752.

p.s. I should be glad to have once more an oportunity to board with you, but I can't tell, wether and when?

---

1. This letter is probably written to Peter Livingston whom Mühlenberg had met on his trip to New York in August 1750; see *Journals* 1:249f. Livingston is never explicitly identified, however, and Mühlenberg's reference to "young Gentlemen" is somewhat enigmatic since Livingston was born in 1710--making him about forty at the time the letter was written and a year older than Mühlenberg who certainly did not see himself as young at this stage of his life! On Livingston, see also Letter 109 n. 5.

2. Abbreviation of the Latin *videlicet*, "namely."

3. These last three paragraphs are evidently a poem or hymn. The source cannot be identified; one wonders if the author might not be Mühlenberg himself.

4. None of these persons can be identified.

5. Abbreviation of the Latin title *Verbi Divini Minister*, "minister of the divine word."

Letter 111

The Dutch Church Council in New York to Mühlenberg
New York, 17 February 1752

In response to Mühlenberg's letter of 9 January 1752 to C. R. Herttel
(Letter 109), the Dutch Church Council writes to assure him that their
communications with him were not meant to indicate dissatisfaction with him
personally but rather their concern for their congregation that was
struggling along without a pastor. The Church Council expresses its hope
and its confidence that--either on a permanent or interim basis--Mühlenberg
will be able to serve them very soon.
    Text in Dutch: Korrespondenz 1:474-75. *For further textual information,*
see Korrespondenz 1:475.

Most reverend, learned Sir!
We have received Your Reverence's worthy letter of 9 January.[1] We
note in it that you may have misinterpreted some of the content of our
previous letter.[2] Your Reverence should not think that we are dissatisfied
because Your Reverence did not come to us during the winter, for that was
not our opinion. We only wanted to inform you of our serious predicament
of not having a pastor while our opposition party was behaving rather
smugly, saying that they could be provided with another preacher as soon
as they lose one but we cannot![3] It is true that we would rather be without
a pastor than to take up with such sorry specimens. But other congregations
are not aware of this and base their reasoning on hearsay only. We are very
much looking forward to the end of winter and hope to see Your Reverence
here this spring, as promised. It is our wish that the consent of Your
Reverence's superiors will be in place by that time,[4] so that we will also be
able to welcome Your Reverence's beloved family and household! But if
not, we will expect only Your Reverence and we will then wait for the
decision of the powers that be. We think they will not be against our
humble proposal and desire for it is definitely necessary to maintain the pure
evangelical teaching and blessedness which would otherwise totally collapse
if Your Reverence would not be assigned to our congregation. We are
convinced that we cannot find a more appropriate person either here or in
Europe.
    Regarding any concerns about the possibility that Your Reverence's
superiors would not want to upset the Reverend Hamburg Ministerium,[5] this
should not be a matter of consideration. We are convinced that these men

will understand things differently when they receive our letters to them and take their contents to heart. They will understand even better when they see Your Reverence's involvement in the matter. We would rather have two or three years with Your Reverence on an occasional basis--in anticipation of Your Reverence's final appointment--than to call someone else. At present there is great concern both in our congregation and among other good friends over Your Reverence's absence, and they are afraid that Your Reverence will not be coming at all. But we have assured them that this is not the case and we continue to hold to this hope.

New York, 17 February 1752   Your Reverence's
Most obliging friends and
Servants,
Charles Beekman
Johan David Wolf
C. R. Herttel
Jacob Tiedeman
George Peterson
Henrich Schäffer

---

1. Letter 109.
2. No such letter of the New York Dutch Church Council is extant.
3. Philipp Heinrich Rapp was pastor of the German portion of the New York congregation since the autumn of 1751. On Rapp, see Letter 108 n. 6.
4. Mühlenberg had made the consent of his superiors the condition for his return to New York; see his letter to C. R. Herttel of 9 January 1752. For Ziegenhagen's negative response, see Letter 105 and for Francke's response, see Letter 124.
5.   See Mühlenberg's journal entry of 4 August 1751: "I told them [the Dutch Lutheran congregation] that they must turn to the Reverend Ministerium in Holland or Hamburg and send a humble petition to them, for our patrons in England and Germany had burden enough in Pennsylvania and would hardly assume the care of New York" (*Journals* 1:301f.).

Letter 112

To Friedrich Michael Ziegenhagen and Gotthilf August Francke
Providence, 18 February 1752

This is one of the more extensive letters Mühlenberg has written to his superiors in England and Germany. Its tone is highly deferential and self-deprecating. At one point Mühlenberg goes so far in the letter as to identify the voice of his superiors with the voice of God: vox patrum vox Dei!

The deferential tone of the letter carries over into Mühlenberg's expression of thanks and appreciation for sending two men as helpers in ministering to the increasing number of congregations desirous of pastoral care.

Though the letter's tone is overwhelmingly deferential Mühlenberg's defense of actions he has taken in the exercise of his ministry is articulate and forthright. Thus he defends his involvement in the controversy between Johann August Wolf and the congregations in Raritan and Hackensack, New Jersey, even though these congregations were under the oversight of the New York Ministerium. Similarly, he defends the propriety of having fellowship with the Swedish Ministerium and its members even though he is for that reason accused of being a pietist.

But in the discharge of his responsibilities Mühlenberg is not only reactive but proactive. In great detail he recommends to his superiors the establishment of an orphanage and, in connection with it, a school, a small printing press and a retirement home for pastors and teachers who have spent their life and energies in serving congregations.

The letter concludes with a petition to accept a ten-year old son of a strong supporter of the Philadelphia congregation as a pupil in the Halle schools and, in a postscript, with a request to transmit to Mühlenberg income from his legacy so he can pay off his debts.

Text in German: Korrespondenz *1:476-92. For further textual information, see* Korrespondenz *1:492.*

Letter to His Reverence, the Very Reverend Royal Court Preacher Ziegenhagen in London and Doctor, Senior and Professor Franck in Halle.

Providence,
18 February 1752

Very Reverend Fathers in Christ,

Very kind Patrons:

I had completed part of my insignificant comments for the years 1750 and 1751[1] this past November and intended a special humble letter[2] to accompany them to His Reverence Doctor and Professor Franck which I owed him for a long time. The opportunity to do so was lost, however, because the ships departed earlier than usual fearing that winter might set in earlier. Before we realized it the most gracious God gladdened us with two new coworkers, Messrs. Schultz and Heinzelmann[3] by name, as evidence of his grace, long-suffering and mercy which still attends our people and for which his glorious name should be praised forever.

The Very Reverend Fathers will on their own most kindly note that after having brought a thankoffering to God I on my insignificant part have also applied much diligence and attention to inquire from the new colleagues at every opportunity: 1) How matters stand in relation to the kingdom of Jesus Christ in Europe and East India in which Your Reverences have stood until now as pillars! 2) What the situation is especially in relation to your holy office and most worthy persons, labor and suffering. 3) What thoughts it pleases Your Most Highly Regarded Sirs to harbor concerning our poor and lowly institutions in Pennsylvania and especially regarding the New York affair.[4] From the response as a whole I learned that the kingdom of Christ still grows and increases under cross and suffering, that the old foe continues to practise his customary wiles,[5] but that the Lord Jesus also crushes the deceitful intrigues and stratagems[6] of the old serpent when they have reached the limit and that he rules in the midst of his enemies.[7] Hallelujah! To the praise of God and my comfort I learned in particular that the Very Reverend Fathers have been delivered from dangerous illness and that, although under their allotted cross and suffering, they were strengthened for the blessing of the kingdom of Jesus Christ! Concerning the third item, the attitude of the Very Reverend Fathers toward the poor and lowly Pennsylvania institution, their most kind letters, the sending of two new laborers, the most precious consignment of several books and medications—these are the clearest evidence and superfluous assurance that the Highly Regarded Ones had not yet tired of granting your unwavering fatherly supervision, love and pity to our poor United Congregations in general and, though undeservedly, to my colleagues in particular for the sake of Jesus Christ.

Next to this, the matter I primarily wanted to investigate and know in private discourse with my new brothers consisted of the following two items: 1) What the brothers had heard and remembered, particularly in special hearings and dealings with the Very Reverend Fathers, about exegetical discoveries and fatherly admonitions? 2) What the Very Reverend

Fathers might have called to mind in a preliminary way with regard to my involvement with New York? What they communicated to me concerning the first point is dearer to me than many books, although I sincerely wish that everything had been dictated and copied word for word, for I find gaps and see that now and then the train of thought is interrupted and is not always taken up again, something I sincerely regret for their sake and mine. I also recall what our Savior said to those who had heard and seen something but not everything from him, "*See that you say nothing to any one!*"[8] I was unable to ascertain something about the second point as easily but only through one or another round about way did I elict and piece things together. My confused and immature letter from New York[9] could not have been in the hands of our most precious father Franck in Halle yet when the brothers were sent from there. But to my sorrow it came to London to the Very Reverend Court Preacher Albinus. That the precious brother in Christ, with the genuine innocence of a dove, handed the letter over to the Very Reverend Fathers, uncorrected and uncut, I could more than hypothetically conclude from the following: 1) It pleased His Reverence, our most precious Court Preacher Ziegenhagen, in his association with the two new laborers to mention that I was not satisfied with being sent first from London to Ebenezer in Georgia. 2) I was accused of tearing in two the call of a pastor sent from Hamburg.[10] 3) Contrary to the instruction and approval of my Very Reverend Fathers I had involved myself with alien laborers not sent by them.[11] 4) I was no longer satisfied with the poor circumstances in Pennsylvania and sought more favorable ones in New York. 5) Neither one of the two new pastors should be placed in New York because the Very Reverend Fathers wanted to have nothing to do with the Dutch but had sent all pastors for the Palatines. If I now assume that my new brothers had rightly comprehended the important words, and as I know from my own experience that our most precious father Ziegenhagen does not put down one word, one syllable, yes, one iota or comma lightly and in vain but weighs everything carefully, consequently, I would like to respond with childlike simplicity and dutiful obedience with what follows and humbly request that you listen to it, not in an unkindly manner but in accordance with patience and gentleness.

I am certainly well aware of being inwardly and outwardly corrupt and not suited for so demanding an office, that the grace and urging of God through word and spirit have not yet altogether achieved their purpose with me, far less completed it because of my own fault and disobedience! I know and heartily regret that I have committed thousands of mistakes, yes, indeed, transgressions[12] in my office and profession in thought, word and deed against God, my neighbor and myself. I realize that I may have written in an immature, disorganized and impolite though not untruthful manner in the correspondence with the Very Reverend Fathers, especially in the last letter from New York. I do not want to justify myself at all but with reference to the last letter call to mind that it was written during an attack[13] of a serious physical and emotional ailment. Although I do not have a copy of it I can, nevertheless, recall that I complained about thoughts or rather vapours which had emerged, for example, why the Reverend Fathers had not sent pastors to Pennsylvania many years previously, etc., etc. These and other thoughts flowed more from a feeling of my own great inadequacy for such an important office than from a craving for reproach or disrespect toward God's most omniscient guidance and direction of his most precious servants. I know quite well that the Reverend Fathers undergo indescribable pains, anxieties and suffering in the course of such missionary undertakings. However, God in his providence has called them for this purpose and they may not bury the talents granted them.[14] If they do it gladly they are rewarded; if they do not do it gladly, they are still commanded to do it, etc., etc. When I consider my weighty responsibility, my inadequacy and lack of faithfulness in office, I am filled with great fear and I would probably rather be a shepherd in Europe or a farmer here than a pastor. But far be it from me that I should overrule the dear God when my soul is tranquil and conscious of communion with the most blessed God in Christ! But now I cannot proceed farther than to request most humbly that the Very Reverend Fathers for the sake of Jesus Christ, our compassionate high priest, may forgive all weaknesses and errors with which I may have ever offended them, not intentionally but during temptations! In relation to the five points I set forth I especially wanted to call the following to mind: 1) I cannot recall having grumbled on account of the journey to Ebenezer; if so, I beg your pardon! It was indeed difficult and depressing that I had to travel alone from Georgia or Carolina to Pennsylvania. But I must admit that the journey did not bring about injury but rather benefit and edification in body and soul and I revere the gracious providence and wisdom of God for having ordered matters thus and not otherwise! If only I could always say in faith in advance: "I trust your marvellous ways, they end in love and blessing, etc., etc.,"[15] 2) At the request of Senior Wagner[16] in Hamburg at that time I submitted a report, indeed, concerning the whole procedure, concerning the call of Mr. Wolf which was violated by lawyers and made null and void by payment of the farmers—a report I submitted with other letters to the Very Reverend Fathers. While I received news concerning the other letters that they had arrived safely I heard nothing further concerning the report. With reference to the procedure in question I have not yet discovered any reproof of conscience before God. The right reverend gentlemen in Hamburg are far removed from America. They cannot feel the disgrace as painfully as we do which is hurled in heaps on our evangelical religion, church and Ministerium because of one offensive pastor. They cannot sense the need as deeply as we when one sees so many poor ignorant agonizing older people and especially numerous youth pine away in soul and only because they turned to Hamburg with good intentions, encouraged to do so by other pastors and taken care of so badly! Seeing those in dire need, a person's heart could break and bleed if one is not indifferent to but eager for the salvation of souls. Heathen could put us to shame when they maintain the proposition that a true patriot is bound to give his life for the preservation of the republic. But in the twelve-year long Wolf matter, it appeared that the little Raritan republic had to be ruined in body and soul, the evangelical religion, the church in America and the Ministeriums had to be made into a real stench only so that an incapable preacher might eat the bread of strife and cursing when he could support himself in another and better way. The Hamburg gentlemen may judge as they wish. The Lord who tries reins and heart[17] also knows my heart and knows how and for what reasons I have acted in the matter.

In the third place, as far as my involvement with alien laborers and my instruction are concerned, I cannot deny that after maintaining a certain distance I involved myself with one or another of them. Unfortunately, circumstances with their encumbrances[18] made it necessary and did not leave one any other choice than either to see the number of my most bitter enemies increase or to maintain a neighborly friendship until better times with those who were comparatively[19] the most decent and useful so that I could stay with my first congregations and be relieved somewhat of an altogether too great overload. One can explain a complicated matter much easier in theory than in practice. My first instruction was initially very modest[20] and focused on the first most kind letter from His Reverence, our dear and highly regarded father Franck.[21] There it was stated in general that I should serve Philadelphia, Providence and New Hanover and have the liberty to move about freely[22] and all of that only on a trial basis for three years; indeed, I also retained permission to return after the term had elapsed. I have not moved about freely without it being necessary. I have acted in accordance with reason and grace granted to me in the most modest measure of all. Wherein I have failed the Very Reverend Fathers may censure me or have others call it to mind. May they have sympathy with a wooden vessel[23] and pitiable person of this kind who in the beginning was thrust into a sea of confusion and on all sides was deprived of good counsel and had no understanding and previous[24] experience. During the whole course[25] of my being here I have had the deepest respect for my Very

Reverend Fathers and have kept in mind the instruction they gave but I could not act in an unlimited way; but often I had to twist and squirm very much. To put it in human terms, when my enemies had me on the run and I wanted to search for some support in the Swedish Ministerium, it was said, "You are a person suspect of pietism."[26] When I sought refuge in the English Ministerium it was said, "Show us a recommendation from the archbishop of the Society"[27] as the Swedish pastors do when they arrive here. When in case of extreme necessity I sought the protection of government it was said, "We cannot decide your affairs; you Germans are tolerated and there are all kinds of German preachers who boast of having a call; we do not know who among you has the greatest claim and best recommendation for a call! When the ministers of the English Church enter they bring a recommendation from their superiors. When the Presbyterians come they show the same thing from their society. Thus the Swedish ones also enter with nothing less than a recommendation. Show us something like that also, then we shall know better how to decide matters," etc. That was the case[28] when I appeared before the government with Count Zinzendorf on account of the church record book and chalice[29] and in many subsequent cases with Andreae,[30] Neuberg[31] and similar ones.

4) Concerning my poor circumstances in Pennsylvania I must admit that until now I have not yet experienced any actual distress. During the first two years it pleased the Very Reverend Fathers out of undeserved love and kindness to make available fifty pounds sterling.[32] I have kept an accurate account for the remaining seven years, and if required to do so, can show that my regular congregations have turned over to me annually at the most thirty pounds sterling in shillings and pence. At present I own eighty acres of land next to the Providence church which I bought for eighty pounds local currency and I have applied close to two hundred pounds local currency to building a house toward which my father-in-law has given me altogether 100 pounds local currency. I still owe 116 pounds on which I must pay annual interest and I am still fifty pounds in arrears to pay for food and clothing for the past two years. Now, as meagre as my income and as great as my expenses for my family have been until now, the gracious God has nevertheless neither forsaken nor failed me because among other things he has spared my family from serious illnesses and misfortune. In addition, my wife knows how to keep house well and is not ashamed of any work. The accusation in external matters which galls me the most is what I must hear among sects of all kinds, yes, even in German calendars and newspapers.[33] One is a clerical mercenary because every year one strips gullible people of money who are themselves mostly poor and must earn their daily bread by the sweat of their brow. One ought to practice a trade

and, in accordance with the custom of the apostles and early Christians, preach without being paid, etc., etc.[34] Also that I am seldom at home and consequently cannot manage my family well. The first part of the consideration relating to the poor circumstances did not provide the motivation to leave Pennsylvania for several months. Much less could the more affluent circumstances in New York entice me, for if New York and Hackensack raise a lot, it would run to fifty, at most sixty pounds sterling a year. But that will not go as far in New York with a family of seven or eight persons, counting domestics, as thirty to forty pounds sterling in the country. The motivation which persuaded me to hasten to the aid of the deserted church in New York and Hackensack for a time will become somewhat clearer from my observations. I have not yet promised and committed myself to the New York people any further until I have the understanding and approval of our Very Reverend Fathers. I shall also acquiesce completely in their bidding, however it turns out, for I want to have nothing to do with making my own choice. I want rather to be impartial and await the determination of the Very Reverend Fathers if the matter is to be handled rightly.[35] According to my worldly feeling I would rather conclude my remaining few days in Pennsylvania or even spend them in a still more unknown corner of the world where I could rear my poor children in an upright and Christian manner, for my back is already somewhat accustomed to the Pennsylvania cross.[36]

The more recent letter concerning the two new coworkers is very dear to me for I consider the voice of the Fathers to be the voice of God.[37] Following joint deliberation of the Ministerium Pastor Schultz has been appointed as coworker on a trial basis in New Hanover and Providence, and Pastor Heinzelmann has been placed as coworker in Philadelphia in church and school until further insight is gained.[38] The elders from New Hanover and Providence were aroused anew when I went to New York. They examined the list of contributors to my salary and discovered that barely a third of those still remained who had subscribed their amount because some had died, others had changed their place of residence and moved on on account of poverty or because they had no land of their own. And the new arrivals had still done little or nothing. They wanted very much to retain me, to petition for a coworker for me and agree on a certain amount of salary for both. Then after long consultation they came upon a method which appeared most suitable to them, namely, they assigned the chairs and seats in both churches and set a price of several shillings on each and were of the opinion that in accordance with such an estimate they could come up with seventy or eighty pounds in local currency. That amount is what they wanted to contribute for both pastors. Barely had a beginning been made when restlessness already set in among those who do not like to contribute anything and allow themselves to be egged on by those who are contrary minded. I had to take the blame. In Sauer's German newspapers in Pennsylvania and the remaining provinces among the German nation I was exposed to slander as the enclosures show.[39] Now the affair with the chairs is still up in the air but, as the elders say, it is to be continued. In the hope that both congregations with their outparishes can raise seventy to eighty pounds local currency here or forty-five to fifty pounds sterling, I have briefly agreed as much as possible with the Rev. Mr. Schultz in the presence of the remaining colleagues in accordance with the promise I made in a letter to the Very Reverend Fathers in which I reported that I would gladly share everything with an upright coworker. Accordingly, the Rev. Mr. Schultz will be satisfied with forty pounds of local currency here with the following conditions: I am to give him twenty pounds cash and for the remaining twenty pounds I am to provide him with lodging, wood, light, maid service, laundry, food, drink and a horse. He promises to try this contract out for a year. With what remains I am supposed to maintain my family and myself. Perhaps, however, a change may be made because the New Goshenhoppen folks have dismissed their Andreae[40] and have importuned my colleague Brunnholtz[41] in writing that they would like to have Pastor Schultz.[42] He replied to them that Mr. Schultz, along with the remaining colleagues should serve New Goshenhoppen as much as possible from New Hanover until further consideration at the next synodical meeting. Besides, as far as the teaching and life and exercise of the ministry of all of my colleagues are concerned, I have neither the calling nor the mind to judge, beyond the fact that I find they are altogether more able, upright and faithful than I myself am. I also hope that in their letters and observations they will gladden the Very Reverend Fathers, give an account of themselves and not conceal my mistakes.

But what may be noted concerning our present Pennsylvania circumstances in general consists of the following points. 1) In Pennsylvania and the adjacent provinces there are several thousand persons belonging to the German nation and by descent and in name to the Lutheran religion. They increase annually and the newly arrived ones increase their number from year to year. They all have immortal but sinful souls. They have been purchased through the precious blood and death of Jesus and it is above all necessary that they be gathered, instructed and rescued from the dominion of darkness and transferred into the kingdom of Jesus Christ.[43] At least twenty upright pastors and an even greater number of those who conduct school would be necessary if they wanted to deal properly with old and young and lead them to the Lord Jesus! If it is true as I have read in a recently published Dutch journal of the Very Reverend Pastor Slatter, namely, that thirty thousand Reformed persons live dispersed in Pennsylvania and adjacent regions, the number of our persuasion cannot be less but most probably must still be greater. The Dutch gentlemen have considered it worth their while to collect a sum of twelve thousand pounds sterling for the Pennsylvania German Reformed people. They have ordered that this capital be invested and from the interest a number of pastors and those who conduct school be supported, and churches and school buildings be erected as one has learned from the letters to the authorities here. God has blessed Mr. Slatter's journey abroad and his effort.[44] May he also grant that thereby the true kingdom of Jesus Christ may be built up! Through the prayers and gifts of our Very Reverend Fathers and so many patrons, the gracious and merciful God has effected a way and open door[45] so that eight pastors[46] and two catechists[47] are presently laboring in common among the dispersed and erring sheep of the evangelical flock. The places where they labor are: Philadelphia, Cohansey, Germantown, Providence, New Hanover, Piketown, Shippack, Oley, Molatton, Heidelberg, Nordkiel, Tulpehocken, York, New Goshenhoppen, Old Goshenhoppen, Indianfield, Tohickon, Fork, Saccum, Upper Milford, Racheway, Lesly's Land and Gebirgte.[48] The congregations, including the small ones, at the places previously mentioned have until now held together. 2) Now, as long as there still are and remain among all of these groups one or more persons of means who can and want to support the pastor and the one who conducts school in terms of their most basic needs, the undertaking will continue for that long but with trouble and not without obstacles. The obstacles are not related to the freedom to teach, for one can teach openly and exclusively without external pressure and without the least fear and one can admonish everyone day and night with tears and extol practice as well as theory. But people are widely scattered and live far from one another. Consequently, the many little groups which are very scattered over large areas have to be brought together so they can raise the most necessary support for the pastor because the number of those who are able to do something beyond meeting their own need is really small. However, there are so many poor servants, as well as widows and orphans, who have nothing and nevertheless would like to be saved. We united pastors probably have barely half of all the so-called evangelical people. The groups outside our fellowship which are well off take preachers just as they want to and can, at the cheapest price, so they may exercise the episcopal and patronage right[49] in a carnal manner, prescribe their own law and employ and dismiss their hired preachers according to their whim and fancy. Other poor groups are entirely deserted and lapse into heathenism because they do not have the resources to support a pastor or they employ one or another corrupt school teacher or craftsman who can say something from memory and distribute the sacraments for as many pounds or shillings as they in their poverty can raise, etc., etc.

3) For several years we have already discussed a church constitution but we do not yet know how to strike a true balance so that pastors do not dominate congregations and congregations also do not dominate pastors. As long as our most prominent congregations are still mired in debts and have pastors whose gifts they admire and through whose correspondence they expect help they are manageable. However, once they are out of debt and have the resources to pay the pastor's salary then they may also do as other groups and say: We have to support our pastor with our own money, consequently we have the right and power to do with him as we wish! In almost all areas of Christianity today matters are such that the well-disposed and fair-minded souls make up the smallest group; they are not always able to outvote the largest group and maintain control. Wanting to receive help from civil authority does not work out well in this country, for civil authority has nothing to do with churches and religious affairs: it does not concern itself with them as long as the matter does not fall under its jurisdiction and the spiritual fathers are too far away. Because of so many parties, sects and enemies and because of our calling we are obliged to assign deeds to our church property in accordance with evangelical teaching according to the word of God and the Augsburg Confession. Next to God, our present congregations are indebted for the advancement of their eternal bliss to our Very Reverend Fathers, namely, the two senior pastors in London and Halle. Now if, as has often been thought, we wanted to obligate our congregations to be wholly dependent on these two places, difficulties and reservations would turn up for it is said, "We do not know how long Joseph will live and reign and what the disposition of succeeding kings may be," etc., etc.[50] Should the pastors here become independent, that would not be salutary and good either, for it is necessary and profitable to remain dependent on upright pillars of the mother church. Should the congregations become entirely independent that would never work, etc. I have often thought that upright pastors should concern themselves with appointing able successors to the congregations and leave the rest to the gracious providence of the chief shepherd and bishop of souls.[51] Something should indeed be done, but I do not yet know what is best and for my small part, I will not undertake anything without the counsel and direction of the Very Reverend Fathers, something which, however should take place soon because the most prominent congregations are still manageable and the oldest pastors are still living. The benevolent collections the Very Reverend Fathers have laboriously gathered and sent here were highly necessary in the beginning

and were applied to the scaffolding so that we could begin to care for so many souls among young and old dispersed sheep. Fruit in proportion to this effort will become evident in eternity, for the saving and instruction of a single soul is worth more than all temporal treasures! "For what does it profit a person to gain the whole world," etc., etc.[52] "The world passes away with its treasures," etc., etc.[53]

But how this good undertaking can be continued best and most safely, we must allow those to judge and counsel who have better insight and experience. Our people and even the well intentioned and honest ones among them here in this country are very suspicious and fearful of forfeiting too many of their liberties to Europe because they are assiduously warned in German calendars and newspapers to beware of the tricks of clerics and their apologists. For example:[54] Before I turned over the first money collected by the Very Reverend Fathers to the elders of the Philadelphia congregation I demanded for my security that they should assign the deed to the church property to the Very Reverend Court Preacher Ziegenhagen, among others, but I could not accomplish it. They did, however, have to give me a bond as though I had lent them the money until the deed and the remaining documents pertaining to the property had been assigned to a congregation of the Augsburg Confession and was thus confirmed.[55] In Providence, too, they were circumspect enough to see to it that nothing would be assigned to me as a person. The procedure was, of course, proper because the collections were not intended for any other use than for the evangelical churches in Philadelphia, Providence and New Hanover in accordance with the Augsburg Confession, etc., etc. As I have already reported on one occasion, the situation is as follows: in the royal countries of Great Britain there is only one established church. The church, in the strict sense of the term, is under the supervision of the archbishop.[56] Now if a piece of land is purchased and a church in this sense is built on it, the archbishop is, without restrictions, responsible for making the arrangements etc., etc. But if other congregations build a church and want to propagate their teaching in accordance with their own confession, the congregations elect one, two, three or more men from their midst. Then a piece of property is bought for the church or meeting house, and the deed is assigned as a private and entailed property to the elected men and their heirs. These owners have to provide a declaration of their own to the other elected men and confirm that the piece of property they have purchased shall be and remain not for their private and absolute use but for the perpetual use of a church according to this or that confession and polity, and so on. We have recorded our pieces of property and churches as evangelical congregations of the Augsburg Confession, etc., etc. In New Hanover they trusted me the most and allowed the church property to be assigned to me and my heirs. I in turn assigned it by deed to two elders, and these two elders assigned it to the congregation in accordance with our confession and polity. The well-intentioned and honest elders were accustomed to say from time to time they would not have second thoughts to make an assignment with life and limb, goods and children to our Very Reverend Fathers and me but they did not know what successors might follow. But I always assured them that all of this would not serve our advantage and that we desired nothing other than to see them and their descendants blessed in Christ Jesus.

Until now one recommendation has been in my thoughts which I wanted to present in childlike simplicity, entirely without presumption and humbly request that the Very Reverend Fathers would not hold to their idea that I was greedy and seeking in these things my own interest. I can assure you before God that I have never wished to become rich but have only desired what was necessary so that I would not become a burden and trouble for others and would be able to rear my poor children in a Christian manner. Should I no longer please the Very Reverend Fathers and my congregations, I will gladly be content to support myself as long as I still live with a trade or farm work and try to rear my children in an upright manner. I am of no account, if only the name of God is hallowed in our America, his kingdom is advanced and his will is accomplished! I wondered whether a modest orphanage could be established on the following basis: 1) In the middle of our congregations, that is, in New Hanover, or wherever it seems most suitable, a considerable piece of land, perhaps at the outset two hundred acres, could be bought with a healthy climate, adequate meadow land, arable land for fruit, woods and water. I could just now buy two such adjacent sites of two hundred acres for four hundred and some pounds local currency which have all of the characteristics previously mentioned and are ready for use. 2) On this site one could first build a part of a large house and gradually enlarge it. A place like that could at first be attended to by a laborer and maid or husband and wife because the meadow and arable land are already in shape, and servants of this kind can be acquired at a reasonable price and for several years. The place could immediately yield annual interest and still more if one were fortunate with the servants. 3) If he lives that long, my father-in-law could put in a word with the proprietor, Mr. Pen[57] so that the institution could be incorporated and also be privileged. 4) But who should be the proprietor of a site like this and to whom should the deed be assigned? The Very Reverend Fathers and patrons in Germany could not really be the proprietors because they have not been naturalized in accordance with English laws. In Pennsylvania they may also not be the sole proprietors for they could abuse their position. It would be most suitable, if the deed were assigned to Court Preacher Ziegenhagen and Court Preacher Albinus and Pastor Brunnholtz or Pastor Handshue.[58] These highly respected proprietors would in return give a counter-deed and declaration to His Reverence Doctor Franck and to one or more trustees, as may be desired. I beg your pardon for being so forward. Highly respected proprietors and trustees would then develop with one another a constitution and issue instructions in accordance with which the institution would be governed and administered to the best advantage of the kingdom of Christ. 5) The proprietor who went to his blessed rest last would sell or bequeath the piece of property in his last will to one or more worthy successors or friends of the same heart and mind to have and to hold, however, on the basis of the first condition and declaration in accordance with the constitution and instructions for this and no other use, etc., etc. 6) The Very Reverend Fathers would most likely hardly come to Pennsylvania unless there were a great persecution and assume the directorship in their own persons; rather they would appoint for a long or brief period one or another pastor in Pennsylvania as agent or inspector in accordance with their will, and as it pleased them. This person would seek to carry out the instructions and laws and give an annual account and answer to the exalted directors. The use of the house and land would be:

1) For faithful pastors and upright schoolworkers in our United Congregations who had sacrificed the strength of their body and mind to the glory of God and who were no longer capable of continuing to endure hardships. For example:[59] Pastor Brunnholtz, Pastor Handshue, Mr. Schaum, etc., etc.

2) For poor upright and pious widows who together with pastors' wives bear the brunt of the more concealed work in a household.

3) For extremely poor orphans of kindred faith who arrive here every year and have lost their parents at sea. Such poor, ignorant, underage worms are given away every year to all sorts of folks, corrupt sects and unbelieving people and are sold at a low price until they reach adulthood. Often they are ruined in body and soul. These extremely poor little orphans could be reared in a Christian way in an institution of this kind and guided to all kinds of useful labor for the common good. The pastors and other workers in this institution could apply their remaining energies, gifts and experience as a great blessing to our congregations, such as:

a) Wisely counseling and managing their own families;

b) Selecting from the poor pastors and schoolmasters and widows' children the most capable and talented ones and gradually preparing them to serve in church and school so our congregations would be provided for and the heavy travel costs could be avoided.

c) They could also have common schools for upright English and German children. Already for many years respected English and German people have wished they could have an institution of the kind where their children could be brought up and educated in a Christian and upright way. They would gladly pay for it, etc., etc.

d) They could annually receive a large number of young people for several weeks who live dispersed far and wide and prepare them for Holy Communion. Otherwise the poor youth have no opportunity to get to that point and all too easily lapse into heathenism or get into injurious groups.

4) A modest book and pharmaceutical store could be maintained in the institution which the blessed institutions in Halle could supply.

5) A small printing press for an annual calendar and a biweekly English and German newspaper would have to be maintained. *Indeed*[60] an institution of that kind could, with the aid of God, be of more help and blessing for our poor, scattered sheep in North America than twelve pastors on the move and would not be far behind the institution the dear Dutch put in place with the German Reformed. In this way our Very Reverend Fathers, patrons and benefactors would have established:

1) A hospital in which the exhausted, faithful servants of church and school could pass their last hours in a blessed and sanctified way.

2) The congregations would have a seminary which would provide them with able pastors and schoolworkers.

3) A place of retirement and edification for the souls of faithful pastors and schoolworkers as well as for poor and pious widows of upright congregation members.

4) An opportunity for well-intentioned English and German inhabitants to have their children instructed in godliness.

5) A refuge for hundreds of orphans where they could be instructed and prepared for Holy Communion.

6) Should an institution of this kind prosper so that it would show an annual surplus after having rendered an account it would serve as an aid and support to the poorest pastors who have inadequate salaries.

A recommendation and plan is developed quickly but where shall we secure bread in the desert for such institutions?[61]

I believe if heaven and earth were moved once more[62] an adequate amount of money would still very well come in for such a highly necessary and salutary institution of this kind. In all of Pennsylvania and the adjacent provinces we could collect money and with the help of God probably gather a couple of hundred pounds of local currency. However, I would not like it if the mites contributed here would be advanced for the purchase of the property so that no one here would have anything to say about ownership.

Furthermore, it is not likely that a rich congregation member would die here who would not bequeath something in his last will. Also country congregations which are out of debt would not refuse to add a part of their Sunday alms which were left over to the fund. Perhaps we could also do without our dear brother Brunnholtz for a year or so; he could be supplied with good references from the government and asked to travel to Europe. Such a journey would perhaps benefit his health, the spa treatment in Europe would be good for him, and the Lord may bless his endeavours, for he has a certain gift for collecting money and also does not have a wife and children who cry after him. If this were undertaken with the approval of the Very Reverend Fathers and if these same highly regarded persons would grant him a good recommendation, the undertaking would be helped along at this point. We could substitute for him for that length of time and assiduously pray for him and his undertaking. Here in Pennsylvania no more would be spent than what is necessary for payment of the site, building the house and the remaining equipment. All of the rest would be put into a fund, invested by the Very Reverend Fathers to yield interest and administered for the benefit of the institution. Also if the respected parties and directors should not experience any benefit and blessing or noticeable contribution to the kingdom of Christ or if land and house are improperly used they could at any time sell land and house again and add the amount to the remaining fund and direct it to something else, or they could change and improve the way it is handled. How many hundred thousand pounds are spent annually for food and drink, and afterwards one is, nevertheless, always hungry and thirsty again! Oh, why should one not spend something for an undertaking whose goal is the eternal welfare of many hundred, yes, thousand souls! In Virginia where Pastor Klug[63] lives, there is a small tract of land where a modest community of German Lutherans lives.[64] A few years ago they sent two to three men to Europe and had them collect money; as I have heard, they received about three thousand pounds sterling. Those who did the collecting took one third for their trouble and as salary and with what was left they built a church of wood and purchased a glebe. The pastor lives on it and benefits in the form of an adequate salary from the estate which is cultivated by eight or nine black slaves. However, only a few benefit from it for it only affects individual matters, etc., etc.[65] The famous Mr. Whitfield[66] went to indescribable trouble in collecting money for the orphanage in Georgia.[67] According to a published English report I saw he spent between five and six thousand pounds sterling on it. The good man lacked the personnel for an institution of that kind; he also did not know as well as our fathers in Halle do, what its benefits are. If he had only spent one thousand pounds here in Pennsylvania for an institution like that and had

had experienced persons available, he could have created something ten times more useful. The English do not understand the administration which is necessary for such institutions. Our prominent English people, the so-called church people in Philadelphia, have also raised among themselves a sum of money and established an academy for young people where a number of professors are retained and many different subjects are taught.[68] My colleagues visited the academy recently and observed their methods but they did not find a single Bible. In response to their question they received the answer that they did not use a Bible in their academy, etc., etc. Perhaps it will be introduced later on when students have completed other matters.

Lastly, I still wanted to include a humble petition to the Very Reverend Fathers on behalf of Mr. Schleydorn, our first and upright friend and benefactor of long standing.[69] He has a son about ten years old whom he would like to have educated in a Christian and godly manner. He has often and in many ways heard all of us praise the blessed institutions in Halle and especially the truly wise and exceptionally beautiful institution of the orphanage for boys. Consequently, it is his single most respectful request and desire before his blessed end to know whether the Very Reverend Fathers would not, as a matter of special love and kindness, deign to accept his child along with boys in the orphanage. The following are the reasons in the father's heart for yearning so much to have his child with the boys in the orphanage: 1) He has heard that in the especially blest institution the most exact and wisest supervision and method exist. 2) Valiant and brave men have already gone forth from the institution and have entered the service of the Lord. 3) Within the past two years he has been very unfortunate in his business and has lost about a thousand pounds, a misfortune which severely limits his external circumstances. 4) Next to God he has placed such confidence in the special character of the orphanage that he is of the opinion he could die far more peacefully in his Savior if he could see his youngest son received there, for here he is exposed to great danger among wicked English young people. He will gladly pay as much as he can; should something be left over after his death, he would remember his son so he could continue his studies if he should indicate promise. We know very well that this is a large request and that there is always a large number of applicants. However, we cannot refrain from interceding most humbly on his behalf and for the following reasons. 1) The father has stood by us in good times and bad and through God's word has allowed himself to be transformed into a faithful follower of Jesus Christ. 2) Until now he has been like our own father to us; he has received us as poor servants in the name of Jesus and has shared his heart and blessings with us. 3) His dear partner[70] has been a mother and nurse for all; especially for our sickly brother, Mr. Brunnholtz; in his serious illnesses she has done almost more than a physical mother. Yes, we may indeed say, and I in particular, that the faithful Savior has richly compensated us, and me, in this home for many years for that which we had to forego because of the great distance that separated us from our dear parents and friends. Now, of course, all of this has happened for our good and refreshment. But we know that the Very Reverend Fathers share in that which has happened to us in good and evil days just as our chief head, Jesus Christ himself, shares in everything which happens to the least of his members. Consequently, we hope that the Very Reverend Fathers will, if possible, grant our request for the sake of Jesus Christ and our dear friends and consent to the same. We cannot repay so great a kindness, not in the least, but we must and will request the Lord Jesus that he may richly reward them!

I beg your pardon for going back once more and catching up on something pertaining to the institution I referred to previously. If the Very Reverend Fathers would consider it necessary, useful and practical to establish an institution of that kind for the benefit of the whole community, the several thousand gulden a wealthy patron kindly promised to advance[71] could immediately be spent for the purchase of a site. I would gladly commit myself to pay the annual interest until his blessed death because, if need be, I could draw the annual interest from the land, I mean, the site without doing harm to the land. But if the Very Reverend Fathers should reject entirely my humble proposal for an institution so necessary, then I would respectfully request that the promised amount from the worthy benefactor devolve upon the Philadelphia and Germantown church, however, in such a manner that both congregations, are made more dependent so they will not misuse it. But I hope that our Very Reverend Fathers, out of fatherly compassion and mercy first care for my poor, weak and worn-out brothers in the ministry and establish a place of their own for their retirement so that they may not become a burden on the poor congregations, objects of ridicule by sects, a mockery for Sauer, the German printer, to scoff at and a vexation to themselves. The land does not lose in value if it has good qualities. Only, I worry lest the best parcels I have in mind in New Hanover might be sold secretly. However, what God has intended for us out of grace will not escape us. For the sake of Jesus Christ, our mediator, he will hear our groaning.

On his own initiative and at the request of his congregations Mr. Weygand[72] wrote to Doctor and Senior Fresenius[73] in Frankfurt a few years ago and solicited a collection for building a church in Raritan. The reverend doctor replied in a letter approximately one and one half years ago and addressed it to the evangelical pastors in Pennsylvania.[74] The content of the kind letter was approximately this: if all pastors and congregations were to join together, lament their plight and concern in a letter, the reverend sir would transmit a petition and supplements to the respective envoys of the estates at Wetzlar with excellent recommendations and try to bring about a general collection in the realm. All of the congregations, however, would have to stand together and be of one mind so that others would not apply once more if only a few receive something, etc., etc. In the month of November just past I wrote to the doctor[75] in the care of a young person who set out from here. Among other things I asked him to confer with the Very Reverend Fathers because I knew that he had special ties with them. Last year we read a sad report in the English newspaper of the conflagration in dear Wernigerode.[76] I thought he would present the plight in one or more congregations in the country which are without debts and take some mites from their alms treasury for rebuilding the church which burned down. Therewith we would demonstrate our good will because many kindnesses for body and soul flowed our way from blessed Wernigerode.[77] In the beginning I could not accommodate myself to the change in location of our dear brother in the ministry, Mr. Handshue,[78] and I was very depressed on account of Lancaster. But now I am completely comforted because I hear that he labors with blessing in Germantown and has patience with the poor circumstances of the congregation and looks to God in faith. The elders of the Germantown congregation grumble from time to time about Mr. Brunnholtz and me and think we do not adequately present their plight to our Very Reverend Fathers because they are also mired down in debts on account of their new church building and have quite a large number of poor congregation members who would gladly contribute something if only they could. I have had my dear colleague Brunnholtz transcribe from the church records here an account of receipts and expenditures of all collections which were handed over to me for the first three congregations by the Very Reverend Fathers. I enclosed the account here with the most humble request that it may please the Very Reverend Fathers to certify in general in a few words under their signature that I have properly handed everything over which was intended for the congregations. I have children and one or another agitator might accuse me and mine and say that I had kept the collections in part for myself, etc., etc. If, however, I have a few lines by an authoritative hand in my safekeeping I can show it and in case of necessity defend myself. I would rather not have had the fifty pounds sterling[79] if I had known of another way to extricate myself. But because the congregations gave me nothing in the first year and provided inadequately in the next year for the most basic necessities and my Very Reverend Fathers granted me the fifty pounds out of special compassion and sympathy, I had to receive it with thanksgiving to God for my daily bread. After all, the Very Reverend Fathers have complete authority to arrange matters as they wish. The elders in New Hanover and Providence had signed in the minutes of their congregations for the receipt of the fifty pounds which had been loaned to me. Mr. Brunnholtz did not want the Philadelphians to know anything about it, so he blotted it out in the minutes saying it was not necessary for them to know it; otherwise they might think the Very Reverend Fathers would give each one that much annually and consequently it would not be necessary for them to care for the support of their pastors. Accordingly, it would be sufficient if it were certified in a few lines that I properly turned the amount of money over which was intended for the benefit of the congregations in Philadelphia, Providence and Hanover.

Finally, once more I request with my whole heart that the Very Reverend Fathers would most graciously pardon and forget for the sake of Jesus Christ all of my mistakes which I have ever made in writing. Of course one should indeed consider to whom one is writing and carefully weigh every word. Because one assumes a child's privilege for whatever reason and one thinks one may without distinction just pour things into the laps of the fathers and write as one feels and is moved at the time, and the many kinds of external affairs and diversions often break off the train of thought, warp and woof become uneven! We have a compassionate high priest who was tempted in every respect[80] and also has compassion and patience with his most miserable creatures; to him and his unspeakable love and mercy I commend my Very Reverend Fathers in their important office and position, along with all their relations. However, myself, my dear brothers in the ministry and all congregations I commend to their unswerving kindness and goodwill and remain with profoundest veneration your

Providence
18 February 1752

Poor servant,
Mühlenberg

P.S.
I would not like to misuse the patience of Your Reverences but I do not know how to help myself in any other way than to add yet another most humble request, namely, whether it would please Your Reverences to have a part of my inheritance[81] in Einbeck made over to Your Most Highly Regarded Sirs and have it sent here by a bill of exchange. With it I would like to pay a part of my debt after the medicines and books which have been ordered are paid from it. May the Lord reward your trouble!

1. See *Journals* 1:234-308.
2. A summary of this letter is contained in an entry into Mühlenberg's diary on 30 November 1751. The letter was not sent until 22 February 1752, See Letter 114 and *Korrespondenz* 1:492 n.1, and on the textual problems of this letter, see *Korrespondenz* 1:505-6.
3. Friedrich Schultze and Johann Dietrich Matthias Heinzelmann arrived in Philadelphia on 1 December 1751. On Schultze, see Letter 89 n.4; on Heinzelmann, see Letter 101 n.3.
4. Mühlenberg had served the Dutch congregation in New York temporarily from May until August 1751. The matter of a more permanent arrangement for a pastor of the congregation had remained unresolved. For more details see Letter 109. See Letter 109.
5. The text reads μεθιοδειάς. The acute accent should be on the penultimate rather than ultimate syllable. See Eph. 6:11,14: μεθιοδείας
6. The text reads *Stratagemata*.
7. See Ps. 110:2.
8. See Mark 1:44; italics in the original text.
9. In Letter 93, dated 16 June 1751, to Gotthilf August Francke and Michael Ziegenhagen, Mühlenberg had complained about feeling ill. Three days later, 18 June 1751, in that same condition, he wrote a letter to Court Preacher Samuel Theodore Albinus. Only the postscript of that letter is extant (Letter 94). On Albinus, see *Correspondence* 1:154 n.8.
10. The reference is to Mühlenberg's involvement in the conflict between Johann August Wolf and the congregation in Raritan. See Letter 72 n.27.
11. For Mühlenberg's involvement in affairs of the congregations in Rhinebeck and Camp being served by Hartwich, see Letter 89 nn. 12 and 13 and Letter 93 n. 31.
12. The text reads παραπτomata, the first half of the word in Greek, the last half in Latin letters.
13. The text reads *paroxismo*.
14. See Matt. 25:14-30.
15. *Ich traue deinen wunder-Wegen, sie enden sich in Lieb und Segen*, from the fourth stanza of Wolfgang Christoph Dessler's hymn, *Wie wohl ist mir, O Freund der Seelen*. See *Liedersammlung*, Hymn 414.
16. See *Correspondence* 1:189 n. 9.
17. See Jer. 11:20 (AV).
18. The text reads *hypothetice*.
19. The text reads *comparative*.
20. See *Correspondence* 1, Letters 8 and 9.
21. The reference is probably to Francke's letter to Mühlenberg in the fall of 1741 which is not extant. See *Correspondence* 1:8 n.3.
22. The text reads *excursiones*.
23. At 2 Tim. 2:20 the Luther text reads *hölzerne Gefässe*.
24. The text reads *a priori*.
25. The text reads *cursu*.
26. The text reads *homo pietismi suspectus*.
27. The Society for the Propagation of the Gospel in Foreign Parts.
28. The text reads *casus*.
29. For Mühlenberg's conflict with Zinzendorf, see *Correspondence* 1: Letters 15 and 17.
30. On Johann Conrad Andreae, see *Correspondence* 1:138-40; 143 n. 10.
31. On Laurentius Thorstonson Nyberg, see *Correspondence* 1:181 n.10; 251-63; 300.
32. See *Correspondence* 1:157; for Mühlenberg's skill as a financial juggler when resources for himself, his family and his congregations were scarce and tight, see *Correspondence* 1:303-4.
33. See *Correspondence* 1:93 n.37; 173; 336.
34. See for example 1 Cor. 9:6; 2 Cor. 11:9; 11:13-14; Acts 18:3 and Matt. 10:8.
35. The text reads *res integra*.

36. See Letter 101.
37. The text reads *vox patrum vox Dei.*
38. This letter is in part the source of the Minutes of the Fourth Convention 12-13 May 1752 which reports the appointments of Schultze and Heinzelmann; see *Documentary History*, p. 35; see also *HN2/1:*78;80.
39. Not extant.
40. See *Correspondence* 1:143 n.10.
41. On Peter Brunnholz, see Letter 71 n.3.
42. At its Fifth Convention in Germantown on 20 October 1752 the Synod appointed Schultze to serve the New Goshenhoppen congregation. See *Documentary History*, p. 39.
43. See Col. 1:13.
44. On Michael Schlatter, see *Correspondence* 1:342 n. 41; Letter 75; *Korrespondenz* 1:503. Michael Schlatter's *Getrouw Verhaal* describing circumstances in the congregations in Pennsylvania was published in Amsterdam in 1751. At a meeting of the Coetus assembly in Philadelphia on 13 December 1750 it was resolved to send Schlatter to Holland. See *Minutes and Letters*, pp. 40-41. There he reported on the difficulties and needs of the Reformed in North America to the consistory. Returning from this journey in July 1752, he brought with him the sum of £12,000 and six pastors to serve congregations in North America. See *Korrespondenz* 1:493 n.26.
45. See Rev. 3:8.
46. The eight pastors are: Mühlenberg, Brunnholz, Handschuh, Schaum, Kurz, Weygand, Schultze and Heinzelmann.
47. The two catechists are: Ludolph Heinrich Schrenck and Lucas Rauss.
48. *Gebirgte* refers to the Hill congregation in connection with Upper Milford. See *Journals* 1:198.
49. The text reads *Jus episcopale und Patronatus.*
50. See Exod. 1:8.
51. See 1 Pet. 2:25.
52. Mark 8:38.
53. See 1 John 2:17.
54. The text reads *Ex[empli] gr[atia].*
55. See *Correspondence* 1:175-76; 228.
56. For the evolving role of the Episcopal Church in the American colonies, see *Correspondence* 1:145 n.4.
57. Thomas Penn managed the proprietary rights of the family from 1732-41 while in Philadelphia and thereafter from England.
58. On Johann Friedrich Handschuh, see *Correspondence* 1:291 nn. 18 and 19.
59. The text reads *Ex[empli] gr[atia].*
60. Text in italics.
61. See Mark 6:35 (AV).
62. See Matt. 5:18; 24:35.
63. See *Correspondence* 1:192 n.7; 342 n.37.
64. See *Lutherans in N.A.*, pp. 31-2.
65. See *Journals* 1:223: "In this month Pastor Klug visited us. For several years he has been the regular pastor of a German Evangelical congregation in the province of Virginia [HN: Some years ago several German men, among them one especially, who was named Stöver, went out from the province of Virginia (also called Spotsylvania) to Germany to collect money. They gathered a sum of nearly £3000. They received a third of it for their traveling expenses and trouble, and with the rest they built a wooden church and bought a tract of land and a number of black slaves. From this land and the slaves the pastor receives a liberal salary and the congregation is not in the least burdened with his support." -See also *Correspondence* 1:192 n.7.
66. See *Correspondence* 1:23 n.11.

67. See Mühlenberg's reference to Whitefield's founding of the orphanage in Savannah, Georgia, *Journals* 1:60; also "A House of Mercy in the Woods of Georgia," in Arnold A. Dallimore's *George Whitefield: The Life and Times of the Great Evangelist of the Eighteenth Century Revival* (Westchester, Illinois: Cornerstone Books, 1970), pp. 445-62. -See also *Correspondence* 1:23 n.11; 111 n. 15.

68. Planned as a charity school in 1740, it opened as an academy in 1751 through the efforts of Benjamin Franklin. In 1755 it received a college charter. In 1779 it became the University of the State of Pennsylvania. It assumed its present name, The University of Pennsylvania, in 1791.

69. See *Correspondence* 1:53 n.22.

70. Elisabeth Schleydorn (1705-85) waited upon and nursed Brunnholz "more tenderly than a mother could her own child." See *Correspondence* 1:301.

71. See *Korrespondenz* 1:494 n.38.

72. On Johann Albert Weygand, see Letter 71 n.21.

73. See *Correspondence* 1:121 n.4 and *Korrespondenz* 1:104 n.4.

74. The letter is not extant.

75. See Letter 106.

76. The greater part of the city, including the Liebfrauenkirche, was destroyed by fire in June, 1751. Rebuilding of the city was undertaken with the help of monetary gifts from other parts of Germany and Denmark. For further information see *Korrespondenz* 1:494 n.42.

77. See *Correspondence* 1:105.

78. Concerning Handshuh's difficulties in Lancaster see *Journals* 1:271; *Correspondence* 1:291 n.18.

79. For Mühlenberg's accounting, see *Correspondence* 1:302-4 and 307 nn. 21 and 22.

80. See Heb. 4:15.

81. Anna Maria Mühlenberg née Kleinschmidt had died in December 1747. Mühlenberg learned of her death only three years later. See Letter 114:236. See also *Correspondence* 1:234 n.13.

Letter 113

To Samuel Theodor Albinus
Providence, 20 February 1752

*Only an excerpt of this letter in the form of a table of contents is extant.
At the time this letter was written to him Albinus[1] was lector at the German
Chapel in London. Mühlenberg's reference to commentaries by John Locke
and Johann David Michaelis is an indication of his continuing occupation
with biblical studies in the midst of his multifaceted ministry.*

Text in German: Korrespondenz *1:494-95. For further textual
information, see* Korrespondenz *1:495.*

1) Certification of his letters[2] sent off to us, in general without designation
of number and dates.
2) Apology for my first letter to him from New York.[3]
3) With regard to my dissatisfaction with Pastor Handshue's change in
location.[4]
4) On Pastor Brunnholz's faithfulness, his relationship with me and his great
frailty in body and vital disposition.[5]
5) Concerning the weakness of Mr. Schaum.[6]
6) With regard to the recommendation of establishing a school and an
orphanage.[7]
7) That our pastors still do not have a firm footing in the congregations.[8]
8) That already our modest institution annoys the devil.
9) Requested to render humble thanks in our names to the Very Reverend
Ziegenhagen for the tracts which were sent.
10) To work out a prompt response with regard to New York.
11) Apology with regard to my way of handling the New York matter.
12) Requested two things from the Very Reverend Fathers: either dismissal
or more adequate instruction.
13) That the trip to New York has improved my health.[9]
14) That by the providence of God I escaped having an accident on the
return journey from New York to Pennsylvania.
15) Sympathy with the physical weakness of Mr. Albinus.
16) Sadness on account of the departure of Lady von Münchhausen:[10]
request for the course of her life.
17) Requested against payment the consignment of Locke's *Paraphrases* of
Paul's letters[11] and Whitby's *Commentary*.[12]
18) Notes concerning Magister Michaelis' *Paraphrases* of letters of Paul;[13]

dated 29 February 1752.

---

1. See *Correspondence* 1:154 n.8.
2. Letters of Albinus in his own hand to Mühlenberg are not extant. However, see Letter 94:133 and 135 n.3.
3. See Letter 94.
4. Concerning Handschuh's move from Lancaster to Germantown, see Letter 93:121ff; 131 n.16. On Johann Friedrich Handschuh, see *Correspondence* 1:291 n.18.
5. On Peter Brunnholz, see Letter 71 n.3.
6. On Johann Helfrich Schaum, see Letter 71 n.9.
7. See also his recommendation in Letter 112:214-17.
8. At issue was the question whether the superiors in Europe were in agreement with Mühlenberg's plan to move to New York a second time for several months. See Letter 112 n.4.
9. See the entry in the diary for 21 August 1751, *Journals* 1:307: "The New York air is very healthy and especially for me because it is situated near the open sea."
10. Wilhelmine Sophie von Münchhausen died October 1750 of dropsy.
11. John Locke (1632-1704), *A Paraphrase and Notes on the Epistles of St. Paul to the Galatians, 1 and 2 Corinthians, Romans, Ephesians* (London, 1705-7).
12. Daniel Whitby (1638-1726), *Paraphrase and Commentary on the New Testament*, 2 vols. (London, 1703).
13. Johann David Michaelis (1717-91), *Paraphrases und Anmerkungen über die Briefe Pauli an die Galater, Epheser, Philipper etc.* (Göttingen, 1750).

Letter 114

To Gotthilf August Francke
Providence, 22 February 1752

Apologizing profusely in the form of self-deprecation for not having written more promptly and citing reasons for this failure, Mühlenberg finds solace in messages of Holy Scripture, aspirations of the Christian faith and in the recent arrival of two coworkers.

Following expressions of gratitude for the receipt of Bibles, New Testaments, tracts and pharmaceuticals, Mühlenberg once again pleads at great length for support in establishing a school and an orphanage in southeastern Pennsylvania. Side by side with Mühlenberg's glowing plans and hopes for these institutions are his involvements in the rough and tumble of carrying his ministry forward. The need to secure financial support for ministers on a voluntary basis from congregation members weighs heavily on his mind and tends to depress his spirit. Also, the need to decide whether or not to leave Pennsylvania and go to New York to minister to Lutherans there must be resolved. Before making a decision on that need he feels under obligation to await the response to his inquiry from his superiors. Furthermore, the Philadelphia publisher, Christoph Sauer, once again irritates him with what Mühlenberg thinks of as irresponsible dissemination of religious falsehoods by which Sauer gives comfort to those who maintain that a preacher should earn his livelihood by engaging in a trade rather than living from the contributions of congregation members.

In spite of difficulties and irritations, Mühlenberg continues to propose dreams for the future of the Lutheran church in North America to his superiors. He knows of wealthy landowners who are willing to provide ample land for a parsonage, a school and sustenance for the pastor to attract settlers from Germany, both Lutheran and Reformed. These settlement plans mesh in Mühlenberg's mind with a way of increasing the number of those who will praise the name of the mediator, Jesus Christ.

The letter, including the postscript, concludes with a number of personal matters to which Mühlenberg alludes: the birth and naming of a daughter, reference to his siblings' inequitable distribution of his mother's bequest, the request of his father-in-law, Conrad Weiser, for a supply of pharmaceuticals and Mühlenberg's desire for several biblical commentaries.

Text in German: Korrespondenz *1:496-505. For further textual information, see* Korrespondenz *1:505-6.*

Very reverend, very learned, very venerable
Doctor, Senior and Inspector, in Christ,
Very favorable Patron and cherished Father in Christ:

Your Reverence justifiably charges me with neglect and ingratitude in observing my duty and obligation because I have neither expressed my condolences nor congratulations in connection with two important changes. However, in accordance with your fatherly love and goodwill I hope Your Reverence will kindly pardon this fault as I present with simplicity and humility reasons which are indeed inadequate but appear important to me. To be honest about it, fleeing the cross and fear keep me back most of all. While suffering from another cross and tribulation, my heart was wounded by the unexpected very painful departure of your wife who was needed for the kingdom of Christ, endowed with extraordinary talents and my kindly disposed patron while living.[1] Already shortly thereafter a new shock followed with the passing of our blessed mother, Mrs. Götz.[2] The first wound was torn open again and depressed me, miserable one, so much that after rightly complaining in my little chamber I wanted to flee from the cross and became fearful of bringing the wound to mind--as well on account of my own melancholy feelings as also an account of fearfulness that, as a result of contact with the sad wound, I would once again bring Your Reverence to tears! However, through a fatherly, very pleasant and undeserved communication from Your Reverence from Pölzig or Pella,[3] dated 29 July 1751,[4] with which I was favored, 18 July 1751 in New York, I was healed and comforted as though it were an ointment which had been poured out. Consequently, my courage increased again in view of the most gracious providence of our heavenly Father which has selected, ordained and granted Your Reverence as wife the baroness[5] with whom I am acquainted in the Lord, her highness before God and men. "In his rule he has not failed to take note of anything," etc.[6] "Happy is he whose help is the God of Jacob."[7] "Should it appear for a time as if God had forsaken his own, Oh then know and believe God will come to their aid! Hallelujah!"[8] May the faithful and all-sufficient God be a mighty shield, a very great reward and glorious crown to the house of the excellent Count Henckel,[9] and their most recent offspring through whose most wise mediation the sad breach in Zion has been healed and the blessed institutions have been provided with a true mother and wet nurse, Exodus 2:9. He has furnished the house of the Lord with an Anna, Luke 2:36,37. The servant of God, overburdened with trouble and work on all sides, he has supported with a Phoebe, Romans 16:1,2. The congregations under your direction have been favored with a Persis, Romans 16:12, and our widely scattered little flocks in East and West have been endowed with a Mary and Tabitha, Romans

16:6; Acts 9:36-9. Gracious lady and true baroness in the Son of God, we on our small part from the desert of the West recall to your mind with a faithful heart, though without comparison on our side, the sixtieth verse of Genesis 24, "*You are our mother and sister, may you and your descendants increase many thousand thousand times*"--if not physically, then spiritually-- "*possess the gates of your enemies.*"[10] I do not envy these two elect ladies[11] their homeward journey and stately rest, for they no doubt had the desire to depart and rather see that which here they believed and hoped.[12] However, on account of the present need, their departure seemed much too harsh to me and more a deserved punishment than a chastisement of us. For it was exactly these two persons who lent our dearest father Franck a hand in his most burdensome ministrations at home and abroad and whose undeserving kindness the Lord directed especially toward me, unworthy as I am, my colleagues and the poor little flocks. But what could I do? I had to place my hand on my mouth and say in my heart, "Because the poor are despoiled, because the needy groan" while the saints decrease, arise, O Lord, and provide help that one may confidently continue to teach, Psalm 12.[13] It is, after all, only a short time after which, for the sake of Jesus Christ, the Lord will take us home from this present vale of tears! Already a very long time ago I had the intention out of a deep sense of responsibility most humbly to wait on the houses of the most worthy counts in Wernigerode and Pölzig in writing. However, I can assure you that I am afraid and stand in awe of them because my style of writing is so easily offensive and unacceptable to persons of such high standing, as Your Reverence yourself at one time was pleased to remind me out of a genuine fatherly love.[14] I do indeed struggle and proceed against it, also pray the dear God in Christ to endow me with better gifts, but I still cannot attain to it the way I would wish. Memory and imagination are always filled with images but the strength in forming judgments is too weak in differentiating between matters and putting each thing in its appropriate place. This is something which must be in one's natural make-up and temperament. Should a melancholy person force himself and act the part of one who is optimistic, an intolerable affectation results, and the reverse is also true. A body has many and various members. Not everything on it can be eye, also not hand and foot. If only all members remain in their order, are sanctified and perform that for which they are intended and suitable a common good is served, be it great or small, considerable or slight.[15]

The two new coworkers[16] arrived safely in Philadelphia on 1 December 1751 to our comfort and encouragement. As we have learned from them, they were guided across the ocean quite gently and quickly as on eagle's wings.[17] They have refreshed us with many beautiful reports regarding the cross kingdom of Christ. It is a real encouragement and new awakening to receive new laborers who come like fattened calves from a healthy, fertile and plentiful pasture and impart everything they have gathered from fathers, young people and children in Christ during the whole journey. Here one finds new material for the praise of God, yes, for all kinds of prayer, intercession and thanksgiving. The Very Reverend Fathers and so many dear patrons and children of God have made provision out of love, mercy and compassion and have established and prepared everything in the Pennsylvanian desert: altars, wood, fire, knives and priests! Now may the covenant God also graciously point out the rams which are caught far and wide by their horns in bushes and brambles[18] so that we and many others whom the Lord has purchased prepare and sacrifice ourselves as a sweet savor! "Then slay and slaughter, etc., place wood on the altar and consume me altogether," etc., etc.[19]

I, for my part, express the most humble thanks of all for the Bibles, Testaments and remaining marvellous tracts of Mr. von Bogatzky,[20] as well as for the medicine. I pray that the Lord Jesus may graciously remember the dear gifts and donors when on his majestic and glorious day of judgment, in the presence of a large number of many thousand angels and the elect he will say, "I was hungry and you gave me food, I was sick and you visited me."[21] I may not let on when I have some of the blessed medicine from Halle at home. As soon as it becomes known I have no peace until the last particle and drop which sticks to the paper and the glass has been dispensed. Oh, if only we had an orphanage and school and in it only a small shop with medicines and a passable physician from Glaucha, we should get a large crowd of people from far and wide and dispense medication for body and soul. The ones who are somewhat well off pay gladly, and in such a way that in case of need one can dispense medication to the poor free if one sells it in accordance with the most recent price. In a joint letter to the Very Reverend Fathers[22] I presented an unpretentious proposal for an orphanage and school. I can assure you that I see no other way by which our congregations could be better assisted and the good cause could be continued. Nothing is impossible for the dear God, he can direct and incline hearts to this purpose! Perhaps it is already a small hint in that direction that a worthy patron has promised to advance several thousand gulden[23] in return for the payment of interest to the end of his life.[24] If there is a need I will gladly stand surety for the interest and mortgage my house although I myself am still in debt, if only the whole enterprise will succeed. The congregations in Philadelphia and Germantown are of course still in debt, but they are on that account obliged all the more diligently to continue the service of God and in a given situation will be even more ready and willing to accept good order for their own and their children's benefit. I am only reporting on things the way they are. For that reason the dear God still has his people and his undertaking among the great crowds; and alongside the work we have in mind, in accordance with his mercy he can guide one little brook or another to both congregations depending on how time and circumstances, need and wisdom stand in proportion to each other. A word to the wise is sufficient.[25] For example,[26] when the Lancaster people were in dire need and leaned toward the precipice there were no more excellent and better pastors than the Hallensians; Magister Wagner[27] and Stöver[28] counted for nothing. But as soon as the yoke and the hangman's noose were gone, the pastors counted for nothing and Wagner and Stöver could attend to matters very well.[29] By this time, as I hear from Lancaster, they have, moreover, built a splendid parsonage and through Mr. Wagner's mediation sent a call to Tübingen, etc., etc.

Your Reverences know more about the ways of the world than I can write. Most people deny the power of godliness and its appearance is used as a cover for sin.[30] The apple of the eye of all of our congregations are innocent children, destitute youth and divinely favored souls who are obedient to the Spirit of God mediated through his word, etc., etc. In the silence of the heart and with the mouth they thank the Lord Jesus that he has inclined the Very Reverend Fathers and benefactors to come to their aid in the anguish of their souls. If precious souls of that kind constituted the largest part and number of people, we would have nothing to fear. Outwardly things would already shine more gloriously but the right time is not here yet. It will surely come, however, when tribulation teaches persons to attend more closely to the word. It is a difficult matter for us in this country that we have to raise our salary from the livelihood of people. Travelling back and forth so much wears out many clothes and ruins horses and health. People have to work hard and for the most part they can just get by or scarcely make ends meet. The ones among whom the word of God takes hold gladly share if they have something. The ones who are well off and at the same time tightfisted and are concerned only with the work as an external act,[31] also give what they promise but they do not do it gladly with singleness of heart,[32] rather they do it before witnesses, turn the money over in their hand two or three times and once they have separated themselves from their dear money, they cast a stoney glance at the pastor and wait to see whether he will extol and praise their charitableness. If the pastor cannot and will not do it, they themselves boast of the great deeds they perform annually. If in accordance with one's office and duty one reprimands them, nothing is gained and the saying goes that the pastor cannot get enough, etc., etc. We live among cunning sects that do not hesitate to make it odious to people. As long as one is single it is still easiest to manage but with families it is still too difficult for the young, poor congregations. I think it might have been equally difficult in Germany and perhaps even more difficult if salaries had not been set[33] and made firm before the Reformation. I regard the young pastors as more fortunate who are not required to expect their support from the livelihood of congregation members. These are simply external matters and yet they have an influence on internal matters. So far the promise of God has still been fulfilled among us, "Seek first the kingdom of God," etc., etc.[34] "I will not forsake you," etc., etc.[35] Giving is in the comparative degree and receiving in time of need in the positive degree.[36] Our dear Savior would easily have changed it if he had not found the arrangement satisfactory as set forth in the Table of Duties.[37] Whoever is not pleased with that should not have any pastors.

In the meantime an orphanage and a school would be necessary, salutary and useful. If the Very Reverend Fathers would approve of it, consider it practical in accordance with their more profound insight and experience, and think it necessary for one of us to come over there, I would indeed not refuse should I be the one who is chosen, if circumstances in my congregations allowed it and wife and children were not too faint of heart. However, I would think my dear colleague, Mr. Brunnholtz, would perhaps be more suitable for such an undertaking because thereby he could hopefully regain his health under the blessing of God and perhaps find and bring back an apt helpmate. It would indeed be hard for us to be without the dear brother for so long a time; however, the dear God would stand by us, especially since Pastor Handshue and Mr. Heinzelman are still available. Travelling cannot be so terribly difficult for us because we are trained in it every day, and we cannot sacrifice our life in any better way than for the glory of God and the general welfare of our neighbor. The institution itself would probably be best situated in the middle of our congregations. However, knowledgeable people could think long and hard and carefully enough where it would be situated best and where to find the most suitable site once things have gotten as far along as to make a beginning. Our old friend, Mr. Vigera,[38] together with his able wife could occupy a place in the bookstore and administration or something along that line. The dear brothers Brunnholtz, Handshue, Heinzelman and Schultz acquired many abilities and aptitudes in the blessed schools and institutions in Halle. With united strength they could gradually design this institution on the same principles once they have obtained the constitution and general arrangement and instruction from the Very Reverend Fathers and the site for it has been assigned.

Concerning the New York affair[39] I humbly request that you kindly consult with His Reverence, Court Preacher Ziegenhagen, concerning the matter and deign to let us have a final opinion as soon as possible. Once I have the response and verdict of my Very Reverend Fathers before me, I can act in a positive and joyful way and satisfy my conscience. Both options are very frightening: to leave Pennsylvania and also to see New York forsaken; to be overhasty and to be negligent. In this matter I do not follow my own will and choice but with all my heart I desire that the will of God be done! Also, in this matter I have done nothing on my own but each time I have consulted with my brothers in the ministry, as my meager notes and the modest correspondence in this instance with my father-in-law[40] demonstrate. I was very worried and anxious concerning Pastor Handshue because things took so sad a turn after his change of location.[41] Now everything has quieted down again and he feels more vigorous in body and soul. He is also of the opinion that the gracious will of God has appointed and directed him to Germantown. Almost every variety of Pennsylvania persuasions resides in Germantown so that one could almost say: there are as many different opinions as there are houses. Most of the members of our congregation live near, around and outside of Germantown and very few in it. He lives in the city and in doctrine and life shows himself to be edifying and exemplary and does not labor without blessing, also among those who are of a different persuasion. It would, of course, be good if, in accordance with Melanchthon's rule, one dealt with quality and concentrated on that instead of quantity[42] which one cannot survey and with which one cannot really contend. Each large congregation would probably very much need two pastors and each small congregation one pastor for itself but, as already noted, the way things are one must rather put several congregations together because we are lacking workers and furthermore the material support is restricted. Sauer,[43] the newspaper publisher, wants to persuade Pennsylvanians at all costs that preachers should engage in a trade and preach to people for nothing. I would gladly do it, if it were the command of Christ and of my superiors. The man promotes a lot of mischief with his printing press and puts perverse notions into the head of unknowing people. A few years ago there was still a German print shop in Philadelphia which belonged to a prominent English printer who had rented it out to a German. But because the German man died a Zinzendorfian rented it and has moved to Lancaster with it. Soon we shall also hear something new from that side. The Lord help us! "Upon the right and the left hand, Help us with vigor to withstand," etc., etc.[44] I wish especially to repeat once more the request I made in the humble letter to the Very Reverend Fathers[45] for our dear friend Schleydorn and his son and most humbly beseech Your Reverences not to look unfavorably upon my boldness. I am told that as many as two hundred applicants are sometimes on hand who are awaiting a place in the blessed institutions. Oh, it would not be surprising if Your Reverences were to tire of my writing for it always consists of complaining, lamenting, begging, excusing! But I cannot help myself in any other way because I am a sojourner in Meshech[46] and, next to God, must at all times take refuge in my spiritual fathers in Christ; they have a sensitive and sympathetic heart which I would not like to misuse but rather please, if only the subject matter for pleasing them were at hand.

After all, there will be a time when wailing and lamentation come to an end! If in this life only we have hope in Christ we are the most miserable of all people.[47] A rest is still available whither in so many thousand years the godly have journeyed, etc., etc.[48] In the past year Your Reverences were very close to this blessed rest and great glory and to the complete possession of them, as I have learned from my dear new brothers! Oh, what, indeed, would Your Reverences desire more than to pass from faith to sight, and how beneficial it would be for your sanctified soul to be freed entirely at some point from a weak body, innumerable professional burdens, from anxiety, worry, sorrow, tribulation, from the arrows and blows of Satan; to be led in triumph out of the kingdom of the cross into the kingdom of glory; to be transferred from the church militant to the church triumphant and into the company of the perfectly righteous who have come there from great tribulations and have made their robes white in the blood of the Lamb;[49] to be introduced to enjoyment of all possible benefits. But for the sake of the present need may the Lord not take you from us yet and punish us so severely!

May the Lord grant you sufficient strength and vigor that you may not sag within and without under the burden of the cross but keep afloat! He provides strength sufficient for the faint, etc., etc.[50] One would think a servant of God of this kind could not fly so high, even if he had the best eagle's wings, because so many hundredweight of official burdens would weigh him down, but the strength of God gives him power to fly. How else in the midst of trials and tribulations would the very blessed Professor Franck have been able to sing, "Ere now my soul has taken wing to you, O Jesus," etc., etc.[51] Be of good cheer, most favored father, a number of pearls and precious stones are still being polished annually in East and West which are to be placed with others in your crown! I know you love the Lord Jesus very much and would gladly do and suffer everything possible and imaginable for him out of love! Here is the best and most suitable time to bear the cross after him out of love; in eternity there is no longer an opportunity to do something of that kind. At present the times are strange and dreadful so that one could very well sing and sigh. Things are gradually reaching the point that the servants of God must lament with weeping and say with sighing, along with Elijah, the precious man of God: The body of those who truly believe is indeed small! Every so-called estate in your Christendom has bowed down in the service and folly of Baal's idols.[52] Very few have not bowed down before pride, greed, impure sensual lust, as you are aware. The head, that is the government, is sick and almost drawing its last breath. One sees the heart, that is the clergy, almost everywhere cast down in impotence. And that which constitutes the body's foundation knows nothing of penitence. The set rules of religion are no longer practiced. By hook and crook every estate has taken as much of your light and right as serves its false purpose and object, thus playing games with sin![53] Times are strange when one considers how during the current decline and wane of Christendom, nevertheless so many faithful witnesses still labor among the nations. God still has three kinds of people on earth: Christendom, Judaism and heathenism. Through the Spirit and Gospel work must be carried forward among all three. The work has a set time for grace and righteousness. Perhaps the Lord will begin to refine and purify his church after preaching has done its share, as one would like to sing, "Attend to all times past/ and to every century/ how the church of Christ was accustomed to do battle/ in times of tribulation and peace?/ It must often be trodden and tried/ otherwise it will seldom be pretty and pure!/ Should God permit it to experience quiet times/ it will become lazy, stagnant and old;/ it has to put up with hypocrites who are neither hot nor cold./ A true clear wine exists when husks of grapes and juice are still as one."[54]

Since I have gotten a little more time and help so that I can collect myself and reflect somewhat better, I recall in my notes of 1750[55] I whined and complained here and there because I was alone, had many distractions and no help. May the Very Reverend Fathers please pay no attention to it and kindly overlook it, also be pleased to have it deleted or corrected by my dear old brother in Christ, Mr. Fabricius,[56] before it is communicated to other worthy friends. I was of the opinion that one had plainly and simply just to write down what is important and unimportant, just as one feels and is moved. I would gladly do better if only I could and knew how. One is not at all times of the same disposition, and just as the poor body is troubled now and then with obstructions so also is the soul in its own way. To this day we laborers have stood fast altogether in brotherly unity and love. Although now and then a small obstacle from "the sin which clings so closely"[57] wants to come between us, we, nevertheless, try immediately to find a remedy insofar as God gives us grace. The best medication to counteract it is poverty in spirit or humility and genuine brotherly love, proper acknowledgment of the variety of gifts communicated for the common good and the like. The great physical weakness I have observed during the last two years in my dear colleague and neighbor, Brunnholtz, and which is getting worse every day still occasions the greatest anxiety in me at the present time. For that reason I could wish that the good brother might be removed entirely for a time from his present burden and circumstances, so that by the blessing of God he could again recover and serve the whole enterprise afresh with his gifts! The best opportunity for such recovery would be in Europe because association with so many different children of God would refresh his soul and treatment at a spa would again restore his body! No one in a hundred understands his illness and weakness, etc., etc.

With other interested persons Captain Herttel, a member of the Lutheran congregation in New York, owns a piece of land consisting of 11,500 acres. He has divided the land into a district in which thirty families of our German Lutherans are to settle. It is situated in the province of New York. He requested me to recommend honest persons to him and also to see to it that a pastor of our communion is placed there. He wanted to allot fifteen hundred acres of it for the residence of a pastor and assign it to him forever so that gradually a property of this kind could be put in condition for a pastor and the pastor could be maintained from it.[58] I have not yet had time to examine the matter, also I do not know whether the Very Reverend Fathers consider my further involvement in it acceptable. Another prominent landowner in New York[59] promised five hundred acres of land as a place for a pastor for another district which is to be laid out if I would recommend nice people from Pennsylvania. One needs to recognize that in part the gentlemen are selling their land to the farmers, in part renting it out at an annual interest rate, and that it is still nothing but woodland. But they want to donate the land for the pastor so people are all the more eager to move there when they learn that provision is made for church and school. That is not the way it is in our Quaker province. The Reformed pastor, our friend, Mr. Slatter,[60] has among other things also proposed to the synod in Holland that they could establish a mission among our heathen nations through the mediation of Conrad Weiser,[61] as I have gathered from the Dutch journal. Our great mediator, Jesus Christ, has given himself for all. Oh, that a message of this kind would be proclaimed and accepted everywhere and his glorious name would become well known to all for their eternal salvation!

My earthly mother who in life was dear to me has already passed into eternity four years ago[62] and only three years later did my friends report this to me. In this connection I also learned that my nearest earthly relatives and siblings were, for the most part, intent on what is material rather than spiritual. I applied about forty reichsthaler of my parents' possessions to my education. In Göttingen I lived on scholarships granted to me by His Excellence, High Sheriff von Münchhauss,[63] from the government in Hannover. In Halle I was in part the beneficiary of the blessed institutions and for the rest I was adequately cared for through benevolent scholarships of Their Excellencies the blessed XXIV Count Reuss[64] and Count Henckel at Pölzig.[65] But my representative, secretary Ernst,[66] together with the majority of my siblings[67] unfairly and unjustly calculated and subtracted three hundred reichsthaler for my education without inquiring further as to how and why. For this reason I humbly beg Your Reverences not to look upon it unkindly that I have taken the liberty to enclose several letters of that nature[68] because I knew of no other way to get my letters to their destination. On 17 September of last year[69] the gracious God delighted me and my wife with a daughter.[70] Since I lost my best and most worthy patron in the blessed Mrs. Francke[71] and still would like to retain and keep in mind her memory and the blessed remembrance of her, I had Mr. Schleydorn[72] and his beloved spouse stand sponsor at the baptism and gave her the name Henrietta. I hope Your Reverences will most kindly pardon such whims and not begrudge me this innocent refreshment! Now I have an Augustus Church before my eyes,[73] a Friedrich Augustus who is godly until now[74] and Henrietta as a blessed remembrance in my house. May God be praised and may he allow his righteousness and peace to increase in us and may his kingdom be advanced thereby! Such whims offend the world and sound weak and lame but the world is gradually crucified to me and I also to it, hallelujah! Of all the benefactions I have received, accounts of the circumstances of the kingdom of Christ in Germany and other places have been the most important and edifying. Everything which is to attain to glory must pass through suffering and struggle.

My father-in-law and his family commend themselves to Your Reverence and gracious wife in kind remembrance before God. He humbly expresses thanks for the kind and welcome communication he received safely last year.[75] On this occasion he wanted to request some of the blessed medicine for twenty reichsthaler, namely, half for life powder and for the other half the remaining elements according to proportion. Similarly, I would obediently make a request for medicine for myself for twenty reichsthaler, namely, life powder[76] for ten reichsthaler and for the remaining ten reichsthaler essence for opening the spleen[77] and polychrest pills.[78] Perhaps more should be added so it will fill a box. If at all possible I would like to have Schmid's volumes dealing with parts of the Bible, for example, the one on geography and the one on medicine, as well as the remaining ones.[79] Finally, I must now close at last with childlike veneration and most humble respect for Your Reverences, your gracious wife, and all of the highly regarded servants of God working at the blessed institutions whom I in part still know personally, in part I do not know but whom altogether I honor and love in Christ. I, as the most unworthy of all, my dear brothers in the ministry and all congregations most humbly commend all the institutions to the infinite love and oversight of the great Savior of the world and to your kindly remembrance and intercession before God. I remain Your Reverence's, my highly regarded father's and superior's in Christ,

Providence   Most obedient Mühlenberg
22 February 1752

1) P.S. If at your convenience I could be honored some time with particulars about the life of the unusually perfected righteous ones, namely, Mrs. Götze, Mrs. Francke and Lady von Münchhauss, I would view that as a special kindness and thank God.

2) In Philadelphia it would be necessary and useful if a service in English could be held on Sunday afternoons without neglecting the service in German and as desired by several of the English people, if the Very Reverend Fathers would consider it favorably.

3) We are still corresponding with our most worthy fellow citizens in Ebenezer, Pastor Boltzius and Mr. Lemke.[80]

Last year I wrote a long letter to them and in it I also complained about one thing or another. Should this letter perhaps at some time come to your attention, then I obediently request you to correct that which belongs to a melancholy temperament.

4) Please extend especially my respect to his Reverence, Deacon and Inspector Niemeyer[81] and Inspector Rüdel,[82] my former foster fathers and bosom friends. Oh, if only I could still be there once more!

---

1. On Johanna Henriette Francke née Rachals, see *Correspondence* 1:113 n.1.
2. Henriette Rosine Götze died 30 June 1749. Following the death of Johanna Henriette Francke she managed the household of Gotthilf August Francke.
3. According to Eusebius of Caesarea (*Ecclesiastical History* 3.5.3) the Transjordanian city of Pella became a place of refuge for Jewish Christians before the start of fighting in the Jewish rebellion of A.D. 66-70. Mühlenberg is drawing a parallel between Pella and Pölzig where Francke had gone for rest and relaxation. See Letter 81.
4. 1751 should read 1750.
5. On Eva Wilhelmine von Gersdorf, see Letter 81.
6. Hymn by Paul Gerhardt (1607-76), "Ich singe dir mit Herz und Mund," (1653), v.17. See *Liedersammlung*, Hymn 499.
7. Ps. 146:5.
8. Hymn by Christoph Tietze (1641-1703), "Sollt es gleich bis weilen scheinen," v. 1. See *Liedersammlung*, Hymn 470.

9. On Count Erdmann Heinrich von Henckel-Pölzig, see *Correspondence* 1:11 n.7.
10. The text is in italics in the original.
11. The text reads εκλεκταις κυριαις without accents, alluding to 2 John 1: ἐκλεκτῇ κυρίᾳ.
12. See 1 Cor. 13:12.
13. The quotation is from Ps. 12:5a while the remaining portion seems to be a free adaptation of Ps. 12:5b.
14. The letter containing this reminder does not appear to be extant.
15. See 1 Cor. 12:14-21.
16. Johann Dietrich Heinzelmann and Friedrich Schultze. See Letter 101 n.3 and Letter 89 n.4.
17. See Jer. 48:40; 49:22.
18. See Gen. 22:1-19.
19. "Drum so tödt' und schlachte hin etc. etc., trage Holz auf den Altar und verbrenn' mich ganz und gar." It has not been possible to identify the source of this hymn.
20. Karl Heinrich von Bogatzky (1690-1774) is known best for his *Güldnes Schatzkästlein der Kinder Gottes deren Schatz im Himmel ist* (Halle: Waisenhaus, 1734; 1761; 30th enlarged edition, Halle, 1776-1786). Anna Maria Weiser Mühlenberg owned a copy of the *Schatzkästlein*. For its place in her devotional life see Helmut T. Lehmann and J. Woodrow Savacool, "Mühlenberg's Ministry of Healing," *Lutheran Quarterly* 6/1 (1992): 62. Bogatzky is the author of the first German missionary hymn, "Awake, O Spirit of the Watchmen," contained in an English translation in *LBW*, Hymn 382.
21. See Matt. 25:35a and 36b.
22. See Letter 112:214-17.
23. See *Korrespondenz* 1:494 n.38.
24. The text reads *ad dies vitae*.
25. The text reads *Sapienti sat*.
26. The text reads *Ex[empli] gr[atia]*.
27. On Tobias Wagner, see Letter 71A n.3.
28. On Johann Caspar Stöver, Jr., see *Correspondence* 1:53 n.18.
29. After Handschuh had been transferred to Germantown (see Letter 93:123f and 131 n.25), Wagner conducted services there every four weeks, beginning in October 1751. See *HN2/1*:176; *Lutheran Church in PA*, p. 321. Wagner's call to the congregation in Lancaster accompanied his letter of 20 December 1751 to the Württemberg Consistory. See *Korrespondenz* 1:506 n.14. See also Letter 91 n.1.
30. See 1 Pet. 2:16.
31. The text reads *opere operato*.
32. The text reads *einfältig*. For the biblical allusion here see *Correspondence* 1:166 n.11.
33. The text reads *Salaria fixa*.
34. See Matt. 6:33.
35. See Joshua 1:5.
36. See Acts 20:35.
37. The May 1529 edition of Luther's *Small Catechism* contained a Table of Duties in an appendix. See Theodore G. Tappert et al., trans. and eds., *The Book of Concord: The Confessions of the Evangelical Lutheran Church* (Philadelphia: Fortress Press, 1959), pp. 337; 354-56.
38. On Johann Friedrich Vigera, see *Correspondence* 1:145 n.3.
39. See Letter 97. For Ziegenhagen's and Francke's response, see Letters 105 and 124.
40. Letter 87 is a fragment of this correspondence. In his diary Mühlenberg remarks, "I wrote a letter to my father-in-law [HD: Conrad Weiser] asking him for advice concerning my intended removal to New York. His reply showed his experience and insight, as may be seen from his questions and answers." See *Journals* 1:270; also *Korrespondenz* 1:506 n.20.
41. In 1751 Handschuh left Lancaster to become pastor of the congregation in Germantown.
42. The text reads *multum ...multa*.
43. On Christoph Sauer, see *Correspondence* 1:93 n.37.

44. Hymn by Martin Luther, *"Vater unser im Himmelreich,"* v.7. See *Liedersammlung*, Hymn 314. The English translation given here is from *LW* 53:298. - Heinrich Miller is the printer Mühlenberg has in mind. Benjamin Franklin rented the print shop to him. Miller was an adherent of Zinzendorf. Beginning 15 January 1752 Miller began to publish *Die Lancastersche Zeitung* or *Lancaster Gazette* with Samuel Holland. Later Miller settled in Philadelphia. See W.P. Adams, "The Colonial German-language Press and the American Revolution," in B. Bailyn and J.B. Hench, eds., *The Press and the American Revolution* (Worcester, MA, 1980), pp. 151-228; also, Benjamin Franklin, *The Papers of Benjamin Franklin*, ed. L.W. Labaree et al. (New Haven, 1961), pp. 259-60. — On Benjamin Franklin, see also *Correspondence* 1:338 and 342 n.36.

45. See Letter 112:218f.

46. See Ps. 120:5a.

47. See 1 Cor. 15:19.

48. See Heb. 4:9.

49. See Rev. 7:14b.

50. See Isa. 40:29a.

51. Hymn by August Hermann Francke "Gott Lob, ein Schritt zur Ewigkeit," v.8. See *Liedersammlung*, Hymn 338.

52. See 1 Kings 19:18.

53. From "Very few have not" to "games with sin" the text is in doggerel.

54. It has not been possible to identify the source of this hymn.

55. See *HN2/1*:503-19; *Journals* 1:234-58.

56. On Johann Sebastian Fabricius, see *Correspondence* 1: 250 n.37.

57. See Heb. 12:1.

58. For this proposal of C.R. Herttel, see Letters 100 and 109.

59. Is this a reference to Peter Livingston? See *Korrespondenz* 1:472 n.4.

60. On Michael Schlatter, see *Correspondence* 1:342 n.41.

61. On Johann Conrad Weiser, see *Correspondence* 1:142 n.7.

62. Anna Maria Mühlenberg née Kleinschmidt was buried 29 December 1747.

63. Baron Gerlach Adolf von Münchhausen, a member of the nobility who supported Mühlenberg with funds for study at the University of Göttingen and at Halle, was the husband of Wilhelmine Sophie von Münchhausen. See also *Correspondence* 1:18 n.18.

64. On Count Heinrich XXIV von Reuss-Köstritz, see *Correspondence* 1:5 n.6; 8 n.5 and 11 n.7.

65. On Count Erdmann Heinrich von Henckel-Pölzig, see *Correspondence* 1:11 n.7 and 17 n.4.

66. See Letter 116.

67. H.M. Mühlenberg had eight siblings, seven of whom were probably still living in 1750. For details see *Selbstbiographie*, pp. 192-94.

68. Mühlenberg is referring to his letter to Krome (Letter 115) and a friend from the time of his youth (Letter 116). Both letters are only extant in the form of copies. Mühlenberg also has in mind a letter to his brothers which is not extant.

69. The text reads *a[nni] p[raeteriti]*.

70. Margretha Henrietta Mühlenberg (1751-1831), who later married Pastor Johann Christoph Kunze. See *Korrespondenz* 1:428 n.2.

71. See n.1.

72. On Heinrich Schleydorn, see *Correspondence* 1:53 n.22.

73. Augustus Church at Trappe (Providence) which was dedicated on 6 October 1745.

74. Mühlenberg's son Friedrich August Conrad (1750-1801) who would later become first Speaker of the United States House of Representatives.

75. The text reads *a[nni] p[raeteriti]*.

76. The text reads *pulv[is] vital[is]*.

77. The text reads *Eröfnende Miltz Ess[entia]*.

78. These were pills made from multiple medicines and combinations, *polychrestum* meaning "having many virtues, considered useful in treating many diseases." For identification of this and some other medicines Mühlenberg used, see Helmut T. Lehmann and J. Woodrow Savacool, "Mühlenberg's Ministry of Healing," *Lutheran Quarterly* 6/3 (1992):66 n.28.

79. The Schmid in question is not Johann Christian Schmid (as in *Korrespondenz* 1:507 n.46) but Johann Jacob Schmid (b. 1691) whose writing includes seven works (1728ff.) dealing with biblical themes. The two works Mühlenberg refers to here are: *Biblischer Geographus, oder vollständige Beschreibung aller in der H. Schrift benannten Länder und Städte, oder zur Geographie gehörigen Oerter und Sachen(1728)* and *Biblischer Medicus, oder Erkenntnis des Menschen, nach dessen natürlichen Leben und wesentlichen Theilen seines Leibes* (forthcoming at the time of Zedler's writing [1743]). See Johann Heinrich Zedler, *Grosses vollständiges Universal-Lexikon* (Graz, Austria: Akademische Druck und Verlagsanstalt, 1961 [1743]), s.v. "Schmid, Johann Jacob."

80. On Johann Martin Boltzius, see Correspondence 1:30 n.9. On Hermann Heinrich Lemke, see Letter 107 n.28.

81. See *Correspondence* 1:33 n.9.

82. Johann Abraham Rüdel (1698-1777) studied theology in Halle and then served as a teacher in the orphanage in Glaucha/Breslau. When the orphanage closed in 1727 he moved to Halle and became inspector of the German schools. He succeeded Johann Heinrich Callenberg (see *Correspondence* 1:315 n.13) as head of the library.

Letter 115

To Theophilus Arnold Krome[1]
Providence, 24 February 1752

Writing to his friend, Krome, who was pastor in Einbeck during his formative years, Mühlenberg expresses his great joy in the attention Krome gave his mother before she died. At the same time Mühlenberg expresses his sorrow that there are so many of his countrymen who fail to recognize the time of grace.

Reflecting on the state of faith and church in Germany, Mühlenberg concludes that there is a failure to discern the true nature of evangelical teaching as represented in the foundation of apostles and prophets and the Lutheran Confessions. In part this failure is due to an inability to evaluate Christian truth by looking beyond the stereotypes of orthodoxy and pietism. Especially the rejection of the revealed word of God and the Savior of the world is galling to him.

As already indicated in Letter 114, Mühlenberg has been taken aback by the unfair settlement of his mother's estate on the part of his siblings which he attributes to a lack of conversion.

Mühlenberg concludes this letter to his friend with a brief account of the number of congregations, pastors and catechists in the southeastern part of Pennsylvania and New Jersey and with the desire for information about church life in Einbeck, the city of his birth.

Text in German: Korrespondenz *1:507-10. For further textual information, see* Korrespondenz *1:510.*

Most reverend, learned and honorable Pastor
and most worthy Colleague:

Words are not adequate to express how pleasing and edifying for me were the two communications of 7 February 1747[2] and 16 July 1750[3] with which you honored me. They have compelled me to shed tears of joy and grief: tears of joy because I could clearly gather from their content that the dimly burning wick I observed in you many years ago has not only not been quenched[4] but has even become a burning light in the Lord which has been placed on a stand in my poor home town to give light to all in the house.[5] This bright light has not been enkindled in Your Reverence's soul by some fanciful notion but by the word which alone saves by means of his Spirit in true repentance. In particular, this light was communicated to my old weak mother in such a way that I hope to find her again at the throne of the

Lamb. No treasure in the world could have pleased and comforted me so much as your blessed report that you cared for my poor mother as far as her soul is concerned in a genuinely fatherlike way, visited her diligently and stood by her with the means of grace until death.[6] I realize that Your Reverence does not desire a tangible and perishable reward. Nevertheless, I hope and pray that the all-sufficient God and Father in Christ will also place my rescued mother as a pearl in your crown of victory when, with Paul and all of the other faithful servants of Jesus Christ in your office and position, Your Reverence fights the good fight, finishes the race[7] and remains faithful to the end! I have shed tears of grief on account of the great blindness and ignorance of my poor countrymen. In part they do not want to hear about the truths concerning the most necessary repentance, faith and blessedness in God; in part they want to obstruct the truth with unrighteousness, forfeit their precious brief time of grace and rather follow their fathers and never ever want to see the light. The poor pitiable worms pass their years like idle talk,[8] are like foolish maidens having lamps without oil.[9] In their hearts they say, "I am rich, I am altogether satisfied and in need of nothing." They do not know that they are poor, miserable, blind and naked until their eyes are opened while they are in the time of grace or perhaps only when they are opened with terror at the last moment of departure into endless eternity!

O my most worthy pastor, give no heed to the high regard of people; shun no suffering, do not expect better times but press on straight ahead! Call out with confidence and do not refrain from doing so! Point out to the poor sheep how dangerous their situation is outside a community of Jesus Christ on the wide path and how well off they can be in time and eternity on the narrow path in believing union with the great Savior of the world, Jesus Christ! The Lord will give you one victory after the other and confess you before his heavenly Father if you confess him before people.[10] It is necessary to suffer and to struggle, as we discover on almost every page of the Old and New Testaments. Indeed, our blessed father Luther speaks of the indispensable afflictions of God's faithful servants everywhere in his marvellous writings. We may not whittle a cross for ourselves at all but only inculcate law and gospel in accordance with Christ's direction and adorn pure doctrine with our life; then the cross will follow of its own accord, meted out, however, under the providence and direction of God and ordained for our best. Our ancient orthodox theologians themselves said, "Where lightning is in life there doctrine is in thunder!"[11] "Arise my spirit, do not tire/ of making your way through the night of darkness!/ Why such anxiety about the loss of strength/ you have been promised!/ How pleasant rest after labor is ended!/ How happy it will make you."[12] We may not start something new at all but only confidently believe, teach, live and remain faithful in accordance with the foundation of apostles and prophets and our Symbolical Books. Then there will be truly evangelical core Christians who may also be called Lutherans, if they would believe and live according to Luther's teaching. But, alas brothers! Luther's core Christians with their true repentance, living faith and daily renewal and sanctification have fallen out of favor so very much that even those related to him in name themselves turn him upside down and would call him a pietist were he to rise again and teach. It is a great pity that our scholars who lack enlightened and disciplined sense do not understand why Satan is called Diabolus as derived from διαβάλλειν because in accordance with his wiliness[13] he confuses everything and likes to pour out the baby with the bath water. We do indeed learn enough according to Aristotle's philosophical distinctions[14] and minor distinctions[15] but divine wisdom is greatly lacking so that we cannot properly distinguish the truly good from evil, what is better from what is good, and the best from the better, etc., etc.

However, from that perspective, too, the struggle will soon be over because a completely new generation is coming to the throne in today's Christendom. This new generation not only rejects privately and publicly the ancient theological writings but also even the ancient, most precious treasure, namely, the revealed word of God, wanting to clear a new way for itself to temporary and eternal happiness without the true Savior of the world. But whether they have hit it right is something they will get to feel one day when eyes give out, hearing ceases, the mouth turns pale, the flow of blood is stanched, when honor, riches and remaining lights leave their little body; when friends and companions laugh from afar, all human help miscarries, the body remains behind and an immortal soul together with its fabricated conscience, understanding and will simply departs for an unknown eternity and is required to give an account before the most holy Supreme Being! At that point the comedy staged here will become a tragedy! We have already had more such brave spirits[16] in ancient and modern times who very much lost their courage and became shamefaced when they have had to exchange the temporary for the eternal. The struggle against an infinite, almighty Supreme Being who can destroy body and soul in hell is not an especially equal one.[17] Whenever David was about to be brought out of sorts by such spirits[18] he entered the sanctuary of God and perceived their end! Psalm 73.[19]

No more of that. May Your Reverence receive my modest thoughts in love and remember me and my colleagues as well as our evangelical congregations in your believing prayer before God. I particularly commend my poor kinsfolk to your special faithful pastoral care, for they are, for the most part, badly in need of true repentance and saving faith, as well as godliness for the rescue and salvation of their souls. I have particularly experienced this in connection with the distribution of the inheritance. They subtracted three hundred reichsthaler for my education, and I did not even receive forty reichsthaler. The most noble town council of Einbeck granted me a scholarship for two years in Göttingen.[20] His excellence the High Sheriff von Münchhauss[21] and their excellencies, the most gracious lords, Count Reus XXIV[22] and Count Henckel[23] provided me with adequate scholarships for my study in Göttingen and Halle. With such shocking procedure my poor kinsfolk demonstrate that they have not yet been converted but have a deceitful spirit and trickery in their heart and put a curse on their own possessions and sustenance. I feel much more sorrow for their poor souls than for the earthly goods.

I can report nothing further for this time concerning our present Pennsylvania circumstances other than that we have twenty-three large and small congregations which are united and are being served by eight evangelical pastors and two catechists. Should I have the honor and pleasure to receive a letter from Your Reverence once again then I would humbly request that in it you would impart information concerning the clergy and the perceptible blessing in their ministry, also concerning schools and especially the conduct of my blood relatives. If permitted to do so, I shall also write from here and similarly make note of matters which are useful and edifying. With sincere compliments and due respect to your spouse and dear children as well as to the whole esteemed family and relationship, I remain Your Reverence's, my especially most kind patron's and colleague's most devoted servant,

Providence　　　　　　　　　　　　　　　　　　　　　Mühlenberg
24 February 1752

---

1. On Theophilus Arnold Krome, see Letter 77, n.40.
2. This letter is not extant but it is referred to in Letter 77:58.
3. This letter is not extant.
4. See Isa. 42:3; Matt. 12:20.
5. See Matt. 5:15.
6. Regarding Anna Maria Mühlenberg's death, see Letter 112 n.81.
7. See 2 Tim. 4:7.
8. See Ps. 90:9.
9. See Matt. 25:1-13.
10. See Matt. 10:32; Luke 12:8.
11. The text reads, *ubi yita fulgur, ibi doctrina tonitru.*
12. Hymn by Christian Friedrich Richter, *"Es kostet viel ein Christ zu sein"* (1704), v.8. See *Liedersammlung* Hymn 228.

13. Mühlenberg may have had Eph. 6:11 in mind, "... to stand against the wiles of the devil."
14. The text reads *districtionen* and probably should read *distinctiones*.
15. The text reads *distinctiusculas*.
16. The text reads *fort Esprits*.
17. See Matt. 10:28.
18. The text reads *L'Esprits*.
19. See Ps. 73:17.
20. Following the establishment of the University of Göttingen in 1735, the decision was made that all cities in hereditary principalities in the electorate of Hannover contribute to a fund for scholarships. Depending on the amount of their contribution they could send one or more recipients of scholarships to the university. The contribution of the city of Einbeck was sufficient to send one recipient. See *Selbstbiographie*, pp. 4-5; *Journals* 1:2.
21. On Baron Gerlach Adolf von Münchhausen, see Letter 114 n.63 and *Correspondence* 1:18 n.18.
22. On Count Heinrich XXIV von Reuss-Köstritz, see Letter 114 n.64
23. On Count Erdmann Heinrich von Henckel-Pölzig, see *Correspondence* 1:11 n.7.

Letter 116

To a Friend from Student Days[1]
Providence, 24 February 1752

Written to one of his three friends who studied with him at the University of Göttingen and shared with him initial impulses toward a piety nourished at Halle, this letter expresses in sharp tones Mühlenberg's anger with his siblings for not having dealt honestly with him in the distribution of income from his mother's legacy. The letter is a fragment; the whole central portion is missing.
Text in German: Korrespondenz *1:511. For further textual information, see* Korrespondenz *1:511.*

Most noble and honorable Forester,
Most kind Patron:
The intimate association which I cultivated with your most noble person from the time of tender youth in school; the first awakenings to a life that is from God which I received in conversations with you as these came in the first flowering of love from the blessed institutions in Halle to Göttingen; and the natural honesty sanctified by the grace of God. . . give my complete inheritance[2] in accordance with what is right and fair and to deduct no more than what I have received and expect what I will give them from it. If they do not want to do that but are obstinate and stubborn, I shall take the 120 reichsthaler with interest for myself and I shall bequeath the remainder somewhere where in accordance with their own claims they will have to care for expenses to the last penny. If I were to leave them what they wrongly took then, etc., etc. Furthermore, I have reported that secretary Ernst[3] should retain nine reichsthaler for his trouble and consign 120 reichsthaler with interest to His Reverence Pastor Franck and take a receipt and transmit it to me.

Dated 24 February 1752   Heinrich Melchior Mühlenberg

---

1. In his autobiography Mühlenberg refers to three young students who, like him, were natives of Einbeck and registered in the University of Göttingen after having spent some years in the institutions of Halle. By their words and in their life-style they communicated to Mühlenberg the possibility and reality of a Christian, virtuous life. See *Selbstbiographie*, p. 6. In his diary Mühlenberg reports that three students admonished him "to forsake evil companionship and turn to the living God through Jesus Christ" (*Journals* 1:3).

2. In Letters 114:236-37 and 115:244-45 Mühlenberg had already reported that his siblings had taken advantage of him at the time of the distribution of the legacy of his mother (who had died in 1747) by assigning to him an expenditure for his studies greater than he had actually received. A letter he had written to his brothers Heinrich Christoph (1702-1786) and Johann Arndt (b.1709) on 7 March 1752 is not extant. On Heinrich Christoph Mühlenberg, see Letter 77 n.35. - On Johann Arndt, after whom Mühlenberg's brother was named, see *Correspondence* 1:315 n.20.

3. In Letter 114:237 Mühlenberg identifies Ernst as his agent.

Letter 117

To the Dutch Church Council in New York
Providence, 21 March 1752

Writing in response to the Dutch Council's letter urging him to serve their congregation in New York, Mühlenberg agrees to come as speedily as possible without his family. Two months after writing his letter he once again began his ministry among Dutch Lutherans in New York. Drawing on a number of verses and images from New Testament writings, Mühlenberg seeks to encourage the members of the church council and, through them, the disheartened members of the congregation while assuring them of his reliance on the Lord to be of service to them.

Text in Dutch: Korrespondenz *1:512. For further textual information, see* Korrespondenz *1:513.*

Esteemed Sirs,
Most honorable Brothers:
I have received Your Honors' esteemed letter of 17 February[1] on 10 March and have learned with joy that the esteemed church council has not let its courage droop entirely, but believes and expects that our small congregation, which at present is like a mustard seed, Matthew 13,[2] and a bruised reed and dimly burning wick,[3] by God's grace and assistance will grow and become the greatest among the shrubs, or at least not be broken off or snuffed out. That is right, esteemed brothers! Whenever we hold fast and immovably to the word of our all-sufficient Savior and build our house on a rock,[4] that is on Christ and his promises, then it shall not be destroyed by storm, flood or wind. For God is almighty and is able to do more than we ask or understand! If God is for us, who can be against us?[5]

If we seek to become righteous through faith, then we have peace with God through our Lord Jesus Christ, through whom we also obtain access through faith to this grace in which we stand. And we boast in the hope of the coming glory, which God shall give. And not only that, but we boast also in the afflictions, since we know that affliction brings patience, and patience brings experience, and experience brings hope: but hope does not lead to being shamed.[6]

For my own most feeble part, I shall not leave off praying for you, and shall come to you without my family as speedily as it may be possible.[7] Finally, my dear brothers, be firm, immovable, and abounding in the work of the Lord.[8] Be faithful, be comforted, have the same mind, be peaceful, so shall the God of love and of peace be with you. Greet one another with the holy kiss,[9] and grant me permission to remain, esteemed sirs, your respectful humble servant

Providence, 21 March 1752   Henrich Melchior Mühlenberg

P.S. I have taken nothing amiss from Your Honors' missive and ask for forgiveness, even if I may have written too much in my letters. Things go on between us as between two patients who on all sides have a tender and sensitive feeling, etc. My dear sirs and much beloved brothers are much perplexed concerning the upbuilding of a poor and forsaken congregation, and I am utterly sick and sorrowful that I am, from all sides, convulsed in order to assist my forsaken and scattered fellows and that I have neither the spiritual gifts nor the ability to do anything if the Lord does not grant it out of grace.

---

1. See Letter 111.
2. See Matt. 13:31-32.
3. See Matt. 12:20; Isa. 42:3.
4. See Matt. 7:25.
5. Rom. 8:31.
6. See Rom. 5:1-6.
7. Originally Mühlenberg had planned to visit the New York congregation in March 1752 but owing to a number of circumstances he had to postpone his visit until May 1752. See *Journals* 1:319.
8. See 1 Cor. 15:58.
9. See 2 Cor. 13:12.

Letter 118

To Balthasar Beil
Providence, 3 April 1752

A conflict between Balthasar Beil, an elder in the Saccum congregation, and Ludolph Schrenck, appointed to serve as catechist there (1750-52), became the occasion for Mühlenberg to attempt to bring about a reconciliation between the two. Whether Mühlenberg's attempt accomplished its intended purpose is not known.

Text in German: Korrespondenz *1:513-14. For further textual information, see* Korrespondenz *1:514 where an alternate draft of the opening part of the letter is reproduced.*

Providence, 3 April 1752

Honored Friend, Mr. Beil:

With sorrow I have learned from your two letters[1] of a misunderstanding which has arisen between you and Mr. Schrenck.[2] I am all the more pained by this circumstance because, in accordance with the measure God has granted each of you, both of you were appointed and directed to promote the best interests of the poor congregations. However, when a pastor and a deacon not only have a falling out but even allow the sun to go down because of their conflict and anger more than once[3] and do not encounter one another with love while there is still time, then the fault must certainly be too great, if not on both sides then nevertheless on one side and sinful hatred must have gained the upper hand. But a situation like that, as can be expected, results in great injury and offense to the congregation whereby the most holy God is angered, the angels are saddened, the congregation is bewildered and our poor children and little tots are misled into heathenism! Oh my dear old friend, Mr. Beil, after all, you know how many a hard ride I took to poor deserted congregations, how sincerely I desired to gather the poor scattered sheep, to safeguard the ewes and to gather the lambs into the bosom of our great chief shepherd Jesus Christ![4] Is all of our effort, pleading and imploring then to be in vain? What will the scoffing hostile sects most likely say which surround us and anxiously await our demise? After all, you have had among you one and another preacher who came running on his own who lived in flagrant vice before we received the congregation into our fellowship.[5] You put up with such people and their vices with patience. Why then do you not want to be patient with our weakness when our intentions are basically honest, we acknowledge our faults and pray God always to make us more capable for this difficult ministry? In this country we have a lot of trouble and hard work; we are surrounded by many spiritual and worldly enemies and have to contend with flesh and blood![6] We bear our treasure in earthen vessels[7] and everywhere have anguish, distress and adversity! Now if even our first and old friends become our enemies and want to contend with us, how then can the congregation be edified and the God of love and peace remain among us?[8] My dear friend, if you still retain a spark of love for me, which I hope, then do not continue in anger but turn around again and reconcile yourself with your brother so that love, peace, gentleness and humility may meet, caress and kiss each other,[9] then the angels in heaven will rejoice and God[10] will have the desire to and the joy of dwelling among us, and Satan will be brought down in disgrace when he is unable to achieve his purpose. The whole past must be forgotten and buried. Love hopes, endures and cloaks all things.[11] But when two persons hate one another they both say the worst things about each other and again make mountains out of mole hills.[12] I cannot render a judgment in the matter until I have both of you together and hear you by word of mouth. If it were possible, I myself would probably come up and reconcile you with each other. But I hope that will not be necessary because you can surely take care of a little matter like that if you want to be disciples and followers of Jesus Christ. I close and remain etc.

Heinrich Melchior Mühlenberg

----

1. Not extant.
2. On Ludolph Heinrich Schrenck, see Letter 78 n.7.
3. See Eph. 4:26.
4. See 1 Pet. 5:4.
5. See *HN2/1*:484-85; *Journals* 1:213.
6. See Eph. 6:12 where the phrase "contending against flesh and blood" is used in a different context.
7. See 2 Cor. 4:7.
8. See 2 Cor. 13:11.
9. See Ps. 85:11.
10. The text reads H Θεός, mistakenly employing the feminine definite article instead of the lower case masculine definite article.
11. See 1 Cor. 13:7.
12. The text reads, "*...und machen wieder Elephanten.*"

Letter 119

The Dutch Church Council in New York to Mühlenberg
New York, 6 April 1752

*The Dutch congregation in New York has readied its parsonage for
Mühlenberg so he may occupy it during the time he has agreed to serve it.
This announcement is part of the acknowledgment of Mühlenberg's letter in
which he expressed his readiness to come and serve the congregation as
soon as possible.*

Text in Dutch: Korrespondenz *1:515. For further textual information, see*
Korrespondenz *1:515.*

Most Reverend Sir, Mr. Meulenberg:

We have indeed received Your Reverence's welcome letter of 23 March[1]
and with much joy have understood therefrom that we might still likely see
Your Reverence among us this month,[2] for which event all well-wishers of
our poor church have for a long time wished and longed with great anxiety,
hoping that the gracious God will perform and complete all things to his
own glory and to the best and blessedness of our poor souls, for which we
all pray for Jesus' sake. We believe that he will not let our poor distressed
little flock be ashamed. The minister's house is ready to receive Your
Reverence.

We remain,

---

1. See Letter 117.
2. See Letter 117 n.7.

Letter 120

To Samuel Theodor Albinus
New York, 1 June 1752

While serving the Dutch Lutheran congregation in New York on a temporary basis for a second time, Mühlenberg discovers rather suddenly an opportunity to send a letter to Albinus with a ship which is leaving for London, England, the next day. As he himself admits, this unanticipated opportunity results in his writing a letter which is not well organized and diffuse. Moreover, because of the stress and tensions to which he is exposed, Mühlenberg is in a rather depressed and melancholy mood. Nevertheless, in this letter Mühlenberg shares with Albinus his evaluation of his fellow workers whom, with one exception, he praises for the assiduousness with which they discharge their office. The arrangements Mühlenberg made for the maintenance and salary of this man who was the exception were such that sooner or later they were destined to fail in accomplishing what Mühlenberg had in mind. The discouragement Mühlenberg experienced in this relationship when combined with the silence and negative response he received to proposals he repeated once again to establish a printing press and an orphanage makes his occasional mood of depression understandable.

This letter has two different dates and places of origin because a copyist entered "Providence, 29 July." "New York, 1 June 1752" is the actual date on which Mühlenberg wrote the letter because he gives this date in an entry in his journals on 1 June 1752. — See Journals *1:379 and* Korrespondenz *1:522.*

This is the only letter of Mühlenberg extant from his second stay in New York.

Text in German: Korrespondenz *1:515-22. For further textual information, see* Korrespondenz *1:522.*

Copy of a letter to the Very Reverend   Providence, 29 July
Court Preacher Albinus.[1]

Because a ship is just ready to leave tomorrow and I only received news of it today, I did not want to let the opportunity pass by to write something. In the spring of last year I sent off to the Very Reverend Fathers with Captain Budden and the son of Mr. Schleydorn[2] my letters[3] and journals in which I wrote how matters are proceeding under the patience and forbearance of God. Your Reverence will kindly forgive me for communicating my thoughts at present in an offhand way as they arise without observing the proper form and due precision. Shortly after our letters had all been sent off, the fatherly letters of Their Reverences, Doctor and Professor Franke from Halle[4] and London[5] arrived. A letter to Mr. Weiser[6] included especially a letter to me which was duly turned over to me on 7 April of the current year.[7] 1) I was surprised at the precious Reverend Fathers' sincere concern, wisdom, patience, love and earnestness in relation to the Pennsylvania mission and I was ashamed by their kindliness toward me! 2) I am convinced that my confused letter from New York in the past year[8] was not received as ungraciously as I had imagined or supposed. In what follows I shall obediently report how matters stand at present and request further great patience and compassion.

1) In the previous year our dear brother Brunnholtz[9] did indeed experience one and another time of trial and severe temptations but the earnest prayer of our Reverend Fathers and brothers in Europe was victorious. He is again making a complete new start in life! The Lord is his shepherd, etc., etc., his rod and staff comfort him, etc., etc.[10] 2) Our dear brother Handschue[11] also lives and labors not without blessing, etc., etc. He is steadily becoming more useful in Pennsylvanian circumstances. 3) Brother Kurtz[12] does what he can in accordance with the gifts God has given him. 4) The dear, poor worm, brother Schaum, is gradually losing his health, has constant pains and is lame on one side. He is also beginning to be lame already on the other side and consequently useless for the ministry. The guidance of God is marvellous! During the past winter his father-in-law, Balthasar Pickel,[13] came to him and stayed with him for several months. In the spring Mr. Schaum travelled to Monocacy[14] in Maryland to visit several German people there and to deliver a sermon. In his absence his wife delivered a young daughter and shortly thereafter together with the child contracted smallpox and miliary fever. During his absence she, together with the child, died. Thereafter the old father-in-law took the sick Mr. Schaum with him to Raritan. However, on the way he visited Mr. Brunholz and made a recommendation as can be seen in Pastor Brunholz's enclosure.[15] Old Pickel had assigned to his daughter a legacy of about six or seven hundred pounds. This sum he now wants to bequeath to the Raritan church. During his lifetime[16] the son-in-law may acquire the interest provided, note well,[17] that Mr. Schaum also becomes pastor of Raritan and Mr. Weygand[18] takes Mr. Schaum's place. Circumstances and occurrences[19] of this kind are too difficult for us to make a determination. If only we were aware of the salutary counsel of our Reverend Fathers in these matters. 5) The congregation in Indianfield is not satisfied at all with Mr. Rauss[20] because he does not have the gifts to manage odd people, as can be seen in the enclosure.[21] 6) Mr. Schrenck[22] is still alert and eager to become more

useful in station and office. 7) Mr. Heinzelman[23] is a brave, faithful and humble laborer in school and church. Dear brother Brunholz and Heintzelman have established a nice school which makes me unusually happy because it is something which has a realistic future blessing in view. But poor brother Heintzelman will not endure it for long but will ruin his health. It would be better if instead of Mr. Heintzelmann a qualified schoolmaster were to attend to school work.

8) Dear brother Schultze was appointed to be of help to me[24] because the Philadelphians immediately cast an eye on Mr. Heintzelmann and one was also of the opinion that Mr. Schultz was more suited for circumstances in the country. At a fraternal conference[25] it was agreed upon and I also promised that he should receive half of my salary which it was hoped would be better in the future. The deacons of both congregations had made a probable estimate of eighty pounds in Pennsylvania currency. Consequently, I promised him[26] forty pounds with the condition that I would give him food, drink, laundry and lodging for twenty pounds and in addition keep a horse free of charge. The remaining twenty pounds he was to receive in cash. I know with complete certainty that annually it would barely add up to seventy to eighty pounds even when taking into account all coins from perquisites. But Mr. Schultze was not very well satisfied with my counting twenty pounds for his maintenance. He was of the opinion he could get by more cheaply because he saw that people now and then on feast days would bring me a cake and a pound of butter. For that reason he promised to accept the contract at first for half a year on trial. Over a period of two years I was very much in arrears on account of the limited salary so that I really still owe around sixty pounds for food, without capital debts for land and house. I had to live within my means. He began in accordance with the contract, gradually became dissatisfied with food and drink and laundry and that sort of thing. Here and there he appropriated some perquisites, visited one and another congregation in the hill country in the hope of acquiring perquisites on the side. He told me of dear father Ziegenhagen's judgment of my covetousness on account of New York. Now and then he spoke disrespectfully of the blessed institutions in Halle. He studied the calendars of Sauer[27] more than the Bible. He began to dabble in medicine or be an empiric. He seized meagre perquisites from the schoolmaster in New Hanover[28] for, because of great poverty, I had allowed him to enter the names of baptized children into the church book for which one or another well-off person was accustomed to pay him a shilling. But Mr. Schultze himself wanted to enter the names of children he had baptized and get a shilling from the poor as well as from the well-off without making a distinction between them, etc., etc. No longer could he drink a modest beer,

but he wanted always to drink brandy mixed with water and sugar, which was not healthy for him and too expensive for me, etc., etc. Self-love and conceit began to ferment so much in this little man that no theologian was good enough any longer and we, his poor brothers, were all only inculcators of the law. He alone possessed the true gospel from a volume patched together from the writings of Hollaz[29] and the postils of Mr. Schubart.[30] I attempted to bear everything in love and did not omit kind recollections but I could not sense any brotherly trust in him because he was of the opinion that I was making a profit at his expense and he was making me rich. In this way I did indeed have help in my burdensome office but my outward circumstances were very trying. After he took on New Goshenhoppen[31] he devoted half of his work to it, and I retained the benefit of the other half of his service. The people of Goshenhoppen promised him twenty pounds for serving them every second Sunday or half of his service. Consequently, for the other twenty pounds I had to provide maintenance and keep the horse free of charge. But since he did not want to be satisfied with me I requested Pastor Brunholtz to come to Providence in the month of April. Then I entered into another written agreement and promised him twenty pounds for the year, if he would preach in my congregations every second Sunday. Thereupon he would have to provide board and sustenance on his own. He consented to this with the condition that his salary should start 1 December of the previous year[32] even though he had only come to me toward the end of December, that I would not charge him for the sustenance he had had during the time which had passed until April and that I would let him keep the perquisites from performing marriages and the like in my congregations. I agreed to his request and had dear brother Brunholtz put it in writing. He has now moved into the schoolhouse in New Hanover and scrimps so much on food and drink that I fear for his health. That, however, is not necessary at all for one person can get along very well in the country on forty pounds and perquisites if one makes a beginning accordingly.

What I have written here is confidential and a most charitable construction is to be placed on it. Herewith I am not passing judgment on my dear brother Schultz but I am only putting this in writing to demonstrate how in this country one is subjected to greater or lesser temptations, especially when a person entering the ministry is young and is not acquainted with the enemies who tempt us. Already for a long time I was afraid of that. Alone I am too weak and I am incapable of withstanding the hardships any more. I am unable to discharge my ministry satisfactorily in my country congregations, much less to satisfy my conscience, and then when I beg for a helper or coworker the salary is not adequate. It is contrary to my nature to complain about my earthly livelihood; nevertheless, need compels me to say something about it. My family increases,[33] my salary decreases. I cannot rear my children because I am seldom at home. The ones who are well off in the congregations do what they can and for the poor it is impossible to hand over both mites. I am not exaggerating. In the German newspaper I simply must appear exposed altogether if I want to have what is merely necessary. In their last communication to me the dear Very Reverend Fathers have written in such a moving and immeasurably kind and fatherly way that I am ashamed when I think of it because I am not worthy of half so many comforting words and deserving of again as many cuffs. Especially His Reverence the dear Court Preacher Ziegenhagen has also driven a new nail from the Letter to the Hebrews into my conscience and so seriously advised me to remain in my country congregations that I do not know how to help myself! If I am to be a sacrifice for New Hanover and Providence then I will apply my remaining strength in the name of the Lord until I break down! Under circumstances like these I cannot rear my children but must commend them to the providence of God. Should the Very Reverend Fathers out of pity want to release me from discharging my office which at present has become impossible for me, then I shall remain with one or no congregation. I would remain in my house, by the grace of God look after my family in spiritual matters and attempt to supply earthly sustenance through an honest occupation. Thus I would not be a burden to anyone here, but I would also not be anxious about the groaning alms from Europe. I cannot do anything beyond my power. However, as much as is within my power by the grace of God I shall gladly do and in case of emergency be of assistance generally as well as to my brothers. Were I to retain both congregations then I must keep horses and I cannot be without hired help, my wife cannot be without maids on account of the children and the management of an extensive household. The management of a household that extensive costs me at least eighty, ninety, yes, up to one hundred pounds annually and even at that I remain a poor slave.

I was not sick this past winter whereas in almost every other winter I have had to endure sickness. That was the case because during the last winter I was assisted by Mr. Schultz. If by chance a letter from me has come to the Very Reverend Fathers from dear old brother Boltzius, I beg you to apologize for me to the Very Reverend Fathers. Last fall I sent a long letter of complaint[34] and among other things I had the notion to come to Ebenezer with wife and children and spend my last hours quietly if perhaps I would no longer get along here in Pennsylvania. These are passing hindrances one encounters from time to time when the weather is dismal. I hope you will forgive me and sympathize with me. Sometimes a person is of the opinion that the dear God has forgotten something in his providence and one wants to be of assistance. It is also somewhat difficult to maintain a balance so as not to become careless and become a burden to one's neighbor but also not to become anxious. "Cast your burden on the Lord," etc., etc.[35]

I have a rather dull and shortsighted vision, can see nothing in advance; however, I have always thought that a small printing press would be necessary and useful. My idea and proposal of an orphanage[36] will probably come to nothing because poverty reigns everywhere in Europe also, and there are too many expenditures for good causes, etc., etc.[37] If I should live on and have to remain in my country congregations I thought once more of urging Their Reverences, our dear Fathers, to supply me at their pleasure with a printing press for publishing a German calendar and a broadsheet or newspaper.[38] At present a fine young man is available who knows the art of printing and who could at the same time be of service to me as schoolmaster. I could obtain type here. Perhaps the safest way would be to send it via Holland because many ships with Germans come from there every year; in case of need it could be insured because it might otherwise ruin me if it were lost. In addition, I would also like to keep a supply of the blessed Halle medicines, etc., etc. Such an arrangement would give me the opportunity to some degree to keep a coworker in the congregation and to manage my family better, assuming that nothing comes of the orphanage and the Very Reverend Fathers find the proposal acceptable. I want to do nothing without advice according to my own will, because my notions are too precarious and shortsighted.

The matter with New York is very much in my heart and conscience. I arrived here again on 8 May of the present year.[39] To me it seems more than likely to find in New York and Hackensack a small mustard seed which in the course of time may become a tree. Lutheran teaching, as we inculcate it in accordance with God's grace in weakness, is valued highly and finds acceptance among the Dutch and the English as one or another of my present observations[40] will soon show. Resistance on the part of the disorderly Germans is not lacking but I do not find that strange. The Pennsylvanians will lose nothing if I should live here with my family for a few years. It appears that Mr. Schultz will probably accept the congregations in Old and New Goshenhoppen and Indianfield. Mr. Brunholtz is getting stronger and has Mr. Handschue in Germantown at his side. Mr. Heintzelman could conveniently and with blessing serve Providence and New Hanover. I could rear my children better and have a better opportunity to study and to counsel my poor desultory soul. In case of necessity I could come to the aid of my brothers in the ministry because from Hackensack one could be in Philadelphia or Providence in two and one half days. And, nevertheless, all of this would only be a trial for two or three years, if I should still live that long.[41] I still cannot understand why the deacons in New York and Hackensack are so very wrong when they no longer request some one from Hamburg. One truly does not dally with such matters of soul and conscience. The gentlemen in Hamburg have now had the supervision of the poor Palatines[42] and Dutch under New York's government between thirty and forty years but what did they accomplish with their squabblers and stinkers whom they sent here? Here in this country the largest evangelical congregations could be planted and built up but now our evangelical polity looks like a ravaged city, like a booth in a pumpkin garden, etc., etc. Very little has been left over, etc., etc. Isaiah 1:9.[43] Now, should the few poor hungry souls be forsaken and repudiated for the sake of those in Hamburg? This time I still had to come because I promised to do so in the previous year, and permission was granted at our synodical conference.[44] However, I will not make another move a third time to that place without having the permission for it from the Very Reverend Fathers. It is a matter of indifference to me in which I do not follow my own will. If it pleases the Very Reverend Fathers to say that I should go, I will go, if not, I will not go. In any case, my conscience has been freed for I am no longer fit for anything. I gave the deacons to understand in advance that it pleased His Reverence Court Preacher Ziegenhagen in his last letter[45] to advise that I should not go to New York. However, theirs is a firm hope, and they think that the letter they transmitted and my narrative report will produce a more favorable result. Should they, however, contrary to their expectation be deserted by our Reverend Fathers and not be accepted, they may be obliged to follow a course of last resort.[46] The commissary of the English Church, Mr. Barclay,[47] intimated with a single word that he would recommend them to the bishop of London who in turn would seek out, ordain and send out a suitable individual from His Excellence, the Count of Wernigerode or Bergen Cloister or Göttingen because these newer upright theologians agreed more with the English Church in their writings and teachings than the old Wittenbergers and would not have scruples of conscience about being in communion with it. The matter is beyond me and I cannot render a judgment concerning it because it is too important. The English Church grants sufficient freedom in matters of conscience and it lacks nothing more than able, diligent laborers in the harvest. In it true piety could be taught and promoted more freely and better than in some places in Germany under our Lutheran polity. Ten years ago I almost landed in jail in my earthly fatherland when I wanted to say a kind word to my friends as a farewell in private.[48] That is not the way it is in the English countries, etc., etc. O most worthy sir and brother, please reckon my ideas for my benefit and put the best construction on them. The people in New York and Hackensack expect an answer from the Very Reverend Fathers with great longing, and I myself am in an uncertain situation until a final declaration from the Very Reverend Fathers arrives. However it turns out, I am willing to accept it, put my hand on my mouth[49] and to remember, "Whatever God ordains is right," etc., etc.[50]

Indeed, should the course of destiny turn out in such a way that I would have to remain in New York for a time I would establish a German print shop in New York. The little that is still left over from my inheritance I probably need to defray somewhat my debts. However, I sincerely leave the option open so that His Reverence, our dear father Francke, may retain it, as indicated previously, as part-payment for a printing press provided the Very Reverend Fathers find the proposal acceptable. Indeed, not my will but the will of God and my fathers be done! As for the rest, I want to close by still referring to several minor details. Our so-called synodical conference has been postponed until I return from New York, if I live.[51] From the enclosed letter of dear brother Brunholz[52] I see that Mr. Schultz may have ideas about marrying Heinrich Kreb's daughter in New Hanover. Krebs is a deacon in New Hanover, and his oldest daughter is about twenty years old. I confirmed her. As a person she is quiet and has been raised in accordance with the social position of farmers here. There is no wealth. Nothing can be said against her as a person; she loves God's word and is probably suitable for a farmer or craftsman, etc., etc. I am not pleased with Mr. Schultz getting mixed up with the practice of medicine here because it takes away time and opportunity from exercising properly one's ministry to which one is called. In case of necessity one may indeed do something, namely, with our blessed Halle medicines, etc., etc. Also, Mr. Schultz does not understand it from the ground up, etc., etc. He pretends to know all of the secrets and prescriptions of the Halle medicine but it is nothing but hot air. He has heard the bell ring but he does not know where it is hanging. I hope he will gradually finish sowing his wild oats and become more discreet. However, it is to be feared that people will receive adverse impressions and make inferences from the particular to the universal,[53] for they take note of one or another mistake in others very accurately and remember it. The poor brother will fare like that overhasty hunter who shot the powder from the powder-pan when he caught sight of game before he had loaded the gun or thought about it. All of us are bunglers and inexperienced millers who have still not tied many sacks shut, must have patience with one another and come to the true physician. Things are much safer when they run their course without excess so that one observes one's own mistakes through a magnifying glass and those of the neighbor through a telescope. However, it is safest according to our Master's rule to remove one's own log and then the speck of the neighbor's, etc., etc.[54] My most worthy brother, now I have poured out my thoughts in a hurry. Should you communicate any of them to our Very Reverend Fathers then I beg you to delete what may offend our dear Fathers and to correct the rest. With due humble respect to all, I remain

Your,

Mühlenberg

---

1. On Samuel Theodor Albinus, see Letter 76 n.50. See also *Correspondence* 1:154 n.8.
2. On Heinrich Schleydorn, see Letter 98 n.1. See also *Correspondence* 1:53 n.22.
3. Letters 112-116.
4. Five letters of Francke from the fall of 1751 to the Pennsylvania pastors are extant (Letters 99; 101-04).
5. Letter 105 from Friedrich Michael Ziegenhagen in the form of a postscript.
6. On Johann Conrad Weiser, see *Correspondence* 1:142 n.7.
7. The text reads *a[nni] c[urrentis]*.
8. The text reads *a[nni] p[raeteriti]*.
9. On Peter Brunnholz, see Letter 71 n.3.
10. See Ps. 23:1,4.
11. On Johann Friedrich Handschuh, see *Correspondence* 1:291 nn. 18 and 19.
12. On Johann Nicolaus Kurz, see *Correspondence* 1:154 n.5.
13. On Balthasar Bickel, see *Correspondence* 1:201 n.4.
14. Monocacy is the name of a river and a region north of Frederick, Maryland. For a listing of some names of places which are antiquated and have been modernized or have been given other names see *HN2/1*:722:23.
15. Bickel had recommended that Schaum should go to Raritan instead of Johann Albert Weygand with the understanding that the legacy of his deceased wife should benefit the Raritan congregation. This arrangement would be made with the condition that the congregation would care for Schaum for the rest of his life. See *Korrespondenz* 1:522 n.7. See also Letter 71 nn.9 and 21.
16. The text reads *ad dies vitae*.
17. The text reads *N[ota] B[ene]*.
18. On Johann Albert Weygand (1722-70), see Letter 71 n.21 and *Pastors and People* 1:162-63.
19. The text reads *casus*.
20. On Lucas Rauss, see Letter 76 n.72.
21. A letter of Brunnholtz reports the Indianfield congregation's dissatisfaction with Rauss. See *Korrespondenz* 1:522 n.8.
22. On Ludolph Heinrich Schrenck, see Letter 78 n.7.
23. Johann Dietrich Matthias Heinzelmann (1726-56) arrived in Philadelphia in 1751 after having been ordained previously by the Wernigerode Consistory in that same year. As assistant to Peter Brunnholz in the Philadelphia congregation he proved to be especially effective in its school and before long was elected as its second pastor. See also Letter 101 n.3.
24. On Friedrich Schultze, see Letter 89 n.4.
25. The entry in Handschuh's diary for 15 January 1752 has a reference to a decision reached at a conference of Brunnholz, Schultze, Heinzelmann, Handschuh and Mühlenberg to appoint Schultze as Mühlenberg's assistant in New Hanover. See *HN2/2:80*.
26. See Letter 112:210

27. On Christoph Sauer, see *Correspondence* 1:93 n.37.

28. Michael Walther, successor to Jacob Loeser in New Hanover, whom Mühlenberg was not able to use as a preacher. See *HN2/1*:587.

29. This is probably a reference to David Hollaz (1648-1713), not to his grandson by the same name (1704-71), who was a leading representative of declining Lutheran orthodoxy. The elder Hollaz's emphasis on inspiration in the order of salvation marks a transition to Pietism. In the course of time he developed connections with the Moravians and published devotional writings akin to their spirit.

30. Andreas Christoph Schubart (1629-89), author of the postil to which Mühlenberg refers and the title of which probably was *Evangelische Lehr=Tempel, in welchem XIV Lehr-Arten über die Sonn- und Festagsevangelien enthalten, nebst dem Anhang 6 sonderbahrer Predigten*, Halle, 1672.

31. Schultze served New Goshenhoppen 1751-56. See *Pastors and People* 1:124.

32. The text reads *a[nni] p[raeteriti]*.

33. At the time of the writing of this letter the Mühlenbergs had four children: Johann Peter Gabriel, b. 1 October 1746; Eva Elisabeth (Betsy), b. 29 January 1748; Friedrich August Conrad, b. 1 January 1750; Margretha Henrietta (Peggy), b. 17 September 1751.

34. Letter 107.

35. Ps. 55:22.

36. Mühlenberg had presented his proposal previously in Letters 112:214-17 and 114:230.

37. The text reads *ad pias causas*.

38. See *Correspondence* 1:229; 340. See also Letters 93:126-27 and 107:187-88.

39. The text reads *Maii a[nni] c[urrentis]*.

40. See *Journals* 1:321-41.

41. In his diary on 5 July 1752 Mühlenberg states, "Today I received sharp letters from Pennsylvania--from my older colleagues and my wife--which indicated that I should return to my congregations in Hannover and Providence and forsake New York. They also declared that Mr. Rauss is unwilling to relieve me here and that Mr. Schrenck is unable to do so at present. These letters troubled me very much; to think of forsaking New York depressed me, etc." (*Journals* 1:339).

42. For the Palatines in New York, see *Lutherans in N.A.* pp. 22-24; also John P. Dern (ed.), *The Albany Protocol: Wilhelm Christoph Berkenmeyer's Chronicle of Lutheran Affairs in New York Colony, 1731-1750* (Ann Arbor, 1971; republished by Picton Press, Camden, Maine, 1992).

43. The allusion is to the German text in the Luther Bible which in translation would read, "...a little has been left over." The previous references to "a ravaged city" and "a booth in a pumpkin garden" seem to be a free adaptation of "like a booth in a vineyard" and "like a besieged city" in Isa. 1:8.

44. Johann Friedrich Handschuh's report of the "Transactions and Resolutions of the United Preachers and the delegates of their united congregations in their Synodical Convention, May 13, 1751 at Philadelphia" makes no explicit reference to the permission granted Mühlenberg at this conference to serve the congregation in New York. The report only says that "Rev. Mühlenberg promised, in answer to the many requests of the delegates, to return as soon as possible, but in the meantime his congregations are to be cared for by the Rev. Messrs. Brunnholtz, Handschuh, and the other United Preachers" (*Documentary History*, p. 34). Letter 90 tells us explicitly of Mühlenberg having consulted with "the Ministry of our Church" about accepting the call of the Dutch Church Council in New York. Handschuh's report assumes knowledge of this previous conference.

45. See Letter 105.

46. The text reads *ultimum refugium*.

47. A graduate of Yale College in 1734 and ordained in London 1737/38, Henry Barclay (1712-64) was rector in Albany and, from 1746 until his death, rector of Trinity Church, New York.

48. For a brief discussion of the difficulties Mühlenberg encountered during leave-taking in Einbeck, see *Correspondence* 1:17-18 nn. 16 and 17; *Journals* 1:12-14.

49. See Judg. 18:19.

50.   Hymn by Samuel Rodigast (1649-1708), "Was Gott thut das ist wohlgetan." See *Liedersammlung*, Hymn 410 and *LBW* 446.

51. The conference was held in Germantown 2 October 1752. See *Documentary History*, pp. 36-40.

52. The reference is to Brunnholz's letter of 20 May 1752. See *Korrespondenz* 1:524 n.28.

53. The text reads *a particulari auf das universale*.

54. See Matt. 7:3-5.

Letter 121

Gotthilf August Francke to the Pastors in Pennsylvania
Halle, 31 July 1752

By the time Gotthilf August Francke became the head of the Halle institutions these enjoyed an international reputation for the books they published and distributed, for the society which published and distributed the Bible and for the production and distribution of pharmaceuticals. These enterprises, the last one in particular, proved to be profitable enough to enable the Halle institutions to finance to a considerable degree their eleemosynary and missionary undertakings. In this letter Francke presents the overarching purpose of these enterprises and the procedures the Pennsylvania pastors should adopt in ordering, receiving and accounting for the various materials like books, Bibles and medicines. Perhaps most interesting in Francke's communication is the selection of Brunnholz as accountant and overseer of the transactions under consideration.

Text in German: Korrespondenz *1:524-26. For further textual information, see* Korrespondenz *1:526.*

To the Pastors in Pennsylvania   31 July 1752

Reverend,
Dearly beloved Brothers in the Lord:

An answer to several points must indeed still be given and I shall now attempt gradually to attend to everything adequately and to communicate it. Herewith I only want to write what is necessary concerning the boxes which have been sent containing medicine and books. From all of the letters I have gathered this much that the books and medications which have previously been shipped for sale have not been unwelcome. Furthermore, you have given me to understand that trade of this kind might continue. Consequently, I have arranged for shipping a substantial portion of both again, accompanied by specifications and invoices, a copy of which has also been enclosed in the boxes. Furthermore, from this copy it is possible to establish at the same time that also all other things which were desired in addition have also been packed in these boxes. However, to put this matter in good order so that neither the main purpose is neglected on account of secondary undertakings of this kind nor also that my dear brothers as well as the orphanage should incur any harm in the process, I find it necessary in this connection to call the following to mind:

1. In this process the main intention must remain to promote edification through distribution of good publications and to serve the neighbor.

2. In part, the distraction is not well suited for the pastors themselves and would require too much time and effort; in part it would also give some people too much opportunity to want something for nothing, and this might not only become troublesome for you but also occasion annoyance when you cannot satisfy the desires of the people. For that reason my advice is that you assign to this business a person suited for the task who should manage the whole undertaking.

3. The whole present supply would be handed over to him and accounts settled with him so that gradually when he had sold up to a certain amount he would pay so and so much of what he owed to Pastor Brunnholz[1] as the present bookkeeper of money in the collection treasury. As often as might be necessary the person would have to determine what books and medicines and how much of each should again be sent out, after he sees that there is more or less a demand for this or that. He would have to see to it that there is especially a supply at all times of the principal items so that inquiry for them would not be in vain. Matters could be set up in such a way that a statement of particulars would be handed in to Pastor Brunnholz separately for medications, again separately for Bibles and separately for the remaining books. Pastor Brunnholz would sign these statements of particulars and the boxes would also be shipped to him.

4. The bookstore, the Bible society and shipping center for medications have assumed the costs for transportation from here to Hamburg. Beyond that the latter allows the seller a discount of ten percent. The remaining expenses for shipping from Hamburg to Pennsylvania must be added on to the price and beyond that a profit has to be factored into the price of the Bibles and books. The pastors could get the price or they could permit the seller to calculate it and present it for approval so that the seller could not change it without their prior knowledge. They could also print a price list and put the price of each item on it which, however, in the case of future shipments could change after expenses rise or fall.

5. As far as payment is concerned, one would indeed wish that God would want to let so much flow together in the collection treasury that from it the debts in the bookstore, the Bible society and the shipping center for medications could be covered. But because it is uncertain at the outset,[2] and in time the deficit could increase, therefore the amounts which exceed the supply in the collection treasury must be forwarded via exchange to England. It is also for this reason that the requisite expenses for the goods have to be added on. In this connection it is of help to know that if the exchange rate of English currency does not change, one pound and one

shilling sterling or one guinea is to be calculated as worth six reichsthaler. On this basis settlement of accounts with the orphanage can be concluded at any time. In the meantime in the bookstore, the Bible society and the shipping center for medications accounts are kept until the charges have been paid.

6. Whoever desires something else and wants to order it, orders it only from the seller so that everything is recorded on one bill and can be attended to in one stroke.

7. In general the seller must with all diligence assume the settlement of accounts, the placing of orders, etc. Only he must present everything to Pastor Brunnholz or all the pastors in advance so that they may retain control of the matter and the seller can do nothing without their prior knowledge.

8. You yourselves will see to it that you do not come to grief from the seller. For that reason do not only give attention to how he conducts his business and if he is spending money or running up debts but also at least reserve the right for yourselves from time to time, if you find it necessary, to examine his supply to see whether he is embezzling the money received.

9. Because Mr. Brunnholz has written[3] that binding in Pennsylvania is so expensive, we have consequently had all books bound here. In the future it must always be stated clearly[4] how each book is to be bound.

10. Should inquiry be made for books which have not been sent along, the seller orders them at the next opportunity.

This is as much as has occurred to me for now. Now you yourselves must see how best to arrange matters. I remain

Halle   Your,
                                                             G.A. Francke

---

1. On Peter Brunnholz, see Letter 71 n.3.
2. The text reads *a priori*.
3. The letter is dated 16 March 1752. See *Korrespondenz* 1:526 n.1.
4. The text reads *distincte*.

Letter 122

Gotthilf August Francke to Peter Brunnholz,
Johann Friedrich Handschuh and Mühlenberg
Halle, 31 July 1752

*In his letter of 18 February 1752 (Letter 112) Mühlenberg had appealed
to Francke to accept the young son of Heinrich Schleydorn as a pupil in one
of the Halle schools. In this letter Francke confirms the arrival of the
Schleydorn boy without, however, identifying him by name. Because he was
not an orphan the boy's enrollment in one of the schools presented a number
of problems. In the process of dealing with the problems in this letter
Francke affords us an insight into some aspects of the administration of the
schools, and, incidentally, into aspects of the social life in them.*
*Text in German: Korrespondenz 1:526-29. For further textual information
see: Korrespondenz 1:529.*

To Pastors Mühlenberg, Brunnholz and Handschuch

31 July 1752

Reverend,
Dearly beloved Brothers in the Lord:
Among the letters[1] transmitted those have also turned up in which you
recommend the dear younger son of your very, very worthy benefactor and
patron, Mr. Schleydorn,[2] and give your reasons for proposing and
requesting that he be placed with a group of children who are really
orphans. On the journey the Lord has also cared for him very well and
toward the end of June just passed has happily brought him here. I have
been moved most of all by his worthy father who has, from the time of the
arrival of Pastor Mühlenberg, proven himself to be a faithful friend, yes, a
father and provider to him and afterwards to all who followed him. With his
good counsel and assistance Mr. Schleydorn has fostered the work of God
in all sorts of ways, as I have gathered not only from your previous
communications but also anew from your present letters in several ways.
Just as I view all love which my worthy brothers encounter as shown to
myself, so I request that you thank this dear friend most sincerely above all
also in my name for all goodwill shown until now. Although far removed
from me, he has willingly served you on my behalf as you permitted
yourselves to be sent out for the sake of God's work to the forsaken
congregations in Pennsylvania. Assure him that I cannot be insensitive to

what he has done; in particular, however, I am sincerely glad that you have certified a number of times that he not only serves the servants of God gladly and seeks to foster what is good but he himself has experienced God's grace in his heart and seeks to abide in it. For that may his name be praised! May God then reward him in his own soul by the demonstration of his sincere love through ample refreshment and blessing. Next to this may God in a fatherly way watch over the outward circumstances of Mr. Schleydorn and his dearly beloved ones. May God especially allow the blessing of godly parents to pass on to his dear children that they may be brought to a living knowledge of Christ to his heartfelt joy.

But as far as the dear youngest son is concerned whom we now have with us: the new coworkers[3] did indeed have good intentions in that they believed he would be looked after best among the orphans. However, to let this pass without saying that it is essentially contrary to the basic laws of the institutions to place the child of a father who is living and not altogether impoverished among orphans, I must reject such a proposal on the recommendation of some best friends, indeed, several distinguished patrons, and protect myself with the argument that this is not done. Also, the dear friends have not considered another aspect. In view of his youth and natural alertness sufficient care cannot be taken for a child like this for which one has a special love and which also is in need of special supervision. The large number of orphans in the classes entrusted to the supervision of one preceptor, even with the best possible arrangements, does not allow sufficient care to be taken of them as in the Latin pupil quarters. In these only three or four pupils live with the preceptor who can then take care of a child like that especially in the light of all circumstances and can in particular[4] concern himself more precisely with his health, pay closer attention to his conduct and ward off what may perhaps be harmful to him, also in all circumstances come to his aid. By way of contrast it is easy to observe that a preceptor of orphans who has to care for fifty children[5] (in both combined classes), even if he wants to be completely faithful, nevertheless, cannot possibly make the rounds and does not even have the time properly to assume special care[6] for an individual child. This is especially true since so many changes occur among preceptors who have one and all departed within the year. Thus a new preceptor can barely acquaint himself properly with the special circumstances of each child before he leaves again or goes to another class. Also, not every one has a gift for this task; more than faithfulness is required of the one selected for it. But in the pupil quarters one can more easily arrange it in such a way that one can assign a child like that to a really good preceptor who has a gift and liking for special care. One can also give him good fellow pupils and with that end in view transfer them from one quarter to the other. But especially also do I request you to take this into consideration in addition: in view of the large number of orphans, it cannot be otherwise than that they must be much more carefully restricted. It is also not possible with any ease to grant as an exception[7] one or another freedom which might otherwise not be harmful. Something like this may indeed very well be acceptable with peasant children who are mostly poor. However, for a somewhat more tender child who was reared in greater freedom and in addition had been so far removed from his parents at such a tender age this arrangement would have become too burdensome and depressed his spirit very much. I also believe it would have been distressing for the parents themselves, if their dear son would have had to be among poor children who are still for the most part naughty (because he would still have had to be placed with the smaller ones) and would have the same treatment.

Pastor Brunnholz himself reported[8] that if it were not possible to place him immediately with the orphans one might in the meantime place him in a pupils' quarters. After consideration of all circumstances of this kind, I have arranged for his placement in a room for four where there is not only a good preceptor but there are also pupils who behave quite well. Out of special love I will give him free room, wood and light. Along with that I have initially provided him with a free evening meal in the orphanage, being of the opinion that it would not be difficult or contrary to the wishes of the worthy parents to pay nine groschen[9] weekly for the noon meal. However, I also experienced that my previous concern was not without foundation. For initially it was decided to place him in quarters for eight pupils where there is also a good preceptor. Because this could not be arranged for immediately he was placed for only a few days in the interim in the quarters for four pupils, referred to previously; when we wanted to move him after a few days, he cried terribly because that was already too burdensome for him. Indeed, he was also not completely satisfied with the free evening meal which is basically not less than or only a little less than the evening meal for fourteen groschen. He could especially not become accustomed at all to near beer, etc. (which is the regular beverage of orphans who never receive beer). For that reason he did not cease asking to be allowed to eat at the fourteen groschen table until we agreed to that arrangement; he assured us that this would not be contrary to the wishes of his dear parents. They will, I do not doubt, without having to deprive themselves too much in the light of their circumstances, still be able to bear the limited costs for board, bedding, laundry, books for which others must be paid and which do not accrue to the advantage of the orphanage, as can be seen in the enclosure.[10] From time to time a bill concerning these items will be sent. From this last arrangement, however, it becomes especially evident that the portion[11] of food the orphans receive would have been insufficient because, as has been mentioned, not only do the orphans not get beer but they also receive meat only once a week and never a roast. In the meantime I request that you greet his parents sincerely from me and assure them that I myself will especially look after their dear son; also the inspectors and preceptors will care for him in particular.[12] I remain

Halle...July 1752[13]   Your,

                                                        G.A. Francke

P.S. I also beg you to inform Mrs. Schleydorn of the gratitude I owe her for the preserved fruit she sent and I only wish I had an opportunity to provide evidence of my love for her. However, we have not been able to establish, also not to learn from her dear son, what kind of fruit it really is. For that reason I beg you when an opportunity presents itself to provide me with some information concerning it.

---

1. See Letter 112:218f; Peter Brunnholz's letter of 10 March 1752, see *Korrespondenz* 1:529 n.1.

2. On Heinrich Schleydorn, see *Correspondence* 1:53 n.22.

3. Friedrich Schultze and Johann Dietrich Matthias Heinzelmann. On them, see Letter 89 n.4 and Letter 101 n.3.

4. The text reads *in specie*.

5. Instead of *a 8f* the text in the letter's manuscript reads *auf*.

6. The text reads *curam specialem*.

7. The text reads *per exceptionem*.

8. This is again a reference to Peter Brunnholz's letter of 10 March 1752. On Peter Brunnholz, see Letter 71, n.3.

9. The text reads "9. gg.," i.e, *neun gute groschen*.

10. Not extant.

11. The text reads *ratione*.

12. The text reads *in specie*.

13. After having dated the letter the "24th" of July 1752, Francke deleted the date. See *Korrespondenz* 1:529 n.8.

Letter 123

Gotthilf August Francke to Mühlenberg
Pölzig, 5 (or 9) August 1752

Written on a blank page of a letter no longer extant of Court Preacher Albinus, this letter in the form of a postscript is intended to correct a misunderstanding of what Friedrich Schultze and Johann Dietrich Matthias Heinzelmann reported of their conversation with Court Preacher Ziegenhagen.
Text in German: Korrespondenz *1:529. For further textual information, see* Korrespondenz *1:529.*

9 August 1752[1]

To Pastor Mühlenberg. To be written on the blank page of the letter of Mr. Albinus.

P.S.

The most worthy Court Preacher Albinus has kindly communicated the preceding letter for examination to me. As I suspected immediately from the outset or rather concluded with reliable certainty, I learn from it the opinion Court Preacher Ziegenhagen expressed in the first five points of your letter.[2] The opinion was not understood correctly or also, as I now moreover conclude, even more so from your most recent letter to Mr. Albinus[3] which you sent me, was rather twisted by Mr. Schultze.[4] Consequently, herewith I am transmitting it immediately so it can be sent to Your Reverence even though the letter to Mr. Albinus just referred to shows that you have already been assured anew of Court Preacher Ziegenhagen's fatherly feelings. That assurance notwithstanding, this letter can nevertheless give you encouragement. I am now in the process of replying to everything that is necessary and with the next mail I hope to be able to transmit my detailed answer.

Pölzig, 5 August 1752

---

1. This date has been entered by another hand.
2. This is a reference to Mühlenberg's letter of 18 February 1752 in which he recounts what Schultze and Heinzelmann had told him; see Letter 112:205ff.
3. See Letter 113.
4. On Friedrich Schultze, see Letter 89 n.4.

Letter 123A

To Richard Peters
Providence, 25 August 1752

Having expresed his gratitude profusely to Richard Peters for his intervention with Pennsylvania's governor in securing a passport, Mühlenberg takes the opportunity in this letter to complain about the behavior of some neighbors in Providence for their involvement in dissolute conduct. Through referral of this complaint to Peters as secretary of the province of Pennsylvania, Mühlenberg hopes that a way can be found to curb excesses he considers immoral.

Text in English: Muhlenberg College, Allentown, Pennsylvania. A copy of the letter is in PM 95-D5. This letter, written in English, is given here in its original form.

To Richard Peters

Reverend Sir,[1]
being called home from Newyork[2] because my family was indisposed, and my Congregations grew uneasy, and coming save to Philadelphia, I endeavoured to wait on Your Reverency, but hearing of Your being abroad with his Honour, our gracious Governor,[3] I could[n]'t perform my duty and was obliged to go home and leave my duty untill the next oportunity. I met with some blessing at Newyork, and a door was opened unto me,[4] so that I could gather and regulate there a pretty small Congregation and another one at Hackinsack 17 Myles from New York, of the german=Lowdutch and English peopel. It is a pitty I could not find nor spare a faithful Minister, perfected in the Lowdutch and English Language, to send and to settle there, because the people seem to have a true desire after the sincere Milk of the Word,[5] that they might grow thereby. Deus providebit.[6] But alas! Reverend Sir, it grieveth me and makes me very uneasy, that I am in no ways able to rendre most humble and real thanks for Your more then fatherly care and Affection. You pleased to bestow on me, the most unworthy Creature, in Affording a passport[7] and Recommendation of His Honour, our Gracious Governor and Your blessed Heart and Hands! If there was any thing in my soul, body and little Estate, which could humbly serve but in token of the least degree of thankfulness, it should surely as far as possible, at the first hint, be ready for your service! Deus providebit sibi agnum at [!]

immolandum.[8] The state and Condition of some English and german Neighbours here at Providence groweth worse, because Abr[aham] de Haven[9] continues to abuse the granted licence by enticing one after another into a dissolute and wicked life, Surfeiting, Drunkeness, playing Cards and dice, fiddling, dancing, cursing, swearing, fighting, scuffling and such like, will hardly cease on the Lord's days! He has had several Sondays in my absence horse=race, before, during and after divine Worship, on the Road, before his tavern, to the great offence of old and young people, who had been hitherto sober and honest! On the 19th of July last, being the Lords day he detained a Company of young people, coming out of the Church, and gave them too much Rum and punch, so that they got fuddled and beat one another bloody, behaving themselves in a scandalous Manner! Two of 'em, lay on the road before his door hurted, when our Justice Mr. Owen Evans[10] past by. He saw them and told Abraham to present him at the Court. Mr. Evans can be the best Evidence, if not too partial. There is to[o] little Inspection here about, and grievous to see, that in a Christian Country, the all mighty and most gracious God must be denied, the Excellent laws and Constitutions notoriously violated, old and young people infected, the fear of God and Magistrates abated, by a young robust and Idle Man, that could find his livelyhood by way of trading or Working like other honest people. Every one of our sober Neighbours, is afraid to present him to the Court, because they have no fortifications about their houses, barns and Cattles against the Revenge of loose people. They plague me to inform our superiors against him, thinking a Minister should first of all, be not afraid of them, that could only, when permitted hurt the Body.[11] But what is a poor Minister in Pennsylvania and Who is next after God my tutelar Angel in this Wilderniss in whose bosom I may pour my Complaints with Confidence besides Your Reverency? though I am sensible and very afraid I may tire your patience and loose Your Affection, by writing and complaining beyond the limits, and interrupting Your precious time, appointed for the buisiness of State and Academy[12] and innumerable Affairs of higher Moments. I have therefore sent a letter[13] and laid my Complaints to and before Thomas Laurence Esq to see wether, through the Assistance of God, a remedy could be found for the disease. May the Lord grant unto me to remain the least of Your Clients and

Providence
Aug: 25th 1752

Reverend Sir
Your most obedient
servant Hr: M.

1. Richard Peters served as secretary of the Province of Pennsylvania and its Council. He was also Commissary of the Church of England and president of the Academy of Pennsylvania. For details concerning Peters, see Hubertis Cummings, *Richard Peters: Provincial Secretary and Cleric* (Philadelphia: University of Pennsylvania Press, 1944).

2. In unambiguous terms Friedrich Michael Ziegenhagen advised Mühlenberg not to leave his Pennsylvania congregations to accept a call to New York (see Letter 105). Similarly, Gotthilf August Francke expressed the opinion that the Pennsylvania congregations remained Mühlenberg's primary responsibility, not New York (see Letter 124:281-82). While serving the Dutch congregation in New York from May until August 1752, Mühlenberg was under pressure from his wife and his colleagues who wanted him to return to Pennsylvania (see Letter 120, nn. 34 and 37).

3. James Hamilton was the governor of Pennsylvania from 1748-54.

4. See Rev. 3:8.

5. See 1 Pet. 2:2.

6. Text in Latin: "God will provide." See Gen. 22:8 (Vulgate).

7. The passport is preserved in PM 95 Z10.

8. See Gen. 22:8 - The text is in Latin: "God will provide for himself the lamb for a burnt offering." Mühlenberg's citation diverges from the Vulgate text.

9. Mühlenberg refers to a person by the name of Abraham de Haven as helping with construction of a well in Providence. See *Journals* 2:758.

10. Mühlenberg performed the marriage ceremony when Owen Evans married Eleonor (Eleanor) Lane. See *Journals* 3:505.

11. See Matt. 10:28.

12. See n.1 above.

13. Not extant.

Letter 124

Gotthilf August Francke to Mühlenberg
Halle, 13 September 1752

*Written in response to Mühlenberg's letter of 18 February 1752 (Letter
112), Franke's letter shows a great deal of understanding, empathy, even
warmth for the concerns Mühlenberg had presented in great detail in his
letter to Francke. After assuring Mühlenberg of his appreciation of the trying
circumstances in which he finds himself and sharing with him the need for
reliance on the guidance and patience of God, Francke responds to (1)
Mühlenberg's proposal to establish an institution for orphans, a seminary for
the education of pastors and teachers and a retirement home for them; (2)
his inquiry about what to do about serving the Dutch congregation in New
York; (3) his complaint particularly about Friedrich Schultze's distortion of
what was said in conversations with Francke in Halle and Ziegenhagen in
London; (4) the difficulty Mühlenberg has in making salary adjustments to
accommodate Schultze as his assistant; (5) Mühlenberg's desire for
establishment of a printing press; and finally (6) the request to use what is
left of his inheritance to defray a part of the expenses for the purchase of a
printing press. Francke closes his letter with greetings from him and his wife
to Mrs. Mühlenberg and her parents, the Weisers.*

Text in German: Korrespondenz *1:530-38. For further textual
information, see* Korrespondenz *1:538.*

To Pastor Mühlenberg
at New Providence

13 September 1752

Reverend,
Very highly esteemed Friend
in the Lord:

As much as possible I herewith want to try to answer briefly Your
Reverence's esteemed letter of 18 February of the current year.[1]

As far as the beginning of the same is concerned I, for my part, want to
thank you sincerely for your cordial interest in God's work near and far in
which the dear Court Preacher Ziegenhagen and I have been used by the
Lord until now as instruments for its advancement. Also, no less do I want
to thank you sincerely for your cordial interest in our health, in outward and

inner suffering and trials and the help of the Lord, in conflict and victory. In the course of these I also thank you for praising the name of the Lord and calling upon it. To no less a degree I assure you that I frequently imagine your circumstances as present and acknowledge the labor of your worthy colleagues and coworkers in the Lord. I sympathize with your suffering, trials, troubles, hardships, diminishing strength and dangers you have endured. For blessing and victory bestowed until now I praise the Lord and acknowledge that the Lord has selected you as an instrument for Pennsylvania circumstances through which he wants to bring his work to pass in this region. Already he has also given his blessing to your work in such a manner that through it he has placed his seal of approval on your ministry and sanctioned it. In this respect I also sincerely rejoice that he has given you the wisdom to act wisely in several confused circumstances in the course of which I and others in the beginning were filled with misgivings as to how things would turn out. In this respect also I do not judge you in those matters in which I wished that you had acted otherwise and in which I would have acted differently according to the nature of the circumstances as I envision them. For one thing, I know very well that it is impossible to obtain from letters a complete overview of all interlocking circumstances. Accordingly one can very easily be mistaken in the conception of them and consequently in the judgment based on it as is said, "The least circumstance can change the matter."[2] In addition, we also have a gracious Lord and Master who also has gracious patience with the actual failings and oversights of his servants in the process and nevertheless constantly keeps the plan of his work and the main thread of his wise rule in his hand in such a way that he wards off all harm. Even those things which we consider failings and oversights or which actually are such nevertheless are turned into something good and an actual advantage for his work. In what I just said here I wanted to make every effort to explain more clearly our attitude on these matters. I do this so you may interpret my mind accordingly when I occasionally brought something to mind and disapproved of it or still call it to mind. Do not let this perhaps dishearten you but apply it in such a way that you can make use of it in future cases.

In the remaining part of your letter, however, I find the following points require a more detailed response. 1) It would be necessary that the work which has been started among the congregations in Pennsylvania should be put on such a sound footing and maintained in such order that in future times as well it will endure and congregations as well as pastors can always be kept within limits appropriate to them. For that reason you have included a recommendation for an institution which is to serve as an orphanage, a seminary for churches and schools and at the same time a hospital for retired persons among those who serve in church and school. All of this in its own way[3] would be quite good if it could be brought into being as quickly as it is conceived and the necessary means are available for the establishment of the institution as well as the required workers and managers were available. But since we are still lacking all of this no other way remains than that one first of all continue to look still more closely to the hands of the gracious God and pay attention to his guidance. We must see how he will indicate to us procedure, means and opportunity and show us footprints whether and in what way one or another institution of one or another kind can be established through which spiritual care of the Pennsylvania congregations as a whole can be provided.

Senior Fresenius[4] has proposed an application for a collection from the body of evangelicals[5] as a whole in Regensburg, and you have struck upon the idea of sending a pastor from your midst who might undertake a collection in Germany. Both proposals, however, are still subject to many difficulties and beset with many risks. On account of previous abuses,[6] collections in Germany are seen as odious and create frequent offense through adverse opinions through which perhaps more harm than good may accrue to the affair. Both kinds of collections may not be adequate for establishing a fund which is considerable and sufficient for the future; they may, however, seal off the hearts of some benefactors and give rise to the idea that now an adequate fund already exists. As one then has also seen that which went to Amsterdam was not even reflected upon. But in the meantime it may not prove harmful for all pastors in common to compose a letter to Court Preacher Ziegenhagen and me in which you would present in detail the existing need and ask for the advancement by Christian patrons of charitable contributions of this kind. The contributions would be applied to pay church debts, the sending of necessary pastors, the maintenance of several teachers in churches and schools in poor congregations, the care of your widows and orphans, also the education of poor orphans, etc. However, nothing should be mentioned of the plan of an institution of the kind you proposed unless God were to provide something. If the debts had been paid off, then one would think of such an institution. On the one hand, one would first look to God in faith in the actual establishment of one institution or another and have no doubt. If he makes our heart certain that we should begin with this or that out of merciful and compelling love, he will not abandon us when he himself more precisely shows us the footsteps for that purpose, even though we do not yet completely foresee the means. On the other hand, however, we must also see to it that we do not outrun God and thereby commit ourselves to these or other projects which can miscarry while carrying them out if we do not have the footsteps of God preceding us. Also in this respect experience has shown this to be true, "To him who has will more be given."[7] Among other things the Lord has laid on the faithful use of what is small and insignificant--on the institutions here, for example—such a blessing that he gives a further one! In this matter it is especially important to keep in mind how carefully my blessed father tested the ways of God and was careful not to start anything in which he did not clearly see his footsteps leading the way.[8] With this in view I cannot advise starting something with debts (especially before previous church debts are paid). However, if debts were paid off first and God pointed particularly to a man of a kind through whom one could carry out a project like that and at the outset also placed something in your hands, then I would not want to advise you against something for which the Lord had given you the cheerfulness of faith confidently to take the risk.

In the present circumstances which are still so miserable it can serve to comfort and strengthen faith that the Lord has already shown us a footstep of his help in advance through funds which, having been offered from Italy, now appear to be materializing after various difficulties. At first the benefactor had arrived at an entirely different decision and assigned his funds to East India, as I have already reported.[9] Afterwards he was nevertheless again persuaded to dedicate them to the Pennsylvania congregations. As he spoke in the beginning of only 10,000 reichsthaler so now he is actually offering that many reichsthaler. For his security he has approved the proposal made concerning the reservation of the interest until the day of his death[10] in accordance with which the funds are to be invested in Germany in a secure mortgage or for repurchase.[11] However, we must wait and see whether an acceptable opportunity for this purpose can be found and something else might not otherwise intervene. In the meantime I, for my part, will omit nothing to make the matter a reality even though thereby no small burden accrues to the orphanage in view of the extensive complications already present. Following the benefactor's death the use to which the fund is to be put is to be left to the discretion of the directorate of the orphanage. Thus with the help of God this money can become a good beginning for a fund for the Pennsylvania congregations. In this way the Pennsylvania congregations are bound to the direction of those who care for them. Thus also in the future the work can be carried forward the way in which it was begun. In this connection one can also see to it especially that worn out workers are cared for so that they do not have to live by the grace of congregations which are often ungrateful. Now I would indeed be pleased if the money could be invested and turned safely to good account in Pennsylvania after the benefactor's death for he has already expressly objected to transferring it during his lifetime outside of Germany so that it would yield full interest and the director of the orphanage alone would have control over its administration and use. For this purpose the acquisition of a plantation would of course be the best means since you give the assurance that interest could be drawn annually from the property. In the meantime, however, the opportunity will likely slip through your fingers unless perhaps through your worthy father-in-law you could encourage a man of means to buy the property referred to for the Pennsylvania congregations. Through his own administration he himself would draw the interest of his money until one could pay it off to him. This procedure would allow him to use the interest for himself and consequently you and your worthy colleagues would not thereby be exposed to a risk. However, such a person will scarcely be found. For that reason it will probably have to depend on God's provision in the future. In the meantime we can take this much for our comfort from the raising up of this benefactor to contribute this capital: in this way the Lord wants to provide evidence of our beginning of his gracious provision and to strengthen our faith so we may not lose courage when we see so many obstacles and miserable circumstances ahead of us. Especially in carrying out his work it becomes apparent that, with the exception of the cross,[12] all of his promises are to be understood as those which always have their beginning under much pressure and must pass through pressure. However, when his work really passes through the cross from the beginning it is thereby validated all the more and, as experience demonstrates, has the most staying power. Accordingly, we do not want to allow ourselves to grow weary or faint-hearted[13] in our confidence in God. We shall also trust him to continue to support our dear brother, especially since you have already consumed your energies in his service very much, and faithfully to care for you and your dear loved ones.

2) The second most important point concerns the circumstances in New York. I see this much clearly from all reports when taken together: (1) That you have entered the affair with sincere integrity and simplicity and in doing so you have sought your own advantage as little as you could expect outward improvement from it in your material circumstances. (2) Here too there would be a field in which good could be accomplished as there are hungry souls here and the local congregation could in the course of time be brought into good order again. (3) It is true that from all points of view it is questionable whether this field should be entirely abandoned after one has once begun some work in it. At least, provided God would only present an opportunity to do so, one would want to demonstrate in several ways that one would like to continue the work once it has been begun as long as the congregation itself does not reject the word. On the one hand I understand very well that one is charged with a lack of constancy and that also among

others confidence could be quashed; on the other hand, a field like that could be left to unfaithful laborers and move poor souls to moan. (4) However, we also cannot do more than God gives us the ability to do. For we are only his instruments and may not outrun him but must await his hint and command as to what he wants to place in our hands. We cannot be faulted for anything as long as we are ready on our part to carry God's work forward and take advantage of all opportunties God indicates and do with them what we are able to do. (5) In this connection one also ought to consider that we are not only to be much concerned that much is started but rather that what is started is continued with constancy, put into perfectly good order and maintained therein. (6) Accordingly, Pennsylvania and the congregations already established in that region rightfully remain our primary concern so that we do not again surrender a field which we have cultivated to this point for the sake of a new field that is not as well developed. So in connection with the work of God we need especially to observe what has been brought forth.[14] Furthermore, I assure the dear brother, as I am well aware indeed, that I cannot put a check of any kind on your insight or expect you to act contrary to the same in accordance with my instruction, for in any case I cannot bind you but only serve you with my frank counsel and rightly leave it to you to examine it before God. Also, you have assured me in advance that what you do is done with sincerity and integrity to the glory of God. (8) If now in accordance with what has been said I should state my opinion according to my present best insight concerning the matter then, taking into account as much as I know of the context of the circumstances, I cannot find the cheerfulness yet from where I am to advise you to accept the call to New York for the following reasons which I want to cite so that you can better examine them. a) In my opinion your presence[15] in Pennsylvania is still necessary at this time to hold the Pennsylvania congregations together. For although the Lord has given you colleagues who are not lacking in wisdom and zeal for the glory of God, the congregations, nevertheless, look primarily to you because you were the first one who broke the ice. If you remain together in Pennsylvania you can maintain the congregations in a much better condition. Together with your reputation you can lend much greater weight to matters than if you were separated,[16] especially since you are the most familiar with all circumstances from the beginning. For that reason you can be more useful with your good counsel on various matters to the Pennsylvania ministerium than can others. In your last letter to the worthy Mr. Albinus[17] who furnished me with a copy of it, you do indeed write that the Pennsylvania congregations would lack nothing because you could reach Philadelphia and Providence from Hackensack by land in two and one half days. You also say that you would move to New York for only two or three years on trial and during that time would turn the congregations in Providence and Hanover over to Mr. Heintzelmann.[18] Nevertheless I fear that you could still not deal as forcefully with matters as when you would be present. However, should you nevertheless feel yourself compelled to move to New York, then I would only request this: that in the beginning and in accordance with what you have proposed this would take place temporarily and that you would arrange matters in such a way that now as before you would remain in connection with the Pennsylvania congregations, be present at their conferences and otherwise in all respects assist in word and deed. As Mr. Weiser with good insight has already called to mind,[19] the first point is probably the most important one. Whatever else has occurred to me as open to question in this matter is not decisive but must, nevertheless, be considered. For exampble, b) the many changes may occasion ever more worry and harm for the dear brothers also in material circumstances and on account of the upbringing of their dear children (in connection with which I sincerely request, moreover, that they also fortify themselves in faith in God's care especially for the future and not allow themselves to become too depressed through sundry worries about the future). The New Yorkers could also again change their minds, if they allowed themselves to be stirred up by others against you. If that happened you also d) might not find any refuge in your previous congregations, especially if Mr. Heintzelmann had administered them for several years and had found his way into the circumstances such that he could not again very well be dislodged. Similarly, e) you have in mind the establishment of a good institution in the Pennsylvania congregations for which your presence and remaining there appear to be indispensable. Consequently, you will want to ponder in the fear of the Lord all of this as well as what your father-in-law has already given you to consider in the letter he furnished you. Now if in the course of considering these reasons you are convinced that it is the will of God for you to remain at your present post one should still then consider whether and how one could be of help to this congregation in another way so that it might receive an able pastor who could establish and maintain order in it under your supervision and that of the Pennsylvania Ministerium. The question is, since Mr. Weygand[20] has already served the congregations as vicar and, if the congregation was satisfied with him, whether he could not be placed there for at least one or more years on a trial basis until one perhaps could find another solution. Since through carelessness he has pretty well closed off access in Raritan and if he has become more careful and found himself after having sown his wild oats he may labor with greater benefit at a third place. Or perhaps Mr. Heintzelmann could at least be transferred there in time.

For he will hardly be able to remain in the present circumstances as it would be too difficult for Mr. Brunnholtz[21] in the course of time to share his income with him. On account of his set ways, however, I would have wished that he could remain with you in Pennsylvania. To be sure, an assistant pastor would also be necessary in Philadelphia if arrangements for paying his salary can be made without being a disadvantage to the pastor who as it is has already lost the subsidy from Germantown. May the Lord of the harvest himself by all means prepare and still send several faithful laborers into the Pennsylvania harvest which is still so extensive![22]

3) I am greatly saddened by what I have seen concerning Mr. Schultz[23] in your previously mentioned letter to Mr. Albinus. On account of him I have been put in a position of considerable concern because of various circumstances since he accepted the call to Pennsylvania almost too readily. I am sorry that my concern only turned up too soon. Before his journey I spared no pains in firm admonition and he still pretty well accepted every thing from me with becoming obedience. Herewith I am also enclosing a serious reminder in writing[24] to him which is to be handed to him and request that you yourself add what is necessary as reproval. God grant that he will allow himself to be helped and to be put right.

4) However, you now also need an assistant as relief in view of all circumstances, if you remain with your congregations in Pennsylvania. Moreover, the support of such a one from your own small salary is in any case not possible, especially since as it is you are already up to your neck in debt. I therefore think it proper in this case to seize the opportunity given with the call received from New York and to apprise your congregations of the fact that you have sufficiently demonstrated that you were not seeking your own advantage--as the congregation itself can see--that you are no longer equal to doing the work alone in view of diminishing energy. Consequently, the congregation itself would recognize that it would be necessary, if you were to remain with them, to make an arrangement whereby you could receive an assistant without it being a burden for you. Failing this you could not know whether it might not be necessary for you to accept the call to New York.[25] So if the neighboring congregations at Goshenhoppen (if it is feasible) as an outparish were given a coworker of that kind such an arrangement would be easier. You, dear brother, with sincere self-denial wanted to grant such a helper half of your own income. The faithful God will also not abandon you with your dear family in view of your disinterested nature but will allow you to experience his care all the more abundantly. In the meantime, it is also appropriate to remind the congregations of their responsibility and that due provision be made for who will come in the future. Negotiations with the congregation in this matter

could perhaps take place through your colleagues Brunnholtz and Handschuh.[26] If the matter of a gift of money in the amount of 10,000 reichsthaler, referred to previously, should, as it appears, soon become a reality, I shall get a communication off to the congregations.[27] Among other things I shall raise in it the point concerning arrangement for salaries.[28] Through this you will be given the opportunity to put the matter on an ever more solid and permanent footing. In the meantime I request your opinion concerning the advisability of telling the congregations already now of such a gift and also concerning what you consider useful and necessary in writing to them and what conditions should be demanded if they want to enjoy these gifts in the future for the maintenance of their ecclesiastical affairs.

5) With regard to the printing press: I indeed promised in my previous response[29] to the letter you sent from New York that if you would still want the printing press, I would be of service to you in the matter. However, after further reflection I nevertheless find many obstacles which in turn have suggested other ideas. (1) I still do not consider it advisable to become involved again in many rejoinders to slanders because the behaviour of Lutheran pastors is becoming increasingly known everywhere and in this way legitimizes itself. Consequently, everyone who has common sense will and can be convinced of the falsehood of such slanders, whereas rejecting them in print can always easily provide an opportunity for further animosity and slander. (2) I fear a printing press could become more of a burden for you because afterwards one cannot let it stand idle without suffering damage. In that case it would become a heavy yoke for you if you would always have to worry about having to prepare enough material for printing while you are otherwise overloaded with work. To reprint one or another book there would also not be advantageous, because we can send you printed books from here more easily than you can print the same books there yourselves. (3) Our treasury for the collections is so depleted that it is still in debt to the orphanage. But now you request that some of what you still expect from Einbeck should be applied to payment for the printing press. However, since you still are in debt I can by no means advise you to involve yourself still further in complicated details. You still do not know sufficiently whether you can again recover the costs and whether you might not suffer loss from the undertaking. For that reason I would rather advise you to take what you are still supposed to receive from your inheritance and to apply it to the payment of your debts, as far as it will go.

6) I have transmitted your letters to Einbeck[30] to Pastor Krohme[31] at that place and sent a letter with them. Although he has forwarded several letters of your loved ones to me to look after[32], nothing is mentioned of disbursement of some money for you to me. For that reason I shall refer to

this point in my reply to Pastor Krohme and ask him for information on the status of the disbursement of the money.

For now this is as much as I wanted to report by way of response concerning the most necessary points. May the faithful God graciously continue to see us through, the God whose work we carry forward, whose servants we are and whose faithful preservation of his church and servants has been marvellous since time immemorial even though it remains a kingdom of the cross. May he help us through, clear obstacles out of the way, himself help to bear all burdens and allow his work and kingdom to prosper perceptibly under our hands to his praise. May he also especially show my dear brother the way clearly, assure you of his will so you may know that what you do is his leading and guidance. Moreover, may he also increase your strength, care for your needs and bless your dear family. May he sustain you and all of your helpers and unite you ever more closely in the bond of true love where one or another wants to stray far afield here or there, may he right it and ward off all harm. With cordial greetings to your worthy beloved wife and dear parents-in-law from me and my wife, I remain with all sincerity,

Your,
G.A. Francke

---

1. The text reads *a[nni] c[urrentis]*.
2. The text reads *minima circumstantia variat rem*.
3. The text reads *sui modo*.
4. See *Correspondence* 1:121 n.4; 310 n.10.
5. The text reads *Corpore Evangelicorum*. For details of Fresenius' plan to collect funds for the Pennsylvania congregations see *HN2/1*:655 n.99. The high hopes Fresenius had for the collection were not realized when the body of evangelicals assembled at Regensburg rejected the plan. In 1749 he succeeded in securing a collection for the Pennsylvania congregations in Darmstadt where he had been court preacher from 1736-41 (*HN2/1*:460 n.147).
6. This is probably a reference to the collection Johann Christian Schultze, Johann Daniel Schöner and Daniel Weissinger undertook in Germany in 1733-34. See *Correspondence* 1:135 n.8; 168 and 169 n.6.
7. See Matt. 13:12; Mark 4:25; Luke 8:18.
8. See August Hermann Francke's *Fusstapfen des noch lebenden Gottes*. Halle, 1701, published in translation in *An Abstract of the Marvellous Footsteps of Divine Providence*. London, 1706.
9. See Letters 99 and 104.
10. The text reads *ad dies vitae*.
11. G.A. Francke had been informed of Sigismund Streit's change of mind in January 1752. Streit had decided to allot 15,000 pounds to Pennyslvania and an equal sum to the churches in Madras, India. *Korrespondenz* 1:538 n.7. For further information concerning Streit see Letter 99 n.1.
12. The text reads *cum exceptione crucis*.
13. See Heb. 12:3.

14. The text reads *parta tueri*.

15. The initial formulation reads, "Your presence and authority." See *Korrespondenz* 1:538 n.8. See Letter 105 and *Journals* 1:301-2.

16. The initial formulation reads, "For although we may indeed not be overbearing before God on account of our standing, we must nevertheless make use of it in proper order to foster his glory." *Korrespondenz* 1:536 n.9.

17. On Samuel Theodor Albinus, see *Correspondence* 1:154 n.8.

18. On Johann Dietrich Matthias Heinzelmann, see Letter 101 n.3.

19. Conrad Weiser's opinion is not exant. On Weiser, see *Correspondence* 1:142 n.7.

20. On Johann Albert Weygand, see Letter 71 n.21.

21. *Correspondence* 1:154 n.4.

22. See Luke 10:2.

23. On Friedrich Schultze, see Letter 89 n.4.

24. Not extant.

25. See Letter 97 n.1.

26. On Johann Friedrich Handschuh, see *Correspondence* 1:291 nn.18 and 19.

27. Francke directed a communication to deacons and elders of Lutheran congregations in Pennsylvania on 15 September 1753. See *Korrespondenz* 1:538 n.15.

28. The text reads *salariorum*.

29. Francke's letter of 20 November 1751 (Letter 102) had been written in response to Mühlenberg's letter to New York of 15 June 1751 (Letter 93).

30. Letters 115 and 116. Francke may also have had Mühlenberg's letter to his brothers, not extant, in mind. See Letter 116 n.2.

31. On Theophilus Arnold Krome, see Letter 77 n.40.

32. These letters are not extant.

Letter 124A

To the Congregation in Germantown
Providence, prior to October 1752

In addressing the leaders and members of the congregation in Germantown Mühlenberg admonishes them to record their names and thereby indicate their willingness to contribute to the improvement and maintenance of their church.

Text in German: A fair copy of this letter is located in the Lutheran Archives Center in Philadelphia, St. Michael's Lutheran Church in Germantown, Box A Folder I.4.

Dear Friends and Brothers:

The gracious God has helped you, the deacons, elders and dear congregation members, to secure a small church.[1] In accordance with God's forbearance the light of the Gospel can shine in it and the holy sacraments can serve you and your descendants for your everlasting comfort. We must care for this precious possession and see to it that everything is done that ought to be done for its reception, improvement and preservation. Our church does not have enough room, especially if after some years it should be enlarged because of our congregation's growth and ultimately also be combined with a parsonage and schoolhouse. Immediately beside our church a half an acre of land is for sale. Consequently, out of love the deacons, elders and congregation members should provide for themselves and their descendants by not letting this opportunity slip through their fingers and kindly sign their names thereby testifying to what they intend to contribute out of kindheartedness to the improvement and maintenance of our churches and schools.[2] May the Lord rule in the hearts of all of you and not allow them to be flighty but increasingly concentrate on what is necessary and be united in love and humility. This is the wish and desire of your pastor and intercessor

Heinrich Melchior Mühlenberg

---

1. While the early history of the congregation in Germantown is shrouded in uncertainty, its existence by 1728 is firmly established (*Lutherans in N.A.*, p. 30). Prior to Mühlenberg's arrival in 1742 the congregation was served by a number of persons the validity of whose orders was for the most part open to question. Thereafter Mühlenberg and his colleagues served the congregation as best they could. Regularity in serving the congregation began with the arrival of Johann Friedrich Handschuh in 1751 and the consecration of its church on 1 October 1752 in connection with the

annual conference of the United Congregations (*Documentary History*, pp. 36-40). Although outwardly peace and harmony prevailed in the congregation at the time of the consecration of the church, rumblings of dissension and conflict were in evidence already prior to it. Shortly after the consecration the conflict burst into the open with a vengeance. For details of this dissension see Mühlenberg's letter of 24 August 1753 as reproduced in *HN2/1*:700-6. However, in view of the dissension which surfaced shortly after the consecration of the Germantown church, Mühlenberg's letter dated "prior to October 1752" must have been written before 1 October since it assumes the existence of a congregation that is still one in spirit.

2. The back of the letter has a list of the names of contributors and their respective contributions, the total of which comes to 12 pounds and 4 shillings. Several names in this list support the view that the letter was written prior to 1 October 1752. For example, Matthias Genzel is listed as contributing 5 shillings, an average contribution. Mühlenberg refers to him as one of the spokespersons of his opponents (*Korrespondenz* 2:43). In the list his name appears as "Matthias Ganseler." Michael Ege is also one of the leaders of the opposition to whom Mühlenberg refers (*Korrespondenz* 2:208). In the list this name probably appears as "Michael Haege." The name of Jacob Müller, also an "antipietist," appears in the same list.

Letter 125

To Johann Philipp Fresenius
Providence, 16 November 1752

After having taken up a good deal of space with compliments to Fresenius, Mühlenberg reports in this fragmentary letter on his own well being and that of his colleagues, on the arrival of two coworkers and of five preachers who are without a call and whose deportment resembles that of mercenary imposters. He also points out that his friend, the Reformed pastor Michael Schlatter, has arrived in New York with six Reformed pastors.

Text in German: Korrespondenz *1:539. For further textual information, see* Korrespondenz *1:539.*

To Doctor and Senior Fresenius[1] in Frankfurt.

16 November 1752

Very Reverend Doctor and Senior:

In childlike simplicity I took the liberty last year of getting a letter[2] off to Your Reverence through a young person from here. In it I reported on the external circumstances of our poor congregations in Pennsylvania, Jersey and New York. I should indeed have waited with writing further until I received permission by word of mouth or in writing from Your Reverence for taking such liberty . . . the most important correspondents must be satisfied if they receive no reply, to say nothing of being able to expect the slightest letter from your heart and hand in response to my meagre letters from the West. I also do not desire to have more than a favorable remembrance and your intercessions on my behalf, my colleagues and our poor congregations. At present I only wanted to report most obediently that all of us united pastors are still living and that the gracious God cheered us on 1 December 1751 with two new laborers from blessed Halle, namely, Messrs. Heinzelman and Schultze.[3] After this I also wanted to report that five preachers without a call arrived here this fall with their families amongst the German people.[4] They rove through the whole countryside and search for a livelihood, either driving us out or having us go begging in disgrace. One has his meagre livelihood in Lancaster for a year until perhaps others come from Tübingen for whom Magister Wagner has written[5] while others still rove about and scavenge for a livelihood. To people of that kind to whom the true Christianity we recommend appears an unbearable burden, the scavenger preachers are very welcome because they proclaim a super gospel without repentance and sanctification for a handful of barley, etc., etc. I hear that merchants in Holland permit recruitment of such disorderly preachers and grant them free passage so that common people will board the ships all the more courageously when preachers are with them. Finally, I must also faithfully report that the Reformed Pastor Slatter arrived in New York on 26 July just as I was there with six new Reformed pastors. He brought me the greetings of Your Reverence[6] which comforted and refreshed me in my toil and trouble very much. However, the poor honest Mr. Slatter . . .

---

1. At the time of the writing of this letter Fresenius was Senior of the Frankfurt Ministerium. On Johann Philipp Fresenius, see *Correspondence* 1:121 n.4; 310 n.10; and *Korrespondenz* 1:104 n.4.
2. Letter 106, dated 15 November 1751.
3. See Letter 112:204.
4. A description of the arrival of these preachers is contained in Mühlenberg's letter to Francke and Ziegenhagen, dated 24 August 1753, and reproduced in *HN2/1*:700, "Gradually ships with German people arrived in Philadelphia and brought five to six so-called Lutheran preachers and a large number of school attendants into the country. Our Pennsylvania newlanders and the merchants in Holland have just discovered this method. The newlanders search out the cheapest preachers and students in the course of their trip through Germany and bring them to the ships to use them as worms on their rods for fishing and in this way the ships are loaded all the sooner." On "newlanders," see above, p.20 n. 12.

Presumably the five Lutheran preachers who came to Pennsylvania without a call were the following: Johann Georg Bager (1725-91) arrived in Philadelphia 23 October 1752. Only after he had accepted a call to the New York congregation in 1763 was he accepted as a member of the United Congregations even though he had studied in Halle. See *Pastors and People* 1:17-18. Johann Theophilus Engelland (d. 1775) arrived in Pennsylvania in 1752 or 1753. He had studied at the University of Tübingen. Though he ministered to a large number of congregations in southeastern Pennsylvania he was never received into membership of the United Congregations. Mühlenberg looked upon him as a very ill-disposed preacher. See *Pastors and People* 1:35. Johann Joseph Roth (d. 1764) arrived in Philadelphia in 1752 and began an irregular ministry in 1755. In 1762 he was received into the membership of the United Congregations. See *Pastors and People* 1:111. Jakob Friedrich Schertlin (1696-c.1718) arrived in Philadelphia 27 September 1752 when he was already in his middle fifties. He attended one meeting of the United Congregations and was invited to others but for one reason or another did not come and never became a member. He had been dismissed from his last parish in Germany. See *Pastors and People* 1:116-17. Heinrich Gabriel Wortmann arrived in Philadelphia 3 November 1752. After serving Pennsylvania congregations for only a brief period of time he ministered to congregations in Virginia and South Carolina with rather indifferent results. See *Pastors and People* 1:167-68.
5. On Tobias Wagner, see Letter 114:231 and Letter 71A n.3.
6. See *Correspondence* 1:340 and 342 n.41; Letter 112:211 and 223 n. 44; *Journals* 1:342. The following were the six Reformed pastors Schlatter brought with him: (1) Philipp Wilhelm Otterbein. See *Pastors and People* 1:101-3. (2) Johannes Waldschmidt. See *Pastors and People* 1:157. (3) Johann Jakob Wissler. See *Pastors and People* 1:167. (4) Theodor Franckenfeld. See *Pastors and People* 1:40. (5) Johann Caspar Rubel. See *Pastors and People* 1:112-13. (6) Heinrich Wilhelm Stoy. See *Pastors and People* 1:144-45. See also *Minutes and Letters*, p. 44. In connection with his trip to Europe in 1750 Schlatter also visited Fresenius twice in Frankfurt. See *Minutes and Letters*, p. 44.

Letter 126

To Johann Conrad Weiser
Providence, 21 December 1752

In this letter to his father-in-law, Johann Conrad Weiser, Mühlenberg enumerates ten charges that have been made against him in a letter written to Johann Nicolaus Kurz. Mühlenberg writes that these charges have been made by "a former friend" who is also a "father-in-law, grandfather, impartial judge and a son of the universal church." In other words, the charges have been made by none other than Conrad Weiser himself. Thus, this letter documents a conflict between Weiser and Mühlenberg that has received little attention. See also Letter 127 for Mühlenberg's further reflections on this conflict.

Text in German: Korrespondenz *1:540-42. For further textual information see* Korrespondenz *1:542. In this letter Mühlenberg uses abbreviations to identify himself with* Mb., *Pastor Kurz with* K. *and Pastor Wagner with* W..

Title omitted without prejudice,[1]
Dear Mr. Weiser:[2]
In a letter to my good friend Mr. Kurz,[3] dated 8 December of the current year,[4] a former friend after much reflection on the Lutheran congregation in Reading[5] has sharply accused me and laid at my door the following charges, namely:

1) Mühlenberg's undertakings are supposed to have as their purpose luring the congregation to his side.

(2) One is too quick to judge.

(3) An old grudge against Mr. Wagner supposedly dwells in Mühlenberg's heart.

(4) Mühlenberg is supposed to be glad for the opportunity to unseat Mr. Wagner.

(5) Once something like that is supposed to lie at the bottom of the heart more than enough may turn up to find fault with a neighbor.

(6) Mühlenberg considers himself to be a far better Christian and more experienced pastor than Mr. Wagner.

(7) It would have been becoming for Mr. Mühlenberg to speak to Mr. Wagner about it; perhaps what he pretends to have heard about Mr. Wagner is not true.

(8) In Reading there is not supposed to be a great hunger for the word of God. This may well be true of all of Pennsylvania.

(9)   He who likes to fish in troubled waters, as Mühlenberg presumably does, can cast his rod there at the present time.

(10) Thereupon the worthy friend takes leave of all parties and takes a pledge to be and remain a son of the holy universal Christian church until death and leave it all in Mühlenberg's hands.

Besides, let anyone who wants to, preach and administer the sacraments in Reading, etc., etc.

The above judgment of me was not written in haste but after much reflection; it is magnified and corroborated by being rendered by a father-in-law, grandfather, impartial judge and son of the universal church. If charges of this kind could be proven and judged by a court of law Mühlenberg would come off before human society as an archhypocrite and exceptional scoundrel. He would rightly be defrocked, yes, stoned by those who are truly impartial and without sin. However, because I still know a judge who tries the hearts and reins[6] and judges fairly I am confident before him and unconcerned before human beings about how or what they think, say or write about me. Princes are human beings; there is no help in them.[7] At most they can only kill the body if God should permit it, etc., etc.[8] In cases like this no argument avails even if one has in one's possession the best credentials and evidence. I had rendered an account of the proceeding,[9] presented the same to my brothers and requested Dr. Busse[10] to pass along a copy of it to Mr. Weiser. Whether or not this occurred I do not know, it is also a matter of indifference to me. I was almost forced against my will into the Reading affair. I also hoped that my sermons and those of Mr. Kurtz would not have poisoned the people. Because I have been saddled with the above judgment without proof I find I have no recourse other than

1)   to avoid the appearance of involvement and, for my part, to sever my connection with the Lutheran congregation in Reading entirely;

2)   to let others fish in troubled waters who know how to do it better and have entered for that purpose;

3)   to leave the responsibility to the one who has forced me into this affair;

4)   and to avoid the appearance of involvement and suspicion I beg you, dear sir, that you would give my lot and that of John Peter to others.[11] Allow me to commend you, each and all, and especially with your worthy family to the endless love and mercy of God and the working of his good Spirit through word and covenant seal which Peter, Paul, John, Thomas and the remaining sons of the church universal found necessary and needed until death.

Providence,

21 December 1752   Mühlenberg

P.S. As far as the letter[12] of Magister Wagner is concerned, I should like to return it when a secure opportunity presents itself because I am afraid it may get lost and later may be abruptly demanded of me; consequently, I could not entrust it to just anyone.

P.S. Thirty-four years I had . . .[13]

---

1. The text reads *S[alvo] T[itulo]*.
2. Johann Conrad Weiser, Mühlenberg's father-in-law, had moved to Reading a few years prior to 1752. See *HN*2:2:201; see also *Correspondence* 1:142 n.7.
3. On Johann Nicolaus Kurz, see *Correspondence* 1:154 n.5.
4. The text reads *8 dec: ac*.
5. When the congregation at Reading came into conflict with Tobias Wagner in 1752 it turned to the synod for help and asked for another pastor. With the agreement of his colleagues Mühlenberg went to Reading to bring about a reconciliation between the congregation and Wagner. Wagner interpreted Mühlenberg's effort as intervention and published the pamphlet referred to against him. See also Letter 71A n.3.
6. See Ps. 7:9 (AV).
7. See Ps. 118:9; 146:3.
8. See Matt. 10:28; Luke 12:4.
9. Not extant.
10. It has not been possible to identify him; however, see Letter 127.
11. This is a reference to the parcels of land Mühlenberg had acquired in his name and that of Johann Peter Gabriel; see Letter 127.
12. Not extant.
13. At this point the manuscript breaks off.

Letter 127

To Dr. Busse
Providence, 21 December 1752

Presumably Dr. Busse was a resident of Reading and member of the Lutheran congregation there, as this letter of Mühlenberg to him implies, for in it Mühlenberg repeats most of the charges and complaints he communicated in his dispute with his father-in-law, Johann Conrad Weiser, in a letter having a date identical with this one. This letter goes beyond the contents of the previous one in that here Mühlenberg makes some recommendations for settling the dispute in the Reading congregation in the hope that Dr. Busse will be instrumental in carrying them out. The depth of Mühlenberg's feelings in this whole Reading affair surfaces in his employment of ironic images sprinkled with intermittent phrases in Latin.
Text in German: Korrespondenz *1:543-44. For further textual information see* Korrespondenz *1:544.*

Very noble, very learned Doctor, worthy Patron in Christ:
Already twice Your Excellency has honored and made me beholden to you with two favorable letters.[1] I am not in a position to thank you for your efforts and being well-disposed toward me, to say nothing of responding in deed. For that reason I ask that the Giver of all good and perfect gifts[2] may richly reward you. I regret that due to my fault Your Excellency has in an innocent way become entwined in this affair and I hope it will cause you no harm. Discipline makes good soldiers, and sympathy demands that members who are bound together should suffer and struggle together. On 19 December in addition to a letter from Philip Meyer[3] Your prudent[4] Excellency received one from Pastor Kurtz.[5] Among other things a letter from Mr. Weiser[6] was given me in which he accuses and judges me beyond limits[7]. I want to put the charges down here confidentially;[8]

1)   It is supposed to be Mühlenberg's intention to lure the congregation in Reading to his side.[9]

2)   One judges too quickly.

3)   Mühlenberg is supposed to harbor a grudge in his heart against Mr. Wagner.

4)   Mühlenberg was supposed to be glad for the opportunity to unseat Mr. Wagner.

5)   For such bad reasons Mühlenberg sought to find fault with Wagner.

6)   In Reading there was simply no great hunger for God's word.

7)   I sought to fish in troubled waters in Reading. From these and other unproved charges Your Excellency can see that I have had a complete falling out with my father-in-law and become entangled in bitter conflicts on account of an otherwise innocent and imposed proceeding. As far as my poor person is concerned I have therefore firmly resolved to sever my relationship to the Reading congregation completely. I would most respectfully ask Your Excellency to add one more service of love to the pains you had earlier and deign to disclose to the elders confidentially:[10]

1)   that they leave me personally out of consideration;

2)   that they try in every possible way to get along with Mr. Wagner;

3)   or if that is not possible that they send a few lines to Pastor Schultz,[11] our collaborator, and invite him to conduct the service on the New Year's festival.

4)   If in the future the elders have something to report they should no longer write to me but to my colleague in Philadelphia.

5)   Should the elders be in trouble on account of the building costs for the church[12] and of necessity would need to borrow forty or fifty pounds but could not get them up there then Pastor Brunnholtz in Philadelphia has kindly offered to plead on their behalf with Mr. Allen.[13] He would obviously advance something if the most prominent members of the congregation would stand surety for it.

6)   If they would like to have some order in the matter of elders and deacons, they could do this when a pastor again conducts the service. After the service they could be elected by all the congregation members and presented by the pastor. All this could take place without me.

My most worthy patron and brother! Though you have only been in Pennsylvania a short time, you will, however, surely discover abundantly that the method of arguing among rustics and magistrates of the people[14] is worthless.[15] Whoever wants to proceed on the basis of revelation and reason will hurt himself and be trampled under foot, etc., etc. Nevertheless, truth must prevail even if it is overthrown for a time. Fear God, do what is right and be afraid of no one is a good watchword. I have now been in Pennsylvania for ten years[16] like a black and white target at which friends and foes shoot their arrows of jest and scorn. As far as the account[17] is concerned I observe that Your Excellency does not find it advisable to communicate the same to Mr. Weiser. Your Excellency does indeed have the welfare of the whole in mind and views matters with impartial eyes. Hence I humbly ask that you act in the affair in accordance with your better understanding of it; whether you proceed or refrain as you think best is a matter of indifference to me. I have written Mr. Weiser and responded to his charges in a reserved tone.[18] I have informed him that I for my part want to sever my connection with the Reading congregation and leave responsibility in the affair to him. To avoid all appearance and suspicion of fishing in troubled waters I have for good measure given notice of ridding myself of the two house lots assigned to me for otherwise it could become a Pennsylvanian or rather Wagnerian syllogism from grammar:[19] whoever builds a cottage near Reading or the church is a common preacher; therefore[20]. . . it sounds almost as good as when the old Germans governed their syllogisms in accordance with the law of the jungle. Enough, however, of these unedifying matters! Nothing would please me more than to be in a position to reward Your Excellency's prudent efforts in proportion to their merit. However, since this is still impossible I will have to make do with the old customary compliment and confess that I am Your Excellency's, my most faborably disposed patron's most obliging servant

Providence,
21 December 1752   Mühlenberg

---

1. Not extant.
2. See James 1:17.
3. The letter is not extant. In his diary Mühlenberg refers to Philipp Meyer who was formerly a pastor in Tulpehocken. However, it is not certain that this is the Philipp Meyer referred to here. *Journals* 1:152.
4. The text reads *cordates*.
5. Not extant. On Johann Nicolaus Kurz, see *Correspondence* 1:154 n.5.
6. Not extant, however, see Letter 126.
7. The text reads *extra terminos*.
8. The text reads *sub rosa*.
9. For more details see Letter 126:293 n.5.
10. The text reads *inter privatos parietes*.
11. On Friedrich Schultze, see Letter 89 n.4.
12. Building the church was begun in the spring of 1752 and dedicated in October of that same year. See *HN2/1*:101.
13. William Allen (1704-80) served as chief justice of Pennsylvania (1750-74) and in 1765 helped Benjamin Franklin in securing the repeal of the Stamp Act.
14. The text reads *inter rusticos und tribunos plebis*.
15. The text reads *cum vaculo*.
16. On 15 March 1752 Mühlenberg was honored with a certificate of gratitude in recognition of ten years of service in Pennsylvania which was signed by elders and pastors. *Korrespondenz* 1:545 n.3.
17. This account, already referred to in the previous letter, is not extant (see Letter 126 n.7).
18. See Letter 126.
19. The text reads *e[x] gr[ammatico(?)]*.
20. The text reads *Atq.[ue] Ergo*.

INDEX OF SCRIPTURAL REFERENCES

Religious scholars and other serious researchers will find the following Index of Scriptural References found anywhere in this volume to be of great value. Biblical references are noted in the standard form of book (in bold type), chapter number, followed by verse number.

INDEX OF NAMES AND PLACES

The following Index of Names and Places covers all the names and places found in this volume, including the endnotes.

301